COCOA AND CHOCOLATE, 1765–1914

Cocoa and Chocolate, 1765–1914 focuses on the period from the Seven Years War to the First World War, when a surge of economic liberalism and 'globalisation' should have helped cocoa producers to overcome rural poverty, just as wool transformed the economy of Australia, and tea that of Japan. The addition of new forms of chocolate to Western diets in the late nineteenth century led to a great cocoa boom, and yet economic development remained elusive, despite cocoa producers having certain advantages in the 'commodity lottery' faced by exporters of raw materials.

The commodity chain, from sowing a cocoa bean to enjoying a cup of hot chocolate, is examined in *Cocoa and Chocolate, 1765–1914* under the broad rubrics of chocolate consumption, the taxation of cocoa beans, the manufacture of chocolate, private marketing channels, land distribution, ecological impact on tropical forests, and the coercion of labour.

Cocoa and Chocolate, 1765–1914 concludes that cocoa failed to act as a dynamo for development largely because of official support for owners of estates and slaves, market manipulation by large planters, and excessive taxation and protectionism. Where liberal policies prevailed, cocoa held out a real promise for the future.

William Gervase Clarence-Smith is Professor of the economic history of Asia and Africa at the School of Oriental and African Studies, University of London. He is the author of *The Third Portuguese Empire, 1825–1975* (Manchester University Press, 1985) and edited *Cocoa Pioneer Fronts Since 1800* (Macmillan, 1996).

COCOA AND CHOCOLATE, 1765–1914

William Gervase Clarence-Smith

London and New York

First published 2000
by Routledge
11 New Fetter Lane, London EC4P 4EE

Simultaneously published in the USA and Canada
by Routledge
29 West 35th Street, New York, NY 10001

Routledge is an imprint of the Taylor & Francis Group

Typeset in Times by Taylor & Francis Books Ltd
Printed and bound in Great Britain by
St Edmundsbury Press, Bury St Edmunds, Suffolk

British Library Cataloguing in Publication Data
A catalogue record for this book is available from the British Library

⌡К *Library of Congress Cataloging in Publication Data*
A catalog record for this book has been requested

ISBN 0–415–21576–5

TO KEIKO AND SARAH

CONTENTS

LIST OF ILLUSTRATIONS

Maps

Tables

Figures

PREFACE

When I saw my first cocoa tree in Cameroon in 1966, little did I guess that I would spend long years researching the history of this handsome little tree, which, oddly, bore its pods directly on its trunk and branches. Nevertheless, I already wondered how the estate could bear the high costs of its French manager, who drove a fast car and lived in a palatial mansion. The question was raised in a more acute form by a visit later that year to Fernando Póo (Bioko), where the cocoa estates of Spanish corporations dominated the agrarian landscape of this beautiful volcanic island. Chocolate was an even earlier memory, as my favourite tea-time snack as a child in France was squares of plain dark chocolate on bread.

An academic interest in cocoa and chocolate grew out of writing about the economics of modern Portuguese imperialism. I was struck by the contribution of the tiny islands of São Tomé and Príncipe to Portugal's balance of payments in the period before 1914, underpinned by a thinly veiled slave trade that strained diplomatic relations with Britain. My first project was thus to investigate the economic viability of colonial cocoa plantations in Africa and Asia from the 1880s to 1914, giving rise to a series of articles and chapters in edited collections.

The stimulus to considering the world cocoa economy from a global perspective came from organising an international conference on cocoa and development in 1993, together with Gareth Austin, my friend and colleague from the London School of Economics. Editing the book which resulted from the conference sharpened my conviction that primary production in the tropics was not a cause of underdevelopment, a conviction born of teaching a first-year course on development in the Third World. Cocoa was rather an opportunity to resolve the problems of rural poverty. It seemed that there was no inherent reason why cocoa should not help to transform the economies of tropical countries in much the same way that wool helped to develop Australia, wheat Canada, or tea and silk Japan.

My original intention was to cover the nineteenth and twentieth centuries, but I became aware that there was a chronological 'black hole' between the Seven Years War and the First World War, a period when liberalism should have favoured economic growth. As cocoa in the twentieth century had already been explored in such detail, it made sense to concentrate on the earlier century and a half. Filling this 'black hole' entailed an attempt to reconstruct over a century of world cocoa exports, which only existed in any systematic form from 1894. When I first embarked on this project, I had no idea of the magnitude of the task that I had set myself. The series remain full of gaps and weaknesses, but I hope that it constitutes an empirical step forward, which could be emulated for many other commodities.

By concentrating on the liberal era, I moved my focus to Latin America and the Caribbean, a part of the world outside my usual academic remit. However, research on the slave trade and Portuguese emigration had already led me to work on aspects of New World history, and teaching a course on Third World development had made me familiar with the general literature. Moreover, a knowledge of Spanish, Portuguese, French and Dutch opened many doors. Nevertheless, I beg the forgiveness of specialists in the field for crass errors that may have crept into my portrayal of their continent's history. I have made myself all the more vulnerable by not only looking at the main cocoa exporting regions, but also trying to cover areas that consumed chocolate.

ACKNOWLEDGEMENTS

Global history is by definition an exercise in scholarly cooperation, including cooperation across the disciplines, as I learned by attending seminars organised by Patrick O'Brien at the Institute of Historical Research in London. I have indeed been fortunate in receiving much support from numerous friends and colleagues, who generously provided me with papers, theses, references and statistics. Some even furnished me with unpublished statistical data that they had painstakingly dug out of archives. To a greater extent than for most books, my debts are thus legion. François Ruf, Gareth Austin and Steven Topik have been a source of inspiration, and their ideas permeate this book. Nikita Harwich launched me on my quest for Latin American sources, Wim Klooster saved me from the morass of pre-metric weights and measures, and Ray Delahunty laboured to make the precious volumes of *Der Gordian* available to me in time.

My warmest thanks are extended the following, who provided me with valuable research materials on the areas indicated in brackets: Tony Lass (general), Jan Rus (Chiapas), José Antonio Fernández (Central America), Julie Charlip (Nicaragua), Luis Martínez Fernández (Hispanic Caribbean), Walter Cordero and Michiel Baud (Dominican Republic), Christian Schnakenbourg (French Caribbean), Mats Lundahl (Haïti), D. R. Butler (Grenada), Kathleen Phillips Lewis (Trinidad), Wim Klooster (Dutch Caribbean), Alex van Stipriaan and Johannes Postma (Surinam), Nikita Harwich, Magnus Mörner and Eugenio Piñero (Venezuela), Malcolm Deas, Eduardo Posada Carbó and Thomas Fischer (Colombia), Michael Hamerly and Paul Henderson (Ecuador), Carmen Parrón Salas (Peru), Fernando Rocchi (Argentina), Mary Ann Mahony and Victor Bulmer-Thomas (Brazil), Hille Toxopeus (Nigeria), Max Liniger-Goumaz (Equatorial Guinea), Claudia Roden and Simone Bass (Middle East), Norman Owen, Dan Doeppers, Doreen Fernández and Felice Santa Maria (Philippines), Jürgen Schneider (Europe), Gilbert Buti, Jean Touton and Juan Antonio Lalaguna (France), Marisa Morell (Spain), and the Ghirardelli Chocolate Company and the Guittard Chocolate Company (United States). My apologies are due to anybody whose help I have omitted to note here through oversight. Furthermore, this book depends to an inordinate extent on those who performed the often thankless task of indexing with due care and attention. I can only hope that my own efforts follow worthily in their footsteps.

My gratitude is due to the Leverhulme Trust and the School of Oriental and African Studies for financing a year's sabbatical, vital to pressing ahead with this book. I would also like to thank the staff of the archives listed in the references section.

Last but not least, I owe a great debt of gratitude to my wife, Keiko, and my daughter, Sarah, who put up with my endless bashing at the computer and numerous absences. As my wife commented on seeing a draft, 'behind every long book there lies a neglected family'. This book is dedicated to them.

1

THE COMMODITY CHAIN

Studying a commodity chain is like cutting a cross-section through history (Gereffi and Korzeniewicz 1994; Topik and Wells 1998; Mintz 1985; Roseberry *et al.* 1995). The focus on a single product engenders a concentrated beam of light, illuminating hidden corners of the past, revealing unexpected connections between apparently discrete phenomena, and testing general theories against irreducible particularity. The main concern here is to understand the wealth and poverty of nations, using the cocoa-to-chocolate commodity chain in the liberal era as a litmus test for theories of economic development.

The nature of this commodity chain is best explained by extending Appadurai's metaphor that commodities have a 'social life' (Appadurai 1988) to the idea that they also have a life cycle. Borrowing a title from a popular book on coffee, the life cycle of cocoa went 'from plantation to cup' (Thurber 1881). As chocolate was principally drunk rather than eaten before 1914, this is an apt summary of the chain that led from sowing a cocoa seed to the final enjoyment of a cup of hot chocolate.

In its 'youth', cocoa was a small and handsome tree, raised in hot and humid equatorial lands, and subject to the vagaries of tropical climates and diseases. The ways in which it was grown, and the economic advantages that rural areas derived from it, only partly depended on the skills of cultivators. The social relations regulating access to land, labour and capital, together with the mental models of social groups, profoundly affected this stage of the commodity chain. Cocoa might be grown on large estates, with slave labour, and as an intense monoculture. Free smallholders might also tend clumps of trees dispersed through the forest, which an outsider would not recognise as agriculture at all.

In 'middle age', cocoa took the form of fermented and dried brown beans, which could only be stored for about a year in the tropics before deteriorating. These beans were used as small change in Mesoamerica, giving rise to the quip that in this instance money really did grow on trees. More usually, sacks of beans of between 50 and 100 kilos were taken to workshops and factories. Far from being in an impersonal market place, these

1

precious sacks were caught up in a network of social and political institutions, which determined how they were traded, transported and taxed, often in journeys that took them halfway around the world. Each agent in the chain attempted to maximise tolls, rents and profits, in the series of transactions that nudged sacks along from field to factory.

In its 'old age', cocoa was transformed once again, acquiring the name of chocolate. The British confusingly refer to many chocolate beverages as 'cocoa', but this book follows the traditions of the Spanish-speaking world, reserving the term cocoa for the raw material and semi-manufactures, and the term chocolate for what is consumed. To make chocolate, the beans were roasted, ground, and mixed with sugar and other ingredients. Chocolate might then be further transformed into a multitude of products by the beverages, confectionery and baking trades. Once ready for sale, chocolate was subject to more taxes, and passed through another network of wholesalers and retailers. Then chocolate 'died', in the act of being consumed.

The origins: producers, the state and development

At the beginning of the commodity chain, the chief question is why cocoa cultivation seems to have failed to generate economic 'take-off'. Bulmer-Thomas (1994) notes that Latin American countries faced a 'commodity lottery', resulting from the specific characteristics of commodities and the contexts in which they were produced and traded. Embroidering a little on his thesis, one can say that the ideal agricultural staple yielded numerous forward and backward linkages, significant transfers of technology and skills to other sectors, and a supply of foreign exchange. Sold on the local market, the crop eliminated imports and lowered the cost of living, and thus the wage rate. In terms of the wider economy, it yielded ample revenues for a developmental state, and good incomes for entrepreneurs willing to invest locally. More widely still, the ideal staple did not damage the environment.

In terms of linkages, narrowly conceived, cocoa ranked rather low. There were few backward linkages, as simple hand tools sufficed for cultivation, and rare attempts at mechanisation of field operations failed. Forward linkages were potentially more substantial, and yet were often disappointing. Even new transport links were not of much significance before 1914, as a relatively high value-to-bulk ratio favoured pre-industrial modes of transportation. The mechanisation of primary processing, often attempted, rarely enjoyed much technical success, and generally failed economically. Chocolate factories represented the greatest forward linkage, promising skilled employment, a stimulus to the maintenance and manufacture of machinery, a lower cost of living in chocolate consuming countries, and export revenues. There were more chocolate factories in tropical countries before 1914 than is usually appreciated, but fixed capital formation was generally low, and they never exported on any scale.

2

The bright side to this picture was that low inputs and imports were a tremendous advantage for poor countries chronically short of capital and foreign exchange. However, this advantage was lost when intensive production on estates was attempted. As there were no economies of scale in cultivation and primary processing, such estates pushed up the import bill and leaked profits abroad, with no compensating increase in productivity.

From a dependency perspective, international power relations should have cheated 'peripheral' governments and entrepreneurs of most export proceeds (Gereffi and Korzeniewicz 1994: 2–3, 17–50). However, Western governments did not intervene with the intention of reducing the price of cocoa, even though their fiscal and protectionist policies at times depressed demand for chocolate, especially before 1850. At other times, supply and demand worked well, and cocoa provided bountiful returns. Paradoxically, it was planters based in the tropics who did the most to reduce returns from cocoa exports, through misguided attempts to force up prices in the short term.

Bad governance was more of a problem. Independent states were prone to squander money deriving from the 'golden bean', whereas colonial authorities lacked vision as to how to invest the proceeds. Harmful policies included failing to protect the forest, favouring estates, allowing labour coercion, discouraging savings, restricting immigration, allowing cartels, and interfering in marketing. Over and above all this, many governments taxed heavily and indiscriminately, while failing to provide essential public goods.

The ability of cocoa to generate a steady flow of capital for the wider economy suffered from marked price volatility. The root cause was sharp variations in supplies, a problem common to all tree crops. Vulnerable ageing cocoa trees fell victim to sudden and unpredictable natural disasters, causing prices to shoot up. This incited producers to plant new trees in a rush, but there was a lag of several years between planting and full production, longer for cocoa than for many other tree crops. Prices thus stayed high for some time, provoking a surfeit of new planting. This eventually led to gluts and brought prices right down. If producers then compensated by ceasing to plant, the cycle moved in reverse, eventually pushing prices up to dangerously high levels again. This endogenous cycle might have levelled out over time, as producers learned to anticipate its effects, helped by better communications and more transparent markets. Unfortunately, exogenous factors kept setting it off again, not least when attempts were made to boost prices by withholding stocks or limiting planting.

Another liability of cocoa was its voracious appetite for virgin forest, possibly greater than that of any other tropical tree crop. Pioneer cocoa cultivators clearing virgin forest held the trump cards. They benefited from fertile virgin soils, further enriched with the ashes of burned vegetation. The initial clearing of the land could be quite expensive, but this was offset by sales of timber and firewood. Few weeds grew in recently cleared soils, giving young cocoa seedlings a good start in life, and such lands enjoyed low concentrations of the many pests and diseases specific to cocoa. When large expanses of forest remained standing within the region, rainfall may also have been more abundant and better distributed across the year. Producers seeking to replace decrepit old trees in the same location faced a diametrically opposed scenario, necessitating substantial and costly additional inputs of labour and capital. Even planting cocoa in lands previously used for other crops was rarely successful. Land could be left fallow for twenty years or more, but forest regenerated slowly and incompletely, and it was usually more economical to use it for other crops or for pasture (Ruf 1991; Ruf 1995; Clarence-Smith and Ruf 1996).

The existence of this 'forest rent' had unfortunate consequences, in terms of both markets and ecology. Cocoa cultivation was effectively a wasting asset, rather like mining, and the cocoa frontier was driven restlessly along, sometimes 'jumping' huge distances from one continent to another. This exacerbated uncertainties in supply, contributing to price volatility. In the longer term, cocoa represented a threat to the very existence of the tropical forest, and thus to gathering activities, biodiversity and climate. To be sure, the ecological impact of the cultivation of cocoa and other tropical tree crops has only recently reached a crisis point, but negative effects were experienced in limited areas as early as the eighteenth century, notably in small tropical islands (Grove 1995).

The missing links: traders and shippers

The intermediary stages in any commodity chain are usually the most obscure (Laan 1997). There are several published histories of cocoa plantations and chocolate manufacturers for the period before 1914, but those on intermediaries are few and far between (Greenhill 1972; Greenhill 1996; Harwich Vallenilla 1996). Historians attracted to the world of intermediaries have rarely looked at their role in handling a single commodity. Thus a magisterial study of eighteenth-century Bordeaux has a single passing reference to cocoa, leaving the reader to guess who dealt in this commodity (Butel 1974).

Too little is known about the peddlers and storekeepers who bought cocoa beans, or the muleteers, boatmen, cask-rollers and porters who brought them to commercial centres. The same can be said of the merchants who exported beans, and the shippers, who usually hired their services but sometimes owned the cargo. However, even less is known about commercial networks in importing countries, and their ramifications overseas. Merchants, or dealers, bought cocoa to sell to manufacturers, sometimes selling beans that they had not yet acquired. Brokers did not own beans, but earned a commission by arranging sales, sometimes representing both sellers and purchasers. Agents acted for one of the parties, usually chocolate manufacturers (Dand 1993: 97–100).

4

Intermediaries were potentially vulnerable to being cut out by producers of either chocolate or cocoa. Chocolate manufacturers sometimes purchased beans directly, and occasionally invested in plantations. Conversely, owners of some large estates marketed their beans, and one enterprising Surinam planter set up a chocolate factory in the Netherlands (Schrover 1991: 183). However, complete vertical integration was rarely attempted and never successful. Even the adoption of intermediary functions by manufacturers or planters was relatively uncommon, as the economic logic of specialisation told against the practice.

From the information available, accusations of speculation at intermediary levels in the cocoa chain were rarely well founded before 1914. There were attempts to corner the market, and further research would probably unearth more examples, but barriers to entry were low and competition was intense. Indeed, traders and transporters may have been the most efficient links in the commodity chain. Only when estate owners intervened to push up cocoa prices from the 1890s was there major malfunctioning in the market.

Intermediaries were open to accusations of collusion and speculation, because they formed small and tight knit communities of trust. Given high risks and delayed returns, problems which were only slowly and incompletely resolved before 1914, the question of agency was crucial. Relying on ethnic and religious norms, communities threatened members with exclusion, equivalent to 'social death'. Once the danger of untrustworthy agents was reduced, the costs of doing business fell. However, the widespread notion that competition was thereby eliminated is false. No entrepreneurial community could survive unless it encouraged fierce rivalry, not only with other specialised communities, but also within its own ranks (Dobbin 1996).

The end of the line: manufacturers and consumers

Accusations of cartelisation have been as frequent, and somewhat better documented, at the stage at which cocoa beans were turned into chocolate. Small workshops prevailed initially, and large Western chocolate companies only began to emerge from the 1850s, exploiting new economies of scale in roasting and grinding. They produced finished chocolate, cocoa butter and cocoa powder, the latter two sold to other manufacturers. Unsweetened plain chocolate was bought by a plethora of confectioners and bakers, many of them self-employed.

This process of concentration did not automatically entail collusion and cartels. The only exhaustively studied national chocolate industry is that of Britain, where the three largest firms reached agreements on pricing and advertising, assisted by close ties between inter-related Quaker manufacturers. However, these agreements were limited in scope and not very effective prior to 1914 (Fitzgerald 1995). Moreover, the links between British

5

firms were exceptional in their intensity, and were not replicated in the chocolate industries of the Netherlands, Switzerland or the United States (Schrover 1991; Heer 1966; Brenner 1999). The existing evidence points to equally loose connections in other countries.

Chocolate was subject to unpredictable whims of fashion, much affected by competing products. The Western temperance movement was a powerful ally, springing originally from Protestant strictures against 'demon alcohol'. However, the temperance movement also favoured tea and coffee, and other non-alcoholic beverages were popular in some corners of the globe. Technical change played a part in the never-ending competition for market share, albeit a lesser one before the 1880s than is generally claimed. Product diversification and advertising, the latter precociously developed in the case of chocolate, had equal roles to play, although both were costly and risky strategies.

Chocolate was prey to fiscal pressure and protectionist regulations. Customs duties on cocoa beans and sales taxes on prepared chocolate were crushing in the mercantilist era, as luxuries were deemed fit to bear a heavy burden. Although liberalisation began to gather pace from 1765, it suffered a temporary reversal in the wars of the end of the century, and its tempo was highly diverse, both geographically and chronologically. The temptation to tax this discretionary item in people's consumption was always there, only tempered by a fear of political unpopularity.

The liberal era as a unit of study

The age of liberalism is of special interest because it provided cocoa's best chance of acting as a dynamo for development. The gradual freeing of commodity markets, the growing mobility of labour and capital, and an ever more stable single currency (gold), offered cocoa producers a chance to benefit from rising Western consumption of chocolate, itself driven by the impact of free trade. To be sure, the extent to which this opportunity was seized was conditioned by a gap between the liberal ideal and the reality on the ground, but it mainly reflected the ability of historical actors to grasp this prospect.

The onset of the liberal era was not clearly marked. Reforms in the Spanish empire, by far the largest cocoa producer at the time, began in a small way with the accession of the Bourbon dynasty in 1700. However, it took humiliation in the Seven Years War of 1756–63 to give Spain a new sense of urgency. The 1765 Spanish decree on colonial trade is thus taken as the starting point for this book. To be sure, reforms went into reverse with the outbreak of the French Revolutionary Wars in 1793, and recuperation after the wars was painfully slow. Free trade did not really prevail until the middle of the nineteenth century, and its triumph was incomplete. The doctrine was increasingly questioned from the 1880s, although some of its fruits continued to develop up to 1914 (Capie 1994).

Another reason for focusing on the century and a half from 1765 to 1914 is a curious gap in the historiography of cocoa. Much has been written about pre-Columbian cocoa, the Spanish destruction of the Mesoamerican economy, Baroque Europe's love affair with chocolate, and the Iberian privileged companies of the eighteenth century. A slowly thickening fog then falls over historical writing, becoming most dense during the depression of the 1820s to the 1840s, and only dissipating slightly during the subsequent partial recovery of the world cocoa market up to the 1870s. Indeed, cocoa forms one of the greatest gaps in the post-independence economic historiography of Latin American commodities (Bulmer-Thomas 1994: 36). At the same time, the spread of cocoa to Africa and Asia prior to the 1880s has been neglected. The great boom of the 1880s to 1914 has been better covered, although the world's first specialised cocoa journal, *Der Gordian*, was written in German, and thus remains a neglected source for many authors from cocoa-producing countries.

The existence of this 'black hole' is particularly unfortunate, for the commodity chain altered dramatically in this era. As the volume of cocoa production increased prodigiously, techniques of cultivation actually became less intensive. Whereas cocoa was mainly grown by slaves on estates in 1765, coerced labour was fading away by 1914, and it looked as though estates were going the same way. The individual merchant, controlling the chain from the purchase of beans to final sale, was replaced by a host of specialised intermediaries. Productive units evolved from small pharmacies and workshops into large mechanised factories, employing thousands of people. In the West, chocolate was transformed from a heavily taxed luxury for wealthy aristocrats into a moderately priced item in the weekly budgets of industrial workers. This process was quickened and deepened as chocolate became widely consumed as a food.

These tumultuous changes were accompanied by great shifts in the geographical location of cocoa production. The Iberian conquest of the New World had already spread cocoa cultivation from its Mesoamerican origins to northern South America, turning Venezuela into the world's main producer. The onset of the liberal era witnessed the triumph of Ecuador, with the Brazilian Amazon jostling for second place. As the nineteenth century wore on, a trio of New World territories challenged for the number one spot: the Brazilian state of Bahia, Trinidad, and the Dominican Republic. A greater threat came from Africa. The Portuguese island colony of São Tomé and Príncipe briefly became the world's largest producer in 1905, and The Gold Coast [Ghana] took a sustained lead in 1911. However, confident predictions that the Asia-Pacific zone would prove a formidable contender failed to materialise at the time.

Geographical shifts in output were paralleled by equally revolutionary changes in the spatial distribution of consumption. Following the Iberian conquest of the New World, consumers were mainly located in southwestern Europe and the lands bordering the Caribbean, with the Philippines as a distant outlier. This pattern only began to change from around the 1860s, as industrialisation and urbanisation turned the northern zones of America and Europe into the largest industrial transformers of cocoa beans. There were no surprises in the position of the United States, Germany, Britain and France among the top half-dozen customers for cocoa beans in 1914, but the presence of the Dutch and Swiss in this charmed circle was more unexpected. It was due to the spectacular growth of exports of drinking chocolate from Netherlands and eating chocolate from Switzerland.

The liberal era was brought to a violent conclusion by the First World War. Historians of Latin America tend to place the break later, around 1930, but such a periodisation seems ill conceived in the case of cocoa. Although there were attempts to salvage something from the wreckage of liberalism after 1918, the 'war to end all wars' brought to a head a number of major discontinuities. There was a steep and durable fall in the real price of cocoa, often missed because of inflation engendered by the war. There was also a marginalisation of large estates, a long-lasting shift in the centre of production from Latin America to West Africa, more trade within currency blocks, greater public intervention in marketing, new restrictions on the free movement of entrepreneurs and workers, and greater cartelisation of the chocolate industry.

Glib talk about globalisation conceals the fact that the international environment remains in many ways less free today than it was in 1914, despite much liberalisation since 1945. If coerced labour is now marginal, both workers and entrepreneurs face huge obstacles in moving freely over frontiers. There have been ill judged attempts to resuscitate estates, even to set up state farms, and government meddling in marketing lingers on. The world payments system has not yet returned to conditions prevailing under the gold standard, and protection and cartels of all kinds persist, ranging from 'fortress Europe' to shipping rings. Worst of all, governments continue to form associations to drive up the cocoa price, unwittingly bringing it down in the medium- and long term. Far from being in the uncharted seas of globalisation, we have yet to catch up with the world as it was before the cataclysm that broke out in 1914.

Conclusion

Topik and Wells (1998: vii) consider that exporting primary commodities was a 'dead end', but that is too harsh a judgement. The removal of mercantilist shackles from the world economy brought real benefits to cocoa producers and chocolate consumers alike. To be sure, liberalisation was partial, hesitant and strongly opposed by vested interests. Moreover, there was no take-off into self-sustained economic growth. However, liberalism was no mere trick on the part of dominant countries to sustain the exploitation of weaker ones at lower cost. As long as liberal policies were hegemonic, the economies of most cocoa-producing countries were moving in the direction of a sustained rise in incomes per head, the closest there is to a working definition of development. As liberalism collapsed, that evolution stopped or went into reverse. Policy makers of today could do worse than to ponder the successes and failures of the liberal era.

2

THE CONSUMPTION OF CHOCOLATE

It might seem perverse to begin at the end of the commodity chain, but demand for chocolate, or even addiction in the case of 'chocoholics', can be seen as the prime mover of the whole chain. There was a favourable long-term trend in demand for chocolate up to 1914, embedded in cultural preferences, and occasionally affected by shifts in taste, production techniques, availability or cost (Burnett 1999; Barr 1998). This chapter concentrates on changing fashions and competing products, while the themes of manufacturing and state intervention are taken up later.

A psychoactive alkaloid, theobromine, makes chocolate mildly stimulating and slightly addictive. This brings chocolate into competition with similar beverages, governed by complex social rituals. Theobromine has a less violent effect on the nervous system and is possibly less addictive than alkaloids in rival products. Coffee and tea both depend on caffeine for their impact, as do maté and *guaraná*. Stimulating alkaloids are also found in products that are smoked, such as nicotine in tobacco, or chewed, such as caffeine in kola nuts and cocaine in coca leaves (Coe and Coe 1996: 28–34; Macmillan 1925: chs 24–5; *http*: 'A modern herbal').

There is a long tradition of distinguishing between stimulants, on the one hand, and drugs and alcohol on the other. However, this distinction is fraught with difficulties, reflecting social attitudes as much as scientific evidence (Sherratt 1995). Cocaine is a prohibited alkaloid today, whereas Sigmund Freud regarded it as a useful stimulant. Similarly, opium was widely consumed in East and Southeast Asia as a stimulant, to combat physical fatigue and hunger (Newman 1995). The distinction between 'good stimulants' and 'bad drugs' was nevertheless of vital historical importance, as temperance campaigners championed the former and attacked the latter.

Many products could replace 'demon drink', but beverages made with boiled liquids enjoyed a great hygienic advantage over cold drinks. It was not until the advent of chlorination, pasteurisation and industrial production methods in the late nineteenth century that rivalry became more intense. Alkaloids extracted from coca leaves and kola nuts were added to industrially produced soft drinks from the 1870s, most famously in Coca-Cola, launched in Atlanta in 1886 as a temperance drink and a 'brain tonic', albeit losing cocaine from its formula in 1906 (Burnett 1999: chs 1–2 and 5).

Unlike most hot beverages available before 1914, chocolate had great nutritional value. Its high fat content, together with some protein, bridged the gap that often existed between stimulants and food. Drinking chocolate thus acquired a particular association with cold climates and seasons, even though the beverage originated in tropical Mesoamerica and was sometimes taken cold. At the same time, excessive fat in chocolate posed problems of solubility and digestibility, not overcome till cocoa butter was regularly and effectively pressed out in the late nineteenth century.

A little chocolate was eaten as a snack throughout its history, but eating chocolate only developed a truly significant market at the end of the nineteenth century. This helped consumption to grow faster than that of tea, coffee and other established competitors. The invention of milk chocolate brought about a convergence of interests with the dairy industry, and the incorporation of chocolate into sweets, biscuits and cakes strengthened links with sugar and wheat. However, chocolate was probably still more drunk than eaten as late as 1914.

The unique taste of chocolate is its final, and most elusive characteristic. Although partial substitutes have been found for cocoa butter, no product has ever been discovered to match the subtle taste of cocoa powder. The roasted pods of the Mediterranean carob tree, probably eaten since antiquity as 'Saint John's bread', come closest. However, the use of carob as an alternative to chocolate is quite recent, the result of concerns about fat and alkaloids in chocolate (*http*: 'Carob').

Apart from its physical properties, chocolate was vulnerable to changing social perceptions. Entering the industrial age as a prestigious luxury for Western aristocrats and an article of daily necessity for Amerindians, chocolate was often rejected as decadent in the West and uncivilised in Latin America. The image of chocolate reached its nadir in the first half of the nineteenth century, when it was typecast as a superannuated and indigestible beverage. A generation later, chocolate was rescued by temperance campaigners, technical change and advertising magic. Pressing out cocoa butter made chocolate drinks a wholesome alternative to alcohol, chocolate bars became a weekly treat in proletarian households, and attractively wrapped chocolate confectionery became an esteemed gift.

The spread of chocolate and its competitors

Spanish expansion in the sixteenth century widened chocolate consumption, both socially and geographically. When the Spaniards arrived in Mesoamerica, cocoa beans were a currency and chocolate was drunk cold or hot, unsweetened, and mixed with strong spices, including chilli. Sumptuary and ritual restrictions dictated when it could be taken, and by whom. The

Spaniards swept away these restrictions and diffused a novel beverage, sweet-ened with cane sugar and flavoured with vanilla or cinnamon. In this form, the drink had its greatest success around the Caribbean Basin, and across the Pacific in the distant Philippines (Coe and Coe 1996: chs 2–4; Harwich 1992: chs 1–3). Chocolate made less progress south of the equator, where it tended to remain confined to Spaniards and wealthy Creoles. However, chocolate was banned by the Jesuits in the River Plate area in 1677, together with similar substances, indicating that it must have been a temptation to some (Garavaglia 1983: 41, 51–2, 54–5, 92). Rich and poor drank chocolate in Quito, but the Amerindians of the Andes hardly touched it (Arosemena 1991: II, 545).

Chocolate's main competitors in the New World were plants related to the common holly and containing caffeine. The Spanish conquest trans-formed an Amerindian infusion made from the parched and broken leaves of maté (*Ilex paraguayensis*) into an item of mass consumption. Mainly collected from forests in eastern Paraguay and neighbouring parts of Brazil, maté was domesticated by the Jesuits. It was exported on a large scale to southern ranching zones, Chile, the mines of Peru, and the Quito highlands. In contrast, little maté was consumed in the heartland of Brazil, the viceroy-alty of New Spain or Europe (Garavaglia 1983; Linhares 1969). A related plant, guayusa (*Ilex guayusa*), grew in the Amazonian forests of modern Ecuador (*http*: 'Maté'; Garavaglia 1983: 46). Yaupon (*Ilex cassine* or *vomi-toria*) was another relative. Growing from Florida to North Carolina, it was prized by both Amerindians and immigrants (Simmonds 1888: 201–2; Emerson 1908: II, 438–9; Scott 1964: 109).

Two further pre-Columbian legacies blocked the advance of chocolate in the New World. The indigenous peoples of the high Andes, as far north as Santa Marta in modern Colombia, preferred to chew the leaves of the coca bush (*Erythroxylum coca*). Debilitating addiction was a danger, for cocaine was a stronger alkaloid than caffeine (Garavaglia 1983: 41; Simmonds 1888: 215–16; Eder 1913: 186). Much consumed in northern and central Brazil was guaraná (*Paullinia cupana* or *sorbilis*), a bitter seed with a high caffeine content, from a woody climbing plant cultivated on the middle Amazon. The seeds were dried, roasted, powdered, made into a dough, and then dried again into hard cylinders, to be grated and mixed with water (Simmonds 1888: 181, 213–4; Macmillan 1925: 359).

From the range of stimulants discovered in the New World, Europe embraced only chocolate and tobacco. Indeed, such was the success of chocolate in Catholic Europe that it became part of Baroque civilisation (Coe and Coe 1996: ch. 5). Nowhere was this more true than in Spain, where even servants regularly drank it by the early eighteenth century, and their masters indulged in it, hot or cold, from morning till night. France and regions under Habsburg rule took to chocolate, but Portugal's consumption remained low (Stols 1996: 50–2). The Portuguese had developed a taste for tea from their early contacts with China, which they passed on to their British allies when Charles II married a Portuguese princess (Walvin 1997: 12–14). Competition from coffee and tea was generally stiff in Protestant northern Europe, although chocolate was accepted by Protestant preachers as one way to combat alcohol (Harwich 1992: 65–103; Bizière 1979; Schivelbusch 1992: 22). North Europeans drank chocolate more regularly in their Caribbean colonies, where cocoa beans were cheaper and more readily available (Walvin 1997: 98; Coe and Coe 1996: 199).

With the exception of the Philippines, chocolate failed to make significant inroads beyond Europe. An Ottoman Turkish official in the late seventeenth century pronounced it to be disgusting. In Monsoon Asia, chocolate was chiefly consumed by Catholic missionaries (Coe and Coe 1996: 161–2, 177–8). Chinese scholars accepted it into their pharmacopoeia as an aphrodisiac, but made no great use of it (Pelletier and Pelletier 1861: 123). Alternative beverages barred the way. Tea reigned supreme in the Confucian world of East Asia, and was taken to Russia early in the seventeenth century (Scott 1964: ch. 1). Tea was also favoured in Central Asia, Persia and North Africa, but coffee dominated the central lands of Islam from the sixteenth century, spreading to South and Southeast Asia (Haarer 1956: ch. 1). More anciently established in the lands of Islam was salep (sahleb), a 'nervine restorative', and, like chocolate, a 'fattener' (*EB* 1929: XIX, 876). Originating in Persia, salep was made from the roasted and pounded roots of wild orchids. It was popular from the Balkans to northern India, and had some adepts in the West (Simmonds 1888: 214; anon. 1890: II, 421; *http*: 'A modern herbal').

Masticatories containing stimulants were another barrier to the spread of chocolate in the tropics. Southeast Asians and many South Asians chewed a mixture of areca nuts (*Areca catechu*), betel leaf (*Piper betle*) and ground lime, which released a cocktail of alkaloids (Reid 1988: 38, 42–5). Related to betel was *Piper methysticum*, the root of which was chewed and fermented to make *kava*, the 'national drink' of the South Pacific. The fresh qat leaf (*Catha edulis*) was favoured in South Arabia and adjoining parts of East Africa (Macmillan 1925: chs 24–5; *http*: 'A modern herbal'). Kola nuts, mainly *Cola nitida* and *Cola acuminata*, were chewed over much of tropical Africa. They contained caffeine and a little theobromine, and were nutritious (Lovejoy 1995; Bauer 1963: 381).

The passing of the Baroque age, 1760s–1790s

Although chocolate consumption continued to increase in the second half of the eighteenth century, the threat to Baroque civilisation undermined the commodity's future. Chocolate was associated with the idle clergy and nobility of Catholic and absolutist regimes. A popular motif for painters was the breakfast scene, in which a noble woman, often in bed and revealing much of her ample flesh, languidly took her morning chocolate in the company of a priest and assorted men (Schivelbusch 1992: 85–92). The persecution of the Jesuits, starting in Portugal in 1759 and culminating in the dissolution of the order in 1773, was an early blow to chocolate consumption, and an omen of worse to come (Coe and Coe 1996: 210–11).

Tea and coffee were serious rivals, perceived as incarnating the values of the rising bourgeoisie (Schivelbusch 1992: 85–92; Bizière 1979). Coffee houses spawned newspapers, clubs and radical ideas, although chocolate was often served in these establishments (Schneider 1998: 558, 560, 575–6). Tea and coffee represented 'sobriety, serious purpose, trustworthiness and respectability', contrasting with the feckless excesses of the aristocracy. Moreover, Baroque cuisine was slowly falling out of favour, as strong flavours and smells became unfashionable, whereas lightness and moderation were all the rage (Burnett 1999: 50–1, 95). Chocolate stood accused of being more expensive than its competitors, more time-consuming to prepare, and too oily (Walvin 1997: 97 8).

Spain remained by far and away the most significant Western market for chocolate, albeit seduced by rival beverages. To lack chocolate was said to be the same as being short of bread in France, and some chocolate was eaten with almonds or hazel nuts (Schneider 1998: 550, 552). People of the middling sort commonly partook of a thick chocolate beverage at breakfast, dipping little cakes into it. The habit reached down to the 'common people', seen by some as a 'regrettable extravagance', although most workers broke their fast with alcohol. At the same time, radicals condemned chocolate as part of the absolutist lifestyle, and some people began to take coffee and tea, to appear more European. Coffee houses patronised by men emerged in major towns, although they also served chocolate (Kany 1932: 151–2, 271, 329, 419).

Italy was the land where 'the precious chocolate...was the basis of everybody's breakfast and the evening *rinfreschi*' (Vaussard 1962: 194). Italian cooks showed considerable inventiveness, even adding chocolate to pasta and meat dishes. The Roman Church was among the best customers, and it was rumoured that Pope Clement XIV had died by imbibing poisoned chocolate in 1774. Spanish influence was strong in southern Italy, a bastion of the chocolate habit. In the north, some Venetian artists drank coffee for its radical chic and cheapness (Coe and Coe 1996: 213–20). However, Casanova praised chocolate's qualities, as did other Venetian intellectuals of the time (Bernard 1996: 86; Schneider 1998: 553).

It is not clear how much French social and ideological divisions affected chocolate consumption. It was said of Paris in 1768 that 'the great sometimes partake of it, old people often, but the common people never' (Bernard 1996: 85). The magistrates of Bayonne declared in 1763 that chocolate had long formed part of the 'daily food' of the town, but this ancient Basque centre of chocolate manufacture, much influenced by Spain, was not typical (Léon 1893: 72). The Philosophes defiantly drank coffee in the *salons* where they propagated subversive ideas, even though Voltaire preferred to drink chocolate for breakfast. Conversely, Queen Marie-Antoinette was as fond of coffee as of chocolate for her breakfast. The Marquis de Sade, an icon of aristocratic decadence, was a true 'chocoholic', who pestered his wife from prison to obtain supplies of the 'food of the gods'. A French peculiarity was an early taste for eating chocolate in biscuits, marzipan, desserts, ices and sweets. Even the gritty mass used to prepare drinking chocolate was sometimes eaten by people in a hurry (Coe and Coe 1996: 205–7, 222–6, 231–4).

In the Austrian possessions, Catholic and culturally close to Spain, chocolate spread beyond the aristocracy. In Austria and Hungary, beer and wine vanished from the breakfast tables of the bourgeoisie from the mid-eighteenth century, giving way to chocolate and coffee. However, coffee was the senior partner in 'civilising' the middle class, and it alone was mentioned in connection with artisans (Sandgruber 1986: 75–6, 80–1). Chocolate was slowly losing ground to coffee in the southern Low Countries (Belgium), but the urban poor drank 'little coffee' in 1776, made from roasted cocoa shells boiled with milk, sugar and cinnamon (Swaelen 1996: 61–2; Libert 1996: 78–9).

North Germans and Dutch were the greatest European coffee drinkers, including poor people in town and country, but a number of German poets and writers loved chocolate, notably Schiller and Goethe, and there was quite a market for chocolate in the Netherlands. It is not clear why only imports of coffee and tea were banned in 1768 by Frederick the Great, when he sought to improve Prussia's balance of payments (Schneider 1998: 552–3, 558–63; Slijper 1927: 140–1). Frederick assiduously propagated the virtues of the roasted and ground root of locally grown chicory (*Cichorium intybus*), as a partial or total substitute for coffee, and Prussia boasted the first factory to powder the root in 1770 (Barr 1998: 213; Schivelbusch 1992, 73–9). Chicory had been eaten since antiquity, but its use as a coffee substitute was pioneered in the Netherlands around 1750. Its main disadvantage was that it contained no stimulating alkaloid (Burnett 1999: 84; Smith 1996: 208; *http*: 'A modern herbal').

The reduction of British tea duties in 1784 led to a surge of imports from China, possibly contraband entering legal channels, making tea an item of mass consumption among labourers in southern Britain by the 1790s (Burnett 1999: 31–2, 52–6; Barr 1998: 217–18). The growing popularity of tea led to a 'sharp decline in the sale of coffee, cocoa and chocolate', ruining coffee and chocolate houses (Drummond and Wilbraham 1939: 244). However, upper-class men continued to partake of chocolate inside and outside the home, even if coffee was more esteemed by the 1790s (Burnett 1999: 50–1, 71–5, 79–80). At the other end of the spectrum, the Royal Navy issued slabs of chocolate to seamen in the Caribbean from 1780, spreading an appreciation of the beverage among the poor (Wagner 1987: 16).

Despite the rarity of places of public consumption in British North America, drinking chocolate was available and was consumed by the well-to-do. Boston pharmacists advertised the availability of chocolate as early as 1712, and some leading figures breakfasted regularly on it towards the end of the century (Coe and Coe 1996: 230; Scott 1964: 101). Colonial Virginians made chocolate in the manner of northern Europe, with boiling milk rather than water, although they might add egg yolks in the Spanish fashion. Competing beverages were coffee, green tea, black tea and salep, the latter drunk 'in china cups as chocolate' (Fitchett 1906: 60–7).

Chocolate stood to benefit from the independence of the United States, as tea became a symbol of the iniquities of colonial taxation and regulation. The Boston Tea Party of 1773, the launching pad for the American Revolution, was prolonged by a boycott of tea (Barr 1998: 208; Scott 1964: 108). John Adams, the second president, declared his enthusiasm for chocolate while on a visit to Spain in 1799 (Coe and Coe 1996: 212). Thomas Jefferson, the third president, hoped that nourishing chocolate would become the preferred beverage of the United States (Young 1994: 36). In practice, however, independence allowed free access to supplies of tea and coffee, which poured into the United States in ever increasing quantities. In the great New England port of Salem, coffee was the usual breakfast drink, although hot chocolate or tea were consumed with a light supper (Phillips 1947: 170–1, 347).

Standard accounts of chocolate in this period underestimate the scale of consumption in Latin America, where chocolate was an item of basic consumption (Humboldt 1811: 436). This was especially true of Mexico, where the poor and slaves drank it (Arcila Farías 1950: 40–1, 273; León Borja and Szászdi Nagy 1964: 16–17). Valets, cobblers, muleteers and coachmen took chocolate at least twice a day, sometimes four times or more, and every household possessed a stone to grind cocoa in 1775. Indigenous peoples sometimes consumed their chocolate cold, whereas Creoles and Mestizos preferred it hot (Stols 1996: 44–5). In the dry northwest, missionaries 'ordered large quantities of it annually' (Deeds 1995: 90). Spanish traders breakfasted on it every morning (Brading 1971: 110). A famous Mexican dish for festive occasions was *mole poblano*, turkey or chicken in a chocolate and chilli sauce, allegedly invented in a colonial convent (Lambert Ortiz 1968: 142–3).

Chocolate in Central America had long been 'a basic food staple, drunk in huge, if not incredible quantities by Indians, and enjoyed by the poorer Creoles' (MacLeod 1973: 242). It remained king in Guatemala, drunk at breakfast and after meals, and incorporated into nine different beverages (Rubio Sánchez 1958: 89–90). In Costa Rica in 1785, 'the poor people nourish themselves with chocolate, which they drink at any time', mixed with unrefined sugar. The Bishop of Honduras opined in 1791 that 'even the poorest person drinks cacao twice a day, and many drink it three or four times a day', resulting in imports from other provinces (Fernández Molina 1992: 425–39). Chocolate was among the basic rations issued to labourers on an estate in León in 1773, carefully entered in the accounts (Romero Vargas 1976: 464).

The continuing use of cocoa beans as currency boosted demand in Central America. Repeated attempts to demonetise cocoa in Nicaragua foundered on the scarcity of silver coins and Amerindian preferences (Newson 1987: 280, 296). Guatemala's Maya traders used beans for their commercial operations in 1763 (Solórzano 1963: 185). The exchange rate between cocoa beans and silver was thus officially confirmed in Costa Rica in 1778 (Saenz Maroto 1970: 554).

The threat from coffee was no more than a cloud on the horizon for Mesoamerica. Jesuits arranged a public drinking of the new beverage in Guatemala City in 1743, but it was slow to catch on (King 1974: 91–2). In 1778 the Mexican authorities warned that people might turn to coffee, where imports of cheap Guayaquil cocoa beans were to be restricted, but this was a ploy to put pressure on Madrid (Arcila Farías 1950: 281). Nevertheless, Tabasco was sending coffee as well as cocoa to Veracruz by 1784, and great hopes were pinned on the crop in 1794 (Ruiz Abreu 1989: 70; Florescano and Gil Sánchez 1976: 278–9).

The threat from coffee was greater in the Spanish and French Antilles. Chocolate was the usual breakfast beverage in eighteenth-century Havana (Arcila Farias 1950: 89). The same was true of Puerto Rico, even among the poor (Gil-Bermejo 1970: 189). In Santiago de Cuba, guests who called after the siesta in 1800 were offered chocolate, served with fancy breads and fruit preserves (Wright 1910: 360). The sparse population of Santo Domingo consumed a great deal of locally grown chocolate, although they also grew coffee for themselves by the 1780s (Sevilla Soler 1980: 100). The first coffee house opened in Cuba in 1722, and the island's limited coffee output was supplemented with imports from Puerto Rico in the 1790s (Pérez de la Riva 1944: 18–19, 178–9). The people of the French islands were reported to drink a particularly delicious chocolate, even though Saint-Domingue was the most dynamic coffee producer in the world (Coe and Coe 1996: 222).

The northern marches of South America were addicted to chocolate. Venezuela was estimated to retain about a quarter of its large harvest for local needs (Humboldt 1941: III, 175). Prosperity in the gold mines of the Nuevo Reino (Colombia) resulted in a tenfold increase in imports of beans between 1740 and 1805, brought by ship and mule (Twinam 1982: 69–72; Patiño 1963: 302). The central highlands and coast consumed much chocolate, made from local beans (McFarlane 1993: 44, 47, 176). The usual breakfast and night time drink in Cartagena was chocolate (Walker 1822: I, 499). The wealthy in Bogotá drank chocolate three times a day, brought from Cúcuta and Neiva by mule. Furthermore, chocolate was an 'essential part of the diet of the poor' of the city, who eked out their meagre purchases by adding maize or wheat. After salt, cocoa was the most important article of internal commerce (Brungardt 1974: 91–2).

Chocolate made some progress in the viceroyalties of Peru and the River Plate, especially the former, as political reforms stimulated an influx of Spaniards (León Borja and Szászdi Nagy 1964: 28). One Lima official recorded in his diary that he drank chocolate morning and night in 1790 (Descola 1968: 150–1). Chocolate came to be seen by Creoles as European and progressive, although this reputation was shared with coffee and tea, and Buenos Aires distributed Guayaquil cocoa in the River Plate region (Garavaglia 1983: 54–5, 92–3, 419–20). However, Jesuit fathers of the Mojos missions, keen to sell their cocoa, complained in the 1760s that 'the very Spaniards of Peru, even though they dispose of an abundance of cocoa, prefer maté' (Eder 1985: 151). In 1775, Lima households rarely owned grinding stones to make chocolate (Stols 1996: 44).

Competition came from both old and new products. Coffee arrived in Peru some time after 1760, coming from Guayaquil, where production for local consumption reached a mere four tonnes in 1788. The first coffee house in Lima appeared in 1771, and there were half a dozen twenty years later. However, the novel drink was narrowly restricted to the male urban elite (*MP*: I, 109–10; XI, 168; XII, 169–70). Maté imported from Paraguay was still the usual hot beverage taken at home by speakers of Spanish in Peru and Quito (Parrón Salas 1995: 259, 521, 524; *MP*: I, 110; Walker 1822: I, 500). Exports of Paraguayan maté reached a peak in the late eighteenth century, and some Brazilian maté began to find its way to Spanish colonies (Garavaglia 1983: 83–96). As for Amerindians in the Andes, they stuck to chewing coca leaves (*MP*: XI, 205–57).

In Brazil, the wealthy drank tea from China, copying Portuguese practice, and the maté habit only caught on in the far south (Linhares 1969: 74–88, 113, 164). Coffee houses in Salvador were supplied with locally grown coffee by the 1810s (Spix and Martius 1976: II, 136–9, 147, 151). In the great forests of the north, Amerindians sucked the sweet pulp around bitter unfermented cocoa beans, which they then spat out, while missionaries helped to diffuse *guaraná* (Humboldt 1852: II, 365; Patiño 1963: 271).

Chocolate was well established in the Philippines. By 1810, 'the use of chocolate [was] greatly extended among the natives of easy circumstances' (Comyn 1969: 12). In the independent Islamic state of Sulu, sultan and nobles breakfasted with chocolate in gilded tumblers, in which they dipped macaroons obtained from Manila. Indeed, chocolate had become 'the common beverage of all classes' in Sulu, probably due to the large number of Catholic Filipinos taken as slaves (Moor 1968: 39–40, 44, 50). Elsewhere in Asia, Catholics remained the main consumers of chocolate, such as missionaries and Portuguese traders in Thailand (Coe and Coe 1996: 178).

18

In 1778, cocoa was found in Malaya, growing in the garden of a Portuguese widow in Dutch Malacca (Burkill 1966: 2188).

The impact of revolution and war, 1790s–1820s

Political associations and geographical factors may have done a disservice to chocolate, as the old order collapsed. To the extent that it was identified in the minds of revolutionaries with the decadence and immorality of the nobility and clergy, chocolate seemed destined to be consigned to the dustbin of history (Collet 1996: 10–11). That said, such an issue must have paled into insignificance as the tide of revolution and war submerged Europe. Cocoa also lacked an Asian 'back door' into Europe, unlike tea and coffee. At the end of the eighteenth century, there was a sudden surge in Russia's overland imports of tea from China, much of which was taken on to German markets (Gardella 1994: 38–9; Blanchard 1989: 253). Similarly, Yemeni and Ethiopian coffee could travel overland, although production was too small to take up much of the slack in Europe. (Thurber 1881: 58–63).

The main beneficiaries from chocolate's discomfiture were probably local substances, protected by naval blockades and punitive taxation (Brillat-Savarin n.d.: 117–18). Thus the use of chicory spread from Germany to France (Burnett 1999: 84). Salep, now made from wild English orchid roots rather than imported from the Levant, took the fancy of the labouring population of London. Drunk with milk and sugar, it was not unlike chocolate of the time. Charles Lamb declared it to be an ideal breakfast for chimney-sweeps, taken with a slice of bread and butter (Barr 1998: 214, 251–2; *http*: 'A modern herbal'). A bewildering variety of products was tried in Austria, ranging from roast barley and other cereals, through to acorns, beech masts, figs, and blue lupin beans (Sandgruber 1986: 79–80). However, none of these substitutes contained the alkaloids that consumers craved, with the possible exception of lupin beans.

Disruptions in supplies of cocoa beans in Latin America varied, but only Cuba and Puerto Rico were really vulnerable to naval blockade. In the self-sufficient Nuevo Reino, war had no discernible effect at all (Brungardt 1974: 91–2). There may have been some progress in the consumption of coffee, available locally, and the loosening of the Iberian mercantilist straitjacket facilitated imports of tea, albeit at great expense. In eastern Venezuela, chocolate was drunk first thing in the morning and last thing at night in the 1810s, but coffee was already being taken after dinner. During 'collations' offered by the Caracas elite, chocolate, coffee, tea and Spanish wines were served (Walker 1822: I, 169, 470).

As chocolate was a local drink, consumed by the poor, revolutionaries in Spanish colonies do not appear to have condemned it. Incomes were probably not seriously affected in most countries until the closing years of the independence struggle. In Mexico, chocolate was 'held in high estimation', and there was no sign of a quest for alternatives (Bullock 1824: 285). There were eight cafes in Lima in 1815, but also a guild of chocolate makers (Anna 1979: 116, 118). Tea, easily accessible, was the beverage of choice of Chinese traders and artisans in the Philippines. There was also a sudden spurt in coffee cultivation from the 1790s, spearheaded by missionaries, but this was probably a response to high coffee prices after the Haïtian revolution (Mallat 1983: 123, 247).

The slump of the 1820s–1840s

Hampered by economic recession and a deeply unfashionable image, chocolate faced one of its most difficult periods after the defeat of Napoleon and the independence of continental Latin America. Incomes plummeted in Spain and in newly independent countries, thrown into turmoil for decades. Substitutes adopted during the war years kept some of the market, albeit more because of economic recession than out of choice, as indicated by the frustrated aspirations of consumers in Austria-Hungary (Sandgruber 1986: 76–7; 80–1).

Mesoamerica, the most important New World market, was devastated by independence. Mexican income per head fell from around $73 in 1800 to $56 in 1845, in 1950 US dollars. The collapse of the mining industry reduced demand for foodstuffs, roads were not repaired, and swarms of bandits infested the countryside (Haber 1989: 13–22). Even though excellent chocolate was found in the most remote locations, Mexico's consumption fell sharply in the 1820s (Ward 1828: I, 79; Bologne 1996: 223). This did not reflect any marked changes in taste. People in Yucatán in the 1830s liked to partake four times a day of a traditional gruel made of roast maize, cocoa, sugar and water (Waldeck 1838: 13). Coffee was available in rural stores in Chiapas in the late 1830s, but chocolate was still the normal breakfast drink across southern Mexico and Central America, consumed after the siesta and in the evening (Stephens 1993: 68, 123, 126, 167, 197, 201–4, 223).

Income was again the problem in the northern marches of South America. Venezuelan chocolate consumption slumped to some 750 tonnes of cocoa beans a year between 1830 and 1860, less than half Humboldt's estimate for 1797 (Middleton 1871: 457; Humboldt 1941: III, 175). A decline in gold mining hit Colombia, although cocoa-producing provinces were still the best markets for Bogotá merchants distributing imported goods in the late 1830s (Schneider 1981: I, 173). Coffee was little in demand (Gosselman 1962: 118–19; Mollien 1824: 380–1, 386–7). Indeed, coffee houses were almost unknown around 1850 in Colombia, although the upper classes copied the French habit of taking coffee and the English one of taking tea (McGreevey 1971: 195; Fuentes 1992: 279).

The Andean countries to the south of Colombia were in a state of flux, as Chinese tea began to push maté aside (*http*: 'Maté'). Tea had become the standard breakfast drink in Guayaquil in 1832, 'even among the descendants of Spaniards', whereas locally grown coffee and cocoa were spurned (Terry 1834: 66). That said, chocolate was widely consumed in Quito in 1833, and was allegedly one of the three passions in women's lives in 1847, while maté and *guayusa* were still very popular (Toscano 1960: 269–71, 306, 326). Similarly, people of modest means in the old viceroyalty of Peru drank more chocolate after independence, as a full-fat beverage, taken with milk and sugar (Garavaglia 1983: 41; Romero 1961: 399, 402). Incomes also revived early in Peru, due to the guano boom from 1840 (Mathew 1981).

Cuba under Spanish rule did not suffer from recession, but coffee became the 'national drink', allegedly 'replacing classic Spanish style chocolate' (Pérez de la Riva 1944: 175, 177). Cubans were certainly precocious coffee drinkers, consuming about 6,000 tonnes by the middle of the century (Sagra 1963: 156). However, coffee houses served both coffee and chocolate, and the numerous immigrant Spaniards preferred chocolate prepared at home. Coffee was perceived as a beverage of 'carters, gamblers and people of ill repute', and the authorities cracked down on coffee houses as centres of subversion (Pérez de la Riva 1944: 173, 177–81). Cubans who breakfasted on chocolate tended to be wealthier than those who chose coffee, although chocolate was consumed at all levels of Cuban society, including slaves (Marrero 1972–89: XI, 134; XIV, 225–6; Mangin 1860: 37–9).

The vast empire of Brazil escaped economic recession, but remained indifferent to chocolate and coffee, despite a surge in exports of both. Maté was available everywhere in the country, and in its traditional form was the favourite beverage from Paraná to the south. Well roasted maté was a poor person's substitute for tea in Rio de Janeiro and the centre of the country. The persistence of the Portuguese attachment to China tea was demonstrated by attempts to grow it in São Paulo and Rio de Janeiro, and by the fact that production did not match consumption (Kidder 1845: I, 251–2, 272–3; Linhares 1969: 82–7, 164, 224; Spix and Martius 1976: I, 73–5). *Guaraná*, grown in the middle Amazon and consumed as a cold, sweetened beverage, was of great importance. It was popular in the mines of Mato Grosso and Goiás, other parts of Brazil, and Amazonian regions of Peru and Venezuela (Spruce 1908: II, 449–53).

Chocolate kept a particularly strong position in the Philippines, experiencing an economic boom under continued Spanish rule. Mallat said of the immigrant Spaniard, 'hardly has he opened his eyes, when he asks for his *chicara de chocolate* from the Indio or Negrito serving him'. He took chocolate again after his evening stroll, although tea was a possible substitute. Lower down the social scale, 'the natives take cocoa once or twice a day, in the same way that the Chinese take tea, dipping in it pieces of sugar cane in place of plain sugar' (Mallat 1983: 86, 345, 349). Beyond the areas under

Spanish control, chocolate remained 'the general drink of natives, which rich and poor take every day' in the Sulu sultanate (Anon. 1849: 82, 110).

There are scattered references to chocolate consumption elsewhere in Asia and Africa. Wealthy Makasarese in southern Sulawesi offered chocolate to European guests in the 1820s, made with beans imported from Manila (Olivier 1834–37: II, 214). In Penang, the main consumers in 1841 were Catholic missionaries (Buckley 1965: 361). One Dutch planter in Java drank an exquisite chocolate, made with his own beans (Hogendorp 1830: 174). However, coffee was the usual beverage of Javanese peasants in the 1820s (Elson 1994: 7). Salep retained its popularity in the Middle East and India, and was found, together with coffee, in Yemeni entrepots in the 1820s (Simmonds 1888: 214; Milburn 1825: 75–6). A little cocoa was grown for local use in Sierra Leone, indicating that freed slaves brought New World habits to Africa (Peterson 1969: 273).

Schivelbusch, like so many others, errs when he declares that old-fashioned chocolate 'vanished with the ancien régime', to be replaced from 1828 by defatted beverages and chocolate bars (Schivelbusch 1992: 92–3). In reality, Catholic aristocrats and clerics were reinstated from 1815 to 1848. Moreover, the patenting of Van Houten's famous cocoa butter press in 1828 had no immediate consequences, not even in the Netherlands (Schrover 1991). Unsweetened bars of full-fat Zeeland chocolate were boiled up with milk or water in the Netherlands until 'far into the nineteenth century' (Slijper 1927: 140–1). The mixing of a little dried chocolate mass with hot milk remained typical of northern Europe as a whole, while the poor in Ireland and the Low Countries made do with cheap cocoa shells. Southern Europeans dissolved larger amounts of chocolate mass in hot or cold water, sometimes adding egg yolks for a richer feast (Mangin 1860: 143–4, 160–1; Pelletier and Pelletier 1861: 123–5). The persistence of traditional beverages, frequently mixed with various starchy substances to absorb the fat, partly accounted for the high premium paid for Caracas Criollo, with its good flavour and low fat content (Hewett 1862: 10–11, 48).

Chocolate suffered from an unfashionable image. The Dutch, in their earthy way, declared it a drink fit only for teetotallers and middle class ladies suffering from constipation (Schrover 1991: 179). Balzac vaunted the virile virtues of coffee, airily denouncing chocolate for contributing to the fall of Spain, by encouraging sensuality, laziness and greed. For Musset and Flaubert, chocolate was the breakfast drink of the idle rich (Bologne 1996: 223–30; Bernard 1996: 90). Dickens reflected another old stereotype, portraying a corrupt Catholic cleric as a chocolate drinker (Coe and Coe 1996: 205). However, such pejorative views were not universal. Goethe made 'a cult of chocolate and avoided coffee' until his death in 1832 (Schivelbusch 1992: 92). Moreover, chocolate retained a reputation as a remedy for many maladies, even though its alleged aphrodisiac properties were widely discounted (Barreta 1841: 38).

While France still imported less cocoa than Spain, Brillat-Savarin asserted in 1825 that 'chocolate has become quite normal in France, and everybody has taken it into their heads to prepare it'. He described chocolate desserts and confectionery in loving detail, while noting that chocolate was still mainly a breakfast drink, and that coffee was spreading (Brillat-Savarin n.d.: 117–21). Balzac's novels suggest that the French bourgeoisie had taken up drinking chocolate from the aristocracy, and gave chocolate confectionery to their children (Bologne 1996: 226, 229).

British imports for consumption progressed, but at a lower level than those of France. The Royal Navy replaced breakfast gruel with an ounce of chocolate in 1824, halved the rum ration a year later, and consumed 179 tonnes of cocoa in 1830 (Wagner 1987: 16–7; Barr 1998: 254; Knapp 1923: 24). However, chocolate was still prepared in pharmacies and drunk largely for health reasons. Advertisements stressed its medicinal properties, and Quaker manufacturers promoted it as an alternative to alcohol (Williams 1931: 11–12, 16, 19; Vernon 1958: 131–42). The temperance movement now advocated complete abstinence from all alcohol, not just spirits, but coffee was the main beneficiary. Coffee spread to the working class, and consumption per head rose nearly to that of tea by 1840. It was frequently mixed with cheap chicory, imported from Belgium or produced in England. Moreover, salep remained popular (Barr 1998: 210–11, 290–3; Burnett 1999: 57–61, 81–3).

Iberian contrasts deepened. Spain remained the largest European market for chocolate, as imports recovered in spite of economic and political travails (Prados de la Escosura 1982: 238, 246). In contrast, the value of Portugal's small cocoa imports trailed far behind those of tea and coffee in the 1840s (*MGCP*). Portuguese settlers in Príncipe in 1836, surrounded by coffee and cocoa trees on their estates, preferred to purchase tea at exorbitant prices from the few foreign ships that called (Omboni 1846: 243–4).

Modest recovery, 1850s–1870s

Although economic conditions improved from around 1850, the performance of drinking chocolate continued to lag behind that of its two main rivals. By about 1880, it was estimated that 500 million people drank tea around the world, compared to 200 million for coffee and only fifty million for chocolate. Green tea was dominant in the Confucian world of East Asia, and in the Islamic lands of Central Asia and North Africa. Black tea ruled the roost in Britain and many British colonies, notably India. Russians drank cheap brick tea mixed with melted butter, which looked like chocolate. The domain of coffee lay in the United States, much of continental Europe, the Near East and the Malay world. The only countries where chocolate clearly prevailed were Spain, Mexico, Colombia and the Philippines (Simmonds 1888; Johnston 1865: 223, 236).

Although mainly a coffee drinker, France overtook Spain as the world's largest cocoa importer. Rejecting both the heavy traditional southern beverage and the low-fat variety gaining ground in northern Europe, the French stuck to a little full-fat chocolate mass dissolved in hot milk. They were also unusual in the extent to which they ate chocolate, both assortments, small centres enrobed in chocolate, and plain dark chocolate with bread, a favourite with children at tea time (Fonssagrives 1875–6: 732–4; Debay 1864: 75–82; Lami 1885: III, 338, 346). That said, only around a million people, or 3 per cent of the population, regularly consumed chocolate in 1867, despite growing sales to people of more modest means (Cerfberr de Medelsheim 1867: 19–20). Coffee's greater stimulating effect was highly prized, Michelet writing in 1863 that coffee was 'the sober drink, the mighty nourishment of the brain' (Schivelbusch 1992: 35). Coffee imports accounted for seventy-nine million Francs in 1866, compared to twelve million for cocoa (*Larousse*: VIII, 727; XII, 30).

Britain's take-off came towards the end of the 1860s, stimulated by rising living standards, the temperance movement, and pressing out cocoa butter to make a more digestible drink. Consumption was further helped by revulsion against harmful substances in food, culminating in the Adulteration of Food Acts of 1872 and 1875. Advertising campaigns now stressed the purity and nutritional qualities of defatted chocolate powders (Othick 1976: 77–87; Fitzgerald 1995: 27–9; Williams 1931: 39–41). The large Italian community in London further 'served to extend the sale and popularize the beverage'. Declining sales of coffee may have been a factor, although this was mainly to the advantage of tea (Simmonds 188: 178–9, 211; Bannister 1890: 1051).

Cocoa imports for consumption grew fast from a small base in the United States, possibly linked to the arrival of immigrants from southwestern Europe. The temperance movement also developed mightily from 1841, despite some reverses (Barr 1998: 293, 306; Cook and Waller 1998: 160–1). In any event, the value of chocolate output doubled between 1849 and 1869, although this paled into insignificance beside the phenomenal growth of coffee (Chiriboga 1980: 364; Thurber 1881: 204–9).

Spaniards remained faithful, poor, and conservative chocolate consumers, sticking to the full-fat beverage of earlier times (Pelletier and Pelletier 1861: 124). The country had the highest consumption of chocolate per head of any country in Europe. It was even said that denying a prisoner his chocolate was one of the worst punishments in the country's gaols (Simmonds 1888: 211–12). In contrast, coffee was marginal. Of the European nations, only Russia, tea drinking and impoverished, consumed less coffee per head than Spain in 1879 (Thurber 1881: 243).

Mexican incomes per head continued to fall until the end of the 1870s, due to domestic and foreign conflicts (Haber 1989: 20; Bulmer-Thomas 1994: 69–70). However, the Mexican passion for drinking chocolate was undimmed. Regularly offered to strangers as a mark of hospitality, it was found in the most humble and remote rural inns (Mangin 1860: 18, 132–3). Henri de Saussure was offered chocolate wherever he went in 1854–6. He noted that there was often nothing else for sale in country stores, and joked that revolutions in Mexico lasted as long as stocks of chocolate (Stols 1996: 45). Consumption of coffee was estimated at only 500 tonnes of beans in 1888. Some Amerindians cultivated it for their own use, however, suggesting that coffee was spreading to those seen as most culturally attached to chocolate (United States 1888: 49–53).

Central America, fast becoming dependent on coffee exports, drank more coffee (Thurber 1881: 240; Rubio Sánchez 1958: 104; United States 1888: 56). However, higher incomes may simultaneously have promoted chocolate consumption. Some Nicaraguan families had taken to drinking coffee at breakfast and after the evening meal, but still preferred chocolate with their midday meal, and last thing at night. Furthermore, cocoa beans continued to be widely used as currency for small transactions (Scherzer 1857: I, 124, 134).

Coffee was even more clearly ahead in the larger Antilles, but chocolate retained a clientele. The 1862 Cuban census listed 111 cafes and only nine chocolate shops in Havana, and eleven cafes to four chocolate shops in Santiago, the second city, although chocolate beverages were routinely served in cafes (Pezuela 1863–66: II, 207; III, 348). Cuban 'rich people, or simply those comfortably off, partake of chocolate every day, and at almost any hour'. The wealthy preferred imports from Venezuela, leaving the local variety to poor people and slaves (Mangin 1860: 37). That said, Cuba imported nearly 4,000 tonnes of coffee from Puerto Rico in 1877 (Thurber 1881: 144). Puerto Rico itself continued to consume some cocoa, despite drinking much coffee (United States 1888: 124). Haïti retained around 500 tonnes of its cocoa crop every year for its own needs, compared to around 7,000 tonnes of coffee (Rouzier 1892–3: II, 128; Thurber 1881: 240). Drinking chocolate of a traditional kind was 'in general use' in the Dominican Republic in 1871, where coffee consumption may have been lower than elsewhere (Rodríguez Demorizi 1960: 78, 293).

Colombia was unusual in sticking to chocolate, whereas coffee was clearly in the lead in Venezuela, with some 9,000 tonnes consumed in 1888 (United States 1888: 21). Such was the level of demand in Colombia that traders found it more remunerative to sell cocoa beans in Antioquia and Bogotá than to ship them abroad in the 1870s (Schenck 1953: 50). Colombians liked to partake of chocolate first thing in the morning and last thing at night, especially in cold mountain climates. Balls of an ounce (28g) of dried chocolate mass were boiled with water and whipped to a foam. Usually incorporating sugar, such balls were common items of retail trade, even eaten with dry bread by the poor (Holton 1967: 46, 67–8, 88, 133, 174, 198, 209). To the north of Bogotá, in 1877–8, chocolate was 'the favourite drink of the natives, which even coffee cannot displace' (GCR 1879). For all that, coffee was increasing in popularity in Colombian towns in the 1870s (Beyer 1947: 310–11).

The Andean lands to the south consumed little coffee, and it was China tea that was blamed for the collapse of maté imports (Linhares 1969: 367; Thurber 1881: 240; United States 1888: 21). Chinese traders were reputedly making fortunes in Lima by selling tea, although Guayaquil chocolate and coffee were also on sale in Quito (Orton 1876: 84, 406). Chocolate was proclaimed to be one of the three 'articles of the first necessity and of daily consumption' near Cuzco around 1870, possibly a regional peculiarity (Marcoy 1875: I, 331).

The situation in the Amazon-Orinoco basin was complicated by the relation between chocolate and *guaraná*. Cultivated especially downstream from the confluence with the Madeira river, *guaraná* was drunk as far as southern Venezuela and eastern Bolivia. It was said that 'the natives, particularly up the southern tributaries, are passionately fond of *guaraná*'. However, some chocolate was also made and drunk by Amazonian peoples (Orton 1876: 518, 524–5). Moreover, it was common to add ground cocoa to the dried cylinders of *guaraná*, or to mix chocolate and *guaraná* to make a 'more exciting' beverage (*Larousse*: VIII, 1574). This was probably the origin of the confusing appellation 'Brazilian cocoa', sometimes given to *guaraná*. As for the fiercely independent peoples of eastern Ecuador, they drank *guayusa* rather than *guaraná* (Spruce 1908: II, 453–4).

The inflow of European immigrants led to new patterns of chocolate consumption further south, highly influenced by France and with Buenos Aires taking the lead in 'civilising' Latin American taste (Rocchi 1997: 184). However, maté remained the people's choice from Paraná to southern Chile (Linhares 1969: 105–7, 124, 164–71). Moreover, Brazil was drinking much more of its coffee, retaining some 60,000 tonnes for internal consumption by the 1870s (Simmonds 1888: 199–203; Thurber 1881: 240–1).

The Philippines shared with Mexico and Colombia the distinction of remaining mainly a chocolate consumer. The Spanish and Filipino elite drank sweetened chocolate, made with water, as other nations partook of coffee or tea. Poorer Filipinos mixed their chocolate with roasted rice, or incorporated roasted pili nuts (*Canarium commune*) (Jagor 1875: 94, 97). Monasteries and convents were particularly famous for their excellent chocolate (Loney 1964: 69). As the economy boomed, strong demand drove up cocoa prices in Manila (González Fernández 1875: 238; Clarence-Smith 1998: 98). Chocolate also remained 'the national beverage in Sulu' in the 1870s, including lands claimed by the sultan in northeastern Borneo (Burbidge 1989: 92, 221). However, there were signs that coffee consumption was increasing in the archipelago, and the ever more numerous Chinese population propagated tea (González Fernández 1875: 64, 107–8, 114; Sancianco y Goson 1881: 192).

The rest of Asia probably consumed even less chocolate than before. To be sure, Europeans and *burgers* of mixed race consumed part of the cocoa crop of the Moluccas (Clarence-Smith 1998: 95). However, 'natives' in the Moluccas grew coffee for their own use in 1870, and the government auctioned some 3,000 tonnes of coffee in Java for local consumption in the same year (ANRI 1870a; 1870b).

The great chocolate boom, 1880s–1914

The explosive growth of a mass market for chocolate from the 1880s transformed world consumption more radically than at any other time in history. Chocolate progressed more rapidly than either coffee or tea in the West, and prices held up better (Othick 1976: 77). World imports of cocoa beans grew nine times between 1870 and 1897, whereas those of tea doubled, and those of coffee rose only by about half (Crawford de Roberts 1980: 48). Progress was especially marked in northwestern Europe and North America. Consumption of cocoa per head rose by a factor of nearly six in Britain between 1870 and 1910, while that of tea did not even double, and that of coffee actually fell by half (Othick 1976: 78). Germans in 1907 accounted for more than five times the cocoa imports of 1886, although they still consumed six times more coffee than cocoa (*Gordian*: XIV, 1957–8). A similar pattern of rapid rise from a low base characterised the United States between 1898 and 1908, though coffee imports were worth $73 million in 1905–6, compared to $15 million for tea and only $9 million for cocoa (*Gordian*: XV, 2938; *SYB 1907*: 449–50).

The success of chocolate was partly based on product diversification. While remaining primarily a beverage prior to 1914, sales expanded as lighter and more digestible powders came on to the market, alkalised to improve taste, colour and ease of mixing with liquids. At the same time, Swiss technical break-throughs in the 1870s revolutionised the quality of eating chocolate and created milk chocolate (Fincke 1936; Othick 1976). Urbanisation, falling transport costs and increasing purchasing power created new opportunities. Chocolate, a classic 'impulse buy', was at the forefront of new techniques of advertising (Fitzgerald 1995; Fraser 1981: 135–6, 170–2). One drawback of eating chocolate, however, was marked seasonal peaks in sales, at Easter and Christmas (Schrover 1991: 180). Moreover, Proust considered it too vulgar to serve at tea time (Bologne 1996: 230–3).

The spread of chocolate consumption to the industrial working class was a crucial development (Othick 1976: 77, 82). A survey in 1891 showed no trace of chocolate in the spending patterns of Belgian workers, but in 1910 it had become an established part of expenditure. A Belgian male labourer needed to work sixty hours to buy a half-kilo bar of chocolate in 1893, but only just over an hour in 1913 (Scholliers 1996: 177–8). Consumption had penetrated to 'the lowest classes' in Germany by the 1900s. Shortly before

1914, it was even feared that a rise in the price of the weekly chocolate bar would provoke revolutionary violence on the streets (BAAP 1906; 1908a).

Concerned at levels of alcohol abuse in expanding industrial towns, the apostles of temperance enjoyed considerable success from the 1870s, notably in Britain, Germany and the United States (Fraser 1981: 30, 208–9; Roberts 1984: 42–5; Cook and Waller 1998: 160–1). Chocolate, considered more wholesome than coffee or tea, benefited particularly from falling alcohol consumption, leading advertisers to emphasise nutrition (Othick 1976: 85–7; Knapp 1920: 15, 168–70; Norero 1910: 119). 'British workman cocoa houses' were even built (Diaper 1988: 41). In Germany, chocolate was considered the best drink for labourers, as it had more protein and fat than coffee or tea, and a less negative effect on the nervous system and the heart (BAAP 1906).

Public bodies vigorously propagated chocolate. German troops were regularly issued with it from the 1880s, helping to democratise consumption (Stollwerck 1907: 2; Klopstock 1937: 78). The United States supplied tons of chocolate to its troops in the brief war with Spain in 1898, and the British did likewise during the Boer War of 1899–1902 (Leonard 1973: 51). Even the Prussian Railway Administration encouraged workers to turn to hot chocolate (BAAP 1906). Britain's Royal Navy also did its bit, although it was peculiar in remaining doggedly attached to full-fat drinking chocolate of the traditional Latin American type (Knapp 1923: 24).

The Western boom was not replicated in the rest of the world. An expanding Latin American middle class frowned upon beverages associated with 'primitive' Amerindians. Eager to copy European cultural models, they switched to coffee and tea (Fuentes 1992: 279). That said, more peaceful conditions and rising incomes stimulated consumption. 'Civilised' forms of drinking and eating chocolate also made some headway, especially in the temperate southern cone of South America, even though refrigeration was in its infancy.

Mesoamerican chocolate consumption benefited from a rough doubling of incomes per head in Mexico between 1877 and 1910 (Haber 1989: 20). Cocoa butter was not pressed out from little cakes and balls, which were sold everywhere in Mexico as a convenience food. Rich and poor alike broke their fast with this traditional product, which became more a porridge than a beverage through the addition of pre-soaked maize, sugar and milk (Hart 1911: 250–1). The Tabascan poor made their chocolate with water rather than milk, which was reserved for sick children (Arias et al. 1987: 286). Guatemalans added cinnamon to their chocolate, churned or beaten into a froth before drinking, and contrasting with the poor quality of locally brewed coffee (Brigham 1887: 345–6, 422). Nicaraguans were fond of tiste, cold water with ground cocoa, maize flour and sugar, and sometimes cinnamon (Preuss 1987: 99; Rouma 1948–9: II, 267). In Soconusco, many rituals of the Mam Maya people continued to revolve around cocoa

(Medina Hernández 1993: 442–3). In addition, cocoa beans were still used for small monetary transactions in Guatemala and Nicaragua (Brigham 1887: 425; Dunkerley 1988: 11).

Colombia was the New World country most faithful to chocolate (Arosemena 1991: II, 471). 'Cacao is one of the most important articles of production in Colombia. It is in daily use in every household, rich and poor, in every district of the country, to quite as great an extent as tea is in England' (*PP* 1888: vol. 100). There was hardly a family, rich or poor, that did not drink hot chocolate at least once a day in 1909. Three cups were often taken, especially in the mountains and Cauca, and chocolate was as important to Colombians as beer to Bavarians (*Gordian*: XV, 3081). The millions of trees in the Cauca valley were entirely for local consumption in the early 1910s, and Antioqueños were paying up to twice European prices (Patiño 1963: 311–12). Servants insisted on receiving part of their wages in the form of a daily chocolate ration (*Gordian*: XIII, 1606). Nevertheless, competition from coffee was growing in 1909, and coffee figured alongside chocolate as one of the eight key items of internal trade in 1913 (Beyer 1947: 311; Eder 1913: 135).

Despite the undoubted progress of coffee in Venezuela, people continued to drink much chocolate. Cocoa butter was not pressed out, and the beverage seemed indigestible and unpalatable to Europeans (Preuss 1987: 73–4). In the 1930s, Amerindians still drank *chorote cerrero*, an unsweetened chocolate beverage, while Mestizos drank their *chorote* with sugar and cinnamon, sometimes adding aniseed or pepper (Rouma 1948–9: II, 505).

The non-Hispanic Caribbean predominantly consumed coffee or tea, but chocolate had not disappeared. Landowners in the Cap Haïtien region consumed cocoa from their estates in the traditional manner, crushed into a paste, mixed with syrup, and served on banana leaves (Aubin 1910: 329). Old-fashioned *chocolate criollo* was also popular in the neighbouring Dominican Republic (Thomasset 1891; Deschamps 1907: II). Surinam consumed some fifty tonnes of cocoa in 1914, not bad for only 90,000 inhabitants (Benjamins and Snelleman 1914–17: 187). British Guiana's beans were almost entirely consumed on the spot, and local demand was reported to be 'steady' (Maclaren 1924: 193). Tea was preferred by the better-off in Jamaica, however, and this may have been true elsewhere in the British Caribbean (United States 1888: 110).

Cubans manufactured and consumed much chocolate, but it may have been in the form of confectionery, as coffee was so dominant as a beverage (*EUIEA*: XVI, 820–1). In families and eating houses of the 1900s, coffee with milk was usually taken first thing in the morning, and thick black coffee was drunk at frequent intervals during the day. Indeed, 'coffee in the coffee cup' became a standard promise of politicians (Wright 1910: 110–13, 127–8, 135, 206, 209, 232, 393). While upper- and middle-class Cubans started their day with coffee, the poor downed a glass of rum (Clark 1899: 2–3).

Unusually for this period, Peruvian chocolate consumption may have increased. Upwards of 2,000 tonnes a year of cocoa beans were retained for consumption in 1905–6, much more than in the colonial period, when the figures also included Bolivia (Bonilla 1975–6: II, 228; Contreras 1990: 89). Moreover, the country had a particularly dynamic local chocolate industry (Rippy 1946: 148–51). That said, coffee made inroads into Peru's chocolate market (Romero 1961: 402; Bonilla 1975–6: II, 235). Indeed, Marcoy was offered a cup of coffee after dinner on a cocoa estate in the Cuzco area (Marcoy 1875: I, 358).

Chocolate consumption declined in Ecuador, and possibly in Bolivia. Ecuadorian consumption per head was allegedly one of the lowest in Latin America (Arosemena 1991: II, 547). Cocoa beans retained for consumption averaged only sixty-five tonnes a year in 1905–8, about a tenth of the late colonial figure (Guislain and Vincart 1911: 68–9; Laviana Cuetos 1987: 182, 186). Despite the continuing loyalty of some Bolivian consumers to 'mission chocolate', coffee had become Bolivia's usual highland breakfast beverage by the 1900s. Coffee was offered to visitors in the tropical lowlands, where people also made much use of *guaraná* from Brazil. Grated and added to cold water, *guaraná* was an 'excellent tonic', with a taste 'rather like maté' (Walle 1925: 173, 376; Fawcett 1953: 34–5, 67, 71).

Brazilian consumption of chocolate remained low, although 'cacao soup' was a delicacy in the Amazon, served on the feast of Saint John and similar occasions. Coffee was king for everyday purposes in the Amazon, small strong demi-tasses being taken continuously throughout the day (Lange 1914: 145–6, 365–6). Nevertheless, the dominance of coffee in Brazil should not be exaggerated. *Guaraná* was grown more widely than ever, and was even called 'the most popular non-intoxicating beverage in Brazil' (Fawcett 1953: 71; Emerson 1908: II, 378–9; *EB* 1911: XII, 651). How much cocoa was added to *guaraná* remains a mystery, but the practice was still reported in the 1920s (*EB* 1929: X, 932). Maté producers did not dare attack the country's coffee barons, but they fulminated against tea, 'entrenched in our customs' (Linhares 1969: 149–53, 224).

Despite the passion for maté in the southern cone of South America, chocolate retained a niche. New European kinds of chocolate suited the cosmopolitan and wealthy coastal regions, and there was even demand for the old-fashioned variety in the northern provinces of Argentina, imported from Bolivia (Malaurie and Gazzano 1888: 143). This was not an insignificant market, as Argentina was at this time one of the richest countries in the world (Topik and Wells 1998: 10).

The chocolate habit in the Philippines was only slowly undermined by coffee after the United States take-over in 1898. Early in the American period, it was noted that 'chocolate and not coffee...is the common morning drink among the better class of Filipinos' (Atkinson 1905: 176). Furthermore, 'in every household of any pretensions the afternoon caller is invited to *"merendar con chocolate"*, which corresponds to the English "5 o'clock tea"'(Foreman 1906: 302). By 1920, coffee had become an alternative morning drink, although chocolate remained the usual afternoon beverage (Miller 1920: 77, 289).

Even though there was no breakthrough for chocolate elsewhere in colonial Africa and Asia, the often repeated dictum that Africa produced cocoa but consumed no chocolate is not entirely accurate. The Duala interpreter of the Germans drank chocolate in Cameroon in 1884, a habit probably acquired from his Baptist mentors (Wirz 1972: 203). As Uganda's cocoa before 1914 was 'consumed locally', a small market of this kind existed more widely (Great Britain 1920a: 234). Catholic missionaries grew cocoa for their own use in southwestern India, and sold some to local Europeans (Watt 1889-96: VI-4, 43-4). Station buffets along the Javanese rail network in the 1890s stocked chocolate, and chocolate desserts were popular with Westerners, even if coffee was the preferred drink (Scidmore 1984: 29, 52, 65, 248).

A little chocolate was imported into the lands of the eastern Mediterranean by the turn of the century, largely for a European clientele (*Gordian*: V, 1699-1701). Jewish families were fond of chocolate cakes, made with almonds for Passover, but the habit did not spread to the Muslim population (C. Roden, e-mail, 24.6.1999). Salep was sold as a warming drink by the street vendors of Istanbul in the cold winter months, and Greeks took it, sweetened with honey, as an early morning beverage (*http*: 'A modern herbal').

Conclusion

Economic historians are notoriously suspicious of cultural explanations. They breathe a sigh of relief when the popularity of a commodity can be explained by something quantifiable, especially comparative fiscal burdens (Smith 1996). Technical changes in methods of production are another reassuring stand-by (Othick 1976). While there can be no doubt that both industrialisation and taxation played a part in the consumption of chocolate, as will be seen in the two succeeding chapters, it is surely dangerous to reduce such a complex phenomenon to solidly material and satisfyingly calculable causes.

Debate still rages over whether chocolate is physiologically addictive, and, if so, whether the cause is theobromine or other mood enhancing substances. It may also be that a psychological dependence turns people into 'chocoholics'. In any event, it is clear that chocolate has long been seen as having an effect on the mind, and more research is needed on changing perceptions of this impact. Addiction, or at least a quest for stimulation, must have affected the elasticity of demand for chocolate, however difficult it may be to quantify this for the period before 1914.

Closely related are the ways in which chocolate was perceived in different cultures, and how they changed over time. The obsessions of upper-class Westerners have long been pored over, and social historians have begun to explore the changing tastes of the emerging industrial proletariat. However, we know much less about poor people in the tropics. Chocolate held the greatest wealth of ritual significance for Mesoamerican Amerindians, and yet it is surprisingly hard to trace how this changed in the liberal era, and how coffee found a place for itself beside chocolate in the diet of these societies.

3

TAXATION, REGULATION
AND WAR

The price of cocoa beans reflected the actions of governments as much as the skills of farmers and natural conditions. Warfare was an acute problem around the beginning of the nineteenth century, and fiscal and regulatory burdens remained heavy up to about 1850. The combination of high taxes, vexatious commercial legislation, external wars and civil strife greatly hindered cocoa production and chocolate consumption. Although such factors might modify consumer choice to the advantage or detriment of chocolate, taxation tended to vary in a broadly parallel fashion for all 'luxuries'. Variations in the cost of sugar could also affect consumption, as the two products were closely allied (Mintz 1985: ch. 3).

Fiscal and related costs, borne by cocoa producers and chocolate consumers alike, ceased to loom so large from around 1850, when the ideology of free trade became hegemonic in the world. Many countries significantly lowered taxation, simplified or abolished restrictive regulations, and achieved lasting peace in both internal and external relations. However, the weaker European and Latin American states were more likely to retain high duties and preserve vexatious regulations, and were not always able to keep the peace. Moreover, the late nineteenth century witnessed a hesitant and partial rehabilitation of protectionism across the world, foreshadowing the return to neo-mercantilist policies after 1914 (Capie 1994).

Mercantilism and contraband

The mercantilist policies adopted by all European colonial powers overseas slowed the consumption and diffusion of chocolate for two centuries or more. Cocoa had to be sent in national ships to the metropolis, whence any surplus was re-exported. Countries sought to increase their share of overseas trade through repeated bouts of warfare and licensed privateering, pushing up expenditure on transport and insurance. Contraband flourished, but it also implied high costs.

European interlopers seized small Caribbean territories from Spain, and used them to carry on contraband on an impressive scale. Spanish colonial

33

cocoa was chiefly obtained in Curaçao, occupied by the Dutch in 1634; Jamaica, seized by the English in 1655; and Martinique, claimed by France in 1635. In a second phase, interlopers developed their own cocoa plantations, applying the same mercantilist restrictions that they flouted in the Spanish colonies (Klooster 1998; Fortune 1984: ch. 4; Tarrade 1992: 28–35). Much of this cocoa, whether smuggled or produced in the Caribbean, ended up in Spain, the main European market for chocolate. This too was often a clandestine trade, centred on the French Basque port of Bayonne (Arcy 1930: 14–15).

Spaniards even engaged in contraband within their own empire. The residents of Guayaquil evaded a long series of edicts restricting trade between the viceroyalties of Peru and New Spain (León Borja and Szászdi Nagy 1964). Even the Philippines, an appendage of New Spain, regularly received Guayaquil cocoa on the Acapulco galleon (Schurz 1959: 275). Cocoa was among the products which optimists hoped that the Philippines could export to Spain in 1732, although the islands remained importers (Díaz-Trechuelo 1965: 5–6, 15).

In the eighteenth century, the Iberian crowns created privileged companies for the cocoa trade. The Real Compañía Guipuzcoana de Caracas (Caracas Company), was founded in 1728. It quickly came to monopolise exports of Caracas cocoa to Spain, albeit not to Mexico. The Caracas Company not only stamped out much smuggling of Venezuelan cocoa, but also obtained restrictions on exports to Spain from other Spanish colonies (Hussey 1934; Gárate Ojanguren 1990). The Companhia Geral do Comercio do Grão Pará e Maranhão, or Pará Company, monopolised expanding cocoa exports from the Brazilian Amazon to Lisbon from 1755 (Alden 1976: 124).

Free trade within the Spanish empire, 1760s–1790s

The aftermath of the Seven Years War was a turning point in the commercial history of cocoa. Statesmen may have sought merely to tinker with mercantilism to make it work better, but they opened a Pandora's box. The liberalisation of trade regulations and reductions in taxes were sufficient to marginalise contraband, broadly unify the world market, and give a marked stimulus to chocolate consumption. The main beneficiary was the province of Guayaquil, where the authorities complained in 1796 that the cocoa mania was distracting the inhabitants from growing basic foodstuffs (Arosemena 1991: I, 75, 85–6).

Standard histories underestimate the importance of the New World as a consumer of cocoa, as shown in Table 3.1 below. Estimates for Central America, Venezuela, the Nuevo Reino and Ecuador may be on the high side, but those for Mexico, the Antilles and Peru may be too low.

A 'colonial common market' and reduced taxes boosted chocolate

Table 3.1 Latin American and Caribbean consumption of cocoa and exports to Western markets, early 1790s (tonnes per year)

Region	Exports to the West(1791–95 av.)	Approximate consumption 1790s
Mexico		2,500
Central America		1,000
Spanish Antilles		400
Other Antilles/Guianas	744	500
Venezuela	4,840	1,600
Nuevo Reino [Colombia]	91	1,400
Ecuador	1,265	600
Peru [Upper & Lower]		500
River Plate		50?
Brazil	794	50?
TOTAL	7,734	8,600

Sources for exports: Appendix 2. Venezuela here includes Maracaibo
Sources for estimates of consumption: Ruiz Abreu 1989: 58, 61–2, 66; Peña 1951: III, 926; Arcila Farías 1950: 89, 310–11; Touzard 1993: 40, 42; Marrero 1972–89: XI, 133–4; Paterson 1972: 10; Rouzier 1892–93: II, 128; Mam-Lam-Fouck 1986: 228; Knight 1990: 366–7; Leal 1984: 496; Humboldt 1941: III, 175; Laviana Cuetos 1987: 182, 186; Baleato 1887: 54, 58, 84; Contreras 1990: 89; Orbigny 1992: 312–13; León Borja et al. 1964: 28.

consumption in Spanish America. The 1774 proclamation, of freedom of commerce carried in Spanish ships between Spanish ports in the eastern Pacific Ocean, was the most radical step, coupled with a reduction in dues payable in Guayaquil and Acapulco. The fact that most Guayaquil cocoa destined for Acapulco still went via Callao might suggest that trade had not been truly liberalised (Fisher 1997: 179). However, a closer examination reveals that Guayaquil producers preferred to sell to Lima traders, who disposed of silver for immediate cash payments (Parrón Salas 1995: 222, 236–8, 340). The subsequent 1778 regulations facilitated direct commercial relations between New World colonies in the southern hemisphere. Whereas the Navarrese Basque firm of Ustariz re-exported some five tonnes of Guayaquil cocoa from Cadiz to Buenos Aires in 1769, after 1778 Buenos Aires became the entrepot for Guayaquil cocoa in the River Plate (León Borja and Szászdi Nagy 1964: 28; Garavaglia 1983: 419–20).

Madrid soon had second thoughts about unregulated Mexican cocoa imports, swayed by vociferous protests from established Caracas exporters. In November 1778, Mexican imports of Guayaquil cocoa were limited to around 500 tonnes a year. However, the authorities in Mexico used various time-honoured devices to import more, despite reprimands from Madrid. Mexico City alone imported some 3,500 tonnes of Guayaquil cocoa between August 1779 and November 1782, over twice the total legal maximum for the whole colony. In 1789, Madrid bowed to the inevitable and abolished the quota. Exports from Caracas to Veracruz dwindled, and the price of cocoa beans in Veracruz fell substantially. Despite the lowering of import dues in Veracruz to match those in Acapulco in 1780, Caracas never regained its market share, although some consumers were prepared to pay more for Caracas beans (Arcila Farias 1950: 37–41, 81, 228–30, 270–89, 310–11; León Borja and Szászdi Nagy 1964: 29–39).

Caracas vested interests also secured discrimination against Maracaibo's burgeoning cocoa exports to Mexico, drawn mainly from the Cúcuta valleys of the Nuevo Reino (Colombia). The limit was probably around 250 tonnes, or 70 tonnes if these were really *arrobas* rather than *fanegas*, and it seems to have been imposed at the same time as the Guayaquil quota (Brungardt 1974: 74). Export duties on cocoa in Maracaibo in 1777 were estimated to be 20.5 per cent ad valorem, almost double the amount levied in La Guaira, the chief port of Caracas province (Arcila Farias 1950: 217). Exports from Maracaibo to Veracruz were in the region of 350 tonnes in 1785, when a new quota of 220 tonnes was decreed (McFarlane 1993: 143–4).

The stifling of Maracaibo's exports did not last. The intendant of Venezuela complained in 1791 that the export tax was approaching 30 per cent ad valorem, and that a supplementary duty was levied when cocoa crossed the Venezuelan boundary on its way to Maracaibo. Moreover, import dues in Veracruz were higher for Maracaibo than for Caracas beans (Leal 1984: 493–4, 501–2). In 1793, Maracaibo thus became a *puerto menor*, exempt from many forms of tax in the trade with other colonial ports (Arcila Farias 1950: 83). The large sums yielded by the ecclesiastical tithe in Cúcuta reflected the prosperity of cocoa exports in subsequent years (Brungardt 1974: 78).

Cocoa producers in Tabasco also prospered, sending some 300 tonnes a year to Veracruz by the end of the century (Arcila Farias 1950: 82–3, 310–11). From 1778, it was no longer mandatory for Tabasco's cocoa to be sent east to Campeche for re-export west to Veracruz, although a 1779 request for direct exports to Spain was turned down (Ortiz de la Tabla 1978: 128–31). Villahermosa became a *puerto menor* in 1792, and subsequent decrees in 1793 and 1796 freed cocoa exports from many remaining taxes (Gil y Saenz 1979: 149–50). Some Tabascan cocoa was sent to other Spanish territories in the Caribbean basin, mainly via Campeche to Cuba and to other parts of Yucatán, and possibly even to New Orleans from 1776 (Ruiz Abreu 1989: 58–65, 92–6, 106). There were also overland exports to Chiapas, to make up for the faltering output of Soconusco. The isolated Petén outpost in Guatemala received its cocoa from Tabasco in 1801 (Ruz 1994: 186, 202). A little fine cocoa from northwestern Honduras also reached Mexico (Humboldt 1811: 436).

Nicaragua, which had only been able to meet its own internal demand since the early eighteenth century, was probably exporting around 250 tonnes of cocoa a year before 1796. Exports were mainly directed to

Acapulco and El Salvador, small amounts finding their way to Spain (Newson 1987: 260, 264; Fernández Molina 1992: 425–39; Salvatierra 1939: II, 208). The level of tithes yet again reflected the buoyancy of the cocoa sector (Wortman 1982: 194, 282–3). However, the tithe itself was resented as 'a considerable fiscal imposition' (Dunkerley 1988: 8). Moreover, planters complained about having to send beans by mule train from Rivas to Realejo for shipment. They petitioned for the nearby port of San Juan del Sur to be opened for trade, a request that was never granted (Salvatierra 1939: II, 36–7). Planters retaliated by sending cocoa to the Caribbean coast for sale to British interlopers (Wortman 1982: 199).

Central American producers grumbled that Guayaquil cocoa was invading their own markets, since the opening of the Pacific ports of Sonsonate and Realejo by the 1774 decree (León Borja and Szászdi Nagy 1964: 32, 50). Table 3.2 shows that Guayaquil beans took 56 per cent of the Guatemala City market in 1778, and probably 31 per cent in 1781. At the same time, the maximum price obtained for Costa Rican cocoa in El Salvador fell, from 30 to 25 pesos per *quintal* between 1772 and 1776 (Fernández Molina 1992: 425–39).

The impact of the 1774 decree on Central American imports is hard to evaluate, as local and Guayaquil cocoa were not exact substitutes for one another. Cheap Forastero beans from Guayaquil were popular among the poor, while wealthy residents of Mexico preferred fine Criollo beans from Central America (Solórzano 1963: 185, 194–7, 214–15). Moreover, Realejo accounted for less than 1 per cent of Guayaquil's total cocoa exports in 1791–3, an average of only 17 tonnes a year, and there was no mention of Sonsonate (*MP*: XII, 166–7). Traders in Guayaquil and Callao were only

Table 3.2   Cocoa consumed in Guatemala City, 1778 and 1781 (Tonnes; Pesos per quintal)

Country	1778	1778	1781	1781
	% Amount	Price	% Amount	Price
Tabasco	20.8	54.9	17.2	54.3
Oaxaca	6.3	83.3		
Chiapas			27.6	46.4
Soconusco	2.3	68.7		
Suchitepéquez	6.3	57	22.2	38.7
Costa Rica	6.3	56.3	2.8	60
Guayaquil	55.6	21.9		
[no indication]	2.3	72.4	30.8	37.5
TOTAL	63 tonnes		25 tonnes	

Source: J. A. Fernández Molina, e-mail message 10 February 1999

37

interested in the Acapulco market (Parrón Salas 1995: 227–8). The influx of Guayaquil cocoa was modest, and did not preclude exports to Mexico.

Although the Philippines were excluded from complete freedom of inter-colonial trade, a novel element of competition was introduced. The Acapulco galleon continued to take cocoa to Manila, but the Real Compañía de Filipinas (Philippines Company) was given a monopoly of direct exports from South America to Manila from 1785. This duopoly was bitterly resented by other merchants, although the prize was not cocoa, but rather the lucrative exchange of American silver for Asian manufactures (Parrón Salas 1995: 197, 209–12, 379–84, 395, 400; Díaz-Trechuelo 1965). Manila also received some cocoa from the Visayas and the sultanate of Sulu, the latter sending some 6 tonnes in 1761 (Cruikshank 1982: 225–6; Warren 1981: 65, app. F).

The liberalisation of trade with Europe, 1760s–1790s

Reforms after 1763 also facilitated and cheapened imports of cocoa into Spain, almost eliminating contraband and fostering a current of re-exports to the rest of Europe. Although far behind bullion, cocoa was Spain's second most valuable agricultural import from the New World between 1782 and 1796, after tobacco, but before sugar, indigo and cochineal (Fisher 1985a: 52–3, 56). Spain imported around 3,500 tonnes of cocoa a year between 1767 and 1776, and this shot up to an average of about 6,000 tonnes in the next peaceful period, between 1791 and 1796. The three chief measures adopted were the reduction of taxes, the licensing of ports for colonial trade, and the abolition of chartered companies (León Borja and Szászdi Nagy 1964). Neutral ships supplied Spain with cocoa in times of war, often via the Low Countries (Parrón Salas 1995: 416–18; Lucena Salmoral 1990: 14; Hussey 1934: 286–90).

As a competitor to Caracas on the Spanish market, Guayaquil benefited most from the reform process, mainly sending cocoa via Callao and Cape Horn, a route permitted since 1743. The reduction of import duties in Spain from 33 to 25 maravedís per *libra* in 1776 was a crucial spur to increased exports (León Borja and Szászdi Nagy 1964: 24–31).

Spanish insular possessions in the Caribbean proved a broken reed, although the first reforms of 1765 were aimed at them, authorising trade with nine ports in Spain. Trinidad only began to export a little cocoa to Spain after 1785, when French planters were induced to settle in the island by a suspension of export duties and the tithe. The island's small cocoa exports were then diverted to French ports, under special commercial dispensations (Sevilla Soler 1988: 99–100, 142–6, 153, 174; Newson 1976: 213). Cultivation in Cuba was boosted by a ten-year suspension of the tithe in 1794, but the island remained a net importer of cocoa (Marrero 1972–89: VIII, 222; XI, 133, 137; Pezuela 1863–6: I, 60). Puerto Rico was in the same position (Gil-Bermejo 1970: 189). A trickle of Santo Domingo beans went to Spain for a time, assisted by the 1786 suspension of the tithe for ten years on land newly planted in cocoa, but the colony soon settled down to re-exporting Venezuelan beans to Puerto Rico and Cuba (Sevilla Soler 1980: 100, 126, 182–4, 203–6, and maps).

More cocoa reached Spain from eastern Venezuela, following the grant of fiscal and other privileges to the Real Compañia de Barcelona (Barcelona Company) in 1766, albeit without a formal monopoly. The Barcelona Company was also active in Santo Domingo, Puerto Rico, Honduras and Buenos Aires, but cocoa from eastern Venezuela represented 60 per cent by value of its total imports into Spain between 1758 and 1785 (Oliva Melgar 1987: 36–42, 73, 297–9, 312).

Even though the 1778 'free trade' regulations were not fully applied in Venezuela until 1789, they signalled the beginning of an assault on privileged companies. The Barcelona Company quickly went into decline and was abolished in 1785 (Oliva Melgar 1987). The crown restricted the privileges of the Caracas Company from 1778, ended its monopoly on trade with Spain in 1781, and dissolved it in 1784 (Hussey 1934; Gárate Ojanguren 1990). However, the promoters of the old company were allowed to form the Philippines Company in 1785, which kept substantial commercial privileges in Caracas (Arcila Farias 1973: I, 356–60; Díaz-Trechuelo 1965: 42, 50).

Caracas remained Spain's largest single supplier of cocoa, softening the blow of the loss of market share in Mexico. In 1793, Spain received some 4,500 tonnes of cocoa from Caracas, 500 from eastern Venezuela, 150 from Cartagena and Maracaibo, and 1,350 from Guayaquil (Arcila Farias 1950: 312; Dias 1971: 361–75; McFarlane 1993: 371; Laviana Cuetos, 1987: 186). Cocoa could be sold to traders from friendly and neutral powers in 1780–4, and it proved hard to stop the practice thereafter (McKinley 1985: 39–40, 104–9; Arcila Farias 1973: I, 349, 353–4). A further boon was the authorisation, granted to some producers, to transport cocoa in small boats from the coast of Barlovento to La Guaira (Tamaro 1988: 126–8).

The cocoa sector of Caracas gained no major fiscal concessions. In 1777, the export burden on cocoa stood at 17.5 per cent ad valorem in La Guaira. At best, some minor reductions and simplifications of taxes were enacted in 1794 (Arcila Farias 1950: 229–30). This contrasted with the abolition of export duties on coffee in 1789 (Izard 1972: 93). The tithe was also levied at a full 10 per cent on cocoa, whereas it was reduced or suspended for other crops. However, major cocoa planters often obtained the right to collect the tithe on behalf of the government (McKinley 1985: 86; Polanco Martínez 1960: II, 283; Tamaro 1988: 287).

The decline of contraband trade through the Dutch possessions was one consequence of Venezuelan commercial liberalisation. Curaçao re-exported an average of around 300 tonnes of cocoa in 1769–70, but only around 100 tonnes from 1786 to 1791, and this figure fell even further in subsequent years (Klooster 1998: 159, 187–8). Nor was there any more mention of the smuggling of cocoa along the Orinoco to the Dutch colonies in the Guianas (Patiño 1963: 325–6; Briceño de Bermúdez 1993: 21–7).

The expansion of Brazilian exports followed a similar path of lower duties and greater regulatory flexibility. A decree of 1765 abolished the convoy system for merchant ships, except in time of war, and export taxes were reduced in 1773 (Brito 1821: 67–8). Liberalisation gathered speed after the fall of the Marquis of Pombal in 1777. The Pará Company's charter was not renewed in 1778, and unrestricted trade was allowed between Brazilian ports. Import dues on Brazilian cocoa entering Portugal were slightly reduced in 1790 (Novais 1979: 257). Rodrigo de Souza Coutinho, an admirer of Adam Smith, pressed in 1798 for a reduction in all Brazilian export duties to a flat 4 per cent (Silva 1987: 275–6). About two thirds of Brazilian cocoa was re-exported from Lisbon, mainly to Italy (Alden 1976: 130). Genoa, and to a lesser extent Livorno, were the main importers (Niephaus 1975: 277–344).

Following defeat at the hands of Britain in 1763, the French adopted the *exclusif mitigé*, or moderate colonial pact (Tarrade 1972). Falling rates of taxation and the opening of more French ports greatly improved the onerous conditions earlier imposed on cocoa (Boyer-Peyreleau 1823: II, 40, app. 13). Taxes on colonial cocoa entering France had fallen to 10 centimes per livre by 1775, and cocoa exports from Saint-Domingue were entirely free of duty by 1791 (Mangin 1860: 44; Edwards 1801: 215). French Guiana was allowed to trade freely for twelve years with all nations in 1768, a privilege renewed in 1784 (Girault 1916: 27). Although free ports were established in Saint-Domingue and Saint Lucia in 1767, Martinique remained the main importer of the Venezuelan and Trinidadian cocoa that reached French ports, often in exchange for slaves (Hardy 1947: 96; Tarrade 1992: 28–35; Newson 1976: 213). Marseilles accounted for about two thirds of total French imports of cocoa in 1775, and just under half in 1785, but Bordeaux was fast catching up (Arcy 1930: 16; Casey 1981: 33).

The 1774 decision by the Thirteen Colonies to block commercial relations with Britain worked to the advantage of the French Caribbean, even though trading with North America was formally contrary to mercantilist principles. Even before independence, North American captains often sold their merchandise in British islands for cash, proceeded to French islands to purchase tropical commodities, and declared them to be the produce of the British Caribbean on return home (Ragatz 1977: 89, 165, 180–3, 230–1). Franco-American links were reinforced by alliance in the struggle for independence, formalised in a treaty of friendship and commerce in 1778 (Hardy 1947: 102–3). Cocoa was a regular part of the cargoes that New England ships brought back from the Caribbean (Phillips 1947: 68).

The early phase of the French Revolution led to further liberalisation of cocoa marketing, although it proved ineffectual. France lowered duties and proclaimed free trade within the French empire in 1791, qualified in 1793 by the obligation to use French ships. However, French colonies were wracked with violence from 1791, and then blockaded or occupied by Britain from 1793 (Blérald 1986: 39).

Britain discriminated much more than France against 'the inferior planters' of secondary crops (Smith 1996: 203–6). To be sure, a test case in 1774 determined that a 4.5 per cent export duty, current in the old colonies, was unlawful in the islands ceded to Britain in 1763, which produced almost all the British Caribbean's cocoa at this time. Moreover, planters thwarted later attempts to impose export duties (Ragatz 1977: 128–9). However, this was a hollow victory, for cocoa imports were harshly taxed in Britain, and Navigation Laws prohibited the colonies from legally sending their beans elsewhere (Knapp 1920: 13–14). Furthermore, import duties on cocoa rose during the wars that broke out in the late 1770s (Brizan 1984: 39; Ragatz 1977: 42, 164–6, 353).

Given low metropolitan consumption of chocolate, Britain concentrated on encouraging re-exports of cocoa beans to Spain and France, granting a substantial drawback on import duties in 1763 (Ragatz 1977: 287). Imports of British plantation cocoa for home consumption paid 1.28 pence per pound in 1774, whereas those destined for re-export paid only 0.13 pence (Ragatz 1928: 11). The success of these measures is shown in high re-export figures (Piñero 1988: 84).

The Free Ports Acts of 1766 and 1786 were intended to entice produce from foreign colonies to Britain, although the planters of Dominica initially suffered from their beans being classified as 'foreign grown' (Ragatz 1977: 106–7, 140–1, 202–3). Whether Jamaican exports of Mesoamerican cocoa increased is uncertain, although the Jicaque of northern Honduras sometimes sold cocoa to British interlopers (Floyd 1967: 61). The British Mosquito Coast settlements exported nearly sixty tonnes in 1769, most of which was probably bought from Costa Rica rather than locally grown (Potthast 1988: 386). Costa Rica's Matina planters petitioned the crown in 1776 to form a chartered company to export cocoa to Spain, and turned to contraband dealings with Jamaican traders when their request was ignored (Fernández Molina 1992: 425–39). Jamaica may thus have been the real destination of cocoa officially consigned to Cartagena, when such exports were freed of tax for six years in 1787 (Rosés Alvarado 1982: 271–5).

The Dutch had a more significant cocoa sector of their own, but were also keen to re-export beans from other colonies, legally or illegally. Saint Eustatius thus joined Curaçao as an entrepot for re-exported cocoa (Klooster 1998: 226–7). At the same time, cocoa grown in the Dutch section of the Guianas continued to be directed exclusively to the Netherlands (Goslinga 1985: 39–40, 574–607).

The impact of war and revolution, 1790s–1820s

A new kind of conflict engulfed the world cocoa economy from 1793, lasting to 1815 in Europe, and to 1824 in Latin America. Fighting took on an increasingly harsh tone, as the niceties of aristocratic warfare gave way to the mass mobilisation of nations. The ferocity of hostilities pushed up freight rates, insurance charges and taxes for cocoa producers (Depons 1930: 311–12). There was a resurgence in contraband, and cocoa prices fluctuated violently and unpredictably, temporarily reversing the convergence towards a single world market. World cocoa output probably fell overall, although revolution and war extended their ravages to the statistical record. The scarlet threads running through this period were Britain's mastery of global sea lanes, and the concentration of European chocolate consumption in Spain.

The turning point was Spain's ill judged decision to declare war on Britain in 1796. A brief respite was gained by the Peace of Amiens in 1802, but war erupted again in 1804, and the Royal Navy destroyed the Spanish fleet in 1805. The Spaniards were thus obliged to throw open the sale of cocoa to friendly and neutral powers (McKinley 1985: 39–40, 44, 100, 103–9; Hamerly 1973: 108). Spain issued licences to vessels from the United States, the Hanseatic ports, Denmark, Portugal, Livorno and Genoa (Fisher 1997: 202–4; Parrón Salas 1995: 427, 431–4, 455). While this allowed cocoa to reach Spain by roundabout routes, it was a costly process, causing the retail price of chocolate in Madrid to shoot up after 1796 (Piñero 1994: 155).

The dynamic American merchant navy became the main carrier of cocoa in this first phase (Tandrón 1976: 162–4). Great quantities of beans were brought to the United States for re-export to neutral ports, notably Hamburg and Bremen, or to Bordeaux. American neutrality was not always respected, however, as the British seized Haïtian cocoa on New England ships (Phillips 1947: 113, 169, 171). There was a surge in the value of United States purchases of Spanish imperial cocoa from 1798, falling away in 1803–4 because of the Peace of Amiens, and then rising again until the American embargo of 1807. Over the entire period 1795–1819, cocoa represented 5 per cent by value of all United States imports from Spanish colonies, compared to 15 per cent for coffee and 68 per cent for sugar and molasses (Cuenca Esteban 1984: 51). The United States imported nearly 1,000 tonnes of cocoa in 1801–2, and re-exported over 3,000 tonnes of 'West India cocoa' to Europe between October 1805 and September 1806 (Nichols 1933: 303; Great Britain 1807).

The imposition of Napoleon's Continental System in 1806 marked the beginning of a short but particularly intense phase of commercial disruption. Napoleon's crack-down on neutral shipping elicited a British counter-blockade, followed by a United States embargo in 1807. Napoleon also seized northern Germany, formerly the main conduit for cocoa destined for Spain. Prices were driven sky high in Amsterdam (Posthumus 1946: 197). Hanseatic merchants reacted to this unprecedented crisis by adopting Danish or Portuguese colours to bring Hispanic American cocoa to Europe. A Hamburg firm, financed from the Netherlands and registered in the Danish enclave of Altona, sent two large ships to Cartagena in 1806, bringing back cocoa and other tropical commodities. However, the firm then suspended payments, because of the bankruptcy of a Dutch concern (Barbier 1990: 117–19). Hamburg ships also loaded cocoa in Callao in 1807, destined for Altona and Lisbon, but at least one was seized by British naval vessels (Pohl 1963: 279–80).

Napoleon's invasion of Spain and Portugal in 1807–8 initiated a third phase, bringing Latin America under de facto British naval control, and unleashing Latin American wars of independence. The British outpost of Gibraltar became a back door into Spain for both Spanish and British shipping, usurping the position of Cadiz as the distributor of colonial produce in Spain and around the Mediterranean (Lucena Salmoral 1990: 230, 237–8; Martínez 1988: II, 267; Sánchez Mantero 1981: 77–8). However, much of Spain was occupied by French troops and ravaged by guerrilla warfare, so that the Gibraltar market was easily glutted (Williams 1952: 328). After Creole juntas had declared their independence, campaigns on land and sea caused havoc until 1824, when Spain was left holding only Cuba and Puerto Rico.

The Caribbean basin was the cockpit of naval warfare, and recourse to neutral shipping could not resolve all problems. Costa Rica's cocoa estates were crippled by British attacks, in alliance with Miskito raiders from the north, and Britain seized Trinidad in 1797 (Quesada Camacho 1989: 107; Patiño 1963: 300; Harwich Vallenilla 1996: 34). Venezuelan cocoa exports in neutral ships were authorised in 1797–9, 1800–1, and 1806–10 (McKinley 1985: 40). Of forty-two ships leaving Caracas ports in 1806, nineteen were registered as American, and fifteen as Danish, in effect Hanseatic ships flying the Danish flag and operating out of Saint Thomas (McKinley 1985: 186). United States ships brought essential supplies to Venezuela, notably wheat from Baltimore and Philadelphia. However, the intendant complained in 1806 that Americans preferred to purchase commodities such as indigo, hides and coffee, presumably because of growing difficulties in ensuring re-exports to Spain. This left much cocoa to spoil in storage (Lucena Salmoral 1984: 162, 167).

The cocoa exports of Colombia and Venezuela were hard hit by the outbreak of independence wars in 1811. Cúcuta, on a strategic route, changed hands ten times during the fighting. In 1820, after an orgy of looting, requisitioning and scorched earth policies, it was reported that 'neither man nor beast were available to transport cacao to Maracaibo' (Brungardt 1974: 82–6). Santa Marta's small cocoa exports similarly collapsed by 1818 (Posada and Ibañez 1910: 608). An incipient cocoa boom in eastern Venezuela was halted in its tracks, as Carúpano and other settlements were reduced to ashes (Harwich Vallenilla 1996: 25). Cocoa estates in Caracas province changed hands repeatedly, as the fortunes of war ebbed and flowed, although both royalists and rebels strove to protect this source of funds (Izard 1972: 109–12; Brito Figueroa 1985: 253).

Mexico compensated for vulnerability on the Caribbean flank by stepping up trade in the Pacific. Cocoa imports from Caracas and Maracaibo were badly affected after 1796 (Brungardt 1974: 77, 89; Arcila Farias 1950: 310–11). Even Tabasco's shipments on the short sea route to Veracruz suffered from British naval action, although cocoa from the territory still found its way to many destinations in central Mexico in 1803–7 (Gil y Saenz 1979: 153–4; Ruiz Abreu 1989: 62–3, 95, 102, 118). Imports of beans through Acapulco were at first hardly touched, and Guayaquil cocoa was even transported overland to Veracruz for re-export (Humboldt 1811: 690, 697; Arcila Farias 1950: 310–11). However, Mexican insurgents took Acapulco in 1813 and burned some 750 tonnes of cocoa belonging to Martin Icaza, a major Guayaquil trader (León Borja and Szászdi Nagy 1964: 41–2).

The reorientation of Mexico's trade to the Pacific gave a boost to cocoa output in Central America, even though the region simultaneously imported more cheap beans from Guayaquil. Producers benefited from a decree of 1797 that freed trade with Mexico from all taxes, enabling Central America to increase exports of high quality Criollo cocoa (Benjamin 1989: 13; Bullock 1824: 285). This came partly by land from Guatemala to Oaxaca, and partly by sea from Nicaragua to Acapulco (Carvalho 1994: 77–8, 88, 227; Salvatierra 1939: II, 35–7). At the same time, Realejo and Sonsonate figured more prominently among destinations for Guayaquil's cocoa (Baleato 1887: 59). Guayaquil beans accounted for around nine tenths of Guatemala City's consumption in 1816–17, well up on the 1770s and 1780s (J. A. Fernández Molina, e-mail 10.2.1999).

United States and Hamburg vessels loaded some cocoa in Guayaquil or Callao, although Spain was less favourably inclined towards foreigners in the Pacific. There was little fighting, and a rapidly growing Chilean fleet was available to transport Guayaquil beans within the ocean (León Borja and Szászdi Nagy 1964: 41–2; Hamerly 1973: 108; Parrón Salas 1995: 431–4). Nevertheless, the advent of newcomers reduced the amounts of Guayaquil cocoa going to Callao for re-export to 17 per cent of the total by 1808–13 (Contreras 1990: 80). Guayaquil was only briefly caught up in fighting for independence, between 1816 and 1820 (León Borja and Szászdi Nagy 1964: 41–2). Guayaquil's cocoa exports to Acapulco fell after 1808, but this reflected new opportunities in Gibraltar (Arcila Farias 1950: 310–11).

The trade across the Pacific to the Philippines initially continued unabated, with cocoa reaching Manila on both the Acapulco galleon and

Philippines Company ships from Peru in 1810 (Comyn 1969: 12, app.). Problems only arose when the Pacific ports of Hispanic America fell into the hands of insurgents, leading Manila merchants to seek alternative supplies in Islamic sultanates and Dutch possessions (Clarence-Smith 1998: 95).

Taxes on cocoa producers and traders rose sharply in the Spanish empire, especially from 1804, reversing the trend of previous decades (Depons 1930: 342–9). The Spanish exchequer was empty when war resumed in 1804, leading to harsh new impositions. One of the first acts of the Caracas junta in 1810 was thus to lower export duties on cocoa (McKinley 1985: 141; Lucena Salmoral 1990: 79–80; Izard 1972: 104, 107). Eastern Venezuela's smuggling of cocoa to British Trinidad increased (Humboldt 1941: V, 62). Acapulco's import dues rose in 1804, and again in 1810. There was an 18 per cent import duty in Callao in 1819, with an additional peso per *carga* for cocoa imported for consumption in Peru (Hamerly 1973: 124–9). Nicaraguan planters complained in 1815 that taxes were so high that it was not worth their while to produce cocoa any more (Wortman 1982: 319). The inhabitants of Cartago in Costa Rica pleaded in 1813 for a halving of the tax of one peso per *quintal* on cocoa entering the town, and asked that funds be used exclusively to repair the road from Matina (Saenz Maroto 1970: 100). Similarly, Tabasco protested against increased taxes to fund the war (Gil y Saenz 1979: 153–4).

Brazil benefited from Portuguese neutrality, British naval protection, the opening of the main ports to friendly nations in 1808, stable taxes, and a relatively peaceful transition to independence. Brazilian cocoa exports rose markedly from the late 1790s, profiting from the discomfiture of Venezuela (Alden 1976: 130–5).

Paradoxically, British Caribbean cocoa producers benefited less from the supremacy of the Royal Navy, as they were not permitted to export to neutral ports. At the same time, import duties on cocoa rose so high in Britain from 1793 'that in those Colonies where the cocoa tree would grow it was allowed to die out, and the sugar industry was made the one stock crop' (Bannister 1890: 1040). Trinidadian officials further complained in 1813 that the duty on coffee was unfairly set at a lower level than that on cocoa (Williams 1952: 326–7). Moreover, re-exports of cocoa from Britain were hit harder than those of sugar, coffee or cotton, due to the heavy concentration of chocolate consumption in the enemy nations of Spain and France (Great Britain 1807). It was only supplies from newly conquered Trinidad after 1797 that caused British cocoa imports to increase at all (Ragatz 1928: 22; 1977: 318). This explained the lack of British enthusiasm for cocoa in the occupied Dutch Guianas, where cocoa output declined drastically (Daly 1975: ch. 11; Farley 1956: 95; Reyne 1924–5: 19).

Protection and its opponents, 1820s–1840s

Western cocoa imports suffered from high import taxes in the post-war economic depression, but the situation was not as bad as Schneider's reliance on the Leipzig Encyclopaedia led him to believe (Schneider 1981: I, 39–40). Table 3.3 illustrates gradual recovery, especially as the trough of the 1820s concealed much smuggling into Spain via Gibraltar.

For all the problems of taste and fashion surveyed earlier, the most important cause of depressed Western markets was high taxation, which endured after the Napoleonic wars. Major powers, needing to rebuild their shattered finances, actually raised tariffs after 1815. They only came down slowly and erratically thereafter, as indicated in Table 3.4. Freight and insurance rates benefited from the ending of naval conflicts, but this 'peace dividend' was undermined by anachronistic shipping laws that no longer even sustained a flourishing re-export trade, for countries without colonies could obtain cocoa directly from newly independent producers (Ragatz 1977: 337, 348–53).

British import duties on cocoa came down quite quickly, as set out in Table 3.5, although Britain's fiscal burden was blamed for lower chocolate consumption per head than France (Fonssagrives 1875–6: 360). Duty in 1844 was still equivalent to 21 per cent of the price on arrival for colonial cocoa, and 53 per cent for foreign beans (Great Britain 1848: I). However, cocoa appears to have received the most favourable fiscal treatment of the three competing beverages by 1834, whereas tea remained most heavily taxed (Mulhall 1899: 559). Curiously, cocoa imports from British colonies were smaller than those of foreign origin in every year between 1820 and 1835, despite differential rates of duty (*PP 1835*: vol. 49; *PP 1837*: vol. 49). This may have been because the Royal Navy paid the same duty on foreign and colonial cocoa, and preferred beans from Guayaquil and the Amazon (Wagner 1987: 16; Williams 1952: 330–2; Ragatz 1977: 353, 373).

The increase in French imports of cocoa beans for consumption reflected lower duties than in Spain, as indicated in Tables 3.3 and 3.4. The 1836 French tariff concentrated on protecting national shipping. The advantages granted to French colonial cocoa were not such as to counteract heavy

Table 3.3 Imports of cocoa for consumption into selected countries, 1825–45 (5 year intervals; tonnes)

Country	1825	1830	1835	1840	1845
Spain	882	3,930	6,448	5,451	5,453
France	938	604	1,031	1,664	1,859
Britain	328	443	533	927	1,170

Sources: Prados de la Escosura 1982: 246 [1826 for 1825, 1842 for 1840, 1846 for 1845]; *TGCF* [1841 for 1840]; Historicus 1896: 48; Hewett 1862: 47 [excluding government stores]

Table 3.4 Import duties on cocoa in selected countries, early 1840s (British Pence per pound)

Britain	British colonies	1
	Foreign territories	4
Belgium		0.1
Netherlands		0.3
Denmark		1.3
Sweden		2
Austria		1.9
Russia		6.9
France	Colonial on French ships	1.1
	Foreign Pacific on French ships	2.2
	Foreign Atlantic on French ships	2.4
	Foreign ships and overland	4.6
Spain	Spanish Antilles on Spanish ships	3.8
	Philippines on Spanish ships	5
	Guayaquil on Spanish ships	6.3
	Other foreign on Spanish ships	12.5
	Foreign on foreign ships	25
Portugal	Colonial on Portuguese ships	0
	On foreign ships	9.7

Sources: Great Britain 1845; Macgregor 1843–50: I–II

Note
The rate for Portugal assumes a duty in Reis per kilo

Table 3.5 British import duties on cocoa beans for consumption, 1803–53 (British Pence per pound, not deflated)

Year	*British colonies*	*Foreign*
1803	22	70
1819	30	n.a.
1820	12	30
1825	6	15
1832	2	6
1842	1	4
1844	1	2
1853	1	1

Sources: Knapp 1920: 14; Mulhall 1899: 559; *PP 1835*, vol. 49; *PP 1837*, vol. 49; Great Britain 1845, part 2; Williams 1952: 330-1; Dowell 1888: IV, 242

protection for cane sugar (Girault 1916: 57–61). French possessions thus supplied only 16 per cent of Le Hâvre's cocoa imports in 1831 (*PP 1837*: vol. 49).

Spain still accounted for half of European imports of cocoa beans in the 1840s, representing 6–8 per cent of the country's imports, but stiff taxes on cocoa and chocolate kept consumption stagnant (Izard 1972: 137;

Green 1991: 225–6; Stols 1996: 52). High taxation sprang in part from persistent civil wars and the consequences of the loss of empire (Clarence-Smith 1991: 72–4). Duties on Guayaquil cocoa in 1857 were 4.75 pesos per *carga*, equivalent to nearly half the cost of beans on arrival (Arosemena 1991: I, 193).

Tense political relations between Spain and her former colonies made matters worse, as Madrid decreed a complete trade ban in 1824. Although this prohibition was lifted four years later, differential tariffs channelled trade through Cuba and Puerto Rico, and newly independent states adopted retaliatory measures (Anna 1983: 293; Hall 1824: 41–2; Humphreys 1940: 185). Much cocoa thus entered Spain via Bordeaux, Bayonne or Gibraltar, a trade vulnerable to sudden policy changes (Schneider 1981: I, 187–9, 212, 220, 356–61; Léon 1893: 354–7; Sánchez Mantero 1981: 77–8; Bonilla 1975–6: I, 72). Negotiations with former colonies began in 1835, and direct trade with Venezuela existed by 1837 (Polanco Martínez 1960: II, 186–7). Full diplomatic relations were established with Ecuador in 1840, and Venezuela in 1845, improving prospects for cocoa planters (Anna 1983: 293–4; Banko 1990: 236). However, it took time for trading patterns to adjust, with 1,213 tonnes of cocoa re-exported to Spain via Puerto Rico in 1838, possibly still favoured by tariffs (Palerm Rincón 1982: 136). Five years later, cocoa re-exported to Spain from Puerto Rico amounted to 708 tonnes of Caracas beans, 195 tonnes of Carúpano beans, and 140 tonnes of Trinidad beans (*PP 1847*: vol. 64). At the same time, neither Cuba nor Puerto Rico grew enough cocoa for their own needs, so that some imported cocoa was locally consumed (Mangin 1860: 37, 39).

There was an opportunistic surge of Trinidadian cocoa exports to Spain from the late 1810s, but the boom did not last. Disaster struck in 1828, when the British banned Spanish vessels from bringing non-British goods to Trinidad (Giacottino 1977: II, 422; Williams 1952: 283). There was a simultaneous clamp-down by Madrid on smuggling into Spain via Gibraltar (Sánchez Mantero 1981). British ships could not take Trinidadian produce directly to Spain, so cocoa was shipped to Puerto Rico for re-exportation in Spanish ships, a tedious and costly detour, in open competition with Venezuelan beans (Green 1991: 45, 225–6). It is not even clear who could take beans to Puerto Rico, as the Trinidadian authorities requested permission in 1819 to send cocoa to foreign Caribbean destinations in British bottoms (Williams 1952: 328).

The Navigation Laws, on the statute book until 1849, were the problem for Trinidad. Smuggling cocoa to Martinique was rife in 1818, to avoid British export taxes of over five pence per pound, and to take advantage of much higher prices. In 1817, the Trinidadian authorities pleaded for the abolition of a penny per pound export tax on cocoa destined for the United States (Williams 1952: 327). Following a trade agreement, British Caribbean cocoa exports to the United States rose, averaging 87 tonnes a year in

1822–26. However, renewed American protectionism in 1827 choked off this traffic (Ragatz 1977: 355–61; Schuyler 1945: 122).

Matters were similar elsewhere in the colonial Caribbean. Smuggling of Saint Lucia cocoa to Martinique was reported in 1819 (Ragatz 1977: 351). Dominica's export tax on cocoa was raised to nearly three pence per pound in 1839, to damp down the development of crops that threatened the labour supplies of sugar planters (Trouillot 1988: 109–10). Cocoa's poor performance in Surinam was partly due to the obligation to ship to the Netherlands in Dutch ships before 1848 (Horlings 1995: 109–10).

Markets within the New World were severely depressed by the collapse of the Spanish colonial customs union. Newly independent governments discriminated against imports from sister republics, mainly to raise desperately needed revenue, but also to lessen trade deficits by stimulating import substitution. These 'beggar my neighbour' policies depressed incomes across the continent, by undermining comparative advantage (Bulmer-Thomas 1994: 29, 32).

Mexico, by far the largest Latin American market for cocoa, imposed a standard 25 per cent import duty in 1821, raised to 40 per cent in 1827 (Potash 1959: 30–1, 47). The duty on cocoa was slightly lowered in 1827, against the trend, whereas imports of coffee were prohibited. The duty on cocoa rose again in 1837, climbed to a new peak in 1842, but was then brought down the following year to half the level of 1821 (Cosio Villegas 1932: 46–7).

Although Gran Colombian cocoa producers complained in the late 1820s that these duties were prohibitive, Mexican cocoa imports did not cease altogether (Wills 1831: 28). Mexico imported Maracaibo cocoa on United States ships in 1825, took over half Colombia's small cocoa exports in 1848, and was Venezuela's third market in 1843 (Jong 1966: 333; Schneider 1981: II, 510–28; *PP 1847*: vol. 64). However, the size of the trade shrank. Mexican imports of Guayaquil beans, which had been around 2,750 tonnes a year in the 1790s, fell to 1,400 tonnes in 1825–8, and under 500 tonnes in 1835–44 (Laviana Cuetos 1987: 186; Lerda de Tejada 1853: tables 30–5; Chiriboga 1980: 14). The port of Acapulco suffered from this decline (Guardino 1996: 114). That said, non-Hispanic territories were able to gain legal access to this market, for the Brazilian Amazon supplied 8 per cent of Mexico's imports of cocoa by value in 1828 (Herrera Canales 1980: 90). The British Caribbean also furnished small quantities in the early 1830s (*PP 1837*: vol. 49).

The main producers to benefit from protection were Tabasco and Chiapas. Tabasco adhered to the new Mexican nation with Yucatán, while Chiapas defected from the Central American Federation. The attraction of Mexico's large cocoa market may have influenced these political decisions, although standard accounts do not mention it. The governor of Tabasco proclaimed in 1831 that the state's economy rested chiefly on the sale of cocoa to the rest of the country (Gil y Saenz 1979: xliv). The Tabasco authorities petitioned Mexico City for a complete ban on imports of foreign cocoa in 1830, and complained that their cocoa paid an internal customs duty of 1 peso per *carga* (Arias *et al.* 1987: 88, 143, 187–9).

Sheltering behind the Mexican tariff wall boosted the cocoa output of Tabasco and Chiapas (Lerda de Tejada 1853: tables 32–5; Gil y Saenz 1979: 252). Between 1817 and 1860, the estimated value of Mexico's cocoa output in current pesos was multiplied by a factor of ten, a performance only equalled by tobacco in the country's agricultural sector, although it is unclear whether this takes account of changed frontiers at independence (Coatsworth 1989: 52). In any event, cocoa was undisputedly Tabasco's premier commodity (Scherr 1985: 39). It accounted for twice as many plantations as those devoted to all other cash crops put together in 1831 (Arias *et al.* 1987: 84, 138, 221). The province of Pichucalco, attributed to Chiapas despite strenuous Tabascan objections, derived half a million pesos from the cocoa harvest of 1847–8 (Calderón 1955: 43; Wasserstrom 1983a: 135). Whether this was good for Mexican consumers was quite another matter.

In contrast, Nicaraguan cocoa producers suffered from the secession of the Central American Federation from Mexico, and its subsequent break-up into small independent states, as new countries put up duties against their neighbours (Rubio Sánchez 1958: 103). Costa Rica even banned cocoa imports altogether in 1846, to stimulate internal production (Saenz Maroto 1970: 546). Nicaragua's official cocoa exports contracted sharply after independence, only amounting to 150 kilos by sea in 1841, with twenty tonnes going overland to El Salvador and Honduras in 1844. Some imports of cheap Guayaquil beans also persisted (Burns 1991: 54–5; Lanuza *et al.* 1983: 52, 87–8).

Gran Colombia prohibited cocoa imports in 1821, on pain of the confiscation of vessel and cargo (Mollien 1824: 380–1, 386–7; McGreevey 1971: 34; Humphreys 1940: 245–6). This only became a practical issue after the secession of Venezuela and Ecuador in 1830. A law of 1834 lifted the ban on cocoa imports in Colombia, but set the import duty at 30 per cent, and limited foreign trade to certain ports (Gosselman 1962: 124 5). Ranchers in the eastern cattle plains complained in 1839 that they were cut off for nine months in the year from the rest of the country, and thus wished to obtain cocoa freely from Venezuela (Beyer 1947: 309). In 1842, congress gave special permission to the far southwest of the country to import some Ecuadorian cocoa (Patiño 1963: 302). Colombia was a small net exporter of cocoa and enjoyed much natural protection, so that tariffs are unlikely to have played an import substituting role, even though Tolima cocoa was directed towards Bogotá, Antioquia's output was geared to internal demand, and Cauca cocoa, worth some 200,000 pesos a year, went downriver to Antioquia and upriver to Popayán by 1849 (Brew 1977: 243–4; Brungardt 1974: 93; Hyland 1982: 381).

Influenced by a powerful agrarian lobby, Peru imposed a 30 per cent duty for unspecified articles in 1826, denounced by Ecuadorian planters as 'prohibitive' (Humphreys 1940: 199–202; Wills 1831: 28). This was probably a fiscal measure, as Peru still imported about 150,000 pesos worth of cocoa a year from Guayaquil in the late 1820s, and some 400 tonnes a year between 1835 and 1844 (Bonilla 1975–6: I, 24–5; Chiriboga 1980: 14). In any event, the producers of the Amazon tributaries, dependent on the Cuzco market, enjoyed formidable natural protection. The new province of La Convención was created in 1857, with its capital in Quillabamba, to reflect a booming economy, based on coca leaf, sugar cane, cocoa and timber (Brisseau Loaiza 1981: 35, 39, 161). La Convención at some point produced about half the country's cocoa (Romero 1961: 399–401).

Bolivia grew cocoa in similar valleys, but the political context was different. In a partially successful attempt to break import dependency on Peru and develop a new port in the coastal desert, Bolivia maintained unusually low import duties (Mathew 1989: 412–15). Guayaquil cocoa was thus freely available in La Paz in the 1840s (Dalence 1975: 277). Average annual exports of Guayaquil cocoa to Bolivia were only eight tonnes in 1835–44, but there may have been re-exports via Peru (Chiriboga 1980: 14).

Argentinean import tariffs were solely designed to raise revenue, as there were no local cocoa producers to protect. Buenos Aires had a stiff 20 per cent import duty on cocoa in 1824–5, identical to that on other luxuries, such as tea, coffee and maté. Small amounts of cocoa came from Chile and Peru, probably re-exports of Guayaquil beans (Humphreys 1940: 61). Direct exports of Guayaquil cocoa to the River Plate were only noted in one year in 1835–44 (Chiriboga 1980: 14).

Guayaquil bore the brunt of rampant protectionism, and the port's own high import tariffs made matters worse, as shippers found it difficult to secure a return cargo from Peru (Bonilla 1975–6: I, 24–5). Nevertheless, non-Western markets remained significant for Ecuador. In 1835–44, Latin America and the Philippines took a third of Guayaquil's cocoa exports by weight. Mexico and Central America together only imported a little more than Peru and Chile, reflecting a reorientation of sales to the south (Chiriboga 1980: 14).

A second negative consequence of Hispanic American independence was the raising of export taxes on cocoa beans, notably in Gran Colombia. The new state had a virtual monopoly on supplies of cocoa to Europe, as it included both Ecuador and Venezuela (Anon. 1827: 295). Funds were urgently needed to finance military expenditure and repay loans, so Bolívar proposed a 30 per cent ad valorem export duty on cocoa. This would bring northern ports in line with the duty in Guayaquil, adopted in 1821 as an emergency measure. The proposal was rejected, in favour of a 10 per cent duty in northern ports (Bushnell 1970: 159–60; Hamerly 1973: 132; Arosemena 1991: I, 180). Even 10 per cent contrasted with a ten-year exemption for coffee, sugar and cotton (Mollien 1824: 407–8). High duties were a particular disappointment for Guayaquil planters, who had backed independence to alleviate the crushing tax burden (Chiriboga 1980: 12–13). The closure of many ports to foreign trade made matters worse (Gosselman 1962: 152; Harwich Vallenilla 1996: 30).

A commercial treaty with the United States in 1824, and one with Britain a year later, did not bring the anticipated lowering of export dues (Jong 1966: 71, 109). When tariffs were harmonised across Gran Colombia in 1824, the duty on cocoa was set at 15 per cent, higher than for other products. This was temporarily reduced to 10 per cent in 1826, for fear of competition from Central America (Bushnell 1970: 160, 164). Bolívar then raised a specific duty in Guayaquil in 1827, roughly equivalent to 30 per cent ad valorem (Hamerly 1973: 132–4). On top of all this, the tithe was kept at 10 per cent (Arosemena 1991: I, 229). The more rapid growth of Venezuelan coffee may have been partly due to differential taxation (Bushnell 1970: 164).

The dissolution of Gran Colombia in 1830 provided little immediate relief for Venezuelan producers, as export taxes on cocoa were set at 14 per cent, whereas coffee was exempt. In 1838, coffee was imposed at 30 centavos per *quintal*, compared to 70 centavos for cocoa (Gosselman 1962: 151). However, Venezuela eliminated the tithe in 1833, and cancelled all export duties on agricultural produce in 1841–9 (Polanco Martínez 1960: II, 148, 207). Money was also spent in useful ways, as internal transport costs were halved by the completion of a new road between La Guaira and Caracas in 1845 (Schneider 1981: I, 216).

Taxation fell in the other successor states to Gran Colombia, albeit slowly in Ecuador. The 14 per cent export duty was cruelly felt in Guayaquil in 1832, due to a slump in the world cocoa price (Terry 1834: 66, 85, 251). This had come down to 10 per cent by the late 1830s in Ecuador, and Colombia abolished all export taxes on agricultural produce in 1834, although export subsidies granted to other crops were denied to cocoa (Gosselman 1962: 105, 125). The tithe was retained in Ecuador, more than ever to the benefit of state rather than church (Arosemena 1991: I, 229).

The 1822 export tax in Central America was equivalent to only 2 per cent ad valorem, in the hope of resurrecting the flourishing cocoa sector of earlier centuries (Humphreys 1940: 291). Central American cocoa exports in 1825 were even valued at 1,500,000 pesos, or nearly a fifth of the Federation's total export earnings (Solórzano 1963: 291). This must either have been a fabrication or an inflated estimate of contraband, as Mexican statistics for that year only recorded minuscule imports of Nicaraguan cocoa, valued at under 8,000 pesos (Herrera Canales 1980: 64). In any event, Central America's cocoa exports faded away quickly in the face of competition from Tabasco and Chiapas.

Haïtian export duties were high, but France obtained a 50 per cent rebate in 1825, in return for formal recognition of independence. France thus became the main market for Haïti's low grade cocoa, re-exporting about half of it (Joachim 1972: 1516).

The Dutch were more malleable in Asia than in the Caribbean, as demand for cocoa from the Philippines provided a welcome boost to the languishing economy of the Moluccas. Direct trade with Manila contravened regulations that such trade should be conducted via Java, but Chinese captains adopted the flag of the Sultan of Sulu. Officials turned a blind eye, in part because some had themselves become cocoa planters. Export dues were kept at 6 per cent, for there was competition on the Manila market. As Spanish relations with Ecuador improved, cocoa again flowed legally across the Pacific, although shipping links were irregular, and discriminating consumers preferred Moluccan beans (Clarence-Smith 1998: 95–6). Manila also received unknown quantities of cocoa from within the archipelago (MacMicking 1967: 187; Díaz Arenas 1850: app. 15; Mas 1843: II; Mallat 1983: 201).

The qualified triumph of free trade, 1850s–1870s

The performance of cocoa in the golden era of free trade improved, although competitors such as coffee did better. Vexatious taxes and regulations melted away like spring snow from around 1850, and terms of trade were probably more favourable to primary products than at any other time in modern history. The modesty of cocoa's recovery from the doldrums of the post-Napoleonic world was in large part due to the lack of a mass clientele in the most dynamic and liberal areas of the world, as shown in Table 3.6.

France, briefly seduced by free trade, became the world's main importer of cocoa, as shown in Table 3.6. The government reduced import dues, while maintaining differentials in favour of French ships and colonies (Mangin

Table 3.6 Imports of cocoa for consumption into selected countries, 1850–80 (10 year intervals; tonnes)

Country	1850	1860	1870	1880
France	2,068	4,717	12,189	10,767
Spain	5,847	7,111	4,258	8,471
Britain	1,399	2,079	3,150	4,775
Germany	535	780	1,259	2,019
Netherlands	203	221	534	1,130
Portugal	128	68	na	na

Sources: *TGCF*; Prados de la Escosura 1982: 246 [1849 for 1850]; *AEE* [1861 for 1860]; *PP 1876*, Vol. 77, c. 1634 [may be gross]; *PP 1886*, Vol. 69, c. 4877 [may be gross]; Historicus 1896: 48; Fitzgerald 1995: 49; *Gordian*: II, 522–3 [5 year averages]; Schrover 1991: 292 [10 year averages]; Freitas 1867: 86–7

1860: 154, 186, 190–1, 198). Protectionist demons reared their heads again after Napoleon III's humiliating defeat in 1870, leading to rearguard action by chocolate manufacturer Emile Menier (Girault 1916: 77; Smith 1980: 75–6).

Fluctuations in Spanish imports may have been reinforced by contraband. The reduction of import duties from 1849 led to smuggling into France. Even reduced French duties in 1860 remained high enough to encourage this flow of contraband (Mangin 1860: 197–8; Carr 1982: 277–80). However, Spanish duties on cocoa rose again, as the republican interlude of 1868–74 gave way to renewed protection under the restored monarchy (Carr 1982: 343, 366; Alzola 1895: 80).

Gladstone abolished preference for British colonial cocoa in 1853, imposing a uniform duty of a penny per pound. Chocolate manufacturers welcomed the change, but argued that the duty still amounted to a quarter of the value of beans (Johnston 1865: 222–3). Imports were also sensitive to sugar duties, raised in the 1850s to pay for the Crimean War, reduced in the 1860s, and scrapped in 1874 (Janes and Sayers 1963: 29–30).

The main Latin American purchasers of cocoa lowered duties on imports, but often kept them high on internal trade, for fiscal reasons. In 1856, the Mexican duty on cocoa imports came down to a fifth of the 1821 level, probably 5 per cent ad valorem (Cosio Villegas 1932: 46–7). However, the internal duty on Tabasco cocoa was raised to 2 pesos per *carga*, plus miscellaneous federal and municipal dues. To add insult to injury, cocoa from Chiapas was taxed less, even when it was exported through Tabasco (Arias *et al.* 1987: 248–9). The fall in the number of Tabasco's cocoa trees the mid-1850s may have reflected this fiscal structure (Scherr 1985: 72). Colombia acted likewise, reducing import duties from 1847, and abolishing the tithe in most provinces from 1850 (Bergquist 1986: 11–12, 15; Liehr 1989: 469). However, Manizales traders complained bitterly in 1880 about internal duties on the 500 tonnes of cocoa that annually came through their town for sale in Antioquia (Schenck 1953: 40, 51–2). Colombia imported thirty-one tonnes of cocoa in 1873–4, whereas exports were under a tonne (*AEC 1875*: 183).

Peru both adopted 'aggressively liberal' tariffs and abolished internal duties in the early 1850s (Bulmer-Thomas 1994: 39; Basadre 1963–8: III, 1289). Ecuadorian beans thus sold at half the price of the local Peruvian article in the late 1860s, although quality also affected this differential (Orton 1876: 437).

Export duties and regulations inhibiting sales abroad were on a downward path. Cocoa leaving Guayaquil was charged 0.4 pesos per *quintal* by 1860, about a quarter of the 1827 level, although the government still levied the unpopular tithe at a full 10 per cent (Arosemena 1991: I, 229). The opening of the port of Carúpano to foreign trade in 1846 gave a considerable boost to cocoa exports from eastern Venezuela (Harwich Vallenilla

1996: 30–1). The triumph of the liberal cause in Venezuela two years later consolidated policies favourable to exports (Lombardi 1971: 24–5, 107). Export duties were even abolished altogether in 1868, to cope with an unprecedented drought (*PP 1871*: vol. 65, c. 232).

Lowering taxes was tried elsewhere. Nicaraguan cocoa producers were exempted from many taxes in 1846, and by 1867 there were an estimated 2.3 million cocoa trees in the Rivas district (Lanuza *et al.* 1983: 83–8). The authorities reacted to the 1840s coffee crisis in Cuba with fiscal measures to stimulate cocoa exports to Spain, notably the reduction of the tithe to 2.5 per cent from 1850 (Marrero 1972–89: XI, 134–5; XII, 339). More effective were differential import duties in Spain, cocoa from the Spanish Antilles paying only 28 pesetas per 100 kilos in 1877, compared to 107 or 72 pesetas for different categories of foreign beans (Alzola 1895: 80).

Brazil went against the trend by increasing export duties, although certain commercial regulations were eased. In particular, the Amazon was opened to ships of all nations in 1867, at a time when cocoa still accounted for 10 per cent of the region's exports by value (Keller 1874: 98). However, producers complained of a 9 per cent ad valorem export tax in Belém, additional temporary taxes, and internal transit dues that penalised areas upriver from Obidos (Orton 1876: 259–60, 354, 363). Arbitrary municipal taxes, licence fees for peddlers, and tolls on canoe traffic all added to the burden (Weinstein 1983: 55, 65–6). Export taxes on Bahia cocoa also rose, from an effective rate of 5.5 per cent in the 1850s to 9 per cent by the end of the imperial period, to which various extras were attached (Freitas 1979: 15; Zehntner 1914: 103–6; Bondar 1938: 30–1).

Commercial restrictions in the colonial Caribbean were swept away, but export taxes lingered on. Whereas British Navigation Laws were abolished in 1849, levels of export tax on cocoa varied from two pence per hundred pounds in Grenada after 1868, to twelve pence, with an additional 15 per cent, in Dominica at the same time (*PP*: various years). The Dutch allowed foreign ships to trade freely in Surinam in 1850, and differential export duties gave way to a flat 5 per cent by 1858, allowing the colony to switch sales to the United States (Reyne 1924–5: 20; Lier 1971: 190; *PP 1861*: vol. 63). The 1861 tariff also liberalised trade in the French Caribbean (Blérald 1986: 43–5).

The two burgeoning cocoa producers of the Gulf of Guinea faced quite different conditions. São Tomé and Príncipe were obliged to ship to Portugal in Portuguese ships, as this was technically an extension of metropolitan coastal trade (Clarence-Smith 1985: 64–5). Duties on the total value of exports in 1869–74 were between 9 and 12 per cent, although coffee exports were still worth ten times those of cocoa in this period (Ribeiro 1877: 454–69). In contrast, Santa Isabel remained a free port exporting mainly to Britain, even though Spain took over direct administration of Fernando Póo in 1858 (Clarence-Smith 1994a: 184).

Liberalisation boosted Philippines cocoa imports, underpinned by a prosperous export economy. Ecuadorian Forastero sold for about half the price
of local Criollo, despite the beans being taken half way round the world
(Jagor 1875: 95–6). Consumers preferred Criollo, however, leading to a
steady growth in imports from the Moluccas, no longer regarded as contraband by either Spaniards or Dutch from the 1850s. Sailing ships flew the
Spanish flag, to benefit from tariff advantages entering Manila, and called
yearly at more ports in the Moluccas. The spread of steamers in the 1870s
made it attractive to ship cocoa to the British entrepot of Singapore, albeit
still for re-export to Manila (Clarence-Smith 1998: 96–7).

Neo-mercantilist temptations, 1880s–1914

Increasing scepticism about free trade, provoked by the recession of
1873–96, had negative consequences in southern Europe and Latin America,
but these were more than offset by an 'open door' for raw materials in the
booming economies of northwestern Europe and North America. A
dramatic increase in overall imports thus coincided with a great shift in the
main markets for cocoa beans, as set out in Table 3.7, while differing import
duties are shown in Table 3.8.

The spectacular rise of the United States to world leadership followed the
abolition of duty on cocoa beans, in 1886 or possibly earlier. This allowed
American imports to grow at an astonishing pace, almost exclusively to meet

Table 3.7 Principal cocoa importing countries, 1885–1914 (5 year intervals; net
imports; thousands of tonnes)

Country	1885	1890	1895	1900	1905	1910	1914
USA	5	8	13	18	32	47	78
Germany	3	6	10	19	30	44	54
Netherlands	1	n.a.	3	6	11	19	32
UK	7	9	14	20	20	25	30
France	12	14	15	18	22	25	26
Switzerland	1	n.a.	2	4	5	9	10
Spain	7	8	7	5	6	6	7
Austria			1	2	3	5	7
Russia			1	2	2	4	4
Belgium			2	2	3	5	3
Canada					1	1	3
Italy	n.a.	n.a.	1	1	1	2	2
Total	n.a.	n.a.	71	98	140	199	267

Sources: Food and Agriculture Organisation 1955; Hall 1914: 405; *PP 1886*, vol. 69; *Gordian*: X,
4198; Historicus 1896, 48; Hart 1911: 244–5

Note
Total includes all other importers

Table 3.8   Import duties on cocoa beans in 1898 and 1913 (German Marks per 100
              kilos)

Country	Remarks	1898	1913
Britain		19	19
Netherlands		0	0
Belgium		0	0
Sweden		6	6
Germany		35	20
Switzerland		1	1
Austria-Hungary	By sea	41	41
Russia		59	59
Italy		80	24
France	Foreign origin	83	83
	Colonial origin	42	42
Spain	Foreign origin	75	96
	Colonial origin	36	40
Portugal		16	16
Canada	non-British 1913	0	13
United States		0	0
Nicaragua		89	122
Colombia		759	376
Philippines		47	30
South Africa		38	19
Australia	Queensland	23	0
	Other states	0	0

Sources: calculated from *Gordian*: IV, 1367–72; XIX, 6332. French and Spanish colonies from
Jumelle 1900: 74; AGA 1905

internal demand for chocolate (*Gordian*: IV, 1579). Free entry for beans
accentuated the partial reorientation of New World exports to the United
States. Thus the Dominican Republic initially shipped to Hamburg, but
switched to New York, which even re-exported some of these beans to
Europe in 1914 (Baud 1982: 75). A commercial reciprocity treaty, signed in
1891, reinforced US-Dominican trade relations (Abel 1985: 341, 344).

    Two small European countries cut import taxes on beans to boost choco-
late exports. Switzerland, with a low duty, became the world's largest
exporter of eating chocolate, while duty-free cocoa underpinned the rise of
the Netherlands as the main exporter of chocolate powder. There could be
no imperial preference through tariffs, and Surinam thus sent most of its
cocoa to the United States, with only 4 per cent destined for the Netherlands
in 1899 (*Gordian*: VI, 2241; XIX, 6497–9). Measures favouring national shipping did bring a large part of Java's beans to the Netherlands, but they were
almost entirely re-exported. Java beans were liked for their colour and butter
content, but were shunned by makers of chocolate powder because of their
insipid taste (Hunger 1913: 451; Roepke 1922: 80–1, 84).

Relying mainly on the internal market, Germany pursued less liberal policies. Import duties were cut and re-exports made free of duty in 1885, and sugar firms secured a further paring of the cocoa duty in 1903 (*Gordian*: VIII, 3468; XII, 1007; Stollwerck 1907: 74–5). Manufacturers resisted attempts to raise it again, requesting that it be scrapped altogether, to stimulate exports of chocolate on Dutch and Swiss lines. This was opposed in Berlin, because of commercial treaties and fiscal necessities (BAAP 1907a).

The German colonial lobby sought free entry for empire beans, but at most received a drawback for minute amounts of colonial cocoa used in chocolate exports in 1892 (Rudin 1968: 264, 278–9). Speculative stocking of São Tomé beans led to further unsuccessful pressure for greater reliance on colonial sources (*Gordian*: IV, 1530). The Kamerun Kakao Gesellschaft was set up in 1896 to market 'pure colonial' chocolate, but it soon collapsed because of the need to blend beans of different origins (*Gordian*: IV, 1623; Preuss 1987: 103). As the Kaiser continued to call for colonial chocolate, one German company made such a product with a German flag on the wrapper (BAAP 1908b). Despite all this, a paltry 2.4 per cent of Germany's cocoa imports came from her colonies in 1912 (Schinzinger 1984: 127).

Britain was in a similar position. Governments refused to scrap Gladstone's penny per pound import duty for fiscal reasons, despite repeated pleas from chocolate manufacturers (Gardiner 1923: 241). However, governments also rejected tariff advantages for colonial cocoa, until the First World War led to both higher import taxes and the reintroduction of imperial preference (Knapp 1920: 14). The raising of British sugar duties in 1901, to finance the Boer War, was bitterly opposed by the Manufacturing Confectioners' Association, dominated by chocolate companies (Fitzgerald 1995: 99). To put this in perspective, Dutch manufacturers paid about ten times more for their cocoa beans than for their sugar in 1913 (Schrover 1991: 176).

Slow growth in French cocoa imports reflected high taxes, which inhibited French chocolate exports (Stollwerck 1907: 69–71). A prohibitive rate of duty fell on cocoa imported from other European ports, particularly São Tomé beans, forced to come to Lisbon by differential Portuguese tariffs. A solution worthy of Kafka was adopted in 1909. São Tomé beans were trans-shipped in Madeira, part of Portugal for the Portuguese, but part of Africa for the French (*Gordian*: IX, 3793; XVI, 3681). French imperial preference was a hollow pretence. Colonial cocoa paid 52 francs per 100 kilos from 1892, whereas foreign cocoa was charged double (Girault 1916: 106–7). However, the ministry of finance limited this concession to a quota, set annually, causing the colonial share of French cocoa imports to fall from 5 to 2 per cent between 1905 and 1913 (Chalot and Luc 1906: 3, 57–8; Sarraut 1923: 265–6). It was only then that France decreed the abolition of all import duties on colonial cocoa, effective in 1914 (Girault 1916: 107). This led to a rise in imports of expensive colonial beans after the war (Campbell 1996: 207).

Spain's stagnation as a cocoa importer was even more striking, with even higher taxes and more effective protection for colonial suppliers. A law of 1882, aimed at fostering trade between Spain and her colonies, progressively reduced import duties on colonial cocoa from 25 pesetas per 100 kilos to nothing in 1888, essentially to Cuba's benefit. In contrast, foreign beans entering Spain paid a high duty of 60 or 64 Pesetas per 100 kilos in 1891 (Alzola 1895: 80–1, 83, 165, 252–3). The loss of Cuba in 1898 was offset by importing cocoa from Fernando Póo, but a duty of 45 pesetas per 100 kilos, imposed to meet the cost of war with the United States, was doubled to 90 pesetas in 1899. This was still lower than the astronomic 120 pesetas on foreign beans, and export duties in Fernando Póo were waived. Nevertheless, a coalition of planters, manufacturers and retailers forced a reluctant ministry of finance slowly to decrease the duty from 1906, albeit only for a quota set annually. In 1914, the duty stood at 50 pesetas per 100 kilos for the first 4,000 tonnes (AGA 1901 and 1904–14). A year later, 49 per cent by value of Spain's raw cocoa came from the island (*EGCEE* 1915).

Latin American importers also raised their tariffs, in a general drift back to protectionism (Bulmer-Thomas 1994: 141). In 1898, a mere 0.5 per cent of Ecuador's cocoa exports went to Latin American destinations, and 1 per cent in the following year (Kaerger 1901: II, 453; *Gordian*: VI, 2428). One exception was Bolivia, denied access to the sea by the fortunes of war, obliged to sign a commercial treaty with Peru in 1905, and thus importing Cuzco cocoa among other foodstuffs (*EUIEA*: XLIII, 1248). However, cocoa imports amounted to a modest 59 tonnes in 1918 (Schurz 1921: 165).

The closure of the Mexican market was exacerbated from 1872, when import duties on cocoa rose sharply. They remained substantial up to 1910, probably between 15 and 20 per cent ad valorem (Cosio Villegas 1932: 46–7). This limited imports from Ecuador to an average of 50 tonnes a year in 1895–8 (Preuss 1987: 102). Conversely, duties on internal trade were abolished in 1896, once again opening up the national market to Tabasco and Chiapas (Arias *et al.* 1987: 267; Haber 1989: 21, 24). The revolution of 1910 led to a further hike in import duties, but a renewed internal duties coincided with rising imports and falling local production (Cosio Villegas 1932: 46–7; Martínez Assad 1991: 116, 118).

Most of Central America went the same way as Mexico, mainly self-sufficient, but importing some cheap Ecuadorian cocoa, and exporting a little valuable Criollo (Preuss 1987: 94, 99, 101–2). Guatemala suspended import duties in 1878, following a particularly bad cocoa harvest, but exacted a duty of 25 pesos per *quintal* four years later (Rubio Sánchez 1958: 93, 103). Costa Rica was the one exception. Protectionist duties, adopted in 1898 and raised two years later, eliminated imports completely by 1905, and the country became the only significant cocoa exporter in Mesoamerica (Quesada Camacho 1989).

59

Colombia's high import duties may have benefited Cauca. In 1892, about 1,000 tonnes a year of Cauca beans were sent to Antioquia, and cocoa had become 'the prime commercial commodity of the Valley' (Hyland 1982: 404). The great surge in Cauca's output was chiefly sent downriver, with Antioqueños paying up to twice European prices for their Criollo beans in the 1910s (Patiño 1963: 311–12). This suggests that Colombian exports consisted mainly of inferior Forastero beans from the coastal lowlands.

Barriers also went up in Southeast Asia. The United States spoke of lowering Filipino import duties on cocoa after seizing the islands in 1898, following a ten-year transitional period. However, the duty remained quite high, as shown in Table 3.8, possibly because the Americans met with no more success than their Spanish predecessors in turning cocoa into an export crop (*Gordian*: VI, 2669; IX, 3714; XIX, 6665). Moluccan cocoa could no longer be shipped directly to Manila, due to Dutch support for a monopolistic coastal steamer company, benefiting European planters on Java (Clarence-Smith 1998: 106). Beans from Batavia destined for Manila went to the free port of Singapore, which also received supplies from the free

Table 3.9 Export duties on cocoa beans in 1912 (German Marks per 100 kilos, rounded)

Country	Amount
Ecuador – Guayaquil	5
Ecuador – other ports	7
Venezuela	0
Surinam	0
Brazil – Pará	6
Brazil – Bahia	17
Dominican Republic	5
Trinidad	1
Grenada	1
Jamaica	0
Dominica	2
Gold Coast	0
São Tomé	5
Fernando Póo	0
Cameroon	0
Congo Free Trade Zone	0
Ceylon	5
Dutch East Indies	0
Western Samoa	0

Sources: Sociedade de Emigração 1915: 104–5, 199, 201; Paixão 1964: III, 164; Hall 1914: 361; AHA 1912.

Notes
Reis converted to marks at 1912 rate for São Tomé; Brazil rates assume an export price of 100 marks per 100 kilos, as in Zehntner 1914

port of Sulu and from Ceylon. From Singapore, most cocoa went to the Philippines, but about a fifth was destined for Hong Kong (*Gordian*: VI, 2667). By the early 1920s, Manila was one of the two largest markets for Ceylon cocoa (Maclaren 1924: 194).

A comparison between Table 3.9 and Table 3.8 indicates that export duties had fallen further than import duties by 1912, illustrating how the momentum towards freer trade sometimes persisted up to 1914. Indeed, some Latin American export taxes may have come down too far for sound economic development (Bulmer-Thomas 1994: 110).

The heaviest export taxes fell on successful producers with little or no political influence, leading Bahians to complain that the authorities were eating up their profits (*Gordian*: XVII, 4914). When the Republicans allowed each state to determine its own export taxes in 1891, Bahia's was promptly doubled from 7 to 14 per cent ad valorem, reaching a peak of 18 per cent in 1902–4, and only coming down slightly to 17 per cent thereafter (Zehntner 1914: 32, 103–6). In 1909, an additional 2 per cent was levied for statistical services, and 1 per cent for the municipal bank (*Gordian*: XV, 3228). Including municipal taxes, the average burden on cocoa between 1889 and 1930 was estimated at 20–25 per cent (Ruf *et al.* 1994: 77).

Bahia's producers also complained bitterly that the state gave nothing in return. As late as 1910, ports were in a state of nature, the state's coastal shipping company had insufficient steamers and yet prevented foreign ships from competing, few and ineffective attempts had been made to improve river navigation, the new railway being built served few properties, roads were abominable, the telegraph network was skimpy, telephones were non-existent, and the postal service was rudimentary. Furthermore, the agricultural institute was useless, and there were no schools in rural areas. Most seriously of all, violence reigned throughout the cocoa zone (Zehntner 1914: 135–52). This dismal litany may have included an element of special pleading, for the Ilhéus railway probably did play a part in stimulating cocoa exports (Tosta Filho 1957: 6).

The Brazilian Amazon, divided into two states, kept taxes on cocoa lower. Treasuries were filled to overflowing with the proceeds of wild rubber, and diversity in exports was desired. State taxes on Pará's cocoa exports were 4 per cent ad valorem by 1895, compared to 22 per cent on rubber. While Pará raised the rate to 6 per cent in the 1900s, freight rates on subsidised steamer services were reduced in the early 1910s. The inland state of Amazonas charged only 3 per cent on cocoa, rising to 5 per cent by 1913 (Weinstein 1983: 112; Le Cointe 1922: II, 425–6). Municipal taxes were an additional burden (*Gordian*: X, 4165–6).

Smallholders in the Dominican Republic suffered, until violent action brought relief. Dispersed small cocoa farmers in the north were politically less influential than a handful of sugar barons in the south, who gained complete exemption from export duties (Abel 1985: 352). The export tax on cocoa fluctuated but was generally considerable, reaching one peso per *quintal* in 1905 (Marte 984: 260; *Gordian*: VII, 2854; Deschamps 1907: II, 65–6). Discontent led to serious riots in 1909, as the world price drifted down (Bryan 1977: 156–7, 413). Although the export duty was halved in 1910, it remained high in world terms (Hall 1914: 378).

Independent Haïti and colonised Cuba, not included in Table 3.9, were also among the fiscal bandits. Supplementary taxes lifted Haïti's rate to around 15 per cent ad valorem in 1893 (Rouzier 1892–3: II, 128). Smallholders paid to service a national debt accumulated over decades of political mismanagement, from which they benefited little if at all (Aubin 1910: xx). Cocoa was particularly valued by the ministry of finance, as low coffee prices reduced the country's overall exports between 1890 and 1912 (Bulmer-Thomas 1994: 69–70). The Spanish regime in Cuba put a multitude of taxes on cocoa before 1898, allegedly enfeebling cultivation (Clark 1899: 198). That said, the 1888 abolition of import duties on Cuban cocoa entering Spain was a concession of some importance (Alzola 1895: 80–1).

Estate owners were divided by crop in Trinidad. The Legislative Council, dominated by sugar planters, caused an outcry by raising export taxes on cocoa and reducing those on sugar during the sugar crisis of the 1880s (Williams 1964: 118). As the owners of cocoa estates improved their relative position, duties on their crop fell to 7.5 pence per 100 pounds by 1902, and about half that a decade later (*Gordian*: VIII, 3173; Hall 1914: 354). Trinidadian taxpayers also got value for money, as rail and road projects actively stimulated the spread of cocoa, and peace reigned in the interior (Giacottino 1976: II, 545–58).

Ecuadorian cocoa planters exercised an unusual degree of political influence after 1875, and their rejection of higher taxes may have dissipated windfall gains for the country (Maiguashca 1996: 81–3). That said, the export tax on cocoa rose tenfold between 1889 and 1912, and many supplements were added on a temporary basis, more than compensating for the abolition of the tithe in the 1880s (Arosemena 1991: I, 370–9). The export tax was also quite high compared to other countries in 1912, as shown in Table 3.9. Moreover, the regime was notorious for wasting money, notably on the army and public works, resulting in heavy debt servicing (Pineo 1996: 37–8). Breaking up large estates might have made more sense than upping taxes.

Taxes fluctuated violently in Venezuela, with strongmen bringing them down. The tyrannical Guzmán Blanco, in power from 1870 to 1888, drastically lowered duties in order to stimulate exports. Political chaos followed his fall, leading to a show of force by Western powers in 1902–3, who gained undertakings for debt repayment (Lieuwen 1965: 39–45). A 20 per cent additional export tax was thus imposed on cocoa in 1900, raised again in early 1903 (*Gordian*: VI, 2284; IX, 3695–6). However, when Juan Vicente Gómez seized power in 1908, he reformed Venezuelan finances, and once again abolished export taxes on cocoa (Hall 1914: 368).

São Tomé and Príncipe's plutocrats were obliged to shore up Portugal's crumbling finances, including transfers of funds to meet fiscal deficits in other colonies (Clarence-Smith 1985: 86). An export duty of 14 reis per kilo was imposed in 1882. This was pared to 12 reis per kilo in 1892 for São Tomé, equivalent to 8.5 per cent ad valorem, while Príncipe was granted duty-free exports for ten years. In both cases, cocoa had to be sent to a Portuguese port in a Portuguese vessel, for duties on exports in foreign ships or to foreign ports were set at prohibitive levels (Nogueira 1893: 77–8, 85–6). The duty was raised to 18 reis per kilo in 1894, to replace a rural land tax that had hardly been collected. Planters complained that they got little in return: fourteen kilometres of railway, a short road, and a rudimentary iron quay (Sociedade de Emigração 1915: 16, 114, 199). The flood of beans entering Lisbon was almost entirely re-exported, on payment of a moderate tax (Moreira Júnior 1905: II, 121). The cash-strapped Republican authorities proposed to lower the export duty in São Tomé to 13 reis per kilo in 1912, but to impose a land tax and a 30 reis per kilo re-export tax in Lisbon. Protests erupted, as it was claimed that this would make the tax burden one of the highest in the world (Sociedade de Emigração 1915: 199).

Governments abolished or reduced export duties to achieve export diversification, especially in times of crisis. Export taxes were suspended in Dominica in 1888, due to the collapse of the world sugar price (Trouillot 1988: 110; *PP 1894*: vol. 92). Costa Rica did likewise for cocoa in 1914, to stimulate the replacement of bananas devastated by disease (Quesada Camacho 1989: 92). The French authorities in the Anglo-French New Hebrides condominium (Vanuatu) reduced duties on cocoa exported to New Caledonia or France in 1901, as part of an attempt to ensure the economic supremacy of French over British planters (Girault 1916: 118). There were 2,672 hectares of cocoa in French hands by the early 1920s, compared to just 122 for the British (Maclaren 1924: 197).

Behind the phenomenal success of colonial smallholders lay official reluctance to collect export taxes in recently conquered territories. Even hut, poll or land taxes were suspect, if sufficient revenue could be derived from import duties. Gold Coast cocoa exports were thus free, until a quarter of a penny per pound was reluctantly imposed in 1916, to cope with the exigencies of war (Maclaren 1924: 181). The authorities turned down a proposition to collect hut tax in 1897, in view of a rebellion in Sierra Leone the previous year. There was thus no direct taxation of Africans on the Gold Coast until 1936. Cautious British attempts to exact such a tax in southern Nigeria in 1912 caused riots two years later (Crowder 1982: 207–8). Similarly, cocoa from German colonies was routinely exempt of all duties in order to stimulate exports (Schinzinger 194: 141; *Gordian*: V, 2175).

Import duties on inputs had a marginal impact, given the low capital intensity of cocoa cultivation, and only occasionally became an issue. Cameroon exempted goods for agricultural use from all import duties, including machines, seed, fertiliser, pesticides, scientific instruments, books and medical supplies (Schinzinger 1984: 140). However, two plantation corporations protested in 1900 against import taxes on food and consumer goods consumed by plantation workers (*Gordian*: V, 2175; VII, 2694). The plea for duty-free entry was rejected, but the companies prevented increased duties on foodstuffs (ABM 1906).

Conclusion

The trend was clearly for burdens imposed by governments to decrease, and this was a factor in the lower price of chocolate, but much remains to be discovered about the details. Regulatory changes have been fairly well explored, but the extent and impact of contraband in the late eighteenth and early nineteenth century still pose considerable challenges to historians, not least on the statistical front. Another area that requires investigation is the cost to metropolitan chocolate consumers of protecting cocoa planters in the colonies, notably in the case of Spain.

Above all, there is a need for systematic series of taxation rates, for both imports and exports, including all the additional and temporary taxes so common in Latin America. Ideally, this should include a consideration of taxes on closely related commodities, especially sugar, and of consumption taxes on chocolate. Indeed, to get a truly accurate picture of the burden borne by producers, it is necessary to consider fiscal policy as a whole. The extraordinary West African boom, which gathered way before 1914, was clearly characterised by remarkably low taxation, but comparisons with other cocoa-producing lands are hard to establish. Such research would help to tackle the burning question of the ideal level and method of taxation for today's cocoa producers.

Similarly, much more consideration has to be given to what 'cocoa actors' received in return for their taxes. An attempt has been made here to suggest startling variations in the quantity and quality of public goods supplied in the tropical world. Colonial regimes tended to score better than independent states, but there were wide variations within both categories. British colonialism probably provided best value for money, although the use of state revenues tended to be quite conservative.

4

THE CHOCOLATE INDUSTRY

Conditioned by demand for its products and the price of cocoa beans, the chocolate industry also responded to technical and managerial changes, as well as state policies towards chocolate. Evolving techniques lowered costs of production, although the historical record is littered with examples of firms mechanising too early or in the wrong way. Another part of the story was the emergence of companies with specific business cultures, and the interplay between these companies. Taxation and regulation also affected the industry, especially the degree of protection offered to manufacturers.

Chocolate suffered from a particular difficulty on its rocky road to mechanisation: the joint supply problem. To make chocolate beverages more digestible, it was necessary to press much of the cocoa butter out of the liquor, leaving a partially defatted 'cake', which could then be powdered. However, the patenting of Van Houten's famous press in 1828 did not signal the resolution of the industry's fundamental difficulty, despite innumerable claims to the contrary, for there was initially no market for cocoa butter. The joint supply problem acted as a drag on technical innovation for a long time, as manufacturers clung to old forms of chocolate, adulterated with starches to soak up excessive fat. The solution depended on the elaboration of new kinds of eating chocolate, which incorporated surplus cocoa butter, in turn giving rise to an international market for cocoa butter (Othick 1976).

As scale of production increased, the chocolate industry split into two distinct sectors. A multitude of firms, many of them very small, used chocolate in confectionery and baking. Increasingly, they bought their chocolate, rather than making it themselves. A few large firms, many of them household names to this day, processed cocoa beans, supplied chocolate to the confectionery and baking sector, and produced beverages and eating chocolate for a mass market.

Large firms were accused of forming cartels, pushing down the price of cocoa beans and increasing that of chocolate, to the detriment of tropical farmers and Western consumers alike. While such an analysis has some value for the period from 1914 to the 1950s, it was not generally true of the period before 1914. There were also complaints that the quality of chocolate deteriorated, as manufacturers purchased cheap beans. However, there was great disagreement as to what 'quality' might mean. Dutch dealers considered Ecuador's Arriba or Nacional, botanically a Forastero, to be the *vin ordinaire* of the world cocoa trade in 1859 (ANRI 1859). Fifty years later, it was listed among the 'fine' beans (Hall 1914: 495). The evolution of processing techniques and the emergence of a mass market changed the requirements of manufacturers over time, but it is hard to spot any conspiracy against producers of fine beans.

The mercantilist background

Producers continued Mesoamerican practices almost unchanged until the eighteenth century, roasting beans and then grinding them with stone rollers on curved stones, sometimes adding unrefined sugar, spices or starches. This was an arduous task, as workers had to kneel for long hours to produce quite small amounts of chocolate. Dried pieces of chocolate mass were an early convenience food, grated to make a hot or cold beverage with water or milk. They were only eaten in unusual circumstances, as they had a dry and gritty texture (Coe and Coe 1996: chs 4–5; Harwich 1992: chs 4–5).

Chocolate was produced at home, by wandering specialists, or in workshops. Many families made their own, especially in Mesoamerica, where every household had its grinding stone. Alternatively, peripatetic artisans carried heavy stones from house to house, grinding beans for a fee. A little Andalusian port had fifteen such artisans in the eighteenth century, as well as three workshops (Stols 1996: 44, 52). Sephardic Jews played a central role in diffusing Spanish methods of chocolate making across Europe, with workshops in Amsterdam, Bayonne and Bordeaux, and probably in London. In Hamburg, however, their activities were hampered by discrimination against Jewish artisans (Israel 1989: 79, 183).

Industrial evolution, 1760s–1790s

The quickening pace of industrialisation in the late eighteenth century affected the making of chocolate. However, it is a wild exaggeration to say that, from 1770, 'the advent of steam power caused the chocolate and confectionery industry to progress rapidly' (Williams 1953: 30).

Even in Britain, progress was slow. Joseph Fry, a Quaker pharmacist, settled in Bristol in 1753, selling chocolate as well as medicines. He bought Churchman's water mill (established to grind cocoa beans in 1729) in 1761, and expanded sales of Churchman's Chocolates. In 1764 he had a network of agents in fifty-three towns, with a warehouse in London, and may already have been exporting to Ireland. This was said to be the only chocolate mill in the country in 1776, when Fry penned a 'humble memorial', pleading for a reduction in the import duty on cocoa and the excise on chocolate. In 1777, he moved into larger premises, and his wife Anna took over the business after his death in 1787 (Diaper 1988: 33–6; Wagner 1987: 12–15).

There were similar stirrings in Continental Europe and North America. Lombart, claiming to be the oldest chocolate firm in France, was created in 1760 (Knapp 1920: 122). The French experimented with pressing out cocoa butter from at least 1760, and the firm of Pelletier appeared a decade later (Pelletier and Pelletier 1861: 50, 137). French manufacturers began to apply water power to grinding and mixing cocoa liquor from 1778 (Bourgaux 1935: 168–9). By 1798, there were chocolate 'factories' in eight German and Austrian cities (Harwich 1992: 79). The Dutch chocolate industry, concentrated in Zeeland, may have used wind power (Slijper 1927: 140–1; Fincke 1936: 19–20). John Hannon, an Irishman who had learned his trade in England, in 1765 installed a factory in an old water mill on the Neponset river, in Dorchester, today part of greater Boston. He met his death on a voyage to obtain cocoa beans in the Caribbean. James Baker, a Dorchester doctor who had provided the capital for the venture, took over the mill as the Baker Company (Harwich 1992: 79–80; Coe and Coe 1996: 230).

Prosperous late-Bourbon Spain and France were at the cutting edge of technical progress, and yet clung to guilds. Steam power was allegedly first used very early to make chocolate, in 1780 in both Barcelona and Bayonne (Rubinstein 1982: 175; Harwich 1992: 79). There was also a mule-driven mill in Spain in 1786–7, grinding cocoa with five rollers of polished steel and two millstones (Coe and Coe 1996: 231). However, the nearly 150 artisan grinders of Madrid formed a guild in 1773, on the lines of those existing in Barcelona, Pamplona and Lisbon. They fixed a six-year apprenticeship, and promised to combat the adulteration of chocolate (Kany 1932: 152). The Basque artisan grinders of Bayonne formed their guild in 1761, excluding Jews and attempting to gain the sole right to manufacture and sell chocolate. A compromise solution was imposed by Paris in 1767, allowing Jews to retain some of the market (Léon 1893: 69–76).

Most cocoa beans continued to be ground by hand, both in the West and in Latin America (Fincke 1936: 19–21). The positioning of heated stones in such a way that labourers could work standing up, producing 6–7 kilos of chocolate mass a day, was probably more important than early experiments with inanimate power (Lami 1885: III, 337). The encyclopaedia of Diderot and d'Alembert, published between 1751 and 1772, illustrated methods of roasting and grinding chocolate that had not changed since Aztec times, even though the *chocolatière*, in which the beverage was whisked and served, had reached a high degree of Baroque elegance (Coe and Coe 1996: 224–5). Workshops in Mesoamerica produced chocolate mass that was regularly sold on markets, but all households were also said to possess their own grinding stones (Stols 1996: 44; Newson 1987: 294; Bullock 1824: 284).

Peru and surrounding areas formed a precocious centre of chocolate workshops, with small quantities even reaching Spain. Chocolate was regularly exported from Callao to Cadiz in 1767–76, ranging between 0.25 and 1.5 tonnes, and there was mention of such exports in later years. A mule train on the Arequipa to Buenos Aires route carried 7.4 tonnes in 1790, while a little chocolate from the Mojos missions came to Cuzco (Parrón Salas 1995: 353–4, 396, 524, 526). Mojos chocolate, laboriously prepared by Amerindian women, was sold in Cochabamba, Santa Cruz and Chuquisaca (Sucre) in 1791, and may have been sent to Spain in this form (*MP*: II, 316; Kany 1932: 152; Orbigny 1992: 301). Guayaquil exported a little cocoa butter to Spain, reaching one tonne in 1788, as producers away from the rivers could not afford to send cocoa beans to the port by mule, whereas it was worth their while to deliver cocoa butter (*MP*: XII, 169–70). There was even a revolutionary proposal, in 1774, that all Guayaquil beans should be ground prior to export, to reduce freight costs and increase preservation (Arosemena 1991: II, 545). Vast amounts of crude raw sugar went into chocolate production in Venezuela, but there was no mention of exports (Humboldt 1852: II, 29).

The uneven impact of revolution and war, 1790s–1820s

The tide of war penalised the French empire and its allies. Access to cocoa beans became progressively more difficult for most of Europe, especially with the imposition of the Continental System in 1806. This caused Bordeaux's flourishing processing of colonial commodities to grind to a halt (Casey 1981: 39–40). As soon as the wars seemed to be over, in 1814, a water-driven chocolate mill was set up in French Catalonia. A year later, Casparus van Houten began making chocolate in Amsterdam, with a mill turned by labourers (Williams 1953: 30–1).

In contrast, British protégés and the United States could continue to make chocolate throughout the long wars. Portugal was particularly fortunate, protected by the Royal Navy and a centre of the neutral cocoa trade (Pohl 1963: 279–80). Lisbon exported a little chocolate in the late 1790s, and had active workshops in the early 1820s (Alden 1976: 131; Balbi 1822: I, 448). In the United States, Mr Welsh's mill, in Boston, turned out over a tonne of chocolate a day in 1794, and there were four chocolate makers for the 40,000 inhabitants of Philadelphia by 1786 (Leonard 1973: 51). In the same year, New York boasted three chocolate manufacturers (Arosemena 1991: I, 179).

British producers benefited from a complete prohibition on chocolate imports, denounced as inimical to colonial interests in 1818 (Williams 1952: 327). Joseph Storrs Fry took over the family's Bristol company from his mother in 1795, but he invested somewhat too heavily in new methods of production. In a purpose-built new factory, he installed a larger roaster and a steam engine to grind beans, stressing mechanical perfection in his advertisements. However, the expenses were such, together with buying a brewery, that he was forced to bring a fellow Quaker into the firm as a partner in 1805, with roughly equal shares in the capital by 1814. It was not until 1822 that Fry felt able to dissolve this partnership (Diaper 1988: 36).

The impact of war and revolution on the Spanish empire remains to be investigated. Exports to Spain were no longer mentioned, but they had been marginal. Only some Caribbean islands would have been cut off from supplies of cocoa, and the violence of the independence struggle was patchy. Chocolate makers were among the minor guilds of Lima in 1815, yielding 6 per cent of the tax income from this group (Anna 1979: 118). In Mexico City in 1823, 'great numbers of females are employed making it; which they do by grinding it by hand, between stones...and it is a laborious process' (Bullock 1824: 284).

The slump of the 1820s to the 1840s

Peace and technical progress in the West should have been propitious to the mechanisation of the chocolate industry, but a stagnant market for chocolate, in the context of a deep post-war depression, ensured that there were many false starts and few real advances. Many famous firms, still known today as brands, originated in this period, but they were tiny compared to what they later became.

The poor performance of the industry has been masked by an extraordinary myth surrounding the patenting of Coenraad van Houten's cocoa butter press in the Netherlands in 1828. On the one hand, the novelty of his invention has been greatly exaggerated. A cocoa butter press of sorts existed as early as 1687, and there had been continuing attempts to develop suitable machines (Bourgaux 1935: 110; Fincke 1936: 18). On the other hand, there was no point in pressing out cocoa butter if there was no demand for it. Van Houten remained a tiny company, only installing its first steam engine in 1850, and the same was true of other Dutch companies (Schrover 1991: 172–3, 182, 268, 297). The lack of a market for cocoa butter and established consumer tastes in a depressed market are sufficient to explain the long hiatus between the invention of Van Houten's press and its widespread utilisation. Secretive business practices and high duties on machinery played no more than a secondary role (Othick 1976: 81–2; Fitzgerald 1995: 20–1; Williams 1931: 24–30).

France was a centre of technical innovation. François Pelletier installed a four-horse-power steam mixer in his Paris factory to great acclaim in 1819, allowing for the production of 75 kilos of cocoa mass in half a day (Harwich 1992: 129). Other mechanical improvements came in the 1830s, including a closer integration of grinding and mixing, although this was not without teething problems (Lami 1885: III, 337–8). The Bordeaux firm of Louit was set up in 1825, and by 1850 the city had a number of little factories with steam-powered machinery (Bonin 1997: 125). Bayonne had thirty-three enterprises for making chocolate in 1856, some apparently driven by steam, compared to twenty-one in 1822 (*http*: 'Chocolat Basque'). A Breton, Jean-Baptiste Létang, established a workshop in Paris to make moulds for eating chocolate in 1832, spurred on by advances in both metal-working techniques and chocolate manufacture (Dorchy 1996: 198–9).

The benefits of mechanisation were far from compelling. Pelletier claimed that his machines lowered the price of chocolate, while admitting that the cost of beans was falling (Pelletier and Pelletier 1861: 22–3). Brillat-Savarin opined that machines made better but more expensive chocolate (Brillat-Savarin n.d.: I, 120–1). Barreta criticised high rates of mechanical breakdown, and championed old manual methods (Barreta 1841: 35–6).

Menier chose a path between Barreta's conservativeness and Pelletier's experiments. Trained as a chemist and from a family of food merchants, Jean Menier began to make medicinal powders in 1821, selling them in a pharmacy in Paris' Marais quarter. Chocolate was initially a side product, used to conceal the unpleasant taste of medicines. Menier used horses to power a mill in Paris, and then bought an old water mill in Noisiel, on the Marne. Chocolate became more important prior to his death in 1853, as he won medals in international exhibitions in 1832, 1834, 1839 and 1844. Menier pioneered the packaging of chocolate in France, wrapping half cylindrical bars in yellow paper. In 1849, he introduced yellow chrome paper, with his signature and pictures of his medals (Jeandelle and Robert 1994: 51–2; *http*: 'Menier-Nestlé').

French dynamism spilled over into neighbouring countries. Chocolate producers in Brussels and Wallonia experimented with small steam machines (Scholliers 1996: 164–5). Steam-driven machinery was installed in Potsdam in 1828, although the venture soon collapsed (Fincke 1936: 21–3). J. M. Lehmann set up in Dresden in 1834, specialising in the production of cocoa processing machines (Fincke 1936: 23). Caffarel of Turin possessed a mill driven by an iron water wheel from 1826 (*http*: 'I nostri 170 anni'). It was from Caffarel that François-Louis Cailler, the Vevey pioneer of the French Swiss industry, learned the art of chocolate making (Coe and Coe 1996: 249). Swiss companies were mere workshops, however, at best employing hydraulic energy. Cailler himself waged an uphill struggle against adversity until his death in 1852 (Heer 1966: 79–81). Bayonne Jews set up industries in the Spanish Basque Country and Madrid after 1840, although chocolate was not specifically mentioned (Léon 1893: 356–7).

For all that, southern Europeans generally resisted innovation. Spaniards allegedly did not even place grinding stones on tables. Their chocolate, made by workers on their knees in the old way, was of poor quality. There was no mention of the modern Spanish mills of earlier decades. Most Italian and French chocolate was made by workers standing at heated stone tables, producing up to 20 kilos a day, and wastefully boiling chocolate liquor to extract cocoa butter. Trieste, Verona and Padua were major Italian

centres, together with Italian-speaking Switzerland, while Paris was dominant in France (Barreta 1841: 9–18, 29–38). There was little specialisation.
Romanegro, a Genoese concern, not only prepared and sold chocolate in the
1830s, but also sweets, sugar loaves, syrups, pastries, liqueurs, coffee and
spices (Teiser 1945: 3).

Even Britain, in the vanguard of the Industrial Revolution, did not do
particularly well. Fry's, a family partnership from 1822, remained the largest
chocolate manufacturer, but employed a mere sixteen workers in 1835 at the
death of Joseph Storrs Fry (*http*: 'Cadbury Limited at Somerdale'). Sales
were flat, and the partners withdrew capital from the firm for social
purposes and to fund other business ventures. However, the three sons began
to turn the business around after 1835, with advertisements in newspapers, a
new warehouse in London, rising sales, and imports of about a quarter of
the cocoa beans processed in Britain (Diaper 1988: 37–8).

Cadbury's remained small, and Rowntree's was still no more than a
grocer's shop in the centre of York, purchased in 1822 (Vernon 1958: 9–58).
John Cadbury sold chocolate as a side-line to tea and coffee in his
Birmingham shop in the 1820s. He rented a small factory in an old malt-
house in 1831 to manufacture chocolate, moving into the somewhat larger
Bridge Street factory, again rented, in 1847 (*http*: 'Cadbury Fact Sheet').
Some of the chocolate making operations in this latter factory were mechanised in 1852, but the steam engines were weak, the mainly female labour
force was small, and the factory was cramped. Indeed, Cadbury's 'seemed in
a fair way to extinction' by 1859 (Williams 1931: 24–30).

Innovation in Britain enjoyed mixed success. Daniel Dunn sold a chocolate powder that could be mixed directly with boiling water as early as 1819,
but it was based on the addition of starches, notably arrowroot. Machines
roasted, shelled and ground beans by about 1860, as well as mixing in sugar
and other ingredients (Hewett 1862: 10–11, 65–7). Early chocolate bars,
available at least from the 1820s, were unsuccessful. If sweet, they contained
too little cocoa butter to be moulded properly. If bitter, they were rejected by
consumers. Moreover, bars had an unpleasant grainy texture, as the chocolate was not mixed thoroughly (Williams 1931: 5–6, 13–14; Knapp 1923:
23–5, 130).

In the United States, Walter Baker, the grandson of James the doctor,
took over the Dorchester mill in 1820. The firm then became known as
Walter Baker and Co., and eventually became by far the largest chocolate
producer in the country (Coe and Coe 1996: 230). Walter Baker advertised
the use of a press to extract cocoa butter, but the date is uncertain (Leonard
1973: 51). It may not have been until after 1866, when a Van Houten press
was adopted in Massachusetts (Williams 1953: 31).

The Mexican chocolate industry did surprisingly well for a country in
turmoil. The 1824 tariff may have helped, by prohibiting chocolate imports
(Cosio Villegas 1932: 22). Mexico's first modern chocolate factory dated

from 1828 (Scherr 1985: 39). The German entrepreneur Frank Alt, one of eleven chocolate manufacturers in Mexico City, used steam-powered machinery in 1845 (Mentz *et al.* 1982: 216, 470). Between 1817 and 1860, the estimated value added in producing chocolate nearly doubled in current pesos, one of the best performances in the food industry as a whole, and far above the average industrial growth rate. That said, chocolate accounted for a mere 1.2 per cent of value added in 1860 (Coatsworth 1989: 48).

An Italian in Peru followed Alt's path. Domenico Ghirardelli, the son of a small Ligurian merchant, was apprenticed to a confectioner in Genoa. Ghirardelli sailed across the Atlantic in 1837, aged twenty and recently married, to seek his fortune. After working for a year in a 'coffee and chocolate establishment' in Montevideo, he moved to Peru and set up a confectionery business in Lima. Although he did fairly well for himself, he left in 1848 to take part in the California gold rush. When he failed to find gold and started manufacturing chocolate in California in the 1850s, he imported his first machines from Peru (Teiser 1945: 3–5, 15). In 1860, Peru exported a small amount of chocolate (Basadre 1963–8: III, 1286).

Bolivia and the Philippines apparently stuck to older methods. Mojos women still painstakingly roasted and ground beans by hand to make chocolate mass as tribute for the government (Orbigny 1992: 300–1). Bolivia even exported small quantities of chocolate to Peru and Argentina (Dalence 1975: 273–4). The Spanish government in the Philippines had some kind of workshop in Bikol, and chocolate was made in Manila (MacMicking 1967: 187; Mallat 1983: 179). However, the most common pattern was for Filipinos and Spaniards to roast and grind beans at home (Jagor 1875: 97).

Slow mechanisation, 1850s–1870s

Although free trade assisted the chocolate sector by cheapening beans and machinery and facilitating exports, the pace of industrialisation remained slow (Klopstock 1937: 74). Van Houten's famous press at last began to be employed, but only from the late 1860s on any scale, and by no means universally. With few exceptions, family firms remained small, employing few workers.

France became the premier chocolate manufacturer in the world, although the country remained a curious mixture of new and old, full of regional contrasts. As late as the 1870s, grinders with 'Aztec' stones, mainly Sephardic Jews, still went from house to house in southern France to offer their services, also producing chocolate mass for local confectioners and pharmacists (Coe and Coe 1996: 236). Nevertheless, machinery became more common in the industry (Debay 1864: 16–17). Machines now divided chocolate into bars, and wrapped them in a kind of foil, with a firm's brand name (*Larousse*: IV, 165–6). These machines were mainly made in France, and there was no mention of pressing out cocoa butter in a description of the late 1860s (Thénard 1868: 360–6). However, other sources indicate that small hydraulic presses were applied to sacks filled with cocoa liquor, rarely extracting more than 20 per cent of the fat content (Pelletier and Pelletier 1861: 49–50). Cocoa butter enriched certain kinds of eating chocolate in the 1870s, but there was little demand for the defatted drink pioneered in the Netherlands (Lami 1885: III, 338, 346–7).

By the time of his death in 1881, Emile Menier had come to dominate not only the French chocolate industry, but also that of the world. Born in 1826, he studied science before inheriting his father's business in 1853. He rebuilt the Noisiel water mill in 1855, and again in 1860–72, installing newly invented horizontal turbines. Such was the splendour of this factory that it was dubbed 'the cathedral'. As his chocolate business expanded, Menier moved his pharmaceuticals business to Saint-Denis, and then sold it in 1879. He integrated vertically to a degree not seen before or since, buying cocoa estates in Nicaragua, chartering a fleet of ships, acquiring a branch railway line and sugar refineries, housing 2,000 workers in a model town, and creating his own chocolate distribution network (Mangin 1860: 147; Jeandelle and Robert 1994: 52–3; *http*: 'Menier-Nestlé'). The Noisiel factory, which acquired steam machines to supplement water turbines, produced 688 tonnes of chocolate in 1853 and 2,502 in 1865–6, equivalent to about a quarter of total French output. This reached some 4,000 tonnes in 1872, much of it exported (Cerfberr de Medelsheim 1867: 19; *Larousse*: IV, 165–6; XI, 30). Menier set up a chocolate factory in London in 1863, which ten years later produced some 500 tonnes a year (Knapp 1930: viii; Fitzgerald 1995: 21). He became an influential politician, combating protectionism in the aftermath of France's defeat in 1870 (Smith 1980: 61, 71–3, 75).

Menier had several rivals in France (Lami 1885: III, 344). Marquis and the Compagnie Coloniale, based in Paris, supplied much of France with their wares in the mid-1860s (Debay 1864: 26–7, 42, 56). The Ibled brothers had a hydraulic factory in the heart of the northern sugar beet region (Mangin 1860: 139). The Compagnie Française des Chocolats et des Thés, set up in Paris by Pelletier in 1853, was unusual in having planters from Venezuela and Brazil among its shareholders, as well as retailers from all over France as its 'associates' (Pelletier and Pelletier 1861: 137–8). Bordeaux's factories, including 'a large chocolate works' in 1870, probably transformed about a quarter of France's cocoa imports (Casey 1981: 85, 149; *Larousse*: II, 996). There were still two old-fashioned Jewish artisans in Bayonne in 1860, and the town's chocolate industry employed 130 workers in 1870 (Léon 1893: 69; *http*: 'Chocolat Basque').

Belgium and Spain both produced mainly for the home market, but otherwise were worlds apart. The Belgian industry, benefiting from rising incomes and demand, increased the number and power of its machines, although it was rare for engines to exceed twelve horse-power (Scholliers 1996: 165). Despite being the world's second importer of cocoa beans, Spain showed no sign of similar mechanisation. Annual average exports amounted to a paltry 71 tonnes of chocolate in 1861–3, nearly all destined for the protected Cuban colonial market (*AEE* 1862–5; *EGCEE*).

Germany's most striking niche was as a manufacturer of machinery. The Dresden firm of Lehmann became the world's foremost supplier of machines to process cocoa beans. The Cologne chocolate firm of Stollwerck also branched out into the manufacture of machinery in 1866, exporting to France, Britain and the United States (Fincke 1936: 23). In the 1860s, the Létang brothers of Paris lost their monopoly of making chocolate moulds to German entrepreneurs, some of whom had worked for the French company (Dorchy 1996: 199–200).

The Netherlands occupied another niche, the manufacture and export of chocolate powder. Van Houten's press now came into its own, seconded by another Van Houten innovation, the alkalisation or 'Dutching' of chocolate powder, apparently discovered in the 1860s. The main effect of 'Dutching' was to make the taste of drinking chocolate less astringent. The process also changed the colour of the powder and made it seem to be more soluble in water (Fitzgerald 1995: 21–2). Manufacturers in other countries found it hard to replicate this technique, so the Netherlands exported much powdered chocolate (Lami 1885: III, 346). The slow spread of alkalisation was also due to suspicions of adulteration (*Gordian*: XVII, 5112–13). Van Houten established a new steam-powered factory in 1850, close to Amsterdam, but still employed only seventy-eight workers in 1881 (Schrover 1991: 182, 297). By 1888, there were a dozen manufacturers in the Netherlands, exporting about 750 tonnes of chocolate powder a year to Britain and Germany, and 100 tonnes to other markets (Simmonds 1888: 211–12).

Britain joined the world leaders when Cadbury's decided to adopt the Van Houten press in 1866, enabling the firm to produce 'pure' drinking chocolate. Cadbury's then ceased to sell tea and coffee, and became a dedicated manufacturer of chocolate (Williams 1931: 18, 37–41). Whereas Cadbury's had employed less than thirty people around 1860, they had more than 300 on their books by 1880 (Cadbury Brothers 1880: 10). Rowntree's made a more cautious start in chocolate in 1862, buying a small business from the Tuke family, also Quakers. These York works only employed about twelve people, and it was not until 1887 that Rowntree's marketed its own brand of low-fat chocolate powder, made with a Van Houten press (Fitzgerald 1995: 47–51, 59–61). There were about a dozen other chocolate manufacturers of importance in Britain (Simmonds 1888: 211).

Fry's rivalled with Menier for the title of largest chocolate manufacturer in the world, and yet delayed marketing its own brand of low-fat chocolate powder till 1883, despite acquiring a Van Houten press in 1868. This reflected the success of the firm's leading line. 'Pearl cocoa' was made with arrowroot to soak up extra fat, and was launched in 1856 at a price suitable for workers. However, Fry's experimented with eating chocolate, copying

French assortments and producing 'chocolate creams' from 1855, one of the firm's most famous and long-selling lines. A chocolate bar was introduced in 1847, followed by a chocolate coated 'cream bar' in 1866. Sales of eating chocolate rose from about ten tonnes in 1852 to over 1,100 tonnes in 1880, although technical problems remained and this was only about a quarter of the firm's total sales by weight. Fry's advertising stressed its royal warrants and its role as sole supplier to the Royal Navy. Fry's also acquired Adolphe Lafont in 1863, a firm whose products were mainly sold on the Continent (Diaper 1988: 37–9, 43, 45; Coe and Coe 1996: 243, 251; Williams 1931: 39; *http*: 'Cadbury Limited at Somerdale').

The United States witnessed promising growth, albeit from a low base. Including secondary users of chocolate, the industry roughly tripled in size between 1849 and 1869. In the latter year there were 949 factories, employing 5,825 workers, producing $7.2 million worth of output, and with a nominal capital investment of $8.7 million (Chiriboga 1980: 364). Territorial expansion brought new opportunities in California, where the Mexican cultural legacy included a taste for chocolate. Etienne Guittard, who had learned how to make chocolate at his uncle's factory in France, took part in the California gold rush of 1848–9. He searched fruitlessly for gold for three years, before heading for San Francisco to engage in trade. After a three-year stint in Paris to raise capital and buy machinery, Guittard returned to San Francisco in 1868 to inaugurate Guittard Chocolate. Starting with a few bags of cocoa beans, he slowly built up the enterprise (Fendyan 1991: 6).

The case of Domenico Ghirardelli illustrates the opportunities and perils of making chocolate in California. Having failed to find gold, he opened a number of shops in San Francisco and surrounding towns, overcame disastrous fires in 1851, and founded Ghirardelli's California Chocolate Manufactory in San Francisco in 1855 or 1856. This small workshop processed less than half a tonne of cocoa beans a year in 1866, and Ghirardelli still ran a chain of provision shops, even peddling ground coffee and spices from a horse-drawn wagon. In 1870 he filed for bankruptcy, and four years later most of his assets were sold at public auction. Ghirardelli's survival as a manufacturer was due to sales of Broma, a chocolate powder defatted since 1867 by heating ground cocoa beans in a bag and allowing cocoa butter to drip out (Teiser 1945: 5–27; *http*: 'Profile – Domenico Ghirardelli'). This method of extracting cocoa butter, which presumably involved some kind of press, resembled early French techniques.

Argentina's modern industry, making chocolate for recent immigrants from Europe, clashed with the staunchly traditional Bolivian product. Frenchmen played a leading role in setting up modern factories in Argentina, competing with imports of Menier's chocolate (Moorne 1893: 104–10; Malaurie and Gazzano 1888: 142–4, 270–2; Corvetto 1886: 60–6). In the more conservative areas of northern Argentina, however, fancy goods from Buenos Aires came up against rough and ready Bolivian chocolate, declared to be 'good for Indians alone' (Rocchi 1997: 184). When a Frenchman set up a simple chocolate mill in Santa Cruz, eastern Bolivia, a rumour was spread that his 'artificial preparation' gave people violent colic. His subsequent bankruptcy left the field clear for Amerindian women, who painstakingly ground the roasted beans in wooden troughs with 'common field-stones' (Keller 1874: 166).

Similar contrasts abounded in South America. Swiss citizens founded a chocolate factory in Venezuela in 1850, probably the precursor of La India, a modern chocolate factory in the city of Caracas, run by the Swiss Fullié brothers in 1861. They imported twenty-six large machines from France and Germany, as well as many smaller ones, with a capacity to produce a tonne of chocolate a day (Cartay 1988: 69; Bell 1922: 173). Medellín, in Colombia, had installations to grind cocoa beans mechanically in 1865, but chocolate was 'generally ground...by the family that use it' on heated stones also used for maize (Ospina Vazquez 1955: 266; Holton 1967: 46). Guayaquil had two chocolate factories in 1863, sufficient for Ecuador's internal requirements (ICR 1863). Several chocolate factories emerged in Peru between 1860 and 1880, including the Fábrica de Chocolate Cavenago y Cortazar, founded in Lima in 1867 (Rippy 1946: 147; Oficina del Periodismo 1921: 184). The Brazilian Amazon lagged behind, with no more than small artisanal work-shops (Orton 1876: 360, 518).

The mechanisation of chocolate production also gathered pace in Mexico. A resident in Mexico City bought machinery and asked for the exclusive privilege to manufacture chocolate by mechanical means in 1853. The concession must have been denied, for others followed his example (*DP*: I, 779). Mexican firms did not sell French-style wrapped bars, carrying a firm's name. Moreover, it was still common to roast and grind beans at home, or to pay a grinder to do it (Mangin 1860: 133). Mexicans often roasted beans in an open pan (Lami 1885: III, 340).

News of chocolate manufacture elsewhere in the tropics was patchy. The greatest break with tradition was a modern factory set up in Manila around 1870, to make chocolate 'in the European way' (Jagor 1875: 97). Little cubes of chocolate for the traditional beverage were made in the Dominican Republic city of Puerto Plata in 1871, probably in workshops (Rodríguez Demorizi 1960: 293; Thomasset 1891). Costa Rica even banned imports of chocolate in 1846 to protect local production (Saenz Maroto 1970: 546).

Cocoa-producing countries exported hardly any chocolate to Western markets, which were protected by tariffs. Even Britain maintained a duty of two pence a pound on manufactured chocolate imports from 1853, twice as high as that on raw beans (Head 1903: 88). That said, the tariff was low enough for Continental chocolate to enter the British market (Fitzgerald 1995: 21). Martinique and Guadeloupe sent a little chocolate to France in the 1850s, peaking at 6 tonnes in 1854, perhaps exploiting some form of imperial preference (Mangin 1860: 268–78).

The great chocolate boom in the West, 1880s–1914

The tremendous surge in chocolate output prior to 1914 partly resulted from diversification, as cocoa beans became a truly significant raw material for the food industry. Consumption of eating chocolate soared after 1879, when Roderich Lindt of Switzerland invented 'melting chocolate'. It was enriched with added cocoa butter, and the texture was greatly improved by repeated mechanical 'conching' of the cocoa mass (Fincke 1936: 24, 248; Stollwerck 1907: 67). Chocolate then became a common ingredient in a bewildering variety of baking and confectionery products (Norero 1910: 116–17; Scholliers 1996: 177). Even though Daniel Peter, also a Swiss, succeeded in adding condensed milk to chocolate in 1875, it took longer for the public to accept this novelty, which only came into its own after 1900 (Heer 1966: 82–5; Williams 1931: 81, 92–3). The rise of new food products tied the fortunes of chocolate more closely to allied inputs, notably sugar, nuts, milk and wheat, prices of which were generally low and declining in this period (Scholliers 1996: 176).

For all the spectacular development of eating chocolate, cocoa remained a major raw material for beverages prior to 1914. These were transformed by the diffusion of lighter and more digestible powders, with much of the cocoa butter pressed out, while new combinations with malt and milk extended the range and appeal of drinking chocolate (Norero 1910: 116–17). The alkalisation of chocolate powder further contributed to this success (*Gordian*: XVII, 5112–3).

As product mixes varied greatly from one country to the next, cocoa butter came to be traded internationally on quite a scale. For many manufacturers, cocoa butter remained surplus to requirements, especially when some was replaced by milk solids (Fincke 1936: 250–2; Dand 1993: 13). Moreover, there was a tendency to use cheaper fats, notably coconut oil, to make inferior types of chocolate (Wildeman 1902: 110; Knapp 1920: 159). The international trade in cocoa butter was regulated by auctions in Amsterdam, for the Dutch specialisation in powdered chocolate made them the world's greatest exporters of cocoa butter (*Gordian*: III, 3584; Othick 1976: 83–4; Schrover 1991: 178). The position in 1910 is illustrated in Table 4.1.

Secondary uses for cocoa butter were marginal, as were sales of shells. Cocoa butter had a high melting point and did not easily become rancid, but it was expensive compared to other fats. Only a little cocoa butter went into the manufacture of suppositories, pessaries, ointments, perfumes and toothpaste (Hall 1914: 35, 504; Watt 1889–96: VI-4, 44). Shells made a cheap beverage for the poor in Ireland and Italy, were added to animal fodder, or

Table 4.1   Main importers and exporters of cocoa butter, 1910 (tonnes)

Country	Imports	Exports
USA	1,572	
Switzerland	1,304	
Austria-Hungary	864	
Belgium	849	
Russia	670	
Italy	338	
Great Britain	338	
France	196	
Australia/New Zealand	170	
Spain	39	
Netherlands		4,371
Germany		2,246

Source: Gordian: XVII, 4280–2

were burned to make a potassium-rich fertiliser (Wildeman 1902: 108–9; Hall 1914: 35–6).

The rise of the modern chocolate factory was underpinned by new machines and sources of energy. A labourer could produce 500 kilos of chocolate paste a day in a factory in the 1890s, compared to 10 kilos a day in pre-industrial workshops (*Gordian*: III, 1108). Of 144 German chocolate factories for which there was information in 1895, 109 were powered by steam, eighteen by water, and seventeen by gas, petroleum or electricity (*Gordian*: IV, 1560–1). Mechanisation in the United States chocolate industry was noticeably more rapid than growth in employment (*Gordian*: XVII, 5006).

German manufacturers remained in the vanguard of mechanical innovation and the export of machinery (Fincke 1936: 23). It was the marvels of Lehmann's machines, witnessed at the Chicago International Exposition of 1893, that inspired Milton Hershey to experiment with making chocolate in Pennsylvania, and he continued to depend on German and Swiss machinery (Brenner 1999: 85, 106, 118; Hinkle 1964: 9–14). Dominance in the production of moulds passed from France to Germany. Anton Reiche, founded in Dresden in 1870, was the largest producer in the world by 1910, employing some 500 workers and pioneering the use of nickel plating (Dorchy 1996: 199–200, 204). Switzerland was another major exporter of chocolate processing equipment (Klopstock 1937: 82). British chocolate manufacturers were in part supplied by Joseph Baker and Sons, a Quaker enterprise founded in 1878, but they also imported much foreign machinery (Fitzgerald 1995: 194; Othick 1976: 88–9).

Despite productivity gains, even the visionary factory built by Hershey on a greenfield site was far from being fully automated, and there was thus a marked rise in the number of chocolate workers (Brenner 1999: 117; *Gordian*: III, 1108; Stollwerck 1907: 52). Employment in chocolate factories of all kinds in the United States went from 5,825 in 1869 to 53,658 in 1914, a near tenfold increase. Over the same period, output per worker rose from $1,236 to $3,183 (Chiriboga 1980: 364). In Germany, the chocolate and confectionery labour force numbered some 5,700 people in 1887 and 27,200 twenty years later (BAAP 1908b). The Swiss firm of Cailler employed 1,373 people in 1905, compared to only eight workers in 1888 (Heer 1966: 80–1).

Workers became increasingly female and juvenile. Cadbury's already employed slightly more women than men in 1879, a preponderance which grew in the 1890s, but then fell back slightly in the following decade. Just before 1914, the firm had some 4,000 women and 3,000 men on its books in Britain (Williams 1931: 277). A slight majority of German chocolate workers were female by the late 1890s, and in 1912 women accounted for some two thirds of the 4,000 workers in Dresden's numerous chocolate and confectionery companies (*Gordian*: IV, 1561; XIX, 6732–3). Similarly, about a twentieth of workers in Belgian chocolate factories were women in 1846, a third in 1896, and half after 1918 (Scholliers 1996: 172). Employers stressed the need for manual dexterity in delicate operations (Knapp 1923: 130–2). Compressing wage costs was probably a significant consideration, although Edward Cadbury was an early advocate of equal pay for equal work (Dellheim 1987: 26).

Chocolate manufacturers were renowned for a paternalistic concern for their workers, especially their female staff. This was particularly true of Quaker firms in England (Wagner 1987: 48–72). Joseph Storrs Fry gave a copy of Mrs Beeton's cookery and housekeeping book to every girl leaving to get married (Diaper 1988: 47). Hershey was not religiously inclined in the manner of the English Quakers, and yet he built a model company town and a famous orphanage. He also carefully segregated his labour force on gender lines, according to task (Brenner 1999: 113–28). The Meniers' paternalistic concern for their workers was equally legendary, even though their religious beliefs, if any, were not stressed (Jeandelle and Robert 1994: 52–3).

Ever larger and more complex factories raised barriers to entry into manufacturing, and the emergence of 'chocolate giants' brought rumours of cartels or trusts. However, these are hard to substantiate. Attempts to fix prices and reduce competition at an international level were rare and ineffective. In 1907, Ludwig Stollwerck of Cologne mooted a 'comprehensive international price-fixing arrangement', but Rowntree's rejected these advances, on the grounds that the British public was hostile to 'Continental-type cartels' (Fitzgerald 1995: 34–41, 106–7). The first-ever international congress of chocolate manufacturers was held in Bern, Switzerland, in 1911, but this was to establish standard definitions of chocolate products across the world. The congress was dominated by French and German delegates. Non-European countries were not represented, even though it was estimated that some 300 firms processed raw cocoa beans outside Europe, compared to 900 in Europe (*Gordian*: XVII, 4607–8).

Fitzgerald's argument for cartelisation is based on Britain alone, but he overstates his case. To be sure, Cadbury's of Birmingham, Fry's of Bristol, and Rowntree's of York purchased some two thirds of all cocoa beans imported for consumption in 1900. Moreover, the three companies were controlled by inter-related Quaker families, and they reached an agreement to limit discounts to retailers in 1889. They fixed a minimum price for certain types of eating chocolate in 1895, and amended this agreement in 1900, 1906 and 1912. A. J. Caley of Norwich was included for some purposes, as was Clarke Nicholl and Coombes, Clarnico, of London. That said, a public outcry against Lever's 'soap trust' made the Quaker firms anxious not to be labelled a 'cocoa trust'. Moreover, the three firms were not prepared to limit competition over drinking chocolate, the key product of the time. Advertising remained a bone of contention, and there were repeated disputes about the detailed implementation of the agreement. (Fitzgerald 1995: 38, 51, 77–9, 97, 104–6, 120; Wagner 1987: 109–11).

Agreements did not prevent changes in the relative positions of the three firms, for Cadbury's overtook Fry's in terms of sales in 1910, and Rowntree's was catching up fast. Joseph Storrs Fry, second of that name and chairman from 1878, was an introverted and deeply conservative man, a 'plain' Quaker who never married and lived with his mother. He could scarcely be accused of failure. At his death in 1913, he was a millionaire, his limited liability private company had an authorised capital of a million pounds, and it was the largest employer in Bristol, with nearly 4,500 people on its books, compared to only around 500 in 1861. Fry's also continued to be a pioneer of eating chocolate, which overtook drinking chocolate in terms of weight in 1885. However, Joseph Storrs failed to keep up with the tide of product innovation, spent less on advertising than his rivals, and exported little. The huge warren of eight main factories and sixteen subsidiary units in the heart of Bristol was costly to operate, and the decision to transfer production to a greenfield site was only taken after his death. One of the Cadburys commented that the firm had become 'complacent' (Diaper 1988: 39–46, 49–51; Wagner 1987: 20, 24; *http*: 'Cadbury Limited at Somerdale').

Selling in overseas markets lay outside the scope of agreements, and Cadbury's did best in this field. By 1914, 40 per cent of Cadbury's total sales were abroad, compared to only 10 per cent for Fry's. Most British chocolate went to the empire, most precociously to Canada and spreading to Australia, New Zealand, India and southern Africa. France and Chile were Cadbury's only non-imperial markets of any significance, while Fry's sold well in the Canaries and Madeira (Fitzgerald 1995: 510–1; Diaper 1988: 40; Williams 1931: 45, 72, 130–9). The United States, the largest market in the world, was considered closed by the tariff hikes of the 1890s, although the Swiss and the Dutch maintained sales there (Stollwerck 1907: 69–70).

At the same time, the cartelisation of the British home market was undermined by chocolate flowing in from abroad. A German observer commented in 1911 on the ferocity of competition in Britain, spurred on by lavish advertising and larger imports than anywhere else in the world (*Gordian*: XVII, 4286). This was the year in which the Liberal government lowered the import duty on chocolate, so as to tax only the raw materials used to make it (Gardiner 1923: 241). The Dutch were unchallenged as purveyors of alkalised drinking chocolate until Cadbury's brought out the Bournville brand in 1906. Even then, Van Houten continued to sell a great deal in Britain. Swiss milk chocolate was only successfully copied by Cadbury's in 1905, and Cailler and Kohler products, distributed by Nestlé from 1904, continued to take a large share of the market. Two other Swiss firms, Suchard and Lindt, sold plain chocolate for baking, while Menier's assortments remained popular. British companies even noted with satisfaction in 1914 that the war had cut off imports from Germany and Austria-Hungary (Fitzgerald 1995: 67–9, 73, 78–9, 103–9, 115–16, 127).

In addition to this flood of imports, there were British manufacturers not party to the agreements. Even Terry's did not join, although it was a Quaker firm. Founded in York as a sweet manufacturer in 1767, Terry's began to make chocolate from 1886. Similarly, Carson had a well established position in Scotland (Fitzgerald 1995: 85, 115; Knapp 1923: 27). Taylor Brothers of London claimed to be 'the largest manufacturers of cocoas in Europe' around 1880 (Collet 1996: 212). Lipton, the great tea firm, set up a chocolate factory in London in 1895 (*Gordian*: I, 68–9).

It was the First World War that gave the decisive impetus to price fixing in the British chocolate industry. Regular conferences were held in Cheltenham from 1917 to coordinate all aspects of the industry between the major companies. At the same time, the partial fusion of Cadbury's and Fry's reinforced the solidarity between Quaker firms (Fitzgerald 1995: 137–8). That said, it may have been the change in mentalities brought about by the war that had the greatest impact on the formation of a more effective cartel.

Cartels were equally ineffective in the Netherlands. Many small Dutch companies used chocolate in the confectionery business, but the processing of cocoa beans was limited to some fifteen firms before 1914. Fierce competition reigned until the founding of the Vereniging van Cacao- en Chocoladefabrikanten in 1901. The association wished to fix a minimum price on the domestic market, and brought together most of the large firms, such as Kwatta, Bensdorp and Driessen. But Van Houten refused to join. At this time, Van Houten employed about a fifth of workers in the industry, and sold a remarkable 90–95 per cent of its output abroad, with offices in London, Leeds, Liverpool, Edinburgh, Glasgow, Dublin, Paris, New York and Chicago. As other Dutch companies also exported a high proportion of their output, agreeing to a domestic price was somewhat beside the point. It was not until 1919 that a more effective national cartel emerged (Schrover 1991: 174–5, 182–5, 190, 208).

Attempts to end competition between Swiss firms suffered from the same drawback of high exports. There were seventeen chocolate companies with a nominal capital of over half a million francs in 1906, of which by far the largest was Suchard with nine million francs. Quite a few paid no dividend in 1907, and Ribet of Lausanne went bankrupt (*Gordian*: XII, 850, 876, 927; XIII, 1185, 1213). Suchard had 'tariff-hopping' factories in Germany, Austria and France in 1909, and planned to open another one in San Sebastián, Spain (*Gordian*: XV, 2650). The gradual fusion of Peter, Kohler and Cailler took a major step forward in 1911, with 39 per cent of the shares of the new consortium owned by the closely allied Nestlé milk company (Heer 1966: 85–9, 105–6). However, three quarters of Swiss chocolate was exported, notably to Britain, Italy and Germany. An association formed in 1907 could only agree to a minimum price for cheap chocolate on the internal market (*Gordian*: XII, 1084–5; XVII, 4372). This agreement soon collapsed, and retailers promised strong resistance to a successor signed in 1913 (*Gordian*: XVIII, 5358; XIX, 6815, 6989).

The German chocolate industry exported little, but it was highly fragmented and regional. This made it quite unable to organise an effective national cartel. There were as many as 178 German firms processing cocoa beans in 1895, of which only fifty-three were members of the Verband Deutscher Chocolade-Fabrikanten (*Gordian*: I, 74–6, 211, 225–7; III, 1027; IV, 1560–1). In 1900, there were around fifty large factories and 110 small ones (*Gordian*: V, 2173–4). The number of firms only increased slightly thereafter. Of around 200 in existence in 1911, twenty-eight were in Dresden (*Gordian*: XVII, 4607; XIX, 6732). A succession of coordinating bodies was formed, but none of them could impose any discipline on this dynamic and dispersed industry. A 'chocolate war' even broke out in the town of Halle in 1897, as rival retailers undercut each other ferociously (*Gordian*: III, 811).

The world's largest chocolate industry, that of the United States, was even more inward looking and a great deal more concentrated. American firms had a vast and wealthy internal market, protected by high tariffs on imported chocolate from 1894, which were raised again in 1897, before being lowered and simplified in 1913 (Stollwerck 1907: 69–71; *Gordian*: XIX, 6696). 'Half a dozen' major factories turned cocoa into chocolate in 1900, at a time when the Walter Baker Company alone bought more than half of the beans imported into the country (Brenner 1999: 87, 105). However, another source states that there were as many as 112 factories processing cocoa beans in 1909 (*Gordian*: XV, 2937). Including factories that used chocolate rather than cocoa beans as their raw material, the numbers were even greater, going from 1,348 in 1904 to 2,391 in 1914 (Chiriboga 1980: 364). There was no sign of price fixing, and entry into the sector remained easy.

Walter Baker did not even supply all the United States. Sales barely reached as far as the Mississippi River from Massachusetts, due to problems in keeping chocolate in good condition over long distances. The two San Francisco firms of Guittard and Ghirardelli held sway further west (Brenner 1999: 54, 74, 109). Ghirardelli slowly recovered from his 1870 bankruptcy. In 1885, the firm processed around 1,000 tonnes of cocoa beans, employed over thirty workers, and exported around the Pacific to Mexico, South America, China and Japan. Expansion was even more rapid after 1892, when the patriarch retired, two years before dying in his native Rapallo. He handed over to his sons, partly educated in Italy, who incorporated the business in 1895 as Domingo Ghirardelli and Co. They acquired the former Pioneer Woollen Mills in 1893 as a site for a new and larger factory, which came onstream in 1897. The company concentrated exclusively on chocolate from 1900, with the quirky exception of mustard. The Ghirardelli chocolate factory was fortunate to escape almost unscathed from the 1906 San Francisco earthquake (Teiser 1945: 8, 24–9; *http*: 'Ghirardelli Square'). Guittard Chocolate's factory was burned down during the earthquake, but Horace Guittard, who had taken over at his father's death in 1899, built a new and larger one to replace it (Fendyan 1991: 6).

The ease with which new firms could enter the sector was shown most clearly by Milton Hershey. A Mennonite sweet maker from Lancaster, Pennsylvania, he began to develop a subsidiary interest in chocolate from 1894, hiring two employees who had formerly worked for Walter Baker. Hershey sold his caramel company for a million dollars in 1900, and built a dedicated factory and company town on 500 hectares of scrub land, which came to bear his name. He gained economies of scale by producing a small number of lines for sale across the whole country, notably the five cent bar, introduced in 1900. Hershey found a way of making milk chocolate, around 1905, which differed from the Swiss method. He benefited from plentiful supplies of local fresh milk, and sober hard-working Mennonites made excellent workers. By 1911, he employed 1,200 people and his sales topped $5 million (Brenner 1999: 74, 83–90, 105–28; Hinkle 1964: 12–14, 22).

European firms provided further competition by jumping the rising American tariff wall. The Menier factory in Hoboken, New Jersey, dated from 1891 (Knapp 1923: x; *http*: 'Menier-Nestlé'). Stollwerck established a plant in Stamford, probably the Connecticut town of that name (*Gordian*: IV, 1579; XV, 2937). The Swiss Peter-Cailler-Kohler alliance did likewise in Fulton, New Jersey, in 1907, employing 150 people by 1913. Half the capital was raised in the United States, and the products were rather misleadingly sold as 'Swiss chocolate', under the three separate brand names (*Gordian*: XIX, 6297).

French industrialisation was sluggish, held back by high tariffs (Stollwerck 1907: 69–71). However, the country kept an international reputation for luxury foods. Manufacturers produced little powdered drinking chocolate or milk chocolate, concentrating instead on high-quality black eating chocolate and assortments (Hall 1914: 496). France was the world's second exporter of eating chocolate by volume in 1912, although the 2,000 tonnes exported trailed far behind Switzerland's 15,000 tonnes (*Gordian*: XIX, 6499).

After the death of Emile Menier in 1881, his sons Gaston and Henri maintained the company's position. They repeatedly extended the factory and company town at Noisiel, using the most advanced architectural techniques of the time, such as reinforced concrete (Jeandelle and Robert 1994: 52–3). Gaston Menier claimed that Noisiel was the largest chocolate factory in the world in 1906, with an output of 20,000 tonnes a year, a fivefold increase compared to 1872. He also boasted that he had twice been the guest of the Kaiser, a privilege not granted to any German chocolate manufacturer (*Gordian*: XII, 891–2). The brothers placed a new emphasis on saturation advertising, developing the famous poster of a little girl seen from behind writing on a board or wall. An extraordinary range of trinkets promoted the company, and tours of the remarkable Noisiel factory proved popular (*http*: 'Menier-Nestlé').

For all Menier's size and reputation, the firm held no monopoly in France. In the southwest, small firms in Bordeaux supplied non-branded chocolate to wholesalers, who in turn sold on to bakeries and confectioners. Among the chocolate firms were the venerable Louit Frères et Cie., with 310 employees in 1920, and the S.A. de Chocolaterie et Confiserie Talencia, founded in 1909 (Bonin 1997: 124–6; Dupeux 1969: 391). Bayonne was in the shadow of Bordeaux, but retained a reputation for high-quality chocolate (*http*: 'Chocolat Basque').

Belgian manufacturers were protectionist but not cartelised. Manufacturers protested about the penetration of French chocolate, and import duties were consequently raised from 30 to 45 francs per 100 kilos in 1885 (Scholliers 1996: 166). In 1898 and 1906, the duty stood at 50 francs (*Gordian*: IV, 1367–72; XI, 446). Belgian firms were thus late in adopting a strategy of exporting high-quality eating chocolate, and nearly two thirds of their small exports in 1913 went to the niche market of North Africa and the Middle East. The industry remained regional and fragmented, with seventy-three chocolate companies in 1910, employing an average of thirty workers each. Machines were small for the food industry, but there was a 65 per cent increase in installed horse-power between 1896 and 1910, compared to only 10 per cent for sugar refining and flour milling (Scholliers 1996: 167–8, 172–5).

Less is known about the stagnant Spanish chocolate industry. The past lived on in Catalonia, where Barcelona workshops displayed employees on their knees, grinding beans on traditional stones in full public view, to avoid any accusation of adulteration (Coe and Coe 1996: 236). Further north, in Gerona, Rafael Comas set up a tiny workshop in 1910, making *tabletas* for the preparation of old-fashioned full-fat beverages (*http*: 'Chocolates y turrones'). At the same time, Madrid boasted three large enterprises and twenty-two small ones in the early 1900s, although quality was allegedly poor (*Gordian*: VIII, 3275; IX, 3665). Betraying deeply protectionist attitudes, Spanish chocolate manufacturers in 1913 called for prohibitive import duties on foreign chocolate, export subsidies, and lower duties on imported sugar (AGA 1913).

The chocolate industry in the Third World, 1880s–1914

The great chocolate boom left the Third World lagging even further behind, despite some progress in industrialisation. In Latin America, consumption of full-fat beverages was still dominant before 1914 (*Gordian*: XIX, 7110). This traditional chocolate sustained home grinding and a network of small workshops, and even modern factories. However, new tastes spreading from the West encouraged both imports and some import substitution. What was conspicuously lacking was any export drive to Western markets.

The coexistence of old and new was particularly marked in Mexico. Protected by a tariff wall, the country only imported between eight and twelve tonnes of chocolate a year in the 1890s (Kaerger 1901: II, 508–9). The number of mechanised chocolate factories grew from the 1880s, with twenty flourishing mills in existence by 1910, and artisanal workshops held their own. The main chocolate centres were in the central highlands, especially in Mexico City, but also in Puebla, Toluca, Morelia, Celaya and Guadalajara (*EUIEA*: XXXIV, 293; Rosenzweig 1965: 357–8). Tabasco had small factories by 1910, selling, among other products, a traditional mixture of ground maize, chocolate and sugar (Kaerger 1901: II, 508–9; Arias *et al.* 1987: 276). However, stone grinders and rollers for home use, unchanged from those of the ancient Maya, were also for sale in 1910 (Hart 1911: 250–1).

Unable to supply their Noisiel factory with Nicaraguan beans, Menier turned to making chocolate for the local market, with more than one plant by 1900 (Medina 1900: 38). These were probably the two factories recorded in Managua in 1914 (*EUIEA*: XXXVIII, 529). The government raised the import duty on chocolate to 0.5 pesos per kilo in 1899, and placed a duty of 0.4 pesos per kilo on milk chocolate (*Gordian*: VII, 2855). While the latter may have been a purely fiscal measure, it may also have indicated that Menier was experimenting with new forms of European production.

Costa Rica's chocolate industry consisted of small workshops turning out traditional products for a minuscule home market. Import duties on chocolate were raised in 1900, to stimulate import substitution (Saenz Maroto 1970: 103–4). But the oldest recorded chocolate factory, La Mascota, was set up earlier, in 1887. It was owned by two Spanish traders, Jerónimo Pagés and Rafael Cañas Mora, who also grew cocoa. More factories were set up after 1900, all in or around the capital city of San José, with about a dozen listed in 1915. The names of the owners were mainly Spanish, but there was one Italian, one French and one English name among them. Typically, these were traders moving into small-scale production with a limited amount of machinery. Imports were not entirely choked off, for about 7 tonnes per year were recorded in 1908–13, mainly from France (Quesada Camacho 1977–8: 82–4, 87, 89–90, 105). Continuing imports reflected the fact that these small mills neither pressed out cocoa butter nor made powder in 1909, simply dividing the dried mass into portions sufficient to prepare a single cup of the traditional beverage (*Gordian*: XV, 2907).

Other Central American processing units were of a similar nature. Guatemala had a few small factories sheltering behind high tariffs, but was unable entirely to eliminate Western imports (Brigham 1887: 345–6; *Gordian*: VI, 2669). El Salvador boasted a single factory for chocolate and confectionery in 1905, and Panama had some small establishments (*EUIEA*: XIX, 834; *SYB* 1907: 1293).

Independent Caribbean islands had some modern installations, but continued to produce old lines. In 1896, thirteen chocolate 'factories' were listed in Cuba, eight of them in greater Havana (Clark 1899: 469, 474, 489, 497–8). This was despite duty-free imports of chocolate from Spain, which reached a peak of 393 tonnes in 1894 (*EGCEE*; Alzola 1895: 199). By 1914, the factory of La Estrella was famous throughout the island (*EUIEA*: XVI, 820–1). In the Dominican Republic, imported chocolate was preferred by some, partly for reasons of social prestige and partly because import duties on United States produce were lowered or scrapped in 1891 (Bryan 1977: 167; Abel 1985: 344). Nevertheless, a Swiss trading company had a modern factory in Samaná in 1907, and there was another one in the capital city (Deschamps 1907: I, 250; II, 316–7). Numerous locally financed workshops turned out *chocolate criollo* of the traditional kind, some of them operated by just two women (Bryan 1977: 166–7; Thomasset 1891; Schoenrich 1918: 240). Haïti's output also appears to have come from workshops (Rouzier 1892–3: II, 134).

A similarly mixed picture was evident in the British Caribbean. Much 'creole chocolate' continued to be made at home in Trinidad, heavily spiced with cinnamon, nutmeg and ginger, and balls or sticks were on sale in markets. The island's first modern chocolate factory was created by Cruger and Leotaud, the latter a major French cocoa trader of Port of Spain. The business went under by 1890, allegedly because of import duties in Britain and a lack of such duties in Trinidad (Moodie-Kublalsingh 1994: 23–7, 228). There were three little factories producing 30 tonnes of chocolate a year by 1942, but it is not clear when they were set up (Great Britain 1942: 65). Georgetown, the capital of British Guiana, had its own chocolate mill in 1901 (*Gordian*: VI, 2604).

There was a steep increase in Venezuela's tariff protection for chocolate in 1896, although imports were not entirely eliminated (Norbury 1970: 136–7). Many Venezuelans roasted and ground their own beans in the traditional way in the 1890s. The chocolate factories of Caracas processed cheap Forastero beans, rather than famous and expensive Criollos from the coast. They did not press out cocoa butter, because it was judged uneconomical to export cocoa butter to the West, and because there was little local demand for Western kinds of chocolate. A sample sent to an esteemed European manufacturer was criticised as substandard (Preuss 1987: 73–4). Nevertheless, La India, the Swiss chocolate factory of Caracas, produced an array of chocolate, sweets, soft drinks and ices (Bell 1922: 173). It became a joint-stock company with a capital of 500,000 bolivares in 1913 (Cartay 1988: 69). There was another chocolate factory of note in Caracas in 1913, and one in La Guaira by the early 1920s (Karlsson 1975: 194; Bell 1922: 138). Nonetheless, the country's output was only between 30 and 40 tonnes a year in the early 1920s (*EUIEA*: LXVII, 1048).

The Colombian authorities provided high tariffs and other support to chocolate manufacturers. One Antioquia mill ground cocoa beans, wheat, maize and rice in 1888, although it later came to specialise in chocolate. Other small enterprises foundered in the face of people's preference for home production, but the successful Antioquia factory of Juan B. Villegas dated from the 1890s (Botero Herrera 1984: 84–5). There was a flourishing chocolate industry in 1914, with factories in most large towns, some of them quite large and expensively equipped. Medellín, capital of Antioquia, had four chocolate factories in 1914, and even boasted an engineering shop chiefly engaged in manufacturing machinery for chocolate and coffee producers. Other factories existed in the Caribbean ports of Barranquilla and Cartagena, as well as in Bogotá (Lévine 1914: 126–7, 131, 151–2, 156–7). Enrique Chaves had a factory in Medellín and another in Bogotá, the latter, Chaves y Equitativa, capitalised at over 150,000 pesos (Botero Herrera 1984: 85; Eder 1913: 219). For all that, most Colombians were still said to roast and grind their cocoa at home as late as 1909 (*Gordian*: XV, 3081).

Ecuadorian chocolate production was dominated by Italians. A considerable turnover of firms masked continuity in entrepreneurs. Of seven chocolate manufacturers in Guayaquil in 1883, all but one had disappeared by 1900, but there were five again in 1906. The most durable family was Segale, which employed fifty workers under the name of La Universal in 1906, and later fused with Norero. These small factories exported little, and the local market was restricted by a small population and low consumption per head (Arosemena 1991: II, 545–7). Guayaquil's best foreign market was Peru, but protectionism was increasing there (Enock 1925: 275; Bonilla 1975–6: II, 149).

A German dismissed Peruvian factories as small workshops, whereas a Spaniard enthused about the, 'many chocolate factories all over the country' (Kaerger 1901: II, 377; *EUIEA*: XLIII, 1251). A 1905 survey showed seven chocolate factories among 'approximately a hundred establishments approaching the status of true manufacturing plants'. The major concentrations were in Lima and Cuzco, with another in Arequipa in the south, founded in 1911, and more in the northern towns of Trujillo and Chiclayo (Rippy 1946: 148–51). 'La Española', a factory set up in Trujillo around 1890, supplied much of the north and interior with chocolate (Oficina del Periodismo 1921: 493). The largest factories were in Lima and Cuzco, protected from the 1890s by a 65 per cent ad valorem duty on imports (*Gordian*: IV, 1367–72; VII, 2855). At the same time, Cuzco firms exported some of their output to Bolivia, benefiting from commercial concessions granted to secure Bolivia's access to the sea after 1883 (*EUIEA*: XLIII, 1248; Walle 1925: 10).

Chocolate confirmed the predominance of northern Italian entrepreneurs in the capital city of Peru. Of four Lima manufacturers represented at the Paris World Exhibition of 1900, three had Italian names, among them one Vignolo, probably of the same family as the co-owners of La Italia chocolate factory in Guayaquil in 1906 (*Gordian*: VI, 2256; Arosemena 1991: II, 546–7; Werlich 1978: 127). Of five Lima firms listed in 1921, three had clearly Italian names, and the other two may have done. In contrast, companies in Cuzco, Trujillo and Arequipa had names that sounded more Castilian or Basque (Oficina del Periodismo 1921: 184, 493, XVIII, LXI, LXVII).

Although Bolivia imported some Cuzco chocolate, the country had its own factories. Santa Cruz was the main producer, with several small chocolate factories recorded in 1912, but the best product was reputed to come from Apolobamba, the old Franciscan missionary centre (Walle 1925: 173, 225, 376). A firm founded by the sons of a wealthy silver miner had a steam-driven chocolate factory on an estate close to Sucre in 1907, packaging chocolate 'in a style similar to a popular French brand' (Langer 1989: 74). At the end of the 1910s, bar chocolate was made in Cochambamba and Santa Cruz, and chocolate creams in Sucre, although there were also imports from the United States (Schurz 1921: 183).

Swiss manufacturers singled out Brazil as one of the most protectionist countries in the world, on a par with Spain and Russia, with an ad valorem duty of 50 per cent on chocolate (*Gordian*: IV, 1242, 1367–72; VI, 2670; VII, 2855). With this, and with other support from the state of Pará, a number of small factories sprang up in Belém from the 1880s. Portuguese entrepreneurs usually financed these plants, which aimed to supply the internal market. One of the most successful was the Fábrica Palmeira, founded by five Portuguese in 1893. It turned out a variety of processed foodstuffs, among them chocolate powder (Weinstein 1983: 91–3). Upriver, Obidos produced chocolate by 1914, and there were three small units in the state of Amazonas (Buley 1914: 154–5, 182). In contrast, the first chocolate factory in Bahia was only set up in 1927, seemingly reflecting the lack of a local market (Garcez and Freitas 1975: 47).

There were chocolate factories close to the numerous and wealthy consumers of southern Brazil, many of them recent immigrants with European tastes. Of the two factories in Rio de Janeiro in 1900, one had a German or Dutch name, and the other a Franco-Portuguese name (*Gordian*: VI, 2670). Chocolats Suisses de São Paulo, a joint-stock company founded in 1912, proved an instant success (*Gordian*: XIX, 7150; XX, 7197). Imports of foreign chocolate continued, however, and attempts at import substitution were judged to be disappointing (Lange 1914: 349–50).

The conflict between traditional and modern forms of chocolate production was acute elsewhere in the southern cone. Small Chilean workshops produced blocks of full-fat chocolate, struggling to meet competition from modern imports, supplied by companies such as Cadbury's (*Gordian*: XIX, 7110). In contrast, immigrants of mainly French and Italian extraction continued to develop a modern chocolate and confectionery industry on European lines in Argentina (Rocchi 1997). The Saint firm produced 500 tonnes of chocolate a year and employed 210 people in the 1900s, while Viuda de Seminario e Hijo had an output of 170 tonnes with forty workers (*EUIEA*: VI, 104). Uruguay had six establishments producing chocolate in Montevideo in 1900, two of which sounded Italian, and one which seemed to be German (*Gordian*: VI, 2666–7).

The British empire was no closed preserve for British chocolate makers, as the campaign for imperial preference failed (*Gordian*: XIX, 6204). Local initiatives were especially strong in the White Dominions. Despite Fry's dominant presence on the Canadian market, two brothers of Loyalist farming stock founded Ganong in 1873, in Saint Stephen, New Brunswick. Claiming to be Canada's oldest independent confectionery company, Ganong worked with chocolate by 1885, and invented the five cent chocolate nut bar (*http*: 'Ganong, our history'; Acheson 1982: 65, 70; Diaper 1988: 40). Richard Hudson, an illiterate English orphan, went to New Zealand to find gold, but ended up making biscuits in Dunedin in 1868. He thought he had produced the first chocolate manufactured in the southern hemisphere in 1884, blithely unaware of the South American past (*http*: 'Our history').

The Philippines had a mixture of advanced and traditional units. Manila's 'steam-power manufactory', probably a Basque concern named La Bilbaina, supplied part of the city's requirements (Foreman 1890: 355; *El Comercio*: 2 November 1901). By 1903, chocolate was the colony's twenty-seventh largest industry in terms of units of production, and thirty-ninth in terms of employment (United States 1905: IV, 506ff.). Small factories, owned by Chinese and a few Filipinos, were chiefly situated in Manila, and did not sell their output under brand names (*Gordian*: VI, 2669). They mixed in unrefined sugar, and often added roasted rice and *pili* nuts (Canarium Commune) (Hall 1932: 493). Manila boasted twenty-nine chocolate 'factories' in 1915, employed 102 people, working an eight-hour day. Contrasting with the usual gender balance in the West, ninety-nine of these workers were men (Miller 1920: 470).

Much Filipino chocolate was not made in such establishments. Peasants roasted their own beans over a slow fire, shelled them, and pounded them into a paste with unrefined sugar, 'using a kind of rolling pin on a concave block of wood'. They frequently mixed in roasted rice and *pili* nuts, whereas the 'civilised' population usually added vanilla (Foreman 1890: 354). Grinders, many of them Chinese, perpetuated the Spanish tradition of going from house to house, preparing chocolate with sugar and spices (*Gordian*: V, 2096; XVIII, 5482; XIX, 6665). The equipment of a Chinese chocolate grinder consisted of 'a small wooden table, made to rest on the knees of the man, who squats down'. On this table, roasted and shelled beans were 'pounded in a small marble mortar with a heated pestle'. The mass was then 'kneaded to chocolate-dough with sugar, peppers and other favourite spices' (Freeman and Chandler 1907: 134).

The French-speaking islands of the southwestern Indian Ocean have a tradition of making chocolate, but it is not clear when it began (Campbell 1996: 208). Workshops in Réunion certainly produced chocolate around 1900. There were complaints that locally produced cocoa was insufficient for their needs, and the island imported duty-free chocolate from France (*Gordian*: VIII, 3330; XI, 506).

Cocoa was processed industrially in colonial territories with weaker or non-existent traditions of local consumption. Plans were laid in 1903 to manufacture both drinking and eating chocolate in the Dutch East Indies (*Gordian*: IX, 3757; X, 4265). This industry was in existence by 1914 (Mitchell 1942: 211). The Peradeniya Chocolate Company was the only one in Ceylon in 1924, the foundation date not being given (Maclaren 1924: 195). São Tomé exported a little cocoa powder for Portugal's diminutive home market by the turn of the century (Moreira Júnior 1905: I, 122).

Exporting chocolate was rarely envisaged. In part, this reflected Western protectionist tariffs, as indicated in Table 4.2, but local conditions and attitudes reinforced this reluctance. Latin American governments protected their internal markets with tariffs and monopolies, neither of which were conducive to competitiveness on the world stage. Western markets were highly sensitive to quality, and most Latin American chocolate was of the traditional full-fat variety. Chocolate products of any sophistication required the blending of beans of various origins, but importing cocoa from other tropical countries was obstructed by high tariffs, and ran counter to established trade patterns. Despite all this, four Lima entrepreneurs entertained hopes of breaking into the European market by taking part in the Paris World Exhibition of 1900 (*Gordian*: VI, 2256). Trinidad's first chocolate factory also intended to export to Britain, and blamed protectionist duties as one cause of its failure in 1890 (Moodie-Kublalsingh: 1994: 26–7).

Table 4.2 further indicates that Western duties on cocoa butter were

Table 4.2   Import duties on chocolate in 1898 and 1913, and on cocoa butter in 1913. (German Marks per 100 kilos, rounded)

Country	Chocolate 1898	Chocolate 1913	Cocoa Butter 1913
Britain	37	14	19
Netherlands	42	42	0
Belgium	40	24	0
Sweden	56	56	0
Germany	80	80	35
Switzerland	24	24	8
Austria-Hungary	102	170	15
Russia	589	198	44
Italy	264	162	24
France	120	243	122
Spain	128	240	160
Portugal	90	91	16
USA	185 (+ 15%)	(50%)	32
Mexico	329	168	n.a.
Colombia	759	284 (+ 70%)	284 (+ 70%)
Brazil	(50%)	690 (+ 50%)	n.a.
South Africa	37	37	37
Japan	n.a.	149	149
China	n.a.	7	n.a.
Philippines	78	63	53
Australia	75	70	39

Sources: *Gordian*: IV, 1367–72; XIX, 6332–4

Notes
Chocolate refers to eating chocolate. Prepared chocolate drinks and basic cocoa powder were often taxed at different rates.
My calculations for 1898 from currency equivalents given in *Gordian*.
Highest duty recorded where a range existed [notably for France, Spain, Russia, and USA].
US duties on chocolate were roughly halved later in 1913.

generally lower than on chocolate. Pressing out cocoa butter was technically easier than making chocolate, and did not necessitate importing beans from other countries. Indeed, exports of cocoa butter have become significant for many tropical countries since the 1970s (Dand 1993: 93–7). However, Latin American consumption of full-fat chocolate did not necessitate pressing out cocoa butter.

Conclusion

The evidence in this chapter, scrappy as it is, scarcely supports allegations that Western firms manipulated prices by forming cartels. Companies occasionally entered into agreements to fix prices, but such agreements were limited in scope and time, and usually collapsed quickly under competitive pressure. That said, there is remarkably little published work on chocolate manufacturing outside England. Company histories of Menier, Van Houten, Stollwerck and Walter Baker are long overdue, together with accounts of the chocolate industry in most of the main producer countries.

Accusations that the West helped to underdevelop the Third World by stifling its industrial development are slightly better founded, but it is far from clear that chocolate firms were chiefly responsible. Import duties on chocolate were clearly not in line with free trade ideals, even in Britain, but it is likely that workers pressed most doggedly for protection, to safeguard jobs. More research is needed on how decisions were reached to impose particular tariffs on chocolate and cocoa butter.

Certain themes in the history of Western chocolate firms could profitably be taken further. The role of advertising needs more consideration, as the image of chocolate may have been as important to its changing historical fortunes as the cost of raw materials or manufacturing techniques. Much attention has already been given to paternalistic labour relations in Britain, but it is far from clear why chocolate firms in other countries enjoyed a similar reputation. Was it inherent in the production processes of the industry, or was a Quaker ethos somehow transmitted around the globe?

Even less attention has been paid to chocolate manufacturing on the periphery. The most basic data are lacking in almost all cases, and at least one old chocolate firm in Latin America has recently thrown away its archives. Far too little is known about entrepreneurs, their strategies and their workers. Nor is it clear why protectionism went so far beyond the needs of 'infant industries' in independent countries, generating an inward-looking mentality. This may have been one of the missed opportunities of development, especially for countries producing cocoa beans. As there have been costly mistakes made recently in trying to set up chocolate industries on the periphery, notably in Ecuador and Nigeria, it would be helpful to know more about the successes and failures of their predecessors.

5

COMMERCIALISATION AND CREDIT

Complaints of shadowy Western speculators forcing down prices of cocoa beans have a long history, but there is little evidence to support such rumours prior to 1914 (Mahony 1996: 175). Although this is the link in the commodity chain about which the least is known, rivalry appears to have been even more marked among brokers and merchants than among chocolate manufacturers. Barriers to entry were low, and manufacturers, sensitive to the cost of cocoa beans, were always ready to cut out intermediaries and buy directly. In view of such accusations, all too often accompanied by racist or xenophobic undertones, it is ironic that the most severe market distortions before 1914 were caused by associations of wealthy planters from the tropics.

Traders in cocoa-producing countries were just as regularly accused of collusion, especially when a few powerful export houses faced numerous, scattered and uneducated smallholders (Greenhill 1996). Indeed, this was a major reason given by governments for assuming marketing functions in the 1930s and 1940s. While there were undoubtedly examples of fraud, they tended to cut both ways, as producers were equally tempted to cheat traders. As long as mercantile networks remained open and competitive, the 'hidden hand' of the market curbed such practices. In turn, the key to competition was the ability of traders to enter the market at any moment (Bauer 1963). The loosening of immigration regulations was thus crucial for competitive marketing, given the lack of commercial expertise on most forest frontiers. The period from around 1880 to 1914 witnessed the greatest freedom to migrate the world has ever known, and specialised entrepreneurial diasporas of every kind seized the opportunity offered to them (Clarence-Smith 1997).

Merchants were also routinely blamed for exploiting credit arrangements to seize the land of smallholders, but this betrays a fundamental misunderstanding of how trading communities operated. While the transfer of land through debt was quite widespread, it was typically rich landowners who engrossed the lands of their weaker brethren. The more specialised an entrepreneurial community was in trade and finance, the less its members desired to acquire land. It was an article of faith for such merchants to keep

93

their funds liquid and concentrate on core activities and skills. If they were forced to foreclose to obtain repayment on a loan, they sold the land as fast as they could (Dobbin 1996).

As cocoa producers did not need to borrow, cheap credit was an attraction rather than a necessity. No initial capital was needed, as long as forested land was free, food crops could be intercropped while cocoa trees matured, simple hand tools were already available, and non-family labour costs could be met out of the harvest. Smallholders thus borrowed to finance domestic and social expenditure. When money was plentiful and cheap, there was an incentive for pioneers to brave the dangers and discomforts of the forest, acquiring a readily mortgageable asset in the form of cocoa trees (Ruf 1995).

Merchants and mercantilism

Early Modern colonial restrictions on merchants were deleterious to cocoa production, although far more emphasis has been placed on shipping and tariffs. Preference was usually given to politically well connected traders born in the metropolis, who obtained monopolies, monopsonies and other commercial privileges. The Spaniards insisted that only Catholic subjects of the Crown 'of pure blood' could enter their colonies, although the Portuguese merely required immigrants to be Catholics (Mörner 1992: 211, 213; 1985: 6–7). North European powers were more liberal, but Jews were tolerated, rather than specifically authorised to reside in colonies.

Sephardic Jews nevertheless played a crucial part in the world cocoa trade from the seventeenth century, helped by their prominent role in chocolate manufacturing in Europe (Israel 1989: 179, 183). Active in the main Western ports outside Iberia, Sephardim used the French Basque port of Bayonne for contraband trade with Spain. They exploited intimate contacts with 'New Christians', Jews officially converted to Catholicism in Iberia, who flooded into the Spanish possessions after the union of the crowns of Portugal and Spain in 1580 (Arcy 1930: 14–15; Israel 1990: 131; Fortune 1984; Klooster 1997). Sephardic Jews were also major providers of credit, even making substantial loans to Spanish cocoa planters in Venezuela (Fortune 1984: 154–7; Emmanuel and Emmanuel 1970: I, 113, 216, 226–7).

The intercontinental cocoa trade from Spanish colonies, legally reserved to nationals, quickly fell into Basque hands. Distinct in terms of language, culture and political status, the community included many French Basques, who obtained Spanish birth certificates when necessary (Douglass and Bilbao 1986). The Real Compañía Guipuzcoana de Caracas (Caracas Company) was founded in 1728, and soon obtained a monopoly of trade between Caracas and Spain. Dominated by San Sebastián Basques, the company cracked down hard on Sephardic smuggling (Hussey 1934; Gárate Ojanguren 1990). Basque merchants based in Lima and Callao mastered the burgeoning cocoa trade of Guayaquil, without recourse to a privileged company (Parrón Salas 1995: 19–20, 159). The Acapulco galleon trade to Manila also appears to have been largely in their hands (Kicza 1983: 69–70; Díaz-Trechuelo 1965: 15).

Basques had less of a monopoly in the internal cocoa trade of the New World. Venezuela's internal trade, and that with Mexico, was largely divided between Basques and Canarians (Arcila Farías 1950; Mörner 1996: 19–22; Tamaro 1988: 196). Yucatán was in a similar position, although Maya traders maintained a lively cocoa trade between Tabasco and Yucatán (Patch 1993: 202–3; Farriss 1984: 153–5). Basques shared Mexico's substantial internal cocoa trade with Montañeses, a term sometimes narrowly applied to people from the north of Old Castile, but more usually embracing Asturians and Galicians (Brading 1971: 106; Kicza 1983: 52). Spanish officials, of varied origins, also purchased cocoa from indigenous Mesoamericans (Wasserstrom 1983a: 35; Newson 1987: 165). Jesuits from all over Catholic Europe controlled much of the cocoa trade of the Amazon-Orinoco Basin, in partnership with unsubdued Amerindians (Alden 1976; Eder 1985; Patiño 1963: 276–93). Across the Pacific, Mestizos of Chinese-Filipino origins bought cocoa in rural areas to sell it in Manila (Dobbin 1996: 27).

Cracks in the Sephardim-Basque ascendancy, 1760s–1790s

The abolition of the principal chartered companies after the Seven Years War left the field open for independent merchants, based in European ports and owning their ships. Problems of agency overseas were tackled by employing ships' captains, partners residing in the colonies, or, most commonly, local traders working on commission. Given high risks, contractual ties were usually reinforced by bonds of kinship, ethnicity or religion (Schneider 1981: I, 33–4). Thus importers of cocoa into Genoa and Livorno were initially Italian, but Swiss Protestants from Geneva began to move into the business from the 1780s (Niephaus 1975: 277–338).

Spain opened a crack in the imperial door for foreigners. Heretics and Jews were allowed to call somewhat more freely, either when exports to neutral and friendly colonies were authorised in time of war, or to trade in slaves. In the case of Venezuelan cocoa, this mainly benefited Sephardim from Curaçao (Aizenberg 1978: 244; Arcila Farias 1973: I, 350). Some Catholics were even allowed to reside in Spanish colonies, notably French merchants who dealt in Trinidad cocoa from 1785 (Giacottino 1976: II, 567). Irish traders, also permitted to settle in Trinidad, concentrated on cotton and sugar (Sevilla Soler 1988: 188–9). A Genoese trader in Lima may have been retailing chocolate in 1790 (Descola 1968: 151).

Spanish reforms occasioned a much larger influx of metropolitan traders, at times stirring up resentment among locally born Creoles. However, merchants tended to see themselves not as Spaniards, but as men from 'little homelands' in Iberia, bound into communities of trust by ties of kinship and neighbourhood. In the case of Basques, Catalans and Galicians, such ties were reinforced by linguistic factors (Mörner 1992: 214–15; Ridings 1985: 6–9).

The Basque grip on Spain's imperial cocoa trade, apparently threatened by reforms, may have been strengthened. The Caracas Company lost its monopoly in 1781, and was dissolved in 1784, but its Basque promoters formed the Real Compañía de Filipinas (Philippines Company). This 'multi-colonial' commercial octopus, with the king as a major shareholder, had interests around the globe. Just in terms of cocoa, the Philippines Company retained commercial privileges in Caracas and Trinidad, obtained a monopoly on exports from South America to the Philippines, and competed on the Callao-Cadiz route. Moreover, Basques continued to benefit from their position as importers and distributors of cocoa in Cadiz, Madrid and northern Spain (Parrón Salas 1995: chs 5–6; Díaz-Trechuelo 1965).

'Down with the Basques!' thus remained a slogan for Caracas revolutionaries (Klooster 1998: 155). Not only did the Philippines Company act as the ghost of its illustrious predecessor, but many former company employees went into trade on their own account (Alvárez 1963: 56–62). A sample of wills indicated that 42 per cent of the merchant elite in Caracas province were Basques, with 19 per cent Canarians, 19 per cent Creoles, and 20 per cent other Spaniards. Basque traders were agents of firms in Spain, traded on their own account in several commodities, and invested in plantations. The exports of La Guaira in 1787 were allegedly manipulated by a Basque cartel, consisting of the Philippines Company, José Escorihuela, and Iriarte Hermanos (McKinley 1985: 14–17, 63–8, 89–91, 97, 103–15, 177, 192). A cartel of two or three cocoa shippers, of unknown origins, was also said to exist in Maracaibo in 1776 (Patiño 1963: 319).

Catalans, possibly the main mercantile group in the Spanish Caribbean lowlands by the 1790s, emerged as dynamic rivals in Venezuela (Farré 1979; Mörner 1996: 2). The Barcelona Company, run by some of the wealthiest entrepreneurs of that city, stationed Catalan factors in the ports of eastern Venezuela (Oliva Melgar 1987: 111–14). After the abolition of the company in 1785, Catalan traders remained well represented there (Alvárez 1963: 62). They spread to Caracas province from the 1770s, and about twenty merchants were established in the city of Caracas in 1800, acting for Barcelona firms (Farré 1979: 24–7, 31). Indeed, Segura y Grasi was the largest single exporter of cocoa from La Guaira in 1795–96, with 11.5 per cent of the total (McKinley 1985: 64, 66–7). Numbers resident in Venezuela remained small, as ships' captains often acted as agents of Barcelona houses. Catalans were reputed to be particularly clannish, using their language to cement relations of trust and exclude outsiders, and more likely to return home than to settle in Venezuela (Depons 1930: 66, 307).

Wealthy Venezuelan planters were tempted to market their own cocoa, but they only bypassed traders to a limited extent, typically selling to ships' captains. Although the great Caracas families had earlier owned ships for the cocoa trade with Mexico, this activity declined from the 1780s, and was not replaced by the riskier trade with Spain. Merchants and planters were closely allied, notably by marriage, and the mercantile element in no way held the whip hand (McKinley 1985: 1–2; 66–9).

Resident merchants in Caracas and other towns were usually Spaniards, who waited for producers to bring them beans, or sent agents to buy them in the countryside. Many Canarians and locally born Creoles were rural traders. Some of the latter were of mixed race, and they often acted as mule-teers (McKinley 1985: 20–1, 66; Tamaro 1988: 196). Catalan shopkeepers were spreading along the Orinoco, where Humboldt and his companion were mistaken for such around the turn of the century (Farré 1979: 25; Humboldt 1852: II, 433). Locally born traders were sometimes accused of buying stolen cocoa from slaves (Brito Figueroa 1985: 116).

The Church was the chief lender in Venezuela, with around 2.5 million pesos of loans outstanding by the turn of the century. The Philippines Company claimed 0.2 million pesos owed by planters to the defunct Caracas Company, although debtors refused to pay. Indebtedness was less than in Mexico, partly because the capital requirements of cocoa production were so low. Planters complained but mostly had little difficulty in paying interest charges, although the Church sometimes foreclosed and sold proper-ties (McKinley 1985: 30–1, 83–4, 114; Tamaro 1988: 289–90). The annual rate of interest was low, at 5 per cent (Lucena Salmoral 1992: 22–3). In Mexico, loans were regularly rolled over in a person's lifetime (Brading 1971: 218–19).

The Guayaquil cocoa trade remained a Basque preserve (Contreras 1990: 73, 78). Representing Cadiz firms and with Saint Francis Xavier as their patron, they were mainly settled in Lima and Callao. Chief among them was Javier María de Aguirre, in Lima from the 1780s. The Elizalde, Irizarri, Icaza and Santiago families were well represented, and the Philippines Company consolidated this Basque presence after 1785 (Parrón Salas 1995: 19–21, 29–30, 238, 321–2, 437–8). However, the remote frontier nature of Guayaquil allowed the rise of Bernardo Roca, a Mulatto from Panama. Arriving in the 1760s, he had become one of the main cocoa exporters twenty years later. Other mixed-race traders in the city acted as agents of Lima and Callao merchants (Laviana Cuetos 1987: 132–4).

Cocoa was a major source of profit for the merchant princes of Mexico City (Ladd 1976: 36). The town was the largest conurbation in the New World, with 180,000 people in 1820, and it acted as a distribution hub for New Spain. While cocoa was important to these merchants, they spread their risks, dealing in European and Chinese manufactures, sugar and cochineal. They also invested in silver mining, bought estates, and found official and clerical jobs for their sons (Kicza 1983: 1–2, 45–7, 60–70). Traders usually acted as individual families, rarely forming partnerships. To avoid the decline of family firms, daughters and widows married able young immigrants. Coming from piously Catholic parts of Spain, they lived lives of almost monastic strictness, attending mass and saying the rosary every day. Riots in 1767 were attributed to the arrogance of these immigrants, denounced as 'so many Jews, ambitious and full of avarice, who came only to rob the people of their riches' (Brading 1971: 102–11).

The merchants of Mexico City, nine tenths of them born in Spain, were divided into a Basque and a Montañés faction in the *consulado*, or merchant guild. Basques were members of the confraternity of Our Lady of Aránzazu and closely tied to the port of Bilbao. Montañeses, mainly adepts of the Christ of Burgos and linked to Santander, were reinforced by Asturians and Galicians. Creoles were found in either camp, probably reflecting the origins of their fathers (Kicza 1983: 52, 66, 69–70; Borchart de Moreno 1984: 31–4, 113–14). Neither group monopolised the cocoa trade, although the Count of Jala, from Santander, was censured by the viceroy in 1749 for attempting to do so (Ladd 1976: 36). Pedro Alonso de Alles, an Asturian who became Marquis of Santa Cruz de Inguanzo, obtained large amounts of cocoa from Tabasco in the 1770s and 1780s (Brading 1971: 99, 105, 372). At his death in 1802, Alles had half a million pesos invested in the cocoa trade, including that of Guayaquil (Ladd 1976: 38, 199). However, the most prominent cocoa trader in the 1760s and 1770s was Pedro de Aycinena, a Navarrese Basque, who bought beans from Guayaquil, Caracas, Maracaibo and Tabasco (Borchart de Moreno 1984: 113–14; Brown 1995: 428–9).

Mexico City merchants were linked to colleagues in other Mesoamerican cities. Navarrese Basque merchants dominated Guatemala City, headed by Juan Fermín de Aycinena, a relative and partner of Pedro de Aycinena (Brown 1995; Balmori *et al.* 1984: ch. 2). Although Juan Fermín de Aycinena's main business was indigo, he also dealt in imported Guayaquil cocoa (Rubio Sánchez 1976: I, 96). This was a time when Basque-speaking Navarrese were among the most powerful businessmen in Spain, including the house of Ustariz that dealt in cocoa (Douglass and Bilbao 1986: 135–8; León Borja and Szászdi Nagy 1964: 28). The Veracruz *consulado*, founded in 1795 and with great influence over the regional cocoa trade, had two Basques among its most active members (Ruiz Abreu 1989: 99–101).

Tabascan traders were not from the top shelf of colonial merchants, as exports were controlled by Veracruz and Campeche. The situation was transitional between Mexico and the Caribbean Basin, for Basques and Montañeses were joined by Catalans and Canarians. Of the twenty-five traders listed in 1766, about half were Creoles and half born in Europe, including a Canarian. Basque names were in a clear minority on this list, and not one of Tabasco's three candidates for a projected Yucatán *consulado* in the 1790s appears to have been Basque (Ruiz Abreu 1989: 28–9, 100–1). A

Catalan trader was active in Tacotalpa as early as 1754, and a Montañés trader resided in Cunduacán in 1790 (Ruz 1994: 212; Gil y Saenz 1979: xxxix).

Indigenous traders continued to trade cocoa in the Maya heartland of Mesoamerica. Two Chontal Maya lay confraternities of Chicbul, near Campeche, organised commercial expeditions twice a year to the booming Tabasco cocoa groves, via a network of inland waterways. They bore images of their patron saints to display to the faithful, and bought cocoa in exchange for religious objects, trade goods and cash. The beans were sold in Campeche or Champotón, and handsome profits made the Chicbul fraternities among the wealthiest in the diocese of Yucatán (Farriss 1984: 153–5, 267). Maya traders in Guatemala drove an overland trade in cocoa in 1763, buying cocoa from estates, and sometimes going as far as Chiapas and beyond (Solórzano 1963: 185–7, 194–8). Similarly, cocoa was sold in colonial towns by the Jicaque people of Honduras in 1799 (Rubio Sánchez 1958: 91).

The southern marches of Mesoamerica were generally a dependency of Guatemala City merchants, but the Nicaraguan cocoa trade was jealously guarded by residents of Rivas, also planters. The head of one of the three wealthiest families in Rivas was a Basque, who arrived early in the eighteenth century (Romero Vargas 1976: 468–70, 476, 528–30). Rivas traders transported cocoa by land to Realejo and then took it by sea for sale in Acapulco (Salvatierra 1939: II, 35). A young Spaniard, apprenticed by his uncle in Guatemala City to a Costa Rican trader for commercial training in 1772, sold cocoa in Honduras and El Salvador fairs. Costa Rican cocoa exports were largely controlled by three men, one of them a Mulatto, and they also farmed the collection of tithes (Fernández Molina 1992: 425–39).

Officials provided unwelcome competition to traders in Mesoamerica. In 1760–5, the *alcalde mayor* of Ciudad Real, Chiapas, made 10,000 pesos from forced purchases of about 70 tonnes of cocoa from Zoque cultivators, equivalent to a seventh of his income. A tyrannical petty official administered public whippings to Zoque who did not fulfil their cocoa quotas in 1768, causing them to neglect the production of foodstuffs. He paid prices that were so low that people allegedly could not afford to buy maize (Wasserstrom 1983a: 35–6, 46–8, 60). Purchases of cocoa by officials were recorded in Guatemala in 1763, in Tabasco in the 1770s, and in Nicaragua at the end of the century (Solórzano 1963: 185–7; Brading 1971: 99; Newson 1987: 165).

The crown attempted to suppress forced purchases with renewed vigour in the 1780s, following a serious indigenous rebellion in Peru (Brading 1971: 115; Parrón Salas 1995: 305–7). The practice proved hard to eradicate, however, as officials simply ensured that they were the only buyers. Chiapas was a particular problem. The *alcalde mayor* of Ciudad Real was criticised by the Church for making forced cocoa purchases in 1779 and 1784. On the latter occasion, he was accused of buying cocoa at the old price of 10 pesos per *arroba*, despite a poor harvest, and selling it in Guatemala City for 75 pesos. However, the newly created intendency allowed for closer monitoring of officials after 1790, obligatory purchases accounted for a declining proportion of trade, and a more self-confident merchant group developed (Carvalho 1994: 159–62, 169; Wasserstrom 1983a: 35, 63–4, 103; Wasserstrom 1983b: 105).

The crown itself ran a system of forced cocoa trade in the Amazon pied-mont of the Andes. Parish priests took over the Mojos missions after the expulsion of the Jesuits in 1767, but officials gained control of administra-tion in 1789, receiving cocoa and chocolate as part of the tribute, and excluding private traders (Orbigny 1992: 162–4). Profitable for the state, the system was burdensome for Amerindians. They had to transport tribute goods for sale by auction in Santa Cruz, and received paltry consumer goods in return (Larson 1988: 250–1).

Traders of mixed race served the internal market in the Philippines, but forced purchases lingered on. Missionaries in the Cagayan valley reported in 1796 that the local population had lost interest in growing cocoa, because local officials were cornering the market (Jesús 1980: 134). In 1800, Chinese Mestizos were accused of hoarding cocoa in Manila, waiting for prices to rise. Partly of Filipino origin, Spanish by language, and Catholic by religion, these Mestizos filled the gap left by harsh anti-Chinese measures following the restoration of Manila by Britain in 1764 (Dobbin 1996: 28).

The rise and fall of privileged companies in the Portuguese possessions was compressed in time. The Companhia Geral do Comércio do Grão-Pará e Maranhão (Pará Company) was set up in 1755 to fill the gap left by the expulsion of the Jesuits from the Amazon, with wild cocoa as its mainstay. Following the fall of the Marquis of Pombal, the government refused to renew the company's charter in 1778, throwing open the Amazon to private trade (Alden 1976: 124–6; Novais 1979). However, lay 'directors of Indians' probably blocked much private trade till their abolition in 1798. Foremen who organised collecting expeditions sometimes owned their canoes and met their costs, but they also worked on commission (Cardoso 1984: 171).

Sephardic Jews from Bordeaux were prime candidates for controlling the cocoa exports of the French possessions. The house of Gradis was installed on the south coast of Saint-Domingue and on Martinique, while that of Raba concentrated on the Cap Français region of Saint-Domingue, all three cocoa-producing areas (Butel 1974: 235–6, 290–1). Jews were also prominent in Jérémie, the most dynamic centre of cocoa cultivation, although these may well have been Curaçao Sephardim, less privileged than French families (Plummer 1998: 80–3). Catholic traders from the French Alps around Grenoble, numerous in Saint-Domingue, were also represented in Jérémie (Léon 1963: 28, 203). The privileged Compagnie de la Guyane, founded against the trend in 1777, had no monopoly over French Guiana's exports, concentrating instead on carrying slaves to Saint-Domingue (Hardy 1947: 91–2, 97, 104).

As British and Dutch cocoa producers in the Caribbean were small planters, they probably sold their harvests to merchants in local ports (Carrington 1988: 30). Sephardic Jews handled about a third of Jamaica's 'secondary staples' in the eighteenth century, in competition with Scottish Calvinists and English Quakers, much cocoa being smuggled in from Spanish possessions (Fortune 1984: 84–6, 165). Sephardic Jews were also prominent in Surinam, together with Calvinists from the provinces of Zeeland and Holland (Lier 1971: 88–93).

The impact of warfare and revolution, 1790s–1820s

Warfare from 1796 brought foreigners into greater prominence in the Hispanic American cocoa trade. Venezuela witnessed an influx of American merchants from Philadelphia and Baltimore, together with Hanseatic Germans, as neutral ships took over cocoa exports; however, they did not settle (Lucena Salmoral 1990: 220; Walter 1985: 50). Catalan merchants almost caught up with their Basque rivals, who retained no more than a slight edge in Caracas province. Typically for newcomers, clannish Catalans specialised in trade, whereas Basques had a stake in agriculture and close links with Creoles. Both communities had a reputation for honesty and prompt payment (Walker 1822: I, 167–8, 467; II, 257, 260).

Mesoamerica's commercial communities were not affected in the same way. The penetration of foreigners remained extremely limited, and the reorientation of Mexico's cocoa imports to the Pacific was initially to the advantage of established Basque traders (Guardino 1996: 23, 63; Kicza 1983: 62). At lower levels of commerce, concentration on urgent military matters distracted the crown from the suppression of forced purchases by officials. A decree of 1803 repeated the prohibition of this practice in Chiapas, but officials were still obliging Amerindians to sell them cocoa in 1819 (Carvalho 1994: 162; Wasserstrom 1983b: 117–18).

The independence struggle proved a rude foretaste of things to come for Spanish merchants. Many were arrested and summarily executed in Venezuela in 1813 (McKinley 1985: 171). One of the slogans of the Mexican rebels in 1810 was 'Death to the *gachupines!*', the immigrants from Spain (Brading 1971: 346).

The exigencies of war put great pressure on the role of the Catholic Church as chief banker to the Spanish empire, albeit more so in Mexico than in Venezuela. The Church had some 44 million pesos out in mortgages in New Spain in December 1804, when the crown took over these loans and forced debtors to pay back the principal within a maximum of ten years, extracting 12 million pesos by 1808. Land prices tumbled, as forced sales rose sharply (Brading 1971: 218, 340–1). However, Venezuela was spared this interference in credit markets, and the rate of interest for rural loans in Caracas only edged up slightly to 5–6 per cent in 1810 (Lucena Salmoral 1992: 22–3).

Slave uprisings and war radically altered the commercial and credit situation in parts of the Caribbean. The French were forced out of Haïti after the slave rebellion of 1791, and most Curaçao Sephardic Jews went with them. The small group of Jews who remained behind were largely of mixed race, and may already have converted to Catholicism. They often had members of the family over the frontier in Santo Domingo (Plummer 1998: 84–5). Elsewhere in the Caribbean, the supremacy of the British navy made life hard for French and Dutch merchants.

The further disruption of mercantile networks, 1820s–1840s

The picture of marketing in the West remains shadowy, but the opening of the sales rooms in Mincing Lane in 1811 enhanced the function of London cocoa auctions. While relatively small amounts of cocoa beans actually changed hands at these auctions, they came increasingly to 'fix' prices of different grades of cocoa (Dand 1993: 83; Knapp 1920: 111–12). Shipping and trade became more clearly differentiated after the Napoleonic wars, as overseas merchants became more independent of Western merchant-shippers, but such changes were slow to impinge on Latin America (Laan 1997: ch. 3; Schneider 1981: I, 33–4).

Upheavals in Spain, still the world's largest single market for cocoa, temporarily benefited merchants in southwestern France. Hostile Spanish relations with former colonies led importing houses to move from northern Spain to neighbouring parts of France. Bayonne and Bordeaux then thrived on re-exporting or smuggling cocoa and other 'colonial goods' to Spain. Many Spanish Basques acquired French nationality, neatly reversing the pattern of earlier years. Sephardic Jewish merchants of Bayonne and Bordeaux experienced a renaissance, as they retained the political and social rights gained during the Revolution. They were much involved in the re-export business, notably the houses of Gradis and Léon (Schneider 1981: I, 51–81; Casey 1981: 1–2, 49, 70, 93, 374; Léon 1893: 15–16, 354–7).

The expulsion of Basque and Catalan merchants caused chaos in much of Hispanic America. As Spain refused to accept the independence of her former colonies, Spanish merchants were obliged to leave. Despite the improvement in political relations in the 1830s, Madrid prohibited emigration to the new republics from 1836 to 1853 (Mörner 1985: 21–2). Spanish Basques were sometimes able to avoid such vexatious restrictions by registering as French citizens, accounting for at least part of the apparent influx of 'French' traders into new states (Mörner 1996: 22). Catalans withdrew to Spain's remaining Cuban colony, a base for future expansion (Marrero

1972–89: XII, 213). By the middle of the century, they had completely eclipsed Basque traders on the island (Mörner 1996: 22).

Freight, insurance and interest rates often soared when Spanish traders were expelled, reversing the trend of the early 1820s (Walker 1822: II, 273–5; Gosselman 1962: 109). In part, this illustrated the inability of foreign merchants to step into the shoes of departing Spaniards. Technical developments in shipping made little difference. North American clippers were fast, but they were expensive to build and crew. Steam navigation was in its infancy, as yet insignificant for trans-oceanic transport (Rinman and Brodefors 1983: 20–31, 182).

A contraction of credit followed the expulsion of Spaniards, worsened by liberal hostility to the Catholic Church (Bulmer-Thomas 1994: 30). Venezuelan interest rates for planters soared to a record 120 per cent in 1829 (Izard 1972: 133). In the Cauca valley of Colombia, however, the Church retained its role as a provider of loans (Hyland 1982: 387–93).

Gran Colombia, the largest cocoa exporter in the world, ordered the expulsion of all royalist or 'disloyal' Spaniards in 1823 (Liehr 1989: 476). It was reported that, 'among the merchants, the principal capitalists were European Spaniards, who have generally emigrated', and that Creoles were unable to take their place (Hall 1824: 37). However, frustration awaited foreign traders who flocked in to replace them. A law of 1822 prohibited foreigners from trading on their own account, obliging them to work through local intermediaries. The resulting rush of applications for naturalisation lasted until congress reversed the measure in 1824 (Banko 1990: 51–3). The focus on selling cocoa internally strengthened the position of Creole merchants in Colombia. Of the sixteen principal Bogotá firms dealing in cocoa in 1841, ten were local, three British and three French (Schneider 1981: I, 172–4).

Repeated commercial crashes led most British, American and Dutch merchants to withdraw from Caracas province by 1848 (Jong 1966: 66–80, 109; Cartay 1988: 261–8). This left exports of cocoa mainly in German hands, together with a few Curaçao Jews and 'nationals' or Frenchmen, whose names betrayed Basque or Catalan origins (Banko 1990: 344–56; 1988). Germans were also preponderant around Lake Maracaibo, although the region's cocoa exports were in crisis from the 1830s (Cardozo Galué 1991: 31). These German merchants were mostly Protestants from Hamburg, but some came from Bremen and Lübeck, and a few were Sephardic Jews (Banko 1988; Walter 1985). Bolívar allowed free entry to Sephardic Jews from Curaçao, who settled in two dozen towns in Venezuela, as well as half a dozen in Colombia (Aizenberg 1978: 245–6, 250–1; Elkin 1980: 20).

Other successful cocoa traders in Venezuela spoke forms of Italian, although Corsicans were French by nationality. Merchants from northern Corsica had established connections with Hispanic America long before being transferred from Genoese to French rule in 1768 (Carrington 1971: 197–8, 223). After the defeat of Napoleon, many Corsicans sought their fortune in Puerto Rico, a thriving centre of re-exports to Spain (Renucci 1973: 139). In the formerly Catalan fief of eastern Venezuela, Corsican merchants quickly built up a dominant position as cocoa exporters (Harwich Vallenilla 1996: 27–31). Genoese traders were mainly in and around Caracas, while Corsicans and Elbans were influential in western Venezuela from the 1830s (Vannini de Gerulewicz 1966: 445–594; Cartay 1988: 265).

The complexities of commercial relationships in Venezuela are illustrated by the career of Georg Blohm, the most successful cocoa trader of Puerto Cabello. Born in Lübeck, he preferred to recruit men from his home town, and eventually retired there. However, he acted as consul for Hamburg, and had strong links with the Danish Caribbean island of Saint Thomas, where he met and married his Danish wife in 1834. Blohm was for a time in partnership with an Italian merchant, Gianbattista dalla Costa. Born in Verona in 1791, lord of the Orinoco trade from his base in Angostura in the 1830s and 1840s, and French vice-consul from 1834 to 1846, Costa had family in the United States and died in Genoa in 1869 (Walter 1985: 174–8; Schneider 1981: I, 231).

The unusual leniency shown to Spaniards in Ecuador preserved the position of Basque cocoa exporters. Foremost among them was a man born in Spain, Manuel Antonio de Luzárraga Echezurría, who arrived in Guayaquil in 1814 as an officer in the Spanish navy. By 1847, he exported nearly half of Guayaquil's cocoa, owned cocoa plantations, ran a bank, and was the richest man in the country (Arosemena 1991: I, 186; Gosselman 1962: 105). He was possibly related through his mother to the Echezurría family of Venezuela, major cocoa traders in earlier decades (McKinley 1985: 64). Other Basques in the cocoa economy were the Orrantia brothers, also born in Spain, Delfin Iturburu, and the heirs of Martin Icaza (Chiriboga 1980: 45, 174; Hamerly 1973: 109, 117).

Guayaquil traders saw off a brief challenge by the English firm of Gibbs, Crawley & Co., with origins in the Exeter cloth trade. This company had its main South American importing business in Lima, and it set up a branch in Guayaquil in 1823 (Mathew 1981: 6–13). In 1832 it was one of the three largest commercial firms in the port (Hamerly 1973: 117). Five years later, Gibbs Crawley was still among the first three, together with Luzárraga (Gosselman 1962: 105). Exactly when Gibbs closed down their branch in Guayaquil is not clear, but it was probably shortly after they had obtained the lucrative guano contract in Peru in 1842 (Mathew 1981: 223–4; Greenhill 1977: 163).

The expulsion of Spaniards from Peru and Bolivia had little impact on the old-fashioned cocoa trade of the Bolivian Amazon, where state trading persisted till 1842. Cocoa and chocolate, part of the Mojos tribute, was auctioned on behalf of the state in Santa Cruz or Cochabamba. Small and heavily taxed private traders came down from the Andes once a year to bid for these goods. In return, the authorities supplied the Mojos with inadequate supplies of consumer goods. Only meagre amounts of privately grown cocoa were allowed to change hands on the margins of this exploitative system (Orbigny 1992: 21–2, 74, 77, 300–2, 309–13; Osborne 1955: 86–7).

The large and opulent community of Spanish traders in Mexico was expelled in three waves between 1827 and 1833, many of them leaving before they were pushed (Sims 1990). However, quite a few remained by connections, naturalisation, the adoption of French nationality by Basques, or drifting back from New Orleans as conditions improved (Bernecker 1989: 93–7, 103). The impact on the cocoa trade of Mesoamerica was thus unclear. Tabasco was more opposed to expulsions than any other state, and although forty-six Spaniards were thrown out in 1829, some of them negotiated their return (Sims 1990: 22, 130, 193). The first governor of Tabasco was the son of a Montañés trader, which may explain this leniency (Gil y Saenz 1979: xxxviii–xxxix). Expulsions from Acapulco were probably more drastic, contributing to disruption in imports of Guayaquil cocoa (Guardino 1996: 62–5, 114–16).

Foreign traders dabbled in the internal Mesoamerican trade in cocoa and chocolate, especially Hanseatic Germans. The firm of Sulzer and Hundeiker, established in Mexico City, Veracruz and Tabasco, probably purchased cocoa, and Frank Alt made chocolate in Mexico City in 1845 (Mentz *et al.* 1982: 88, 90–1, 96, 101–4, 467–70; Bernecker 1989: 103). A prosperous German merchant in León, Nicaragua, received eighty mules laden with cocoa from Masaya in the early 1820s, and had a warehouse with large stocks of cocoa (Burns 1991: 52). British, Italian, Colombian and Mexican shippers temporarily filled the gap left by departing Spaniards in Acapulco (Guardino 1996: 114).

There were no official expulsions from Brazil, but there were sporadic attacks on traders, many fled the country, and immigration from Portugal was prohibited from 1822 to 1837. Belém, the country's main cocoa port, was affected by one of the most violent pogroms, in 1817 (Rego 1966: 20, 29–31, 72, 149–50). Violence in the Amazon reflected Portuguese domination of all levels of commerce, and it culminated in the great Cabanagem Rebellion of 1835–9 (Weinstein 1983: 40). Portuguese merchants in Belém remained wary of the 'nativist' threat for decades after this rebellion (Bates 1969: 16–21). Nevertheless, the Amazon was 'overrun' with Portuguese peddlers in canoes, working for merchants in Belém. Credit was usually in trade goods, advanced to a line of intermediaries stretching for thousands of miles along the great river. Advances were backed only by promises of delivery of wild cocoa and other forest products after a considerable lapse of time, so that interest rates were high (Wallace 1890: 261–3). These peddlers were probably Minhotos from northern Portugal, working on commission for firms in Oporto (Pereira 1981).

Sephardic Jews from Morocco were the main competitors in the Amazon, selling textiles and buying local produce (Elkin 1980: 43–4). They started as humble peddlers, plying the waterways of the region. They founded the first synagogues in Belém, in 1826 and 1828 (Weinstein 1983: 50–2, 287; Wolff and Wolff 1975: 267–8). These Moroccan Jews probably arrived via Portuguese territory in the first instance. A few families came as peddlers to the Algarve, Lisbon and the Azores, following the repeal of anti-Jewish legislation in the early 1820s, and then moved on to Portuguese Africa. A member of the wealthy Bensaúde family, from the Azores, set up as a trader in the Amazon around 1840 (Bensaúde 1936: 53–65; Clarence-Smith 1985: 96). This was a time when winds and currents in the Atlantic linked Belém more closely to Europe than to the rest of Brazil (Kidder 1845: II, 9).

Bahia had a slightly different commercial structure. British exporters were installed in the capital of Salvador, but most commercial intermediaries were Portuguese, who also controlled large and lucrative slave imports (Verger 1968: 449–53). Salvador merchants advanced funds to a dozen or so major Ilhéus planters, who in turn lent to smaller farmers and purchased their crops for shipment to Salvador (Mahony 1996: 237–40, 362–8, 421).

Haïti was unusual in the Caribbean basin in discriminating against entrepreneurs on grounds of race. Merchants, mainly British, had to purchase expensive commercial licences, could trade only through Haïtian brokers, could not engage in retail trade, and could not go inland. However, these draconian regulations were relaxed from 1843 (Plummer 1988: 47–9). The south of the country was a stronghold of local Mulatto merchants, a few of whom were active in foreign trade (Nicholls 1996: 8–9, 34; Joachim 1972: 1516). Elsewhere in the Caribbean, Sephardic Jews obtained full legal equality with Europeans, prospering in Jamaica and Surinam (Knight 1990: 293; Lier 1971: 94–5).

In western Africa, the old structure of merchant-shippers based in Western ports remained almost intact until the middle of the century (Lynn 1997). The minuscule cocoa trade of the Gulf of Guinea islands was probably in the hands of ships' captains from New England and Marseilles, who gained a lien on harvests by making advances in the previous year (Omboni 1846: 243).

Apart from irregular arrivals of Ecuadorian beans, Westerners were only involved in the Philippines cocoa trade as providers of credit. Hokkien Chinese syndicates obtained advances and leased square-rigged sailing vessels of 200–250 tonnes from Spanish merchants, making annual round trips to Sulu and the Moluccas. Selling textiles, they bought cocoa for Manila and forest and marine produce for the China market. Sometimes a single ship came in a year, sometimes up to three. The semi-official Nederlandsche Handel-Maatschappij, founded by the Dutch in 1824, was unable to penetrate this trade (Clarence-Smith 1998: 95–6). Chinese Mestizos bought cocoa in the Visayas and northern Mindanao, sending it to Manila (Mallat

1983: 186–7, 202). Muslim traders fed into this network, bringing beans from Sulu to northern Mindanao (Mas 1843: II). Alternatively, Filipinos in the Visayas pooled their resources to make a locally rigged sailing ship, took cocoa and other produce to Manila, settled their accounts on return to their villages, and took the ship apart for use in the next trading season (Moor 1968: 83).

Growing competition, 1850s–1870s

Trading in cocoa was not yet a specialised activity in the City of London as late as the 1850s. A cosmopolitan group of 'colonial merchants' and 'colonial brokers', established in and around Mincing Lane, dealt in a wide range of tropical commodities, although they tended to concentrate on some particular aspect of the trade. Caesar Czarnikow, a Polish Jew by origin, was not only a sworn broker for the sugar trade, but also had a coffee department, purchased Havana cigars, and analysed various commodities in his *Weekly Price Current*. Czarnikow had access to some of the greatest financiers of his time, including the Rothschilds (Janes and Sayers 1963: chs 2–5).

One French attempt to mobilise banking finance briefly sent the cocoa price soaring in 1857, and was remembered for decades. The Crédit Mobilier, an investment bank created by the Péreire brothers in 1852, was accused of financing the stocking of cocoa to drive up prices, until the commercial crisis of the autumn brought this manoeuvre to an abrupt end (*Gordian*: IV, 1352; Arosemena 1991: I, 192). It may have been no coincidence that Emile and Isaac Péreire were Sephardic Jews, born in Bordeaux and frequent visitors to Bordeaux and Bayonne, centres of the French cocoa and chocolate business (Léon 1893: 335–6).

Influenced by this incident, French manufacturers attempted to cut out middlemen through vertical integration. Emile Menier purchased plantations in Nicaragua in 1862, freighted ships and horse-drawn carriages, and acquired a branch railway line (Cerfberr de Medelsheim 1867: 17). The Paris house of Marquis also chartered ships to secure supplies, and Paris manufacturers engaged agents to purchase cocoa in Trinidad in the 1860s (Mangin 1860: 141; Moodie-Kublalsingh 1994: 228). However, Menier's plantations failed to secure independence from growers, only supplying part of Nicaragua's domestic market (Lévy 1873: 469–70). Internalising transport and trading functions was probably more costly than relying on intermediaries. Thus the Société Roger Touton was set up in Bordeaux around 1850, and prospered as a dealer in cocoa beans (Bonin 1997: 124).

Immigration rules were relaxed and political conditions became more stable in the tropical world, allowing intermediaries to compete as never before, and the specialisation of certain communities in cocoa became more pronounced. Conditions worsened once again for Basques and

Catalans in the 1860s, as futile dreams of reconquest led Spain to participate in the invasion of Mexico in 1861, annex the Dominican Republic in 1861–5, declare war on the Andean states in 1866, and brutally repress a Cuban rebellion in 1868–78. The withdrawal of British and United States traders from tropical Hispanic America also continued, allowing Germans and Corsicans to consolidate their position. Merchants played a greater role as creditors, because liberal governments launched assaults on the Catholic Church, but did not succeed in creating modern banks.

The ascendancy of Germans and Corsicans over Venezuela's cocoa trade was consolidated, and they also provided loans to planters (Rangel 1974: 247–8, 268). In 1876 just four Corsican firms accounted for nearly 90 per cent of the rapidly growing cocoa exports of eastern Venezuela. The oldest and most influential among them, the house of Franceschi, had an office in Paris (Harwich Vallenilla 1996: 30–2). Corsicans were also moving into the cocoa trade of the centre of the country, although Hanseatic Germans kept a large share of exports there, notably the houses of Blohm and Baasch in Puerto Cabello. Elbans had a more modest role as peddlers and shopkeepers in the west (Cartay 1988: 261–8). They may have been Sephardic Jews from Livorno, who played a similar role on Elba itself (Preziosi 1976: 133, 146–7).

Colombia's large internal market for cocoa favoured Antioqueño traders, although Germans were fearsome competitors. Antioqueños controlled their province's growing imports of Cauca cocoa, especially the traders of the thriving town of Manizales, founded in the 1840s. To prevent consumers from gaining information about prices, these merchants were said to have sabotaged the new telegraph line between Manizales and Cartago on several occasions. They travelled to Cauca and Tolima, paying cash on delivery for cocoa, and sending some to the highlands of Bogotá (Schenck 1953: 41–4, 50–1, 62; Brew 1977: 245). Germans gradually encroached on purchasing cocoa from Cauca smallholders (Mina 1975: 71–6, 93–4). 'Americans' were probably Germans naturalised in the United States, like the great Baltic German merchant prince Santiago Eder (Taussig 1977: 418).

Spaniards were pushed aside by Germans in Ecuador, largely as a consequence of war with Spain in 1866. Many Spanish concerns went bankrupt, foremost among them the Basque firm of Luzárraga (Chiriboga 1980: 45, 47, 55, 174). Martin Reinberg took Luzárraga's place as Guayaquil's main cocoa exporter. A naturalised citizen of the United States, he arrived in Guayaquil in 1869 as an agent for his uncle, Santiago Eder of Colombia (Arosemena 1991: I, 277–8; Eder 1959). Other German traders followed him, often from Hamburg, building up successful import-export houses (Weilbauer 1974: 39, 53–4, 110; Pineo 1996: app.). Italians, probably Genoese, moved into Guayaquil in the 1860s, initially as grocers (ICR 1863; 1892). Christian Palestinians selling religious relics arrived in Guayaquil around 1850, pioneers of a wider influx from Greater Syria (Almeida 1996:

90–7). Chinese traders were few in number in Guayaquil, but their commercial acumen was respected (Toscano 1960: 462).

Germans continued to play a part in the internal cocoa trade of Mesoamerica and the Antilles, together with Creoles and Spaniards. The German firm of E. Benecke imported Guayaquil cocoa through Acapulco in the 1850s and 1860s, and had agents in Mexico City, where the firm of Heimbürger sold cocoa (Mentz *et al.* 1982: 453–4). Another German firm, with a branch in Tabasco in the 1850s, probably purchased cocoa for Mexico City (Bernecker 1989: 103; Arias *et al.* 1987: 248). Spanish names graced the list of cocoa traders in Rivas, Nicaragua, in 1867, but they were probably Creoles (Lanuza *et al.* 1983: 86). In a remote Guatemalan highland village, the brothers of the local priest were accused of cornering the cocoa trade in 1857 (McCreery 1994: 133). Spanish traders fell back on the Spanish Antilles, where Catalan traders tightened their grip on Cuba. As they enjoyed a virtual monopoly of foodstuffs in Havana, it is likely that the internal trade in cocoa was in their hands (Marrero 1972–89: XII, 213).

Portuguese traders, mainly Minhotos from the north, continued to occupy most of the commercial niches in the Amazon at wholesale and retail level. Four to five thousand Portuguese entered the states of Pará and Amazonas between 1862 and 1872. Mostly young single males, they were literate, numerate, and had some initial capital (Pereira 1981: 190–204). Cocoa traders were based in Belém, with agents or correspondents in strategic locations. At the confluence of the Negro, traders received small lots of cocoa from all over the Upper Amazon Basin, and bulked them up for dispatch to Belém (Marcoy 1875: II, 415). The Portuguese spread beyond the Brazilian frontiers, reaching into the Hispanic regions of the vast Amazon-Orinoco basin (Patiño 1963: I, 327; Weinstein 1983: 58). They stood accused of holding collectors of cocoa and rubber in 'debt slavery' in the 1860s, concealing commercial information and cultivating political connections (Keller 1874: 102). Such accusations underlay xenophobic riots in 1873–4, when the mob once again violently attacked Belém's Portuguese traders, with the professed intention of driving them back to Portugal (Rego 1966: 32; Orton 1876: 259, 360).

The immigration of Jews into the Amazon, encouraged by Emperor Pedro II, intensified after the sultan of Morocco had decreed the emancipation of Jews in 1863 (Léon 1893: 328; Elkin 1980: 44). By 1890, it was estimated that around a thousand Moroccan Jews had entered the state of Pará (Lesser 1996: 49–50). While emigration was no longer funnelled through Portugal, and many Moroccans arrived as French subjects, the successful Benchimol family had commercial interests in Tangier, Lisbon and Angola (Weinstein 1983: 51; Wolff and Wolff 1975: 267–78; Clarence-Smith 1985: 96).

The opening of the Amazon to foreign shipping in 1867 helped to place cocoa exports firmly in the hands of Denis Crouan et Compagnie, set up in the 1860s to purchase cocoa. Donatien Barreau, the firm's French-born but locally married manager, was elected president of the Belém chamber of commerce in 1876 (Weinstein 1983: 55, 58, 62, 64, 307). Crouan was a Breton based in Nantes, and the firm relied on sailing ships to take its beans to France (*http*: 'Brest96'). Almost all the 3,500 tonnes or so of cocoa leaving the Amazon every year in the 1870s were destined for France (Smith 1879: 112).

The Swiss firm of Keller e Companhia held a similar position in Bahia's capital city of Salvador, through which cocoa was exported abroad, for lack of port facilities in Ilhéus. The company was founded in 1829 by three Swiss immigrants specialising in selling and repairing watches. Another Swiss, Johann J. Keller, became a partner in 1836, and the firm eventually took his name. The firm was unique among Salvador merchants in its early concentration on cocoa, and in having its own purchasing agents in the south. One German agent was in place by 1849, and much of Keller's cocoa business depended on personal contacts with Swiss and German settlers (Mahony 1996: 383–5). Keller worked on a commission basis for trusted partners in Switzerland and Germany, and had his own sailing ships built to send cocoa directly to Europe. He also lent money to cocoa planters and acquired land. It is not clear where Keller hailed from, although most of his compatriots in Bahia were from northeastern Switzerland (Ziegler-Witschi 1988: 153–8).

As cocoa exports expanded, other Salvador exporters began to take an interest. They included a second Swiss firm, two companies with German names, and two British firms with Scottish connections. Unlike Keller, however, these firms purchased from agents in Salvador, and they frequently continued to show greater interest in timber and piassava fibre from southern Bahia than in cocoa (Mahony 1996: 385–7).

Much intermediary commerce remained in the hands of Portuguese immigrants. Four fifths of the nearly 1,500 Portuguese who entered Bahia from 1862 to 1871 were traders (Pereira 1981: 189). They came as single young men, often taking a position in the firms of relatives, and they dominated the coastwise trade between southern Bahia and Salvador. However, patterns of trade in the south itself were more varied. The Portuguese Lemos family was a prominent Ilhéus concern, but Swiss, German and French immigrants, the residue of earlier rural colonisation schemes, played their part in commercialising cocoa (Mahony 1996: 237–50, 359–93).

Trading, planting and credit remained closely intertwined in southern Bahia. Salvador merchants were loath to lend directly to planters. Debts were rarely secured on land, for land legislation and uncertain boundaries made it almost impossible to foreclose. Planters thus lent short term, at rates of interest reaching 24 per cent a year. Loans were secured on the coming cocoa harvest, although this was technically illegal. Two planters with commercial backgrounds were particularly active, occasionally lending on the security of land. Luigi Adami was an Italian, possibly Genoese, who ran a store in Ilhéus in the mid-1840s, and married into the old and powerful landowning clan of Sá Homen del Rei. Pedro Cerqueira Lima was the scion of a Portuguese family that had accumulated great wealth in the slave trade in its last clandestine phase (Mahony 1996: 237–9, 375–6, 387–99, 404–10; Verger 1968: 449–50).

French traders began to enter Haïti in greater numbers after 1843, as restrictions on foreign traders were relaxed (Plummer 1988: 49; Marte 1984: 187–8). Few Frenchmen were willing to bear the hardships of life in Haïti for long, however, so they employed Hanseatic Germans as their agents. Some Germans married into the family of their employers, and began to take over their businesses. French Antilles traders, notably from Guadeloupe, arrived after the second French abolition of slavery in 1848. They found it easier than Whites to obtain trading licences, and even penetrated into rural areas (Aubin 1910: xxii).

The French merchants of Trinidad faced new competitors. The main chocolate manufacturers of Paris had their agents in the island in the 1860s, apparently French traders working on commission (Moodie-Kublalsingh 1994: 6, 228). Scottish Protestants, sent out as single young men to make their fortunes, soon dominated imports of dry goods and began to turn to cocoa. William Gordon, who arrived in 1865, was in the cocoa exporting business by 1872. Chinese shopkeepers, allegedly former labourers, probably dealt in cocoa at a local level (Brereton 1981: 100; 119; Harrison 1979: 65).

The number of cocoa exporters in São Tomé and Príncipe rose fast towards the end of this period, numbering seventy-seven by 1874 (Ribeiro 1977: 608). Traders on Príncipe were often obliged to re-dry the beans that they purchased from smallholders (AHU 1872). Most traders on São Tomé island in 1872 had Portuguese names, and appear to have been mainly immigrants from Portugal, together with some 'sons of the land'. However, one of the foremost merchant-planters was a Spaniard, Francisco de Asis Belard (Velarde), who later drew the Spanish Mantero family to the colony. As in the Amazon, there was also a Sephardic Jewish presence, notably the families of Azancot, Levy, and Amzalak (Ribeiro 1977: 450–3; Mantero 1910: 12, 19; Nogueira 1893: 63–4; Almada 1884: 24).

On neighbouring Fernando Póo, trade was dominated by Britons and Creoles, the latter mainly from São Tomé or Sierra Leone. Although most exporting to Europe was done by the Liverpool firm of John Holt from the 1860s, two pioneering Creole cultivators of cocoa broke into the business. One was a São Tomense Mulatto, Laureano Dias da Cunha Lisboa, trader, planter and Portuguese consul on the island. The other was a Sierra Leonean, William Allen Vivour, a bricklayer by trade, and the owner of the largest estate in the colony (Baumann 1888: 132–3, 136–9).

Hokkien Chinese, numerous in the Philippines after the loosening of Spanish immigration regulations in the 1860s, took over the internal cocoa trade from Chinese Mestizos in southeastern Luzon in the mid-1870s, and in

Mindanao in the following decade (Owen 1984: 103; Wickberg 1965: 92, 105–6). They also had most of the Moluccas-to-Manila cocoa trade in their hands, but Chinese from Makasar and Singapore, together with Hadhrami Arabs and Bugis settled in the Moluccas, took advantage of new steamer routes from the 1860s to redirect some of this trade via Singapore (Clarence-Smith 1998: 97).

The perfecting of marketing channels, 1880s–1914

Shipping costs fell from the middle of the 1870s, as steamers became larger and more efficient, and freight rates fell (Rinman and Brodefors 1983: 42–72, 182). However, they fell less than they might have done because of the growth of shipping 'conferences', or 'rings' (Greenhill 1977). These cartels had particularly negative effects in western Africa, where they were accused of pushing up the price of cocoa (Leubuscher 1962). The least competition existed in the western African colonies of France, Portugal and Spain. Prohibitive tariffs on goods carried by foreign ships, together with restrictive legislation, entailed a de facto monopoly for the Empreza Nacional de Navegação in Portuguese ports, and the Compañia Trasatlántica in Spanish ones (Clarence-Smith 1985: 95–7; 1991). A similar system kept foreign ships out of French colonies, except in the Congo Free Trade Zone, regulated by international treaty (Hopkins 1973: 201; Chalot and Luc 1906: 57–8).

The spread of the telegraph from the 1870s, especially underwater cables, caused a revolution in trading practices. All parties on the telegraph gained almost instantaneous information, homogenising the world price of cocoa through arbitrage, and further increasing the autonomy of merchants in exporting centres (Laan 1997: ch. 4). The telegraph enhanced the role of London cocoa auctions, held every Tuesday at eleven o'clock in the Commercial Sale Rooms in Mincing Lane. The results, flashed around the world, established prices for different varieties of beans, usually bought by private contract for forward delivery (Knapp 1923: 88–9).

There was an ambitious attempt to organise a futures market in Le Hâvre in 1898, with ten-tonne lots of Trinidad beans as the basis for contracts, although this does not appear to have operated for long. Swiss manufacturers made the traditional complaint that speculators, who had never seen a cocoa bean in their life, would determine prices, obliging manufacturers to pay over the odds for their raw material (*Gordian*: IV, 2076). In the event, cocoa had to wait longer than coffee for its first regular futures market, the New York Cocoa Exchange, founded in 1925 (Merill Lynch 1972: 47–8).

In the 1900s, cocoa imports into the West became increasingly concentrated in Hamburg, New York, Le Hâvre and London, roughly in that order (Freeman and Chandler 1907: 128). Lisbon handled much cocoa, but almost exclusively for re-export. Secondary ports were chiefly on Europe's Atlantic coast, in Santander, Bordeaux, Antwerp, Amsterdam, Bremen and Liverpool. The smaller Mediterranean trade went mainly to Barcelona, Marseilles and Genoa, while the west coast of the United States imported through San Francisco (Jumelle 1900: 56; Hall 1914: 490–3; Coe and Coe 1996, 236; Clarence-Smith 1994a: 183–5; Teiser 1945: 24–9). British cocoa brokers thus came to be concentrated in London and Liverpool by about 1910 (Gardiner 1923: 250).

Vertical commercial integration became somewhat more significant, especially as large landowners retained ownership of their beans until sale in the West, usually arranged by a broker (Knapp 1923: 87). Among the world's large producers, Ecuador and São Tomé exported most cocoa this way. Conversely, chocolate manufacturers, notably those in the United States, had agents in countries of production (*Gordian*: IV, 1266). Cadbury's set up an agency on the Gold Coast from 1908, and in Bahia at around the same time. However, Cadbury's operations remained on a small scale in the Gold Coast before 1914, and the Brazilian agency was discontinued (Williams 1931: 147–50). Increasingly competitive and effective intermediaries generally proved a better option.

Ecuador was the main Latin American example of exporting by great planters, although much cocoa continued to be channelled through trading houses. Aspiazu Hermanos was formed in 1891, partly to organise the family's cocoa sales abroad (Chiriboga 1980: 151–2). In the first half of April 1909, five landowners shipped about half the beans exported from Guayaquil (*Gordian*: XV, 2708–9). Much of the rest remained in German or Swiss German hands, even though Martin Reinberg went bankrupt in 1901. North Americans, Spaniards and Italians were also prominent exporters (Pineo 1996: 63–7, 165–75; Weilbauer 1974: 39, 45, 53–4; Arosemena 1991: I, 267, 277–8; II, 545–7). Italian merchants mostly came from Genoa, or more widely from Liguria. Some of them had been driven north by the war between Chile and Peru, and several also made chocolate in Guayaquil. Poor peddlers were from Naples and other parts of southern Italy, possibly Jews (Franceschini 1908: 792–3; Vázquez 1970: 80). From around 1910, specialised cocoa dealers began to emerge below the level of exporters, with names suggesting Spanish or local extraction (Arosemena 1991: I, 283–5).

Chinese and Syrians were initially peddlers and shopkeepers, but at least one Chinese firm with Hong Kong connections exported cocoa after 1900 (Pineo 1996: 63–7, 165–75). As Chinese enterprises flourished, they met with increasing discrimination. From 1899 to 1944 they were forbidden to enter the country, and those already resident were obliged to register with the municipal authorities and pay a special tax (Almeida 1996: 89). Nevertheless, it became increasingly common for owners of cocoa estates to rent stores on their properties to Chinese (Crawford de Roberts 1980: 81; Chiriboga 1980: 216, 218).

North Italians were the dominant entrepreneurial community in Peru before 1914, and their involvement in the chocolate industry makes it probable that they dealt in cocoa beans (Werlich 1978: 127; *Gordian*: VI, 2256). The extension of the Peruvian railway network to Cuzco in 1908 led to an influx of British, Italian and Spanish traders (Brisseau Loaiza 1981: 80, 160–2). Germans obtained a commanding position in Bolivia's commerce from the 1890s, but there was no mention of cocoa in their activities (Walle 1925: 58).

A handful of European exporters, mainly Swiss and Portuguese, dominated the export trade of Salvador, where Bahian cocoa was loaded on to oceangoing ships. The Swiss trader Emil Wildberger took over the firm of Keller and changed its name to his own, exporting about one third of all Bahia's cocoa around 1900 (Ziegler-Witschi 1988: 157). In the early 1910s, the other main Swiss or German cocoa exporters were Hugo Kaufmann, Behrmann, and Westphalen & Bach. The British challenge was reduced to a single company, F. Stevenson & Co. 'Luso-Brazilian' exporters were gaining market share before 1914, notably Valente e Peixoto, Costa e Ribeiro, Oliveira and Agenor Gordilho (Mahony 1996: 382–5, 422–3; Freitas 1979: 29, 67). Connections with Germany were close, for the suspension of payments by two Bahia companies in 1906 brought down the Hamburg firm of Leo Friedrichs (*Gordian*: XII, 757, 768).

Exporting companies had agents in the cocoa region of southern Bahia in the 1910s, but still depended to a considerable extent on intermediaries (Mahony 1996: 422–3). Wandering traders bought directly from producers, while commission houses were established in small towns. The latter were gradually squeezed by the expansion of agents of exporting firms (Instituto de Economia 1960: 190–2). Advances of trade goods, more rarely of cash, were well nigh universal to attract the custom of smallholders. On the Jequitinhonha and Pardo rivers, where transport by water was available, traders bought fresh cocoa beans and brought them to their establishments in small canoes, for fermentation and drying (Zehntner 1914: 60–1, 66). The purchase of dried beans was more common elsewhere (Mahony 1996: 320).

Portuguese traders remained entrenched at intermediary levels. The 3,000-strong Portuguese community in the state of Bahia in the early 1910s consisted almost entirely of traders, albeit with more Spanish and Italian rivals than before (Sociedade de Geografia 1912–15: 134–41, 158–9; Costa 1911: 86). Italian traders were numerous in the small cocoa port of Cannavieiras in 1921 (Fawcett 1953: 236). However, Syrian peddlers were the most fearsome competitors, setting out on foot, on mules or in canoes, alone or in groups of two or three (Aguiar Filho 1978: 72–3). The Syrian community numbered over 12,000 in the state of Bahia by the early 1920s (Hashimoto 1992: 89–98).

The supply of credit was stimulated by legislation in 1885, which validated the use of cocoa beans as collateral and facilitated foreclosure on land for the payment of debts (Mahony 1996: 411–13, 421–3). Given widespread squatting, lending was more on cocoa beans than on land. Intermediaries within the cocoa zone typically purchased the harvest in advance at an agreed discount, or provided trade goods to be repaid in cocoa after the harvest. Debts, at interest rates of over 10 per cent a year in 1909, were rarely subject to written contract, and were usually for consumption rather than production (Zehntner 1914: 24, 66; *Gordian*: XV, 3227; Caldeira 1954: 27). Farmers may have borrowed to register title to land, but most applications came from producers with bearing trees (Mahony 1996: 390).

The Nantes firm of Denis Crouan remained the leading cocoa exporter in the Brazilian Amazon (Weinstein 1983: 55, 62, 64). Crouan acted for the Menier factory, which took about half the Amazon's beans (*Gordian*: X, 4165). Crouan had a seventh three-masted sailing barque built for the transport of cocoa from Brazil and sugar from the West Indies in 1896, and kept it in service for nearly twenty years (*http*: 'Brest96'). Three rubber-exporting firms, Zietz, Singlehurst and Alden, also had a stake in Amazonian cocoa; and renewed interest in cocoa was apparent after the plunge in rubber prices in the early 1910s (Greenhill 1972: 3; Lange 1914: 88–91).

The Amazon was the greatest bastion of Portuguese supremacy in the internal trade of Brazil. The frequently made assertion that more Brazilians participated in commerce from the 1880s is misleading. Table 5.1 actually reflects increasingly liberal naturalisation laws. A sample for 1880–1910 indicated that about three quarters of 'Brazilian' traders were men born in Portugal (Weinstein 1983: 60, 72–5, 288). Over four fifths of Belém's commercial establishments were estimated to be in Portuguese hands in the early 1910s, when the great majority of roughly 60,000 immigrants in the Amazon were from northern Portugal (Sociedade de Geografia 1912–15: 119–29, 212–17).

Table 5.1 Traders paying the *patente* tax in Belém, 1914, by nationality

Country	Amount
Portuguese	1,907
Brazilians	1,159
Turks	242
Italians	172
Spaniards	79
Britons	34
French	24
Germans	11
Chinese	3
Russians	2
Americans	1
Swiss	1
Greeks	1

Source: Le Cointe 1922: I, 68

Absent from Table 5.1 were men like the 'Hebrew who immigrated long ago from Algiers', trading in the cocoa belt of the lower Tocantins in 1912 (Lange 1914: 94). Although 'Moroccans' were important purchasers of Amazonian products, they held Brazilian or French papers (Le Cointe 1922: II, 408; Wolff and Wolff 1975: 267–78). Indeed, naturalised Brazilian Jews, returning to North Africa to marry after seven or eight years, posed delicate diplomatic problems for Western powers there (Lesser 1996: 49–51). Of a sample of thirty small commission firms in the Amazon between 1880 and 1910, seventeen were partially or wholly Jewish (Weinstein 1983: 287). These Jews, 3,000–4,000 strong in 1914, had much trade in their hands, and were pious and orthodox, 'keeping their houses closed to the non-Jewish world' (Katz 1992: 37–8). However, they faced competition, especially from Syrians. Entered as 'Turks' in Table 5.1, Syrians numbered some 20,000 in Pará by the early 1920s (Hashimoto 1992: 89–98).

The advance of Corsican cocoa traders in Venezuela continued. An exodus from northern Corsica intensified from the 1880s, as prices of the island's staple crops fell. Some emigrants returned occasionally to oversee the chestnut harvest, and built large houses for their retirement (Renucci 1973: 139, 149–58). Eastern Venezuela's booming cocoa exports were almost a Corsican monopoly. In April 1909, every shipper of cocoa from Carúpano had an Italian name, among them some of the best known Corsican houses (*Gordian*: XV, 2709). The only non-Corsican cocoa exporter in 1921 was Azancot, probably from a family of Curaçao Jews that entered the region in the 1830s (Rangel 1974: 274; Cartay 1988: 265). Corsican concerns also expanded in central Venezuela, notably in La Guaira (Rangel 1974: 247–8, 269–75; Cartay 1988: 267–8). Further west, the upper levels of trade were firmly in German hands till 1914, although small Elban traders dealt in cocoa and other commodities, retiring to Livorno if they prospered (Bell 1922: 199, 225–6, 274; Franceschini 1908: 801–2, 805).

Immigrant merchants made further inroads in Colombia, but locals benefited from the internal nature of much of the cocoa trade. Antioqueño traders thus dominated Tolima, and purchased cocoa in Cauca, gradually excluding small Black traders from brokerage functions (Eder 1913: 135–6, 200–1, 211; Mina 1975: 92). Syrians were dynamic peddlers, and one of them grew cocoa and rubber in the coastal region in 1899 (Fawcett 1992: 363–4, 370–4). Germans were 'conspicuous' in the export sector as a whole, and may have handled cocoa (Eder 1913: 124, 187, 213).

Spaniards were the masters of Mexico's internal cocoa trade. Bulnes, Martin and Romano were the chief merchants of Villahermosa up to 1910, and the latter also had steamers on the rivers. They kept strong links with their homeland, remitting part of their profits (Arias *et al.* 1987: 270, 278–81). They were probably Catalans, the principal group in neighbouring Yucatán (F. Savarino 1998: personal communication). After the 1910 revolution, many Spanish merchants lost their property and were expelled from Mexico, some losing their lives (Mörner 1985: 79).

The Spanish and German position in Central America was challenged by an unlikely duo: United Fruit and Maya traders. Two Spanish traders and a German one prospered on Costa Rica's Caribbean coast, acquiring cocoa estates, and the Spaniard Vicente Pérez was a major trader and cocoa producer in 1912. However, the United Fruit Company not only shipped and marketed its own cocoa, but also bought some from smallholders, as it shifted its focus from bananas in Costa Rica and Panama (Quesada Camacho 1977–8: 73, 90, 92). German houses in Guatemala only exported tiny amounts of fine cocoa (Trümper 1996: 29; Wagner 1991: 142). In contrast, Guatemalan Maya traders remained very active in Mesoamerica's internal cocoa trade, going as far as Tabasco to obtain beans (Sapper 1897: 302, 305–7).

Hanseatic Germans played the main role in stimulating the meteoric expansion of cocoa cultivation in the northern Dominican Republic. They had controlled the tobacco trade in previous decades, and they survived the reorientation of cocoa exports from Hamburg to New York (Bryan 1977: 169–71, 174–7; Baud 1982: 69–70). Other exporters in 1914 were Italian and Syrian, as well as 'Cubans', almost certainly Catalans. The category 'Americans' meant men from Puerto Rico, probably Corsicans and Mayorcans (Schoenrich 1918: 238–9; Aubin 1910: xxxii; Bergad 1983). Some large planters exported their own cocoa, at times purchasing beans from surrounding smallholders, but this can only have accounted for a small proportion of total output by 1914 (W. Cordero: e-mail, 22.4.1998). Prior to the development of banks from 1909, merchants acted as bankers, notably Santiago Michelena from Puerto Rico, with rural loans attracting an interest rate of 12 per cent. German import-export houses purchased trade goods on credit at 6 per cent, and advanced them at higher rates to local merchants, who did the same to smallholders, on the strength of the next cocoa harvest. More rarely, loans were secured on land (Bryan 1977: 174–83; Schoenrich 1918: 239–40).

Baud states that the internal cocoa trade of the Dominican Republic was mainly in the hands of local men (Baud 1982: 74). This probably means that peddlers and storekeepers were naturalised, such as the Sephardic Jews from Curaçao, long established and quite assimilated, who were accused of 'usurious' practices in the cocoa zone in 1907 (Bryan 1977: 180; Plummer 1998: 85; Elkin 1980: 19; Hoetink 1970: 104–5). Syrians and Italians began to enter the country as poor peddlers in the 1880s, and gradually set up stores (Schoenrich 1918: 238–9). Catalans mounted a campaign in the 1890s to prevent the entry of Syrians, mainly Maronite Christians from Mount Lebanon, but Syrians controlled about half the country's internal trade by 1914 (Nicholls 1992: 339–43, 353; Hoetink 1970: 109–10; Schoenrich 1918: 238–9).

Hanseatic Germans controlled most of Haïti's export trade by 1914, and a growing Syrian challenge to Black and Mulatto small traders led to discriminatory measures from 1903 (Plummer 1988: ch. 5; 1998). Much cocoa now went to Germany, German planters were active, and the cocoa trade may have fallen into German hands (*Gordian*: IX, 3836; XIII, 1161). However, more than half Jérémie's traders in 1915 were Haïtians, and a dynamic colony of Corsican merchants established itself in and around Cap Haïtien (Plummer 1988: 56–7; Aubin 1910: 337–8).

French and Scottish traders dominated cocoa exports from Trinidad, also making loans to planters (Brereton 1981: 92, 119). Of the four main exporters in Port of Spain around 1900, Fabien, Leotaud and Ambard were French (Johnson 1987: 34). French landowners also set up the Cocoa Planters Association of Trinidad in 1905 to market cocoa abroad, controlling about a fifth of the island's output (Giacottino 1976: II, 573). Scots played an ever-larger role, notably William Gordon, who arrived in Port of Spain in 1865, aged seventeen and with only £17 in his pocket. Family connections landed him a job with the Colonial Bank, and he set up Gordon Grant & Co. in 1876. Apart from trade, Gordon owned estates in Trinidad and Scotland, acted for Coutts Bank of London, sat as unofficial member in the Legislative Council, and took a prominent role in the Chamber of Commerce. In 1911 he was one of two representatives sent to Britain for the coronation of King George V (Harrison 1979: 65–70).

Other communities were important at a local level, especially Chinese shopkeepers and moneylenders (Harrison 1979: 64; Giacottino 1976: II, 568). Immigrant Venezuelans acted as intermediaries. One styled himself 'cocoa merchant' in Port of Spain in 1890, claiming to pay 'the highest price for cocoa' (Moodie-Kublalsingh 1994: 26, 230). These may have been the traders accused in 1894 of paying less for improperly dried beans before selling them on without further drying, and of charging an 'excessive' 5 per cent commission (Johnson 1987: 31).

Trinidad's cocoa sector benefited from abundant credit and low interest rates. In 1896, cocoa estates were reported to be borrowing in London at 7 per cent, in return for consigning their crop to designated firms there (*Gordian*: V, 1711). The Colonial Bank, with a banking monopoly but prohibited from lending on the security of property, provided funds to Port of Spain merchants, who obtained further lines of credit from Britain. Merchants lent to owners of large estates, who in turn made loans to small planters. In 1891, one Port of Spain merchant obtained funds from London at 6 per cent, and lent on at 8 per cent to a cocoa broker, who afforded mortgages to nearly 200 proprietors at 10 per cent, together with the exclusive right to buy their crop (Johnson 1987: 28–30).

Many Christian Dutchmen left Surinam for the Netherlands after the ending of slavery in 1863–73, leading a German to write in 1893 that 'Surinam is not a Dutch colony but a Jewish colony, in the full and classical meaning of the word'. However, Jews also began to emigrate to the Netherlands from around 1900 (Lier 1971: 252, 256–61). The merchant community then became more diversified, including Chinese and Portuguese coming from British Guiana (Panday 1959: 108). Independent traders were joined by agents of American, British and Dutch firms, who purchased cocoa from smallholders and some estate owners. Other planters formed an association in 1898 to sell directly to chocolate manufacturers, accusing intermediaries of deceiving them about prices (*Gordian*: IV, 1251).

Consolidation among European commercial firms in West Africa rarely entailed the monopsonistic practices of later decades (Bauer 1963). Exceptionally, the Deutsche Togogesellschaft obtained a commercial monopoly in 1902, denounced by missionaries as inimical to African cocoa producers (Sebald 1988: 366–7). British firms, mostly from Liverpool, Glasgow, Manchester or Bristol, merged and came to agreements among themselves, but their cartels were incomplete and unstable (Pedler 1974; Lynn 1997). European firms only penetrated slowly into cocoa regions, opening branches inland as railways and roads expanded, and working through African agents (Hopkins 1973: 198–206). There was fierce competition between British firms that erected buying depots in Akim (Akyem Abuakwa), and they sought to attract sellers by making advances on the strength of the harvest (Tudhope 1917: 184–7). In Ashanti (Asante), the first mention of advances came in 1913 (Austin 1984: 398). Syrians arrived in the 1880s, finding it hard to gain a foothold in the Gold Coast and Nigeria cocoa trade, but acting as intermediaries in the nascent cocoa exports of Sierra Leone (Crowder 1982: 294–8; Bauer 1963: 148–9, 160; Cole 1997).

European exporters in British West Africa faced strong competition from indigenous merchants, even in the export trade. There were 292 'native' exporters of cocoa in the Gold Coast in 1918, compared to ninety-eight Europeans, although the volume of business was not specified (Maclaren 1924: 180–1). Some Africans certainly exported on a fair scale, and were connected by telegraph to Europe and by telephone to local branches (Harris 1968: 50). Nigeria's Creole planters came mainly from a merchant background, and Jacob Coker employed four or five produce buyers in the Agege region, selling both his own cocoa and that of others in Lagos. From 1907, the Agege Planters Union, in which Coker was a moving spirit, acted as a 'shipping agency' (Webster 1962: 125–7; Hopkins 1978: 89). Many of those who snapped up land in the Gold Coast to grow cocoa were experienced traders, and they often commercialised their beans to the point of export (Szereszewski 1965: 10). Cocoa was also bought inland by independent African dealers, known as 'cocoa contractors' or 'free sellers', including a few Muslim Hausa from northern Nigeria by the early 1920s (Maclaren 1924: 180–1).

The commercialisation of cocoa in Equatorial Africa differed significantly, for the lion's share was exported by large estates on their own account, sometimes in their own ships. The major planters of São Tomé and Príncipe, traders by origin, mainly owned their harvests till they reached

Lisbon, shipping on the steamers of the Empreza Nacional de Navegação (Velarde 1924: 141). Belgian estate owners in Mayombe sold through Antwerp brokers, who also acted for German trading houses in the city (Vellut 1996: 131). The great Hamburg shipping company of Woermann was one of the first to plant cocoa in Cameroon (Rüger 1960: 159; Rudin 1968: 157–61). The largest company in the second wave of German planters, the Westafrikanische Pflanzungsgesellschaft Victoria (WAPV), acquired a fleet of ships and set up its own commercial department (Michel 1969: 206). Landowners of Fernando Póo, both Creoles and Spaniards, shipped directly to Barcelona from the 1890s, sometimes purchasing the harvests of their weaker brethren. At the same time, the monopolistic Compañía Trasatlántica shipping company obtained its own estates on the island (Clarence-Smith 1994a: 184–5).

Fernando Póo's Creoles also lost much of the internal cocoa trade, as European exporters, especially John Holt, moved into purchasing cocoa in rural areas on a fair scale. The Holt papers indicate that the key to securing cocoa from smaller Creole farmers was to provide services, such as credit, secretarial help, and labour at harvest time. To obtain Bubi cocoa, the company was prepared to ferment and dry the beans. Competition from British exporters grew, notably from another Liverpool firm, the Ambas Bay Company, founded by Walter D. Woodin in 1888 (Pedler 1974: 89–90). The Hamburg firm of E. H. Moritz was also a rising cocoa exporter (Mecklenburg 1913: II, 234–5). Cocoa at the Spanish end was initially handled by half a dozen Catalan houses, notably the Casa Huelín, which also made loans to planters (Clarence-Smith 1994a: 195–6). Ambas Bay and Moritz sought to buttress their position by setting up agencies in Barcelona, where they were among the three main cocoa importers in 1909–10 (Bravo Carbonel 1917: 132, 241).

Cameroon was linked commercially to Fernando Póo, although plantation companies exported most of the harvest. The two Liverpool firms of John Holt and Ambas Bay were locked in rivalry, joined by Woermann and Jantzen und Thormählen from Hamburg (Pedler 1974: 89–90). John Holt purchased wet beans at a 20 per cent discount in 1911, or accepted roughly processed cocoa at a 5 per cent discount for re-drying (LCL 1911). The small Debundscha plantation, set up by a Swedish trader, sold cocoa through the Hamburg firm of Ernst Kraft, which in turn supplied credit (ANC 1896). Yoruba petty traders bought smallholder cocoa in 1916, together with a scattering of other Africans, possibly because of the withdrawal of Hamburg firms during the war (Epale 1985: 75–6).

Although the great bulk of São Tomé and Príncipe's cocoa was exported by a dozen great planters, Portuguese traders, including some Sephardic Jews, bought beans from smaller farmers. 'Native brokers' only seem to have bought cocoa from African smallholders, and they were commonly accused of purchasing beans stolen by plantation workers (Sociedade de Emigração

1915: 9–10, 17, 19; Hall 1914: 314; anon. 1907: 53). A few Chinese, survivors of an ill starred attempt to import 'coolies', owned little stores and probably bought some cocoa (UBL 1909).

Estates in Asia marketed their output through agency houses, firms that specialised in arranging services for planters, whereas smallholders sold to expatriate Asians. Chinese traders in the Philippines increased their hold over the internal cocoa trade through the ownership of small chocolate factories (Hall 1932: 493). In Ceylon, Asian traders, possibly Malabar Muslims, bought a little cocoa for export to India (*Gordian*: X, 4195).

Cartels of planters, 1890s–1910s

A small group of wealthy absentee planters wreaked far more havoc on the international market than the dealers and brokers usually put in the dock. *Der Gordian*, the German cocoa journal founded in 1895, began by accusing London dealers of holding stocks and forcing up prices for German chocolate companies. The alleged perpetrators were not reputable specialised houses, but speculators who moved from one commodity to another, as opportunities arose to move markets. A reader countered by pointing out that only 4 per cent of German supplies came through London, and that Continental buyers were unlikely to accept London auction prices if they were seriously out of line with the underlying supply situation. Hamburg had its own well developed commercial structure for handling cocoa by this time (*Gordian*: III, 1119–20, 1037, 1047–51; IV, 1264–6).

After further accusations levelled at dealers in Le Hâvre and Amsterdam, it dawned on the editors of *Der Gordian* that wealthy planters were responsible for price manipulation. São Tomé planters, resident in Portugal, made their first recorded attempt to nudge prices upwards in 1898, although rotting beans in Lisbon warehouses soon ensured the failure of this scheme (*Gordian*: IV, 1295–6; XII, 1105). To stem a renewed market fall in 1901, the planters enlisted the aid of Henri Burnay, a Belgian immigrant and the foremost Portuguese banker of his day. With ample funds to hand, stocks in Lisbon were reported to have risen to around 75,000 bags of 60 kilos, rather than the usual 20,000–25,000 bags, and prices picked up in response (*Gordian*: VI, 2563; VIII, 3523; IX, 3723–4).

Encouraged by this experience, and angered by the continuing downward drift in prices, São Tomé planters launched their most ambitious assault on the market in 1906. The cartel was headed by the Marquis of Val Flor, the wealthiest São Tomé planter, once again in association with Henri Burnay (UBL 1907). The planters raised £600,000 from Lisbon banks to store 50,000 bags, aiming to maintain a price floor of one mark a kilo. It was alleged that German financiers were involved, and that there was some parallel stocking of Bahia beans. Initial success encouraged the cartel to go further, with stocks hitting a peak of nearly 135,000 bags in February 1907, and prices rising in consequence (Hall 1914: 497; *Gordian*: XII, 756–7, 942, 962–3, 1104–6; XIII, 1163–5, 1171, 1267). Environmental factors helped the cartel, resulting in a temporary tightening of supplies from some major producers (BAAP 1907b).

The cartel's fall was as spectacular as its rise, as it came crashing down in 1908 amid a welter of mutual recriminations (*PA*: XVI, suppl., 111). German and Swiss chocolate manufacturers formed the Kakao-Einkaufsgesellschaft in 1907 to coordinate purchases, joined in 1908 by Danish and French firms, including Menier (BAAP 1907b; 1908c). British manufacturers signalled their willingness to assist in breaking the ring (Fitzgerald 1995: 106–7). However, the Dutch pointed to the spoiling of stored beans as the real weakness of the 'trust' (Schrover 1991: 175).

A Trust del Cacao was formed in Barcelona in November 1907, to push up the price of Fernando Póo cocoa in Spain, semi-detached from the world market. Inspired by the success of São Tomé planters, the trust associated the Camara Agrícola de Fernando Póo, representing large planters on the island, and half a dozen Barcelona importers. Although initially successful, the cartel was busted by Barcelona wholesale merchants in 1908, with the help of supplies obtained from the British Ambas Bay Company (Sanz Casas 1983: 189–91).

Broader and more official efforts to shore up prices soon emerged. In 1908, negotiations were reported in Rio de Janeiro between representatives of the cocoa sectors of Bahia, Pará and São Tomé (*Gordian*: XIV, 2056). In the same year, the commercial attaché at the Portuguese legation in Paris initiated talks with his Brazilian and Ecuadorian counterparts to encourage the formation of an international syndicate of planters and merchants, as the three countries controlled about 60 per cent of world cocoa output between them. With access to government guaranteed loans, the syndicate would set a minimum purchase price and build up a stock to achieve this purpose. Indignantly rejecting the label of 'speculators', the proposers asserted that they were merely trying to protect honest producers from the wiles of middlemen and manufacturers (Greenhill 1972: 24–5). In 1908, São Tomé planters attempted to enlist the backing of a Berlin organisation representing the owners of German estates in Cameroon (BAAP 1908d). Trinidad planters expressed interest in the syndicate in 1909, as did planters and merchants from the Dominican Republic (*PA*: XVI, suppl., 110–11).

Disagreements quickly surfaced between the main players. The Brazilians and Ecuadorians accused São Tomé planters of secretly selling beans from stocks in Lisbon. Ecuadorian planters complained that the scheme took no account of the finer quality of their cocoa, while Bahia merchants were apprehensive about the high cost of the enterprise (Greenhill 1972: 24–5; *PA*: XVI, suppl., 110–11).

The great Ecuadorian planter, Julián Aspiazu, attempted to put the cartel on a sounder footing. In late 1910, he mooted a planters' association in

Ecuador, seeking official backing for a mandatory tax of one sucre per *quintal* of exported cocoa, to finance a retention scheme. Aspiazu met in Paris in early 1911 with a former governor of the state of Bahia, and with Francisco Mantero, a wealthy São Tomé planter of Spanish origins. Diplomatic representatives of the three countries gave their backing to the formation of three associations of planters, which would jointly fix a minimum price, set export quotas, and select warehouses to stock cocoa (Arosemena 1991: I, 386–90).

Forming associations was the easy part, whereas finance and discipline proved difficult. The three São Tomé planters elected to run the Portuguese association could come to no agreement on financing the scheme. They even entertained a proposal by a shadowy group of British businessmen to purchase the whole São Tomé crop in advance for three to six years, in return for official permission to buy estates. Finance was also the sticking point in Ecuador, where the government hesitated to impose a supplementary tax on exports. Bahia was the weakest link, for there were few large planters, and merchants were dubious about the scheme. The Bahia authorities refused more than token financial assistance, while the federal government in Rio de Janeiro, facing the mounting costs of coffee 'valorisation', refused a loan. By early 1912, the Portuguese and the Brazilians had effectively dropped out of the 'triple alliance', although it lingered on for a few more years (*Gordian*: XVII, 4363–5, 4736–7, 4912–15; XVIII, 5437).

The Asociación de Agricultores del Ecuador engaged in a final attempt to buck the market on its own. Portraying itself as the champion of producers, it obtained the right to levy one sucre per exported *quintal* of cocoa from January 1913. The Asociación bought about a quarter of the harvest at a guaranteed price, paid half in cash and half in chits. Attempts to force up the world price by withholding stocks failed, however, resulting in heavy losses (*Gordian*: XIX, 6412–14; XX, 7351). In 1916, the government authorised a tripling of the export levy, eroded by inflation, and ever-larger loans were obtained from the Banco Comercial y Agrícola, dominated by planters. The real value of cash payments to producers fell, and the redemption of chits was repeatedly delayed, but the association nevertheless purchased 81 per cent of the country's output in 1917. It stored beans to an estimated value of some seven million sucres in London and four million sucres in New York. The Mercantile Bank of the Americas in New York, the association's agent and main foreign creditor, flooded the market when loans were not repaid, contributing to the world cocoa slump of 1921. When young army officers seized power in 1925, they dissolved the Asociación and the Banco Comercial y Agrícola, bankrupting the Mercantile Bank of the Americas and initiating a long and bitter diplomatic row with Washington (Chiriboga 1980: 376–99; Arosemena 1991: I, 285–314; Maiguashca 1996: 78–9).

The most serious legacy of these ill conceived cartels was the stupendous wave of planting in West Africa and Bahia, stimulated by the price spike of 1907. Given that the millions of trees planted at this time came into full bearing around 1915, and continued to bear for at least twenty years and often more, the real world price of cocoa was dragged down for decades, as William Cadbury had rightly predicted at the time.

Conclusion

Extraordinary freedom for migrants, probably greater than at any other time in world history, unleashed fiercely competitive commercial diasporas around the cocoa-producing countries, and yet historians have tended to ignore or vilify them. Although they were a dynamo for economic development, information about them is extremely scanty. Together with detailed studies of how these communities operated in tropical countries, there is a crying need for research on their home areas and cultures, addressing the elusive question of the roots of entrepreneurship. The rise of Hanseatic, Swiss, Corsican and Genoese cocoa merchants in the early nineteenth century is almost as mysterious as the novel prominence of traders from Syria and China at the end of the century. Of all the major communities that crop up in this chapter, it was hardest to obtain information on the Genoese, Elbans and other Italians.

At the level of brokers and dealers in Western cities, the fog is even denser. It is possible that Sephardic Jews and Basques built on their earlier experience, but even the names of brokers and dealers are almost completely unknown. Eduard Douwes Dekker's unforgettable fictional portrait of Droogstoppel, the Dutch scrooge buying Indonesian coffee, makes one long for good historical research on this topic (Multatuli 1991).

What is abundantly clear is that artificially forcing up the world price was a disastrous policy for a slow-maturing crop like cocoa. It would thus be helpful to find out more about how these early cartels actually operated, so as better to understand the later disruptive impact of Third World governments on the world cocoa market.

6

ACCESS TO FORESTED LAND

The need for supplies of virgin forest engendered complex struggles over rights to land between local people, immigrant smallholders, and owners of large estates. The state attempted to arbitrate, but was usually weak in remote forested areas, and many land disputes have simmered on until our own day. Large landowners, often absentees, mostly obtained official concessions of 'waste lands', while immigrant smallholders sought accommodation with indigenous inhabitants. Some of the original forest dwellers suffered from 'ethnic cleansing', others were outnumbered by immigrant strangers, while yet others became the major local cocoa producers.

Owing to advantages gained from cutting down virgin forest, individuals and corporations tended to seek large blocks of uncultivated land from the state. These usually evolved into 'demesne estates', where owners kept direct control of cultivation. However, a contractor might be employed to establish a cocoa plantation, taking most or all production decisions in the early years. 'Rentier estates' were less common, consisting of many different plots, often non-contiguous and built up by foreclosing on debts or purchasing from small farmers. Production decisions on such estates generally had to be left to cash tenants or sharecroppers, who functioned like smallholders.

Definitions of smallholdings are legion. Those based on the expanse of land, the number of trees, or the size of the labour force, are arbitrary in terms of the organisation of production. The definition adopted here is taken from Surinam, where smallholders were deemed to be cocoa producers who laboured themselves on their lands with family members, and might be assisted by extra-familial labour (Lier 1971: 222). If a smallholding grew, the owner and family members progressively withdrew from direct production. At the point that most labour was performed by people from outside the family, the holding became a small estate. Effective control of land was what mattered, not legal ownership, so that squatters are included in this definition of smallholders. 'Small farmers' might be a better term, but 'smallholders' has become firmly entrenched in the literature.

There were no economies of scale in the cultivation of cocoa, as neither gang labour nor mechanisation brought substantial advantages, while managerial diseconomies of scale were greatly magnified by conditions on the forest frontier (Berry 1975: 181–2). Latin American elites, owning land as much for social prestige as for economic reasons, countered this problem through extensive forms of production, also found in central Java. In a seminal article, Wolf and Mintz called agricultural units of this type *haciendas*, distinguished from intensive 'plantations'. However, they went on to assert that *haciendas* were less efficient, and only produced for the market to a limited degree (Wolf and Mintz 1957). The experience of cocoa suggests that the reverse could be true. *Haciendas* made Ecuador the greatest supplier of cocoa to the world market in the nineteenth century, and attempts at intensive cocoa cultivation ended in tears.

The prevalence of estates helps to explain why cocoa often failed to bring prosperity in its wake. Many of the returns on the 'golden bean' were soaked up in high overhead costs. The profits that remained were concentrated in the hands of a few landlords, who either wasted them in conspicuous consumption, or remitted them to Western banks. High production costs and distorted income distribution were a poor recipe for economic development.

Estate agriculture and its rivals under the ancien regime

Cocoa was mainly grown by European planters on demesne estates by 1765, due to the social influence of landowners and the ready availability of servile labour. However, these estates were generally smaller than for sugar, and quite a few were owned by individuals of mixed race. Moreover, some Amerindian smallholders clung to cocoa, despite appalling death rates, while others took it up after the Iberian conquest. They were joined by poor European immigrants, people of mixed race, freed African slaves, and even enslaved Africans enjoying usufructory rights.

The extent to which cocoa groves passed into the hands of Spaniards after the conquest of Mesoamerica has probably been exaggerated (Gasco 1987: xi–xii, 5, 139, 164–9, 236; Ruz 1994: 187–9; Browning 1975: 121–2). Many Amerindian smallholders initially paid tribute to Spanish *encomenderos*, often in cocoa beans, and then switched their tribute to the crown, as *encomiendas* were abolished in all but the most remote areas. Lay and ecclesiastical cocoa estates emerged when indigenous mortality, due to imported diseases, effectively left land vacant (MacLeod 1973; Gerhard 1979). Small estates were most typical of southern Mesoamerica, modern Nicaragua and Costa Rica, where less of the indigenous population survived and cocoa cultivation developed later (Romero Vargas 1976; Rosés Alvarado 1982).

The bias towards estates was considerable in Spanish South America, where there was no indigenous cocoa growing prior to conquest. *Encomiendas* in Venezuela and Guayaquil involved labour services rather than tribute in kind, encouraging *encomenderos* to carve out cocoa estates from the forests in the late sixteenth century. These were usually recognised by the crown in return for a fee, after a decent interval (Ferry 1989; Hamerly 1973). Amerindians learned to grow cocoa in Venezuela, and were joined as smallholders by people of mixed race and immigrant Canarians. Even African slaves grew a little cocoa, on plots granted in usufruct, and runaway slaves sometimes did so as well (Piñero 1992; 1994; Patiño 1963: 314). Estate and peasant cultivation developed more slowly in the inland valleys of modern Colombia and the Amazonian piedmont of modern Peru and Bolivia (Patiño 1963: 314–15; Brisseau Loaiza 1981: 115–16; Eder 1985).

Portuguese monarchs favoured estates, but it was the collection of wild Amazonian cocoa that developed in seventeenth-century Brazil. Catholic missionaries, especially Jesuits, ran villages of 'tame' Amerindian collectors, and forged partnerships with 'wild' suppliers in the forests. This foraging economy spilled over Brazil's ill defined frontiers, into Spanish territory and the interior of the Guianas (Alden 1976; Patiño 1963: 276–93; Coudreau 1886–7: I, 28; Daly 1975: 18–21, 77, 86).

European interlopers in the Caribbean and the Guianas grew cocoa on small estates from the late seventeenth century. English enthusiasm for the crop waned soon after the seizure of Jamaica, and the largest producers were French Martinique and the Dutch Guianas (Craton and Walvin 1970: 19, 31; May 1930: 94–5; Daly 1975: 68, 77; Reyne 1924–5: 5, 7, 11–12). Cocoa in the islands was typically a crop of small French planters, who often took up coffee at a later date. Resident on their properties and owning few slaves, they were frequently of mixed race (Blérald 1986: 26, 97).

Southeast Asian cocoa was in the hands of indigenous smallholders. Lay estates hardly developed in the Philippines, and clerical estates were of the rentier type, with missionaries teaching converts how to grow cocoa from the 1660s (Mallat 1983: 190, 246; Jagor 1875: 94; Foreman 1906: 301). The Dutch tried to grow cocoa from 1706 on settler properties in western Java, but it failed to prosper and disappeared from the sources (Haan 1910–12: III, 493, 863). The Dutch East India Company then focused on the Moluccas, obliging Amboina (Ambon) smallholders to grow it as a minor complement to cloves from 1723 (Coolhaas 1960: VII, 414, 456, 681; Knaap 1987: 313, 390, 501).

The zenith of estates, 1760s–1790s

A new stress on the benefits of private land became apparent, and Spanish reformers particularly criticised the policy of leaving so much land to indigenous inhabitants, in a separate 'Republic of Indians'. The challenge to the privileges of the Church simultaneously weakened the most effective champion of corporate indigenous land rights. However, estates were not necessarily the intended beneficiaries of reform, as some officials wished to convert Amerindians into 'yeomen farmers' on individual plots (McGreevey 1971: 54–6; McCreery 1994: 50–2; Wortman 1982: 173).

The alienation of Amerindian lands was still proceeding on the marches of Venezuela, but land around Caracas was mainly acquired by inheritance, purchase or marriage (McKinley 1985: 25, 79–88). The development of the dynamic Barlovento pioneer front took place mainly on land claimed by descendants of former *encomenderos*, although displaced Amerindians attacked newly created estates in El Guapo in 1775 (Tamaro 1988: 114).

Individual cocoa estates were generally small, although families might own several. The 1,144 *haciendas* of Caracas province in 1787 contained an average of less than 10,000 cocoa trees each. Even the 200 largest units averaged only about 20,000 trees. Of a sample of sixty-one estates between 1777 and 1811, only seven covered more than 200 hectares, including fallow (McKinley 1985: 46–51). The largest estate in Barlovento for which a fee was paid extended over some 1,250 hectares (Tamaro 1988: 99). Members of the elite intermarried to keep lands in the family, paying 1,500 pesos to the Church to overcome the prohibition on unions between first cousins. Alternatively, they brought wealthy Basque and Canarian traders into the family through marriage. They almost invariably resided in Caracas, and the Marques del Toro even lived in Spain. Wills revealed a few cocoa planters of mixed race, such as Gervasio de Ponte, illegitimate scion of a great Caracas family (McKinley 1985: 20, 28, 79–88, 101–2, 200; Tamaro 1988: 104, 108, 146–65, 236). In the frontier region of eastern Venezuela, people of few means could still assure a decent living for their families by the possession of 30,000 cocoa trees (Humboldt 1852: I, 288).

The official preference for small land grants favoured Canarian pioneers in Barlovento. Two powerful noble landowners of Caracas requested a large piece of land in El Guapo, but it was ceded to a syndicate of Canarians in 1774, to be divided up between them. Canarians tended to live on their estates, on poor terms with the snobbish Caracas elite. Two Canarian brothers, who owned nearly 50,000 cocoa trees between them in the 1780s, were refused the honorific title 'Don' (Tamaro 1988: 36, 120–2, 199–200, 279–80, 283).

The 1787 survey of Caracas province also revealed an 'infinity of plots…not formally *haciendas*', apparently lacking freehold title (McKinley 1985: 49). Such cocoa squatters were numerous on the Barlovento pioneer front. Mainly of mixed race, some were *agregados*, allowed to settle informally on the fringes of estates, in return for labour services. Others, like the community of free Blacks in Curiepe, were autonomous. An elite family won a long legal battle over the ownership of Curiepe in the 1780s, but the free Blacks retained usufructory rights. Most had under a thousand trees, but a few had more. Officials refused them permission to send their beans to La Guaira by boat (Tamaro 1988: 71–4, 109–19, 160–1, 205–7, 260, 281).

The unusual Venezuelan phenomenon of a servile 'cocoa proto-peasantry' persisted, despite planter challenges. The administrators of the Chuao coastal plantation decided to put an end to this in 1771, but it persisted elsewhere (Brito Figueroa 1985: 116–17). Slaves were granted access to plots of estate land, on which they were allowed to grow cocoa. Some sold seedlings to their masters for transplanting, others handed over plots for a fee when trees had reached the age of bearing, and yet others harvested their own trees. Landowners alleged that this encouraged the theft of estate beans and the diversion of more labour time than the one day a week theoretically allocated to slaves for work on their plots. However, managers of estates were reluctant to risk disorder by abolishing the system (Tamaro 1988: 27, 56–7, 226, 239–40).

The output of Amerindian cultivators was small and largely oriented towards subsistence. There was little communal land left in Barlovento, where Amerindians rarely appeared as cocoa producers for the market (Tamaro 1988: 205, 281). However, Amerindians still contributed to cocoa exports from the valleys to the west of Caracas, where the surviving population was concentrated (Piñero 1994: 83; McKinley 1985: 25).

In western Venezuela and the Nuevo Reino (Colombia), estates predominated, but Amerindians played a role. Cúcuta and the southern fringes of Lake Maracaibo were characterised by small properties, intensively cultivated with African slaves (Brungardt 1974: 90; Cardozo Galué 1991: 22–4, 53, 55, 63). Estates also appeared on the Magdalena, above Honda and around Mompós, with one estate in the latter area containing 100,000 cocoa trees in 1787 (Patiño 1963: 308–17; Brew 1977: 243; McFarlane 1993: 41, 78, 139). However, over a hundred Amerindian households owned cocoa farms in Cúcuta around 1750, Amerindian cocoa groves were scattered along the Magdalena basin and across the Darien isthmus, and Amerindian households in Antioquia were ordered to plant ten cocoa trees a year in 1788. One community in the Magdalena was compensated for its cocoa trees in 1752, when the population was forcibly removed to a new site. Other Amerindians harassed colonial planters, notably the Motilones, on the western side of Lake Maracaibo, and peoples of the Darien isthmus (Patiño 1963: 274, 301–2, 307–8, 312–15, 321–2, 326, 333).

Amerindians in the cocoa lands of the Guayas plain had little land left, although a Quito judge was accused of taking some in the Milagro region in 1766 (Chiriboga 1980: 167). Small-scale cocoa cultivation by Amerindians developed in the northern outpost of Esmeraldas, though this was rare in the Guayas plain (Patiño 1963: 312–13). Amerindian communities in the west of the coastal strip owned much land in 1803, but the area was too dry for cocoa (Laviana Cuetos 1987: 150–1; Hamerly 1970: 130).

'Waste land' was easily obtained from the Guayaquil town council, property being granted after thirty years of peaceful and continuous occupation (Weinman 1970: 18). Two thirds of the cocoa trees planted between 1780 and 1787 belonged to just 15 per cent of *hacendados*, indicating that estates were growing in size (Laviana Cuetos 1987: 177–9). Although small in the older production zones around Babahoyo, estates were larger in the new cocoa region of Balao (Contreras 1994: 204–5; Hamerly 1970: 138–9). However, land appropriation also benefited people of mixed race and acculturated Amerindians, as the authorities were well disposed towards small cultivators (Hamerly 1973: 105).

Indigenous cocoa cultivation persisted in Mesoamerica. Tabasco's Chontal Maya accounted for a large share of cocoa output, and had secure title to land (Gerhard 1979: 43). They received numerous concessions from the 1760s, one group paying over 400 pesos in 1797 for land in what became Cárdenas (Arias *et al.* 1987: 33, 37; Gil y Saenz 1979: xxix, 150; Ruz 1994: 241–3). Further west, they planted cocoa along the rivers leading to the frontier with Veracruz (Scherr 1985: 39). Amerindian religious brotherhoods also owned cocoa groves (Ruz 1994: 236–7). Soconusco's Mam Maya also continued to grow cocoa (Gasco 1987: xi–xii, 5, 138–9, 167–8, 236). In Oaxaca, eighty families lived off their groves in one settlement in 1763, although the cochineal boom depressed cultivation (Stols 1996: 45; Mangin 1860: 18–19). Nicaragua's Amerindians grew a little cocoa, with mission support (Newson 1987: 294, 305). The Jicaque of northern Honduras either grew it or collected wild pods (Rubio Sánchez 1958: 91).

Tabasco's cocoa estates were probably growing faster, however, expanding in all directions. There were only twenty-four *hacendados* listed in 1766, with two surviving *encomenderos* (Ruiz Abreu 1989: 28). The wealthiest planter in 1783, the Spaniard Antonio Correa Benavides, owned 52,888 bearing cocoa trees on four different properties. By 1794 there were nearly 200 estates in Tabasco, although they focused on cattle as much as cocoa (Ruz 1994: 185–6). Pioneer cocoa farmers pushed west into Acayucán, part of Veracruz, and even moved up the coast to Tlacotalpan, close to the city of Veracruz (Arcila Farias 1950: 82–3). Complex struggles broke out between lay and ecclesiastical authorities to control the abundant tithes engendered by these settlers (Ruz 1994: 185–90, 252–3). Spanish cocoa planters also went south, founding a new settlement in Pichucalco (Gerhard 1979: 44). Cocoa cultivation may even have been attempted to the east, near Campeche (Pelletier and Pelletier 1861: 40).

Estates prospered elsewhere in Mesoamerica, especially in Nicaragua, which had about 1.5 million cocoa trees by 1800. Mainly around Rivas, they yielded high tithes (Salvatierra 1939: II, 36–7, 206; Romero Vargas 1976: 449–54; Wortman 1982: 194, 282–3). The little cocoa estates in the Matina valley of Costa Rica were reaching a second modest peak in the 1780s (Touzard 1993: 37–8). Concessions had never formally been approved by the crown, but the land was treated as private property (Fonseca 1986: 228–30, 233). In 1768, there were 120 small estates spread over about 12 kilometres (Wortman 1982: 164). Some 190,000 trees produced a harvest of about 150 tonnes in 1776, with another 170,000 trees not yet bearing (Salvatierra

1939: II, 207). Many estates belonged to residents of Cartago, and were worked by tenants, including Mulattos and freed slaves (Rosés Alvarado 1975: 259, 278). The old Soconuscan, Guatemalan and Salvadoran estates suffered from exhaustion and competition from indigo, but there was renewed planting of cocoa towards the end of the century (Solano 1974: 325–6, 340; Touzard 1993: 30–1; Rubio Sánchez 1958: 90–1; Medina Hernández 1993: 466–7; Carvalho 1994: 86).

The Spaniards fostered estate cocoa in their Caribbean islands, albeit in the shadow of other crops. French settlers came to Trinidad from 1776, attracted by the offer of free land and tax concessions. Many of these families, amounting to some 4,000 people in all by 1802, were of mixed race. By 1797 there were sixty cocoa estates on the island, compared to 150 for sugar, 130 for coffee, and 103 for cotton. To make room for the French, the authorities annulled dubious titles and those for uncultivated lands (Sevilla Soler 1988). One group of Amerindians, deemed unable to cultivate their lands properly, were moved in 1785 to make space for immigrant cocoa planters (Newson 1976: 196). In Cuba, large tracts of the central provinces of Remedios and Puerto Príncipe, owned in common as cattle pasture, were partitioned to develop cocoa and other cash crops (Marrero 1972–89: X, 85–6).

Spanish efforts in the Amazon-Orinoco basin enjoyed mixed results. Estates only developed in the deep valleys near Cuzco, producing cocoa at lower levels (Brisseau Loaiza 1981: 115–16; *MP*: XII, 112–13). After the expulsion of the Jesuits in 1767, the Mojos of modern Bolivia paid tribute in cocoa and chocolate to parish priests, and then to officials from 1790 (Eder 1985: 150; Orbigny 1992: 162–4; Chávez Suárez 1944: 430–2, 449–50). The Franciscan neighbours of the Mojos organised their converts to collect wild cocoa, described in 1790 as a major source of finance for charitable and religious works in and around Apolobamba. Independent gatherers from the Spanish Amazon also crossed the indeterminate international boundary to sell wild cocoa to the Portuguese in Olivença, in return for metal fishhooks and other supplies (Patiño 1963: 282–96). Each Amerindian household in San Fernando de Atabapo, on the Orinoco, had its own small cocoa plot around 1800, with mission backing (Humboldt 1852: II, 335).

Collection from the wild predominated in Brazil, although official exhortations to plant cocoa found an echo. After the expulsion of the Jesuits in the late 1750s, their flagship estate in the Amazon, containing 40,000 cocoa trees, was rented out by the state (Patiño 1963: 327). Estates expanded around Santarém, partly because of the excessive exploitation of wild trees, and plantations were reported along the Negro in 1775 (Ross 1978: 203, 208; MacLachlan 1973: 214). In the captaincies of Ilhéus and Porto Seguro, later annexed to Bahia, fierce indigenous resistance restricted agriculture to a narrow coastal strip poorly suited for cocoa. However, the Jesuits experimented with the crop, and the Sá Bittencourt family, which acquired lands

of expelled Jesuits, showed great faith in cocoa. The crown encouraged cultivation, granting settlers the right to organise expeditions to capture and kill
'wild Indians' in the 1770s, but there was little or no progress beyond the
traditional pale of settlement (Mahony 1996: 63–78, 86–117).

Estates in the Guianas did best in Surinam, where a property containing
120,000 cocoa trees was taken as the norm in 1770 (Reyne 1924–5: 196–7). A
great coffee boom, fuelled by incautious loans from Dutch merchants,
collapsed in 1775, allowing cocoa to prosper (Stipriaan 1995b: 74–82; 1993).
Dutch planters also grew some cocoa in Demerara and Berbice (Farley
1956: 19; Daly 1975: 86; Reyne 1924–5: 61–2; Kramer 1991: 56–9). French
Guiana's cocoa exports fell from the 1760s, in part because of competition
from new crops such as cloves and cotton, with a mere 170,000 cocoa trees
left on estates in 1787 (Cardoso 1984: 27; Hall 1932: 355). The colony also
suffered from the expulsion of the Jesuits in 1764, as their Amerindian
wards had been responsible for about half the colony's output in 1760
(Coudreau 1886–7: I, 28).

Small planters continued to dominate cultivation in the French islands
(Dupuy 1989: 26–7; Lasserre 1961: I, 365; Patiño 1963: 326). Martinique
contained over a million cocoa trees by the early 1780s, about four times the
total in Guadeloupe (Schnakenbourg 1977: 60–2). In 1791, about half Saint-
Domingue's sixty-nine cocoa estates were in the southwest, with the rest
along the north and south coasts (Edwards 1801: 143, 212–3). Small planters
frequently grew coffee as well as cocoa, and only two big estates in Saint-
Domingue specialised in cocoa, both in Dame Marie (Moral 1961: 302).

There was a rush to buy land in the small Caribbean islands attributed to
Britain in 1763, with Grenada emerging as the main cocoa producer in the
British empire. However, most cocoa and coffee producers were French,
often of mixed race, while many Britons who came to grow sugar withdrew
after the financial crisis of 1772 (Ragatz 1977: 127; Cox 1984: 64–5; Brizan
1984: 59; Trouillot 1988: 54, 59; Carrington 1988: 13–14). Indeed, French
planters of mixed race migrated to British islands in protest at France's
restoration of legal discrimination against free persons of colour in 1766
(Honychurch 1984: 54–5, 61, 66, 76–7; Lasserre 1961: I, 365).

Cocoa cultivation in Southeast Asia remained limited. The Spaniards
sought to develop export crops, but results for cocoa did not match expecta-
tions (Díaz-Trechuelo 1964). The Dutch obtained new supplies of planting
material from the Philippines for estates in West Java, and cocoa was grown by
Moluccan smallholders in Amboina and Banda in 1796 (Haan 1910–12: III,
863). Cocoa was thriving in north Sulawesi in 1804, with hopes for exports
(Clarence-Smith 1998: 97). It was also cultivated in the Islamic sultanates
lying between the Dutch and Spanish possessions (Warren 1981: 43).

The threat to estates, 1790s–1820s

Gains made by smallholders in the aftermath of the French Revolution were limited and precarious. The woes of estates were by no means always to the advantage of smallholders. Blockades harmed planters in the Caribbean Basin, but benefited rivals in neutral or remote territories. Campaigns for independence ravaged some plantations repeatedly, while leaving others unharmed. Servile uprisings undermined estates here, but fostered them there.

The French ending of slavery in 1794 promised a future as cocoa smallholders for ex-slaves. The sudden spurt in French Guiana's cocoa exports suggests that freed slaves did not simply retreat into subsistence, although it may also have been due to smuggling from Surinam under British occupation (Cardoso 1984: 67, 76). Haïtian smallholders were among the few to make unambiguous gains, as they successfully resisted Napoleon's reinstatement of slavery in 1802. Although military rulers only gradually and incompletely broke up confiscated French properties, they sold the Dame Marie cocoa estates of Galais and Morel in small lots. This was in terms of a law of 1814, which sought to restore production by increasing the number of small proprietors (Rouzier 1892–3: I, 290). However, King Christophe handed out estates to his cronies in a cocoa-growing area of the northern Cap Haïtien region (Aubin 1910: 329).

The Haïtian Revolution simultaneously spread cocoa estates around the Caribbean basin. Some 27,000 refugees had settled in Cuba by about 1820, mainly in the almost empty eastern region around Santiago (Marrero 1951: 608; Marrero 1972–89: XI, 101, 134). Roughly one third were Whites, one third free Coloureds, and one third slaves (Mörner 1985: 17). They came in waves, with six boatloads leaving Port-au-Prince as late as 1813. Those who had not become naturalised after five years of residence were forced to leave in 1808, but many returned from New Orleans and elsewhere in 1814 (Pérez de la Riva 1944: 24–31, 37–8, 142; Wright 1910: 361–2). These French settlers grew sugar in the plains, planted coffee and cocoa in the mountains above, and clung to their language (Aubin 1910: xxx–xxxi, 193; Wright 1910: 361–2). In 1809, another group was growing sugar, coffee and cocoa in the Samaná peninsula of Santo Domingo, too close to Haïti for safety (Vega and Cordero Michel 1993: 39). Around a hundred French families went to grow coffee and cocoa in the mountains of Jamaica (Aubin 1910: xxxi–xxxii). More went to eastern Venezuela to cultivate cocoa and other crops (Harwich Vallenilla 1996: 34).

Later uprisings dispersed French cocoa planters even more widely. After the failure of the Grenada rebellion of 1795–6, many French families emigrated to Trinidad (Brizan 1984: 93–4). The British conquest of Trinidad in 1797 led to a renewed outflow across the straits to the Paria peninsula of eastern Venezuela, where they gave a further boost to cocoa cultivation

(Humboldt 1852: I, 289). The French colony comprised some 7,000 souls in 1804, mainly from Trinidad, Tobago and Grenada (Moodie-Kublalsingh 1994: 153). In 1802, the governor of Cumaná complained that the French were settling on lands legally reserved for Amerindians (Harwich Vallenilla 1996: 34, 36–7). Nevertheless, the French and Spaniards allegedly grew 'all the cocoa' in Trinidad in 1810, accounting for a tenth of the planted area (Williams 1952: 5; Brereton 1981: 47).

Some South American cocoa producers were devastated by the independence struggle. Landowners in eastern Venezuela fled between 1817 and 1820, many to Trinidad, as their homes were sacked and burned, leaving former slaves to take over their cocoa groves (Harwich Vallenilla 1996: 25, 34–5; Moodie-Kublalsingh 1994: 153–4). Similarly, Cúcuta estates were repeatedly ravaged and half destroyed (Brungardt 1974: 82–6). In the lower Patía valley of southwestern Colombia, one Spanish landowner abandoned his forty hectares of cocoa (Patiño 1963: 302). Further south, rebel Amerindians burned down the Franciscan missions of Apolobamba (Patiño 1963: 290).

The impact was highly regional, but nowhere escaped completely. Although agriculture suffered little physical damage in Caracas, victorious forces repeatedly sequestered cocoa estates, doling them out to supporters, or renting them for short periods (Izard 1972: 109–17). Storage capacity also told against cocoa in much blockaded Caracas. Cocoa beans only kept for ten to twelve months before going mouldy, whereas coffee beans survived tolerably well for several years, encouraging planters to switch to coffee (Humboldt 1852: I, 288, 478; Nuñez 1972: 552–3).

Landowners in Mesoamerica benefited from the weakening of Spanish authority, with Tabascan planters stepping up the seizure of Amerindian lands (Ruz 1994: 184, 189–90). In Suchitepéquez, Guatemala, Amerindians owned around three times as many cocoa trees as outsiders in 1799, but by 1818 the situation had been reversed (Rubio Sánchez 1958: 90; Dunn 1829: 271). Estates also expanded around Tapachula in Soconusco, although there were still some 800 'native' cocoa plots in 1820 (Carvalho 1994: 85–6, 228–30; Gasco 1987: 168). There were about 700 small cocoa *haciendas* in the Rivas area of southwestern Nicaragua in 1817, with others in the Nicoya peninsula (Salvatierra 1939: II, 36–7). To be sure, the number of cocoa trees in Costa Rica's Matina Plain in 1814 fell to a third of 1770s figures, most planters had less than 2,000 trees still standing, and the region barely met its consumption needs. However, some planters emigrated to Nicaragua to start afresh (Quesada Camacho 1989: 87, 107; Salvatierra 1939: II, 207).

Some Central Americans argued that cocoa's future depended on small farmers. Guatemala's Sociedad de Amigos del País, founded in 1795 and influenced by Adam Smith, offered prizes to Amerindians planting over 500 cocoa trees in Soconusco and Suchitepéquez (Solórzano 1963: 229–30). The *alcalde mayor* of Escuintla did likewise, further proposing that parish priests should use their influence to promote the crop (Rubio Sánchez 1958: 91–2). One cleric in Guatemala argued in 1799 that dividing up communal lands to the benefit of Amerindian and Mestizo yeomen farmers was the best way to restore cocoa to its former glory (Touzard 1993: 80–2).

Neutral Brazil witnessed a slight shift towards estate cultivation. In the Amazon, cocoa estates were concentrated around Santarém, Obidos and Monte Alegre in 1803 (Cardoso 1984: 127, 173). In what was to become southern Bahia, the defeat and forced settlement of the Camacán in 1806 was a milestone, potentially freeing the forest between the Rio de Contas and the Rio Pardo for settlement. However, attacks by Pataxó and Botocudo continued, and cocoa cultivation actually declined, as the Haïti risings made sugar and coffee more attractive. Indeed, continuing military repression of the Botocudo was mainly undertaken to allow cotton and gems from the interior to pass unmolested to the coast (Spix and Martius 1976: II, 49–50, 138–9, 166–8, 173). Nevertheless, when the pioneer German settler Pedro Weyll received the lands of a former Jesuit mission from the crown in 1815, acculturated Amerindians refused to give up their cocoa groves (Mahony 1996: 447–8).

As abolition progressed, the thoughts of European reformers turned to producing tropical crops in Africa. Sierra Leone was set up as the 'province of freedom' in 1787, and Adam Afzelius, a Swedish botanist, reported seeing cocoa trees in the Freetown and Sherbro areas in 1793 (Are and Gwynne-Jones 1974: 8). Conditions for agriculture were scarcely propitious in the little colony of freed slaves, wracked by internal conflict, attacked by Africans, and pillaged by the French, although cocoa seems to have been grown for internal use (Peterson 1969: 17–80, 273). The Danish crown ordered the planting of cocoa on the Gold Coast in 1788, shortly before abolishing the Atlantic slave trade in 1792 (Dickson 1969: 128). Paul Isert developed small coffee plantations inland, obtaining forest land from the Akwapim council, but there was no mention of cocoa, and these plantations were abandoned in 1802 (Nørregard 1966: 172–83, 189; Macau 1973: 25–7, 40). Dutch missionaries may have been the first to plant cocoa on the Gold Coast, in 1815, but cultivation did not persist (Are and Gwynne-Jones 1974: 7).

The British occupation of most of the Dutch possessions in Asia after 1795 led to experiments with cocoa. In 1798, eight Criollo seedlings from the Moluccas were sent to the southern tip of India. By 1819, there were sixty-seven young plants there (Bhat n.d.: 8). The British found a few cocoa trees growing well in Dutch Malacca, perhaps the source of experimental plantations in Penang in 1802 (Wright and Cartwright 1908: 69; Burkill 1966: 2188; Buckley 1965: 361). British naval blockades simultaneously encouraged production for local consumption in Java, remaining under Dutch rule till 1811, with cocoa estates spreading from around Batavia (Jakarta) into the foothills (Haan 1910–12: III, 863–4).

Estates in an era of stagnation, 1820s–1840s

Independence strengthened the position of landowners, but weak states and economic depression ensured that demand for land remained subdued. Liberals had little capacity to implement individual land tenure and common citizenship for Amerindians, and they were often replaced by conservatives. There was some confiscation of Church property, and officials were sometimes paid with public land, but this was balanced by a cautious defence of municipal and Amerindian rights, for fear of provoking rebellions. Where slavery came to an end, rulers were reluctant to allow former slaves to become smallholders.

The indigenous communal lands (*resguardos*) of Gran Colombia, formerly protected by the Spanish Crown and the Catholic missionaries, were abolished in 1821. Communal lands were to be divided up between Amerindian families within five years, any surplus land was to be rented out, and the old tribute was ended. Waste lands in public ownership (*tierras baldías*) were to be offered for sale at a moderate price. This law was soon suspended in Ecuador, and it was patchily enforced elsewhere, in the face of strong local resistance (Bushnell 1970: 176–7; McGreevey 1971: 63; Mollien 1824: 373).

Venezuelan cocoa cultivation mainly impinged on Amerindian lands in the east. The terms of leases on 'surplus' Amerindian lands were rarely respected, and the official surveyor in Cumaná recommended in 1836 that they should be sold. The progressive reclassification of *resguardos* as *tierras baldías* achieved this objective. A wave of migrants, many from the densely populated but dry island of Margarita, entered the cocoa zone to become smallholders (Harwich Vallenilla 1996: 25–7, 34–7). They were joined by Canarians after the expiry of their labour contracts (Rodríguez Campos 1989).

Caracas continued to dominate the country's cocoa economy. Of 8.5 million cocoa trees enumerated in the early 1830s, 84 per cent were on 356 estates in Caracas, with an average of 20,200 trees per estate. This compared to 103 estates in eastern Venezuela, with an average of 13,500 trees per estate (Izard 1972: 138–9). These statistics exclude production zones around Lake Maracaibo, where there were nearly a million cocoa trees in 1838 (Cardozo Galué 1991: 54–5). They also omit the Orinoco, where there were few planted trees but many wild ones (Briceño de Bermúdez 1993: 38, 68, 146). More seriously, the figures do not include smallholdings. The decline since 1814, when Humboldt estimated that there were 16 million in Venezuela, was thus less than might appear at first sight (Humboldt 1941: V, 160). The eastern parts of Barlovento were experiencing rapid expansion in the late 1830s, making up for decay further west (Tamaro 1988: 70, 74). Even the Chuao coastal estate had 35,000 more cocoa trees planted in 1849 than in 1825 (Brito Figueroa 1985: 264–5).

The location of cocoa estates changed in Colombia, but their dominance was not seriously threatened by smallholders. Cúcuta's sharp decline was balanced by a boom in Tolima, seemingly on estates, to supply the highland market centred on Bogotá (Brungardt 1974: 92–4). At the same time, mine owners developed flourishing cocoa estates in western Antioquia, and grew more cocoa in Cauca (Brew 1977: 243–4; Mina 1975: 54–7; Patiño 1963: 310–13). However, freed slaves and other poor cultivators became more numerous in Cauca, renting land on the basis of informal oral contracts, or simply squatting. Chapels formerly erected for slaves were favoured for new settlements (Colmenares 1989: 165–6). Scattered cocoa smallholdings also predominated on the middle and lower Magdalena and its affluents, with no mention of former estates (Holton 1967: 45–6).

More dispossession of Amerindians in the Guayas plain took place after 1821, when 'surplus' lands were granted to planters. Some remaining Amerindians drifted eastwards, settling in the foothills of the Andes (Chiriboga 1980: 15, 34, 130). The Arosemena, immigrant planters from Panama, purchased such lands (Arosemena 1991: I, 178). However, land alienation did not affect the peoples of the dry west, outside the cocoa zone (Hamerly 1973: 102).

Estate owners were less numerous than smallholders in the two thirds of Guayaquil province covered by the 1832 census, but more numerous in Baba, Babahoyo and Machalá, the main cocoa districts. Some owned over 100,000 cocoa trees, notably the Luzárraga, Icaza, Santistevan, Pareja and Vitores families (Hamerly 1973: 100–9). That said, the Mulatto villagers of Naranjal witnessed landowners abandoning cocoa estates in the slump of the early 1830s (Terry 1834: 66, 250–1).

Forced cultivation and collection of cocoa survived independence in Bolivia. The Mojos continued to be wards of the state, obliged to cultivate cocoa, the second crop after cotton. They delivered dried or ground beans as tribute, which men then had to transport, by canoe or on their backs, to Santa Cruz or Cochabamba. Similarly, as Spanish Franciscan missionaries withdrew, Apolobamba Amerindians were obliged to pick and transport wild cocoa, as part of their continuing 'personal servitude' (Orbigny 1992: 74, 77, 301, 313). A decree of 1842 put an end to these colonial relics (Osborne 1955: 86–7).

Mesoamerican cocoa estates did best in booming Tabasco. All social groups participated in pushing westwards into the Chontalpa, although Amerindians seem to have been less of a force than in earlier decades (Scherr 1985: 39). By 1831, 1,823 cocoa estates were enumerated in Tabasco, well up on late colonial times (Arias et al. 1987: 84–5). In 1831, Costa Rica granted about half a hectare of free land to those planting 500 cocoa trees in the Matina region, which contained twenty-four small estates and 175,000 cocoa trees by the 1840s (Saenz Maroto 1970: 101; Quesada Camacho 1989: 87). On the Pacific side, the Pipil of the Sonsonate area produced cocoa for

El Salvador's internal market, and Mam Maya in Soconusco may have bene-fited from the expulsion of Spanish planters in 1827–33 (Dunkerley 1988: 9–10; 14–16; Medina Hernández 1993: 468–9). One politician owned an immense estate on the shores of Lake Nicaragua in the 1840s, but most of Nicaragua's 45–50 cocoa plantations were small, containing some 40,000 trees (Scherzer 1857: I, 122–3; Burns 1991: 44, 84–5). Amerindian communal lands remained abundant, one settlement in the 1820s being described as having 'rich lands, bearing heavy crops of Indian corn and cocoa' (Dunkerley 1988: 16, 18; Burns 1991: 124).

A violent assault on aboriginal peoples was mounted in southern Bahia, although the revival of cocoa cultivation by German and Swiss settlers remained limited (Bondar 1938: 26–7). The Brazilian government attempted to woo Amerindians with a humanitarian programme, in alliance with Italian Capuchin missionaries (Nembro 1958: 207–9). However, the killing of a settler family in 1830 triggered a return to the harsh methods of the past. Settlers were allowed to shoot adult 'rebels' and enslave their children. With improved firearms and 'tame' Amerindian auxiliaries, pioneers engaged in the 'ethnic cleansing' of much of the land to the south of the Pardo river in the 1830s and 1840s. However, they failed to crush the Botocudo entirely (Hemming 1987: 365–77). An American missionary noted with surprise in the 1840s that the coastal land route between Espírito Santo and Bahia was 'only roamed by savage tribes' (Kidder 1845: II, 14–15).

In the Brazilian Amazon, cocoa estates declined to the benefit of small-holders. The great Cabanagem rebellion of 1835–9 shook slavery to its roots and ruined the few remaining cocoa estates (Weinstein 1983: 40–3). Mixed race and Amerindian smallholders predominated in the late 1840s, rarely owning as many as 15,000 trees (Bates 1969: 142–3).

Large landowners were unusually weak in Hispaniola. Former slaves in southwestern Haïti continued to obtain land for cocoa cultivation with ease, if necessary by squatting without legal title (Street 1960: 170–2, 176). Haïtian rule over former Spanish Santo Domingo, from 1822 to 1844, destroyed the remnants of cocoa estates there (Ciferri 1930: 17). Thus the cocoa trees planted by French refugees in the Samaná peninsula in 1809 had all reverted to bush by 1851 (Vega and Cordero Michel 1993: 39–40). Conversely, the Haïtian occupation stimulated smallholder cultivation of cocoa on individual plots, albeit on a limited scale (Bryan 1977: 45–7, 52, 55–6).

Conditions were not so favourable in Trinidad before the abolition of slavery in 1834–8, although small Mulatto planters were increasingly promi-nent. 'Cocoa was king' in 1818, and there were many applications for land to grow it in the next few years. As the commercial crisis of 1828 erupted, however, enthusiasm evaporated, and estates were more than ever small units owned by men of colour (Williams 1952: 39, 273–4, 277, 283, 326, 331–2, 384).

After the abolition of slavery in Trinidad in 1834–8, many British officials agreed with sugar planters that ex-slaves should remain on estates as wage labourers. Two select committees, in 1842 and 1848, warned that an independent black peasantry could be a threat to Caribbean prosperity, even to its very 'civilisation' (Lobdell 1988: 195–8). In an attempt to keep labour on Trinidadian estates, the minimum plot size of crown land that could be ceded was set at about 130 hectares in 1838, and this was doubled in 1847, placing such land even further outside the financial reach of former slaves (Blouet 1977; Phillips Lewis 1996: 45–7). However, opinions were divided. The governor of Trinidad at the beginning of the 1840s expressed the hope that energetic freedmen would be able to better themselves through cocoa cultivation (Green 1991: 225–6).

In any event, it proved impossible to prevent squatters from growing cocoa in the extensive public forests of Trinidad. Squatters came not only from the island itself, but also from other islands and from Venezuela. Legal loopholes, and the sensitivities aroused by the abolitionist campaign, made eviction difficult to contemplate. Moreover, some landowners drove a roaring trade, selling or renting plots of uncultivated land on the fringes of their estates (Blouet 1977; Phillips Lewis 1996: 49–53; Giacottino 1976: II, 399–401). Former slaves from British territories may have been outnumbered by the 'Panyols' or 'Spanish Peons' from Venezuela, attracted by land, and in some cases freedom (Moodie-Kublalsingh 1994: ch. 1). Panyols disliked work on sugar estates, and were denounced by planter representatives in 1842 as a 'dangerous and objectionable class' (Shephard 1937: IV, 3).

Former slaves on Grenada and Dominica enjoyed more success in becoming cocoa farmers after 1838, as the sugar plantocracy on both islands was smaller, and had been severely shaken by uprisings during the French wars. Between 1838 and 1856, forty-seven Grenadan estates were abandoned, and some were divided into plots and sold to former slaves to grow cocoa. Whether through purchase, renting or squatting, many former slaves left estates and set up their own villages. However, some estate owners in Grenada were unusual in the Caribbean, switching to cocoa quite precociously (Brizan 1984: 129; Milstead 1940: 195). Dominica's House of Assembly already had a Coloured majority by 1838, and estate owners found great difficulty in preventing former slaves from drifting inland to grow cocoa. They were joined by fugitive slaves from neighbouring Martinique and Guadeloupe (Honychurch 1984: 96, 98; Trouillot 1988: 63–4, 90–4, 132).

Elsewhere in the British Caribbean, the situation was less favourable to small farmers. Cocoa was one of the crops that emancipated slaves tried to grow in British Guiana after 1838, but restrictive short-term tenancies directed their energies towards annual crops, notably provisions for the internal market (Rodney 1981: 71, 73, 78). The French landowners of Saint Lucia claimed to have entirely partitioned their island, and officials wanted to avoid upsetting them so soon after having placed them under British rule. European planters on Saint Vincent were also well entrenched, owning nearly all the land (Great Britain 1942: 158–60, 175). Missionaries purchased land in Jamaica to settle former slaves, but coffee was the favoured crop (Eisner 1961: 210–16).

As slavery persisted in the French, Dutch and Spanish Caribbean, there were few free persons able to become cocoa smallholders. Land grants on Martinique and Guadeloupe were for the production of foodstuffs, and what little cocoa grew in French Guiana came from small estates around Cayenne and Oyapock (Blérald 1986: 97, 138; Mam-Lam-Fouck 1986: 227). The Dutch authorities allowed the few ex-slaves to obtain plots in 1842, but they had to pay rent and could only grow provisions (Panday 1959: 161). Cocoa in Cuba was grown on estates, concentrated in the central provinces of Remedios, Sancti Spiritus, and Santa Clara. Officials also promoted cocoa as an alternative crop on estates in eastern Cuba, in the wake of the coffee slump of the 1840s (Marrero 1972–89: X, 89–90; XI, 134–5).

Cocoa in Africa was grown on small estates, after José Ferreira Gomes, a Brazilian Mulatto slave trader, had planted it on Príncipe in 1822 (César 1969: 20–1). Only a quarter of Príncipe was cultivated in the 1830s, and the government sold land cheaply to anybody with labour, although much more coffee than cocoa was grown (Omboni 1846: 239–42). Transmitted to São Tomé around 1830, cocoa also remained subordinate to coffee (Terán 1962: 84; Lima 1844: II-1, 18). Circumstances were similar in the French island of Bourbon (Réunion) in the 1820s, to which cocoa was allegedly brought from Ceylon (Campbell 1996: 197). Sugar and coffee predominated, and this cocoa had the worst reputation in France (Mangin 1860: 125).

Estates remained no match for smallholders in Southeast Asia. A handful of cocoa estates existed in the Philippines, but cocoa remained overwhelmingly a crop of scattered smallholders, especially in the Visayas (Mallat 1983). Many rural Filipinos simply grew enough for their own consumption (Díaz Arenas 1838: 57). In Dutch North Sulawesi, families of European status, often of mixed blood, grew most of the cocoa exported to Manila in the 1820s, but they paled into insignificance next to smallholders by 1857 (Clarence-Smith 1998: 102–5).

The uneven expansion of smallholdings, 1850s–1870s

The heyday of free trade also witnessed the rise of smallholders, although estates clung on in places. The widespread abolition of slavery created many aspirant cocoa smallholders, even though land reform lagged behind. Newly ascendant liberal regimes in Latin America seized indigenous and Church lands, and yet little was distributed to humble farmers. Some great landowners were able to exploit their influence to engross land, partly for social prestige and partly to retain workers. That said, the legalities of land ownership were of little relevance to the flood of small farmers expanding their cocoa groves by squatting.

Ecuadorian estates probably expanded, even though liberal governments from 1845 were sympathetic to modest farmers. There was anecdotal evidence of poor pioneers growing cocoa, possibly including a few slaves freed in 1851. However, Amerindians continued to lose a little land to estates, as in Babahoyo in 1871 (Chiriboga 1980: 27, 34, 177). Acquiring river frontage for a pittance gave a planter de facto access to a vast hinterland, as the extension of concessions inland was unlimited, and dependence on river transport was universal (Mangin 1860: 82; Pineo 1996: 13).

The Amazonian piedmont of Peru was another area where estates predominated. In Jaén, they elicited strong resistance from Amerindians, fiercely independent and long accustomed to gathering wild cocoa for sale (J. Dawe: personal communication, 1998). Germans, settled further south in the Pozuzo region in 1858–9, took to cocoa among other crops (Vázquez 1970: 81). Cocoa estates in the valleys around Cuzco were the main Peruvian producers. Deep in the Amazon jungle, Franciscan missionaries persuaded converts to grow cocoa, but in an area far from densely populated highland markets (Marcoy 1875: I, 333–5, 355–6; II, 112–13).

The assault of Mesoamerican liberals on corporate lands was mainly to the advantage of estates (Bulmer-Thomas 1994: 94). In 1867 just over half the 2.3 million cocoa trees in Rivas, Nicaragua, were on twenty-six estates. The rest belonged to ninety-six owners of between 1,000 and 24,000 trees (Lanuza *et al.* 1983: 85–7). In the early 1870s, cocoa cultivation was 'the most lucrative occupation of the American *hacendado*, both pleasant and aristocratic', although smallholders existed, and tenants and sharecroppers enjoyed considerable autonomy (Lévy 1873: 449–69, 509). Menier purchased thousands of hectares close to Lake Nicaragua in 1862, but his plans to plant 50,000 cocoa trees a year soon ran into difficulties (Cerfberr de Medelsheim 1867: 16–7; *EUIEA*: XXXVIII, 528; Lévy 1873: 445, 461–70). Costa Rica provided free land to small cocoa planters from 1850, together with cash subsidies, albeit with few results (Saenz Maroto 1970: 101–2). Whereas wild or feral cocoa was picked in northern Honduras in the 1860s, it was cultivated on estates by 1878 (Squier 1970b: 140, 161–2; Euraque 1998: 97–8).

In Venezuela, it was cocoa smallholders who surged ahead, following the abolition of slavery in 1854, civil war in 1858–63, and a terrible drought in 1868–9. Although estates maintained themselves on the coast, many Barlovento landowners gave up cocoa production. Two in Caucagua, who each used to produce some fifty tonnes of cocoa, rented land in small plots, often to ex-slaves (Middleton 1871: 454–7). Small cocoa farmers were even more prominent in eastern Venezuela, where a law of 1848 declared wide swathes of 'unused' indigenous communal lands forfeit to the state. Newcomers sometimes bought this land, but more commonly squatted on it.

Local Amerindians melted into the general population, leaving only the names of their settlements as mute testimony to their former existence as separate peoples (Harwich Vallenilla 1996: 37–8).

The advance of cocoa in Colombia's upper Cauca valley violently undermined the landed elite. Forced to free their slaves in 1851, landowners granted them plots of land to grow cocoa, in return for labour services. Over time, services were converted to cash rents, typically paid twice yearly from the proceeds of the cocoa harvest. Such arrangements were oral, a problem when entrepreneurial Antioqueños leased large blocks of land (Mina 1975: 54–7, 68–9, 94). The stakes were high, as land planted in cocoa was worth 100–200 pesos per hectare in 1871, compared to only 6–10 pesos for virgin forest (McGreevey 1971: 120). Violence erupted after the liberals came to power in 1862, culminating in a savage civil war in 1876–7. Landlords accused demagogues of stirring up racial enmity, while smallholders fought to prevent the reinstatement of slavery, cutting down some 60,000 cocoa trees on one estate. By 1880, many large planters were bankrupt, while 'free negroes', growing cocoa and tobacco as cash crops, were in the ascendant (Schenck 1953: 52–4; Mina 1975: 63, 77; Taussig 1977: 417). By the end of the war, cocoa cultivation was overwhelmingly in the hands of 'proletarians' (Hyland 1982: 404).

Bahia's rapidly growing cocoa output came from producers of all sizes, but from the 1860s, migrants pressing inland beyond the pale of settlement tipped the balance in favour of smallholders. The land law of 1850, implemented from 1857, allowed squatters to register claims to cleared and planted land. However, as a tax was payable, squatting prevailed (Mahony 1996: 269–72, 296–7, 304, 311). In 1870, the cost of surveying and registering a plot was estimated to be three times the value of the land (Garcez and Freitas 1975: 25). Botocudo still mounted raids, although they were hunted like vermin by settlers with improved firearms (Métraux 1946: 531–2). Particularly fierce fighting flared up between 1869 and 1872, leading the authorities to back Italian Capuchins as agents of pacification (Hemming 1987: 377–80). These missionaries settled hunter-gathers in villages, where they could produce cash crops. In one mission station in 1856, there were 20,000 cocoa trees and the same number of coffee trees. The 'national colony' for Botocudo, run by Capuchins from 1870, included cocoa cultivation among its activities (Nembro 1958: 294–7, 303–13).

The land law confirmed existing estates east of the pale, where slavery held sway. Pedro Cerqueira Lima was precocious among landlords in grasping that cocoa was the crop of the future. Most of the old colonial families grew some cocoa by the 1860s, while continuing to concentrate on sugar and timber. Smaller properties were more likely to be planted in cocoa, especially those of German and Swiss colonists. Modest farmers rented estate land. *Agregados* paid no rent, but sold their cocoa to the landowner, shopped at his store, and could be evicted at short notice. Even selected slaves were allowed to grow cocoa, on plots granted to them in usufruct (Mahony 1996: 47–50, 183–9, 213, 247–317, 350–6, 380).

Cultivation along the banks of the Brazilian Amazon remained firmly in the hands of Amerindian and Mestizo smallholders (Agassiz and Agassiz 1969: 170–6). There was an unbroken line of cocoa cultivation by modest growers, on the south bank from Cametá upstream to Monte Alegre, and from there on both banks to the neighbourhood of the confluence with the Madeira (Marcoy 1875: II, 427, 438). The frontier of cultivation extended to the confluence with the Negro by the end of the 1870s, when even the wealthiest planters possessed no more than 30,000 trees. Healthy young cocoa trees sold at 15–20 cents apiece, but land itself had no value (Smith 1879: 94, 112).

In the judgement of one scholar, 'the Ten Years War had all but destroyed the *oriental* planter class' in Cuba, even though slavery was not abolished till 1886 (Pérez Junior 1989: 79). The mainly French owners of 'coffee' estates in eastern Cuba, who actually grew more cocoa than coffee, were certainly badly shaken by the war of 1868–78. Many slaves freed themselves, and crops and buildings were burned by both sides in the bitter struggle (Pérez de la Riva 1944: 90–4; United States 1888: 116–19). At the same time, the number of cocoa estates in the centre of the island, the only ones officially described as such, fell victim to the advance of sugar (Pezuela 1863–6).

Hispaniola remained a bastion of smallholdings. Haïtian cocoa farmers prospered modestly in the remote southwest, where much forested land technically belonged to the state (Moral 1959: 114; Street 1960: 175). These farmers were 'rarely visited, and reported to be among the most barbarous of the island' (Saint John 1971: 370). The southwest accounted for about three quarters of production in 1880, with most of the rest divided between Cap Haïtien and Port-au-Prince (Rouzier 1892–3: I, 290; II, 128–9). Smallholders in the northern Dominican Republic remained the main cocoa producers (Hoetink 1988: 161). A little village near Puerto Plata was even called Cacao, because so much was grown there, and cocoa was the third export of Samaná in 1871 (Rodríguez Demorizi 1960: 202–3, 293). Planters from the southern United States also settled in Samaná to grow cocoa after 1865 (Enjalbert 1952–3: 65).

The British showed a new willingness to allow cocoa smallholdings in Trinidad, as supplies of South Asian indentured labour made sugar planters less concerned about losing former slaves (Blouet 1977: 443). The floodgates were opened in 1869, as squatters were encouraged to acquire titles, and crown land was sold in small lots on attractive terms (Phillips Lewis 1996: 46–57). In northeastern districts, Tobagonians and Venezuelans from Carúpano sought land, although the former were more likely to grow provisions (Harrison 1979: 59–61). Indeed, Venezuelans made Spanish the dominant language of some central parts of the island (Moodie-Kublalsingh 1994: 4–5, 227). South Asians successfully petitioned the governor in 1869 for some two hectares of crown land in lieu of repatriation, and they also began to grow cocoa. Some preferred to buy crown land, to be free to choose their plots (Brereton 1974: 33; Blouet 1977: 447). A resurgence in the fortunes of French owners of cocoa estates could also be discerned from the 1860s (Brereton 1981: 93).

Lieutenant-governor Keate was too optimistic when he declared in 1853 that small farmers embodied cocoa's future in Grenada. To be sure, the number of autonomous villages went from over 7,000 in 1852 to some 16,000 in 1870, as more estates were abandoned or sold, following the ending of tariff protection for sugar on the British market. However, some landowners themselves converted from sugar to cocoa. The most valuable estate on the island in 1875 had 238 hectares in cocoa. Three years later, more of the surface area of estates was in cocoa than in sugar (Brizan 1984: 129, 135–45).

The Encumbered Estates Court Act may have acted as a partial brake on the transfer of land to smallholders in Grenada, although the contrasting experience of Dominica casts doubt on this theory. The court, located in London, arbitrated on the claims of creditors. Its jurisdiction was accepted in Grenada in 1866, and in Dominica a year later (*PP* 1884: vol. 55, C. 3982). Smallholders who purchased plots of land from estates could not afford to be legally represented in London, and were thus allegedly discouraged from buying (Brizan 1984: 141). However, an estimated seven eighths of Dominica's cocoa crop came from peasant plots by 1884, despite a discriminatory property tax on top of the encumbered land problem (Trouillot 1988: 95, 110–11; Honychurch 1984: 108–10).

Ex-slaves also took to cocoa in the French and Dutch Caribbean. France's freeing of slaves in 1848 led to a surge in the number of smallholdings, despite the efforts of Napoleon III to protect the labour force of sugar planters. Ex-slaves bought or squatted on fallow land in steep areas unsuitable for sugar, with cocoa as one of their crops. Estates seized for debt were also broken up and sold in small lots (Blérald 1986: 73–4, 93–111, 116–17, 138). Apprenticeship in Surinam only ended in 1873, but the popularity of cocoa among former slaves was already apparent (Lier 1971: 223–9).

José Maria de Souza e Almeida is often portrayed as the cocoa pioneer of São Tomé and Príncipe, but this ignores the contribution of small farmers. A Mulatto born in Príncipe of a Bahian father, Almeida made a fortune in the Angolan slave trade, bought abandoned estates on São Tomé the early 1850s, and was made Baron of Agua-Izé (César 1969). However, most cocoa was grown by smallholders on Príncipe in the 1870s. They rented plots of state land for modest sums, employed little labour, and avoided debt (Almada 1884: 10, 28, 15, 46; Silva 1883: 18). Cocoa was Príncipe's 'tree of the poor' in 1871, and a rush to grow it led to food imports from São Tomé (AHU 1872). Governor Gregório Ribeiro's surprise enforcement of the abolition of slavery swelled the ranks of small producers after 1875

(Clarence-Smith 1993b: 150). However, large landowners also began to increase their cocoa output, reaching 298 tonnes in 1878–9 on São Tomé island, compared to 168 tonnes for smallholders (Almada 1884: 28, 108).

Small estates, owned by Black settlers, were the rule on Spanish Fernando Póo. William Pratt, a Sierra Leonean settler, had earlier seen cocoa growing in the Caribbean, and he brought planting material from the neighbouring Portuguese islands prior to 1850 (Liniger-Goumaz 1979: 408; Sundiata 1990: 24). Sierra Leonean traders on the island then slowly increased cocoa cultivation on their little farms (Baumann 1888: 136).

Experimental cocoa cultivation spread to the mainland, beginning on Angolan estates in Luanda's hinterland from the 1840s (Lopo 1963: 36–7, 50–3). French officials tried cocoa in Gabon's Libreville Bay in the 1850s, declaring it Gabon's most promising cash crop in 1865. Catholic Spiritan missionaries grew it with seed from Príncipe, both for local consumption and for sale to passing ships (Tornezy 1984: 156, 162, 170; Mbokolo 1981: 103). Protestant Baptist missionaries, expelled from Fernando Póo in 1858, brought cocoa to the lower slopes of Mount Cameroon. It was cultivated there on small plots by the Christian community in the 1870s, and a few trees existed near Duala by 1884 (Wirz 1972: 203). A chief from Bonny in southeastern Nigeria planted Fernando Póo seed in 1874, and a Creole merchant of Lagos did likewise in 1880 (Are and Gwynne-Jones 1974: 6–70; Hopkins 1978: 88; Webster 1963: 428). Protestant Basel missionaries, who inherited Danish plantations in the Gold Coast, obtained seed from Surinam in 1857, Cape Palmas in Liberia in 1858, and Cameroon. They still grew some in the 1870s, and distributed seeds to Africans (Dickson 1969: 131; Hill 1963: 170–1; Webster 1963: 428; Epale 1985: 237). Cocoa was also found from the Ivory Coast to Sierra Leone by 1870 (Hill 1963: 171; Hall 1932: 428; Peterson 1969: 273).

South Asian efforts were more limited. The Ceylon Botanic Department had cocoa seed planted in villages from 1866, but peasants showed no interest. Cocoa seed was then offered to estates suffering from coffee blight in the 1870s. However, there was little enthusiasm while coffee prices remained high (Wright 1907: 6–7). Cooperation between autonomous princes led to new experiments on India's Malabar coast in the 1870s (Rice 1876–8: III, 48).

European landowners remained subordinate to smallholders in Southeast Asia. The Dutch authorities placed great hopes on estates in Amboina from the 1850s, but smallholders did better, and government loans to planters remained unpaid. The most dynamic pioneer front, sweeping round Sulawesi's Tomini Gulf, was an exclusively indigenous affair (Clarence-Smith 1998: 102–5). No heed was taken of proposals to include cocoa in forced cultivation, whether in the Moluccas or in Java (Clarence-Smith 1998: 105; Baardewijk 1994: 161). 'Large plantations' were rare in the Philippines, compared to small cocoa 'gardens' for local use (Jagor 1875: 95–6).

Landlords seized the cocoa and coffee groves of Negros smallholders in 1876, but they did so to grow sugar (McCoy 1982: 321).

The attempted comeback of estates, 1880s–1914

The great cocoa boom led to a resurgence of estates, reflecting high profits, pseudo-scientific reasoning, and a hardening of racial attitudes. Technology and gang labour were applied to production, in a racially defined hierarchy of functions. Freshly arrived settlers and employees of corporations were ardent advocates of 'factories in the field', wishing to demonstrate the superiority of Western ways. Intensive methods required costly machines and buildings, and greatly increased the need for labour. The internalisation of transport functions created seasonally under-utilised capacity. Speculation pushed up land prices, and top-heavy administrative structures raised running costs, especially when employing astronomically expensive Western expatriates. Returns from cocoa of slightly higher quality were not commensurate with such lavish expenditure, and debt was a passport to bankruptcy, given high interest rates on the forest frontier. From 1900, the empty pretensions of the 'modern estate' were becoming clear to many people in northern Europe and North America, although it took much longer in France and southern Europe (Clarence-Smith 1995; 1994b; Austin 1996).

Western chocolate manufacturers acquired many more estates than before. From 1897, Cadbury's purchased properties in Trinidad, Grenada, the Gold Coast and Western Samoa. They never produced more than a minute quantity of the firm's needs, were generally unprofitable, and were declared to be dedicated to experimental agronomy (Williams 1931: 146; Freeman and Chandler 1907: 127–8; *Gordian*: VIII, 3173; Austin 1996: 168–9). In 1910 Cadbury's explained that 'we are not intending to increase this section of our business, as we need our whole energy and capital on the manufacturing side' (UBL 1910).

Rowntree's were equally unsuccessful. John Wilhelm Rowntree promoted the idea that the firm should acquire cocoa estates from 1896, to guard against speculators, keep beans untainted by accusations of 'slave grown cocoa', and obtain better processed beans. Rowntree's acquired estates in Jamaica, Trinidad and Dominica in 1899, which proved to be 'a commercial failure: plagued by mismanagement, they were unprofitable from the outset'. At most, they provided Rowntree's with around 8 per cent of its requirements, hardly a useful insurance against speculators. In 1902 the directors decided not to acquire more land, but to continue investing in existing properties. After much fruitless expenditure, Rowntree's finally sold out in 1914 (Fitzgerald 1995: 76, 101, 510, 514–16; Honychurch 1984: 119).

Estates were just as marginal for other Western chocolate companies, and apparently similarly unprofitable. Suchard, the largest Swiss company, acquired an estate with 100,000 cocoa trees in the Dominican Republic in

1890, which only supplied a fraction of the company's requirements (Baud 1982: 70; Boin and Serulle Ramia 1981: 245; Knapp 1923: 87). Kwatta took its name from the Surinam estate of its co-founder, but this Dutch company nearly went under in 1889, and the Surinam connection disappeared under new owners (Schrover 1991: 175, 183–5, 190). Stollwerck and other German manufacturers were more prudent, merely buying shares in Cameroonian plantations (BAAP 1908b). Nestlé made it a matter of principle never to acquire land. This rule was breached only once, for Australian dairy cattle, and the experience confirmed the directors' worst fears (Heer 1966: 101).

Ecuador was a prime example of a local oligarchy manipulating political influence to engross forest land (Chiriboga 1980: 136–40). A small charge of 1 peso per hectare was imposed in 1875, raised to 4 sucres (pesos) in 1896, but 'few bothered to pay' (Arosemena 1991: I, 233; Pineo 1996: 13). However, such purchases had become highly speculative by 1911 (Guislain and Vincart 1911: 66). Ecuadorian planters provided credit to their weaker brethren, accentuating the process of land concentration. Merchants and banks in Guayaquil also lent money at 12 per cent, but generally steered clear of becoming cocoa producers (Pineo 1996: 12–13; Maiguashca 1996; Preuss 1987: 87).

The richest planters were cosmopolitan in their sources of finance and lifestyle. The Aspiazu family, descended from a Basque colonial official, and the Seminario brothers, of Peruvian origins, were the uncrowned 'kings of world cocoa' (Chiriboga 1980: 144–56; Pineo 1996: 62–3). They formed joint-stock companies in Hamburg and London, together with the Puga, Durán-Ballén and Caamaño families (Maiguashca 1996: 74). Pedro Aspiazu was reputed to own three million cocoa trees at his death in 1899, and the Puga family, of Galician origins, eight million in 1904 (Chiriboga 1980: 144–5, 156–8; Weinman 1970: 19). As many as a hundred families fled the pestiferous climate of Guayaquil for part of the year, and about a dozen families lived abroad (Arosemena 1991: I, 271; Chiriboga 1980: 212–13; Crawford de Roberts 1980: 65–8).

The degree of concentration in Ecuador's cocoa sector has nevertheless been exaggerated. In 1901 there were 4,287 estates, with an average of only 12,130 cocoa trees per property (*Gordian*: IX, 4103). Although it was common for a family to own many estates, smallholders clearly did exist. For a start, the nearly sixty million trees enumerated in the 1901 census left out the smallest units of production (Pineo 1996: 10). These were probably the farmers called 'micro-producers' in 1911 (*Gordian*: XVII, 4258). The Asociación de Agricultores del Ecuador estimated that smallholders produced a fifth of cocoa output in 1913 (Chiriboga 1980: 140). Chiriboga suggests that the figure was inflated to make the association seem less like a rich men's club, but there were many 'micro-producers' on the Asociación's ledgers, such as a man who exported a mere 300 kilos in 1915 (Arosemena 1991: I, 288–97). The eastward movement of the cocoa frontier may have given more prominence to smallholders. Poor 'whites of the mountain' migrated from the Andes to grow cocoa in the foothills, bartering forest land for rum with Amerindians (Ruf 1995: 70–1).

Under Porfirio Díaz, estates made all the running in Mexico, in part because companies surveying 'unused national lands' were granted a third of the area covered, providing both a motive and a mechanism for land alienation (Haber 1989: 19). Chiapas, after partitioning Soconusco with Guatemala in 1882, set taxes low to attract investors, and sold vast amounts of forested land for 2–5 pesos per hectare (Oficina de Informaciones 1895: 11–13). From 1892 Amerindian communities were broken up and the population placed in nucleated villages. Much land went to German coffee growers, but cocoa estates in Pichucalco were in the hands of Spaniards and Mexicans (Baumann 1983: 12–13, 22; Benjamin 1989: 39, 87). United States corporations buying virgin forest in Palenque produced a little cocoa, but their main crop was rubber (Wasserstrom 1983a: 115). There were 115 *plantaciones* of cocoa in Chiapas by 1912, with no indication as to size, compared to 124 in Tabasco (*EUIEA*: XXXIV, 290).

Tabasco had a lower concentration of land ownership than most Mexican states, and the 200,000 hectares owned by Spanish and French nationals in 1923 amounted to less than a tenth of privately owned land (Martínez Assad 1991: 120–3). To be sure, wealthy landowners lived in Mexico City, and Policarpo Valenzuela owned an estimated 15 per cent of the state (Arias *et al.* 1987: 253, 268–70, 334–5). Nevertheless, estate owners complained that the lower orders could easily buy forested land, sold by the government at 3 pesos per hectare. Most cocoa producers were local farmers, White, Mestizo, or Amerindian, and Chontal Maya remained heavily involved in cocoa production to the west of Villahermosa (Kaerger 1901: II, 492–509). In the 'old' Chontalpa, the main problem was the subdivision of land through partible inheritance (Scherr 1985: 43).

Costa Rica, the only substantial cocoa exporter in Central America, more or less handed over the sector to foreign planters. Between 1881 and 1929, some 8,500 hectares of waste land in the coastal plains of Costa Rica were ceded or sold on easy terms for banana or cocoa cultivation, mainly to Spanish, German, British, American and Jamaican planters (Quesada Camacho 1977–8: 66–71; Saenz Maroto 1970: 103–4). Estate cultivation of cocoa was boosted by the decision of the United Fruit Company, of Boston, to diversify out of bananas because of disease. Starting on a small scale in 1905 in the Puerto Limón region, United Fruit exported 579 tonnes of cocoa from Costa Rica in 1915. The transition in the Almirante area of Panama, bordering on Costa Rica, began in 1913. By the early 1920s, United Fruit rather improbably claimed to have become 'the world's largest cocoa raiser' (Wilson 1947: 190–2, 212, 214, 239; Bergman 1957: 44, 46; Hall 1932: 10).

The pattern of despoiling Amerindians and favouring foreign estates was repeated across Central America, but coffee for export was dominant, and cocoa for the local market was poorly documented. Foreign domination was clearest in Nicaragua. Three Menier estates covered 8,000 hectares by 1914, and another large cocoa estate was sold to a Hamburg firm in the 1890s (*EUIEA*: XXXVIII, 528; Preuss 1987: 95). Guatemala's 1871 revolution sparked off a sustained attack on indigenous communities, and low coffee prices from 1895 encouraged Germans and Americans to produce a little cocoa (Wagner 1991: 160; *Gordian*: XI, 33).

The Amazonian piedmont of the Andes was another domain of estates. Bolivian estates specialising in cocoa were small, rarely over thirty hectares, and lay mainly in the southern Yungas (Walle 1925: 171–3). In the upper reaches of Peru's great valleys, cocoa was grown by settlers, including Britons and Germans, although unsubdued Amerindians still gathered wild cocoa in the jungle (Enock 1925: 155–60, 164, 235).

Estates made no more than a partial comeback in Colombia. Those that emerged in the Atlantic lowlands were often owned by French investors, and produced mainly for export. However, cocoa remained a secondary crop, as bananas swept the board (Posada Carbó 1996: 49–51; Eder 1913: 185). There was also a swing back towards large estates in Cauca, with some properties containing 300,000 cocoa trees, but in the 1910s most output still came from small farms (Patiño 1963: 311–12). Landlords increasingly demanded cash rents from those who claimed to own their plots, whether individually or communally. After the bitterly contested War of a Thousand Days, 1899–1902, landowners became bolder. They upped rents and evicted tenants, often turning land over to sugar cane (Mina 1975: 56–7, 88–91). Despite this onslaught, descendants of slaves remained independent cocoa farmers on small plots in the inter-war years (Taussig 1977: 424–5).

Unsubdued Amerindians and militant small farmers posed problems elsewhere. The Compañía Agrícola e Industrial de Rionegro, associating thirteen prominent Bogotá capitalists, began planting 15,000 cocoa trees and 200,000 coffee trees to the west of the city in 1889. The company was dissolved in 1891, because small farmers successfully asserted their rights as squatters on public lands. However, a court later decided in favour of the company (Bergquist 1986: 32–4). Some 4,000 Motilones, along the northeastern boundary with Venezuela, prevented the development of cocoa production, and other 'savage Indians' did likewise for valleys further south (Eder 1913: 186–7, 215). The Amazon basin's thousands of hectares of wild cocoa were neglected in 1914, due to hostile Amerindians, poor communications, and labour competition from wild rubber collectors (Lévine 1914: 104).

The scale of production in Venezuela probably continued to decline, for it was estimated that there were as many as 5,000 cocoa *haciendas* in the country in the 1900s (*SYB* 1907: 1594). Smallholders were in the ascendant in eastern Venezuela, where there were many squatters. Most *haciendas* there were modest affairs with 20,000 cocoa trees or 30 hectares, although León Santelli owned over 700,000 trees in 1917 (Harwich Vallenilla 1996: 37–8). Rangel considers that estates still dominated cocoa production, even though not to the same extent as for coffee (Rangel 1974: 244–5). The coastal region was probably most firmly in the hands of large landowners, and there were still absentee owners of cocoa estates living in town in 1911 (Preuss 1987: 64–7; Guislain and Vincart 1911: 71).

Smallholders certainly powered the extraordinary cocoa boom in the Dominican Republic (Ciferri 1930). Cocoa ran neck-and-neck with sugar as the most valuable export from 1905, and the country became the world's fourth largest exporter in 1906 (Abel 1985: 341, 346; Schoenrich 1918: 154–5). Officials complained of a human exodus leaving for the cocoa frontier, stimulated by a law of 1874 that exempted men growing over 5,000 cocoa trees from military service (Marte 1984: 243). Grants of uncultivated land by the state appear to have been free of charge until around 1900. Northern smallholders abandoned tobacco in the 1870s, and by 1888 there were nearly five million cocoa trees (Bryan 1977: 45–7, 52–6; Baud 1982: 65–72). The commitment of some smallholders to cocoa was considerable, for they purchased most of their food in 1910 (Boin and Serulle Ramia 1981: 217). However, many producers owned less than 1,000 trees in 1904 (*Gordian*: XI, 156).

A law of 1876 authorised grants of waste lands to foreigners for cocoa cultivation, and some German tobacco exporters invested early in cocoa farms (Marte 1984: 248; Baud 1988: 90). French, Swiss and Spanish immigrants then carved out large properties in the 1880s and 1890s, but they remained islands in a sea of smallholdings, and ceased to expand after 1900 (Boin and Serulle Ramia 1981: 38–40, 215–17; Thomasset 1891; Baud 1982: 69–71; Bryan 1977: 128–30). Although some cocoa lands owned by small farmers were seized for debt before 1914, merchants made no serious attempt to become planters (Bryan 1977: 179, 183).

Plans to turn the clock back and develop vast modern cocoa estates in northern Haïti miscarried. Foreigners could not own land, but they sheltered behind local wives or men of straw. A German planter thus obtained 400 hectares near Cap Haïtien around 1901, mainly to grow cocoa (*Gordian*: IX, 3, 836; XIII, 1160–1). A handful of cocoa estates were in German hands in 1914, but the bulk of production still came from smallholders in the southwest (Hall 1914: 431). Indeed, these decades were known as the *belle époque* of Jérémie's cocoa smallholders (Moral 1959: 114).

Bahia also owed most of its dynamism to smallholders, although not quite to the extent that local mythology would have it. The Republicans handed over public lands to individual states after the 1889 revolution, and the 1897 Bahia land law stated that all former Amerindian lands belonged to the state (Mahony 1996: 428, 441–2, 448). It was these lands that were so attractive for slaves freed in 1888, together with drought-stricken migrants, who poured in from northern Bahia and further north (Caldeira 1954: 11, 29, 38). The speed and scale of colonisation was impressive, with small-holders responsible for about three quarters of Bahia's soaring cocoa output by 1911 (Zehntner 1914: 70, 73). Those who applied for title deeds were generally squatting on a fair amount of land, and already had bearing cocoa trees, enabling them to pay expensive survey and registration fees. Of the 1,573 Ilhéus applications for title from 1899 to 1920, only 206 were for plots of less than 10 hectares (Mahony 1996: 453–7).

Greater safety from Amerindian raids also underpinned the dynamism of Bahia's cocoa pioneer front. The Republicans refused to tolerate 'savages' who stood in the way of 'order and progress', but they were ideologically opposed to missionaries, especially foreign ones. They thus crushed an Amerindian rising in 1893, and tolerated 'ethnic cleansing' with a new gener-ation of firearms (Hemming 1987: 382–4). However, they were unable to clear Amerindians completely from the forests, and endemic raiding persisted (Mahony 1996: 311). Such raids were noted as late as 1921, when the Botocudo remained effectively independent along the undemarcated frontiers between Espírito Santo and Minas Gerais (Fawcett 1953: 226–36).

Estates maintained a significant presence in southern Bahia, even though 'cocoa kings' with a mere 200,000 trees in the 1910s cut a poor figure next to millionaires from Ecuador and São Tomé (Knapp 1920: 38). Some twenty families still wielded great influence in 1914. Colonial aristocrats who had converted effectively from sugar to cocoa figured in this charmed circle, together with descendants of German and Swiss settlers. They were joined by nouveaux-riches, derided as 'Mulatto peasants', who moved into mansions in Ilhéus or Salvador. These new men were likely to own 'rentier estates', haphazard collections of small plots accumulated through foreclo-sure and purchase (Mahony 1996: 288–94, 431–7, 486–8).

Conflicts over land intensified as the cocoa boom gathered way. Violent outbursts in 1888 were due to ex-slaves claiming ownership of plots that they had formerly enjoyed in usufruct (Pereira Filho 1959: 49). Landowners surveyed their properties, whereas they had earlier relied on bills of sale and sworn statements, and began to evict squatters, terminate tenancies, and foreclose on land for the settlement of debts. They manipulated the judicial process to their advantage, or hired armed thugs. Indeed, as Mahony puts it, the repeating rifle was as essential as food on the Bahian frontier. The state was weak, and private armies abounded. Violence was multifaceted, comprising feuds between large landowners, attacks by large farmers on their weaker brethren, common banditry, and clashes with Amerindians. Shootings were commonplace, and properties were sometimes burned. Fighting climaxed in a 'battle' in 1919, when one of the contending parties fielded up to 300 hired guns (Mahony 1996: 310–15, 442–84).

Whether concentration of land in fewer hands sprang from this violence is quite another matter. Countervailing tendencies were strong, notably the influx of squatters while high cocoa prices lasted. Moreover, mortality and partible inheritance quickly fragmented holdings, despite sales between siblings (Mahony 1996: 470–1). Debt was probably more significant in the changing scale of ownership, and probably only after 1914, when real cocoa prices fell sharply and immigration slackened (Monbeig 1937: 291; Caldeira 1954: 29–30; Pereira Filho 1959: 84–6).

Most squatters in the Brazilian Amazon were unenthusiastic about gaining title to their land after 1889. The average plot contained less than 2,000 cocoa trees in the 1910s, although one person might own several plots (Le Cointe 1922: II, 132, 473–4). One rubber tapper on the lower Tocantins in 1912 owned about 200 cocoa trees planted close to the river, and claimed rights to some 800 wild ones scattered in the forest behind. In the same area, a mixed-race community made up for falling rubber incomes by selling cocoa to the local trader (Lange 1914: 110, 116, 407–8).

The remaining cocoa and coffee estates of eastern Cuba were swept away by the abolition of slavery in 1886 and the anti-Spanish insurrection of 1895–8. In 1898, a small group of planters took refuge in the French consulate in Santiago, begging the consul to lend them $80,000 to make a new start (Pérez de la Riva 1944: 97–8). The main cocoa growers were now Afro-Cuban smallholders, for some two thirds of land planted in cocoa in 1898 was owned or rented by people of colour, nearly all of it in the east (Sanger 1900: 558). Attracted by the possibilities of growing cocoa and coffee in the vast expanses of forest that remained, ex-slaves squatted on public land, rented, or bought shares in communal property. After Spain's defeat in 1898, even larger numbers headed for the sparsely settled eastern forests, including quite a few poor Whites. The population of Oriente rose from 327,715 in 1899 to 455,086 in 1907, the increase being greatest in cocoa and coffee areas. However, legislation prohibited the common ownership of land, and squatters faced land syndicates financed from North America, seeking to settle Americans and Canadians along the line of rail to grow citrus fruit. Syndicates might grant squatters title, or accept them as tenants, but they evicted many. Moving away into more remote forests, some of them took to banditry (Pérez Junior 1989: 79–85, 102–17, 133–9, 156–8; Wright 1910: 447–8, 455–60).

British rhetoric in favour of cocoa smallholders was not faithfully imple-mented in the Caribbean, despite Royal Commissions calling for peasant land settlement in 1884 and 1897 (Lobdell 1988: 198–200; Great Britain 1942: 79). Trinidad, undergoing the greatest cocoa boom in the region, was an example of the fading liberalism of 'men on the spot'. British officials after 1875 proved more attentive than before to the special pleading of large landowners. The acquisition of forest land was made administratively more burdensome for smallholders, while it became easier for estates hit by the sugar crisis (Phillips Lewis 1996: 57–61). French cocoa planters experienced an economic and social renaissance. They specialised in selling their existing lands to British sugar companies, and obtaining concessions of virgin forest, or buying plots with young cocoa trees (Brereton 1981: 91–3; Shephard 1937: IV, 3).

A few Asians owned estates, although most were smallholders. Indentured labourers from South Asia ceased to obtain free land grants in lieu of repatriation in 1890, but they continued to acquire land, drawing on cash bonuses and savings. Between 1891 and 1896, about a third of crown land sales were to South Asians, a few of whom built up substantial cocoa estates (Brereton 1974: 33–4; Northrup 1995: 134). South Asians had nearly 23,000 hectares planted in cocoa by 1915, accounting for a little over half the land that they cultivated on the island (Williams 1964: 120, 216). There were also two Chinese registered as owners of cocoa estates in Trinidad in 1889, probably traders (Giacottino 1976: II, 568).

Creole smallholders were far from disappearing from the scene. Former slaves were among the estimated 24,000 people who owned cocoa farms of up to 8 hectares in 1897, and some were remarkably successful. Johnson's argument that these smallholdings were destroyed through debt is not entirely convincing. To be sure, there was a quickening pace of judicial transfers of land to new owners for unpaid debts. Many merchants disliked holding land, but it was clearly profitable to re-sell cocoa groves quickly. Moreover, some merchant creditors became cocoa planters on a fair scale, notably William Gordon. However, Johnson himself notes that those who lost their land often simply moved deeper into the forest as squatters (Johnson 1987: 27–8, 30–5). There were still squatters in the northeast of the island in 1920, despite a land survey in 1888, intended to eradicate the practice (Harrison 1979: 60, 62–4, 67). Nor did the transfer of land to estates necessarily indicate foreclosure. Venezuelans specialised in establishing cocoa plots for sale to estates, and their reputation for selecting the best land and seed enabled them to sell at a considerable premium, before moving on into the forest to start again (Shephard 1937: IV, 6).

Debt was perhaps more of a problem for estate owners. A few cocoa planters of French or Spanish origin lost their lands in this way before 1914, sometimes emigrating to Venezuela (Johnson 1987: 30). Planters lived above their means, educating large families privately in Europe and making frequent visits there. They also preferred to buy new blocks of forest, rather than repaying debts. Creditors incautiously lent them funds at rates as low as 6 per cent, and even more incautiously rolled over loans (Shephard 1937: IV, 5–7). In return, debtors sold beans to creditors, sometimes located in London (*Gordian*: V, 1711). The crash came in 1920, when real cocoa prices collapsed. As one unsympathetic observer put it, these planters 'had lived off the fat of the land' (Brereton 1981: 93, 208–9).

Grenada, second only to Trinidad as a Caribbean cocoa producer, continued with a mix of estates and smallholders. Estate owners restored their fortunes by moving into cocoa and nutmeg, turning their backs decisively on sugar from 1886 (Brizan 1984: 296). Despite a land settlement scheme for smallholders from 1909, it was estimated that by the inter-war years about 60 per cent of cocoa production came from estates. Many beneficiaries of the settlement scheme continued to reside and work on estates, treating their plots as allotments for part-time cultivation (Great Britain 1942: 142, 145, 150). South Asian indentured labourers, not numerous on the island, often accepted grants of virgin forest land in lieu of repatriation, on which they grew cocoa, nutmeg and bananas (Mahabir 1987: 373–4).

Estates fared poorly elsewhere in the British Lesser Antilles. The building of a road into the interior of Dominica in 1902 persuaded 30–40 European settler families to take up cocoa, and the governor himself bought an estate on the new road. These enterprises struggled against falling cocoa prices, and were eliminated by the great hurricane of 1916 (Honychurch 1984: 117–21, 124; Trouillot 1988: 63–4, 132). A hurricane and a serious volcanic eruption ruined large estates on Saint Vincent between 1898 and 1903. The authorities acquired some 4,000 hectares and sold them off as small plots, contributing to a resurgence in cocoa exports (Great Britain 1942: 158–60, 166, 168). Saint Lucia's cocoa, once a preserve of estates, was mainly grown by smallholders in 1909 (*Gordian*: XIV, 2474).

Despite all this, the Jamaican elite considered cocoa 'too sophisticated a crop for peasant farmers to cultivate'. Worthy Park alone owned 12 per cent of the area planted in cocoa in 1893, and was the third largest producer in 1910 (Craton and Walvin 1970: 250). Land settlement policies to turn squatters into smallholders, launched in 1895, initially yielded indifferent results, for the crown chiefly sold exhausted lands forfeited by estates. Moreover, bananas attracted more attention than cocoa (Eisner 1961: 170–1, 221–4). Smallholders took to cocoa slowly, but they came to grow all the island's small crop by the 1930s (Great Britain 1942: 19).

Smallholdings in Martinique were often micro-holdings. The crisis in sugar from 1886, and a devastating volcanic eruption in 1902, led to the forfeiting of properties to the state. Estates in hilly regions, suitable for cocoa, were broken up and sold to smallholders (Blérald 1986: 138–9). There were 3,960 cocoa cultivators registered in 1903, for only 334 exported tonnes of cocoa. Some of these households, unable to make ends meet, sent out members to work on sugar estates or in town for part of the year (Légier 1905: 22, 177–8, 184).

Former slaves in Surinam took to cocoa in a major way, after the ending of apprenticeship in 1873. By 1898 there were 1,107 cocoa smallholdings, compared to seventy-seven small cocoa estates (Have 1913: 116). Ex-slaves achieved a modest prosperity without government assistance, some acquiring 'medium-sized holdings'. Most families obtained plots of 2–3 hectares from the Dutch authorities, at no cost for a period of six years. They could become owners after two years, if deemed 'deserving', and paid land tax after six years. In Coronie, bankrupt cotton and sugar companies

sold ten estates to their workers on reasonable terms. This land was subdi-
vided into private plots, with cocoa secondary to coconuts (Lier 1971:
223–31; Panday 1959: 161–2, 167–8, 174, 187).

The outbreak of witches' broom in 1895 dampened enthusiasm for cocoa.
Smallholder output began to decline from 1901, although the share of
exports peaked at nearly half the total in 1906, before falling back to around
a third in 1912 (Benjamins and Snelleman 1914–17: 187). Creoles diversified
into rice and citrus fruit, and an observer still spoke admiringly in 1917 of
their 'small cocoa plots along the banks of the Saramacca and Nickerie
rivers'. Disease also discouraged South Asians and Javanese from entering
this sector, after the expiry of their indentures (Lier 1971: 229–32, 235;
Panday 1959: 159, 188).

Little estates were mainly located on the Suriname and Commewijne
rivers (Preuss 1987: 19). The smallest harvested half a tonne in 1896, and the
largest 125 tonnes (*Gordian*: III, 1210). As witches' broom spread, many
were sold for knockdown prices (*Gordian*: XI, 156–7). Between 1911 and
1916, only nine out of seventy-one cocoa and coffee estates made a profit,
while the rest had a combined deficit of some 3 million guilders (Lier 1971:
238). In 1910, the harvest of seventy-five cocoa estates was worth far less
than that of five sugar estates (Have 1913: 116).

Estates dominated the great cocoa boom in Equatorial Africa up to 1914,
and this was the only part of the cocoa world in which forced cultivation
was tried. Both facts were related to sparse population, and a lack of significant agricultural or commercial enterprise prior to colonial conquest, except
for slave exports. Nevertheless, free smallholders were by no means
completely absent.

Cocoa on São Tomé and Príncipe was briefly a crop of African Creole
smallholders. In 1882–3, they produced 328 tonnes on São Tomé island,
compared to 177 for estates (Nogueira 1893: 29, 32). Many small farmers,
scattered in a semicircle around the capital city of each island, owned their
land (Banco Nacional Ultramarino 1890: 619, 664–6; Tenreiro 1961: 81,
87–8; Mantero 1910: maps). Others rented Church land, had access to
communal holdings, or simply squatted, generally producing most of their
own food (Sociedade de Emigração 1915: 17, 67–8; Guedes 1911: 24–6,
186–8). Around 1908, Creoles still produced 16 per cent of the colony's
cocoa output and owned 9 per cent of the cultivated land (Mantero 1910:
app.). They rarely employed contract labour, and were routinely accused of
stealing cocoa from Europeans (Nogueira 1893: 32; Anon. 1907: 66).

Official policy from around 1880 was to sell state land to well capitalised
Portuguese immigrants, deliberately restricting Creole opportunities
(Almada 1884: 15–17). Although sitting tenants on publicly owned estates
had a right to buy, most could not afford to do so (AHU 1880). As leases
and tenancies ran out, the state sold properties by auction (Silva 1883: 369).
The authorities also turned a blind eye to extortionate and violent methods

employed by settlers to gain control of land (AHSTP 1900). The Angolares in the southwest of São Tomé, descendants of maroons, lost large areas on which they had squatted for centuries (Dias and Diniz 1988).

Huge latifundios grew up, mainly owned by men who had come to the islands as traders. In 1907, one observer affirmed that, 'a ring of planters run it absolutely in their own interests, and the government is practically excluded from any possibility of mismanagement' (UBL 1907). Foremost in this 'ring' was José Constantino Dias, who came to São Tomé in 1871 to work in a shop, a poor lad of sixteen from the harsh interior of northern Portugal. By 1910, he was Marquis of Val Flor, lived in luxury in Lisbon and Paris, owned a domain of over 10,000 hectares, employed 4,700 workers, and produced some 3,500 tonnes of cocoa a year (*GEPB*: XXXIII, 856; *Gordian*: III, 1170; Mantero 1910: app.).

A few great planters were locally born men of mixed race. Jacinto Carneiro de Souza e Almeida, son of the Baron of Agua-Izé, lost his lands to the Banco Nacional Ultramarino, but founded another great estate in the southern tip of São Tomé island, at Porto Alegre. He lived a life of luxury in the capitals of Europe, and became Viscount of Malanza. When he died in Lisbon in 1904, his properties were seized by Belgian creditors (*GEPB*: XV, 994; César 1969: 121–6; anon. 1907: 54). José Ferreira do Amaral, ranked second to the Marquis of Val Flor as an individual planter in 1903, was a Mulatto, illiterate in his early life (UBL 1903). The prominence of a handful of 'native' planters was noted as late as 1914, one having recently left £6,000 'for the education of the children of San Thomé' (Harris 1969: 249).

While the example of the Viscount of Malanza illustrated the growing importance of corporations, it was unusual for foreign firms to own estates. The Banco Nacional Ultramarino, founded in 1864, had a monopoly of banking in the islands, and it acquired many properties through foreclosing on mortgages (Banco Nacional Ultramarino 1890: 771, 791, 881). Joint-stock companies became more common, but they were nearly all registered in Portugal (Mantero 1910: app.).

Germans obtained more or less fraudulent land grants for vast areas on the slopes of Mount Cameroon, as soon as the ink was dry on the protectorate treaties of 1884–5. Hamburg shipping companies founded the first estates, together with resident Swedish and German traders. When Jesko von Puttkamer became governor in 1895, he cleared the local Bakweri from most of the best lands around Mount Cameroon, and persuaded a handful of Rhenish industrialists and Berlin bankers to found well financed plantation companies. They soon turned the region into a handful of estates covering some 90,000 hectares. At the centre of a spider's web of interlocking directorates was Max Esser, decorated by the Kaiser for 'fructifying Cameroon with capital', but ousted in a boardroom coup in 1907, shortly after Von Puttkamer's recall to Berlin (Clarence-Smith 1993a: 190–4, 197–200; Hausen

1970: 220–2, 310–15; Michel 1969). Estates accounted for 84 per cent of the colony's cocoa exports in 1912 (Wirz 1972: 217).

Creoles and similar groups held a subordinate position in Cameroon. Some Viktorianer Creoles continued to lease plots from missionaries on the slopes of Mount Cameroon, while others obtained freehold. The dynamic Duala were not strictly speaking Creoles, as they had not been through the uprooting experience of enslavement. However, they were profoundly marked by European culture, and grew cocoa on estates. They obtained land informally from chiefs, exploiting established marital and commercial relationships. The German authorities refused to recognise such properties as freehold, although they made them land concessions from 1911. Duala estates were usually small, but Rudolf Manga Bell owned a property of 200 hectares in 1913 (Clarence-Smith 1993a: 194–6, 204–5, 212–13; Monga 1996: 125–8; Austen and Derrick 1999: 119–20, 165).

Non-Creoles produced a tiny proportion of Cameroon's cocoa. The Bakweri, having lost their best lands to plantation corporations, came closest to Berlin's post-1906 ideal of *Volkskultur*, African men employing family labour on communal plots of land (Clarence-Smith 1993a: 212). South-central Cameroon was opened up late. The Germans transformed segmentary Beti society into a hierarchy of chiefs, who began to produce cocoa with forced labour and inflated numbers of 'wives', but this system only flourished after the war (Eckert 1996: 144–5).

The Mayombe cluster of estates was politically partitioned between the Congo Free State, Portugal and France. Planters obtained some 200,000 hectares from King Leopold, although nearly all of them lost money in cocoa (Vantieghem 1996: 159; T'serclaes de Wommersom 1911). These Belgian planters resembled those of Cameroon, a mixture of politically influential nobles, industrialists, and local adventurers (Vellut 1996: 126–30). When King Leopold was forced to cede 'his' Congo to Belgium in 1908, he was promised 40,000 hectares of land as his personal cocoa estate in Mayombe (Waltz 1917: I, 257–8). Over the frontier, the Companhia de Cabinda, founded in 1903 in Lisbon, had a virtual monopoly, with half a million cocoa trees in 1910 and some 22,000 hectares of land in 1914 (Companhia de Cabinda 1973; Lopo 1963). French Congo estates were smaller and more cosmopolitan. A Dutch trading company gained an early lead, but gave up cocoa fairly quickly (Jumelle 1900: 193–5; Chalot and Luc 1906; Vennetier 1968: 205–6; Coquery-Vidrovitch 1972: 470–2). Further north, sixteen small estates in Gabon's Libreville Bay covered between 20 and 70 hectares in 1905, with 25,000 cocoa trees on the largest one (*Gordian*: XI, 480).

Forced cultivation was an alternative strategy, although it accounted for a small proportion of Equatorial Africa's cocoa. From 1897, Congo Free State officials obliged Africans to grow cocoa and coffee, on the notional basis of a twentieth of their labour time, despite tremendous pressure already placed on them to collect wild rubber (Poskin 1900: 24; Jumelle 1900: 192). Officials received 25 centimes for every cocoa tree a metre or more high, resulting in badly planted and poorly maintained groves along the Congo river and some of its affluents. Premiums ceased to be paid when the Belgians took over in 1908, but 'administrative pressure' was still applied along the Aruwimi in 1917 (BAAP 1908e; 1917). The number of cocoa trees peaked at just under half a million in 1900 (*Gordian*: X, 4257). The French imposed forced cocoa cultivation in Gabon in 1907, claiming that 1.5 million cocoa trees had been planted by 1911 (Coquery-Vidrovitch 1972: 471–2).

Fernando Póo was transitional between Equatorial Africa and West Africa. The land cultivated in cocoa was roughly equally divided in 1914 between Creoles, Spaniards and indigenous Bubi. The outstanding Sierra Leonean Creole planter was Maximilian Jones, a carpenter by trade, who retired to Spain and educated his many sons there. Spaniards, mainly Catalans, arrived in increasing numbers from the 1880s, often setting up plantation companies. With Catholic mission support, Bubi cultivators took out individual title to their cocoa groves and prospered. Their success was remarkable, given that they had lost so much land to immigrants (Clarence-Smith 1994a; Sundiata 1996).

The West African cocoa boom came slightly later, was more dynamic, and was different in nature. While Creoles were often pioneers, it was indigenous smallholders who made this region the new centre of the world cocoa economy. Europeans tried to set up estates, but failed abjectly.

Explosive growth on the Akim (Akyem Abuakwa) pioneer front of the Gold Coast was due to immigrant smallholders. From the 1880s, Akwapim, Krobo and Shai migrated to this thinly populated area. The unusual speed with which the pioneer front progressed owed much to resources accumulated in earlier ventures in palm oil and wild rubber. 'Stranger farmers' purchased land outright from local chiefs, a down-payment being followed by instalments. Matrilineal Akwapim purchased land as kin groups, families enjoying usufructory rights. Patrilineal Krobo and Shai, together with patrilineal Akwapim, formed syndicates not based on kinship. These were usually dissolved soon after land had been fully paid for, members receiving a share of land in proportion to their financial contribution. They could sell the land at will, but kin rules continued to govern inheritance, so that land tended to be absorbed back into kinship structures over time. A few local Akim people, often women, also grew cocoa on little plots of up to 1.5 hectares (Hill 1963).

Ashanti (Asante), accounting for about a tenth of Gold Coast cocoa exports by 1911, was different. After the British conquered this powerful kingdom in 1896, a railway, built for gold mining, opened up the region for cocoa. Chiefs controlled land strictly, and themselves became substantial cocoa farmers. However, commoners also became producers, as they only needed to make a token payment to gain access to land, and the British quashed attempts by chiefs to collect rent of a penny per bearing cocoa tree. Chiefs refused to sell land to strangers, who could only gain usufruct by paying a third of the cocoa harvest to chiefs (Austin 1984: 22, 224–7, 267, 397–8, 427, 460–1, 466, 522–5).

Europeans played hardly any role in the Gold Coast, and Creoles a smaller one than elsewhere. Few European cocoa plantations were laid out, and all of them came to grief. British officials initially believed in the superiority of estates, and tolerated a speculative wave of land purchases in the 1890s. However, they feared unrest, and refused to intervene when Africans challenged the terms of land deals. By 1912, many officials backed smallholders as the most effective cocoa growers (Austin 1996; Phillips 1989: 11–12, 27, 59–75, 111–13). Ga merchants of Accra, Creoles in the same sense as the Duala, bought land in freehold, often selling on to other Africans. The wealthiest Ga cocoa farmers were D. P. Hammond and William Solomon, the latter owning seventy-nine farms when he died in 1936 (Hill 1963: 26, 221–5, 238–40).

In contrast, Lagos Creoles were the pioneers of cocoa cultivation in southwestern Nigeria. Although freed slaves, most were of local Yoruba origin, facilitating access to land. Poor trading conditions induced Creole merchants, notably Jacob Coker, to develop cocoa farms in the Agege region from the 1880s, and their example was followed by teachers, ministers and clerks. The Agege Planters Union, formed in 1907, was dominated by a dozen large Creole farmers and had some 200 members. Despite success in this period, the Creoles of Agege foundered in the inter-war years, when the real price of cocoa fell dramatically (Hopkins 1978; Webster 1962).

The further spread of cocoa in Yoruba states followed the imposition of British paramountcy, more or less complete by 1893, and the extension of the railway. Chiefs benefited from their control over forest land, freed for cultivation by the ending of internecine wars between Yoruba states. Immigrant farmers were of some significance, but they were usually Yoruba from other states. The new crop was diffused by networks of Yoruba clergymen, traders and labourers, many of the latter returning from spells of work on cocoa estates in Agege or Fernando Póo (Berry 1975: chs 2–4; Hopkins 1978; Webster 1962: 129).

Britons tried to set up cocoa estates in Nigeria, but all failed. They initially plumped for southeastern Nigeria, where rainfall was too high (Johnson 1917: 189–90, 195). The merchant John Holt and the shipper Alfred Jones were better advised, purchasing 50 square miles (130 sq km) near Lagos, in 1893. However, disagreements emerged as to what land rights had been ceded to the syndicate, and this venture also failed (LCL 1893–9). A subsequent legal case established that 'under native law strangers cannot obtain freehold rights – only occupancy rights' (Harris 1968: 159). Written consent from the High Commissioner was necessary for 'non-natives' to acquire land in the protectorate after 1900, and this was interpreted in a restrictive manner (Berry 1975: 32–3).

German companies grew cocoa in Togo from 1897, but acrimonious disputes also erupted over land purchases, and they had a mere 50,000 cocoa trees planted by 1913. In contrast, Africans, many of whom had worked in the cocoa orchards of Akim, had about a million trees planted by 1911 (Sebald 1988: 363–73, 426–30).

Smallholders grew most of the small amounts of cocoa coming from the rest of West Africa. French trade rules and alternative employment in maritime jobs snuffed out a Kru pioneer front, straddling Liberia and the Ivory Coast, which developed in the 1890s (Chauveau and Léonard 1996: 178). Workers returning from Fernando Póo later laid out little cocoa farms in Liberia, and probably in Sierra Leone as well (AGA 1914). Anyi in the southeastern Ivory Coast grew cocoa on their own initiative from the late 1900s, but the French imposed unpopular obligatory cultivation on communal village plantations in 1912, delaying the onset of a cocoa boom in this region (Chauveau and Léonard 1996: 178–9; Groff 1987). Failure attended French estates in the Ivory Coast and Dahomey (Bénin), where the few planters clinging to cocoa produced at a loss in 1909 (*Gordian*: XV, 2744; Fréchou 1955: 57–9). Some Americo-Liberian Creoles around Monrovia switched to cocoa, following the fall in coffee prices in the late 1890s, but on a small scale (Great Britain 1919c: 37; Davis 1976: 58).

In the vast area stretching from East Africa to the South Pacific, cocoa was promoted as an estate crop, which could become a world leader by stressing quality. Instead, estate production and fine cocoa proved to be a losing combination when the world price came crashing down after the war.

European companies dominated production in the western Indian Ocean. French companies raised a little fine cocoa in northwestern Madagascar and the Comoros. Réunionais Creoles grew cocoa on their own island, and established little estates along the east coast of Madagascar from the 1880s, but with techniques that were deficient. Malagasy smallholders took to cocoa much more slowly (Campbell 1996: 199, 202–3). Cocoa hardly progressed beyond an experimental stage in the Seychelles, on British estates in Uganda, or on German East African estates near the coast (*Gordian*: VIII, 3330; Brown and Hunter 1913; Tetzlaff 1970: 131).

A blight of Arabica coffee and falling coffee prices led British planters in Ceylon to develop cocoa to a greater extent. Estates had some 12,000 hectares planted in cocoa in 1909 in the foothills of Ceylon's southern mountains, compared to around 2,500 for smallholders (Hall 1914: 396–7). However, rubber generally proved more attractive at lower altitudes (*Gordian*: XVIII, 5719). Other Ceylon planters migrated to Malaya, where they grew a little cocoa as a subsidiary crop to coffee from the 1880s (Jackson 1968: 178–80, 185).

The number of cocoa estates in the Dutch East Indies rose steeply from the 1880s, almost all on Java and in reaction to the same problems with coffee. Land was generally obtained on seventy-five year leases from the government. As disease and competition from rubber and Robusta coffee choked off this boom from around 1900, cocoa typically became one crop among many grown by resident planters, locally born, sometimes of mixed race, and mainly in central Java. In 1919 about 6,000 hectares were planted in cocoa on twenty-eight Javanese estates, twenty of them in the centre. West Javanese cocoa estates, much smaller, were sometimes owned by Chinese or Hadhrami Arabs (Roepke 1922). In the Moluccas, Europeans grew mainly coconuts, leaving cocoa to a few smallholders (Clarence-Smith 1998: 102–7). There were also scattered smallholdings in Java (Hunger 1913: 390, 394–5; Roepke 1922: 6).

Cocoa in the Philippines continued to come from smallholdings, as estate owners were put off by ecological difficulties (Foreman 1890: 354–5). The cocoa frontier moved into the large southern island of Mindanao, where the Jesuits propagated cultivation among their converts. It also spread fast in the Muslim Cotobato region on Mindanao (Ileto 1971: 22–3, 26–8; Blair and Robertson 1903–7: XLIII, 224, 243, 252). The island of Negros witnessed another minor cocoa boom, in the mountains above the sugar plains (Echaúz 1978: 3–4, 68, 71, 90, 94). Smallholders elsewhere were mainly content to grow cocoa for their own consumption (*Gordian*: IX, 3714, 4089; XIX, 6665; Hall 1932: 493).

The final frontier lay in the South Pacific, especially Western Samoa, where smallholders overwhelmed estates by 1914 (*BII*: XII, 477). A German company grew cocoa as early as 1883. However, the status of the islands was disputed and some early cocoa planters were British, notably the Scottish writer Robert Louis Stevenson, who ended his days there (Hall 1932: 493; McLynn 1994). Missionaries distributed cocoa seed and encouraged Samoans to grow the crop, and the German authorities supported this initiative after their rule was established in 1900 (Wright 1907: 10; Keesing 1934: 299, 302–3).

Cocoa enjoyed little success elsewhere in the South Pacific. A 'modern estate' on the mainland of German New Guinea failed disastrously in 1890, although copra traders did better with small plantations in the Gazelle peninsula of New Britain (Neu Pommern) from around 1905 (Sack and Clark 1979: 50, 142, 144, 188, 207, 234, 285). Reserves were created in the peninsula from 1899, but the local Tolai people stuck to coconuts and market gardening (Firth 1982: 63, 113, 118–20). French cocoa estates in the New Hebrides (Vanuatu) began to take off just before 1914. In the Solomons, New Caledonia, Fiji and Queensland, however, there was little more than experimentation on estates (Hall 1914; 1932; Wright 1907: 7, 13).

Conclusion

The scale of cocoa production cannot be analysed in narrowly economic terms, for culture and politics need to be considered at every twist and turn of this complex story. As there were no advantages to be gained from producing cocoa on estates, the liberal era should have witnessed their decline, as governments gradually adopted the role of night watchman. This progression was far from universal, and estates made a comeback in the decades before 1914. Two processes underlay this: the ability of elites to manipulate the allocation of land rights, and the rise of pseudo-scientific and racist ideas about tropical agriculture. Both these phenomena have been studied in their own right, but they need to be better integrated into the history of cocoa cultivation.

More obscure are the processes whereby indigenous forest dwellers were pushed aside by immigrant cocoa pioneers, at least in Latin America. Indeed, there is a startling contrast between the wealth of analysis on West African cases, and the underdevelopment of the genre in the historiography of Latin America. The expansion of cocoa cultivation often took place at the expense of Amerindians, and yet it is remarkably difficult to extract this story from published accounts. The problem is general, but it is most glaring in southern Bahia, which became by far the largest New World cocoa producer after 1914. Moreover, the hunter-gatherers of these forests resisted the expansion of agriculture more fiercely than anywhere else, leading to 'ethnic cleansing' of a particularly vicious kind. Much of the detail of how this happened lies buried deep in Portuguese and Brazilian archives.

Another problem that needs solving is the 'stickiness' of land reform following the abolition of slavery. The issue has been discussed for the Caribbean, albeit often with an underlying assumption that estates were more efficient than smallholdings, a questionable proposition even for sugar. In the case of Haïti, where sugar disappeared after independence, the focus has been entirely on coffee, even though cocoa did better from around 1895 to 1914. In Colombia and Venezuela, the topic has hardly begun to be broached, although the reasons for this missed opportunity would repay more attention.

7

MODES OF CULTIVATION

Cocoa can potentially be grown over a vast area of the tropics. A lower-storey tree of the equatorial forest in its natural habitat, it requires abundant heat and moisture throughout the year, and shelter from strong winds. Shade prolongs the life of the tree, although it is not absolutely essential. Cocoa tolerates many different soils, as long as they are well drained. It is sensitive to cold, only thriving over about 600 metres in particular microclimates.

Great swathes of forest in the world's equatorial belt are thus suited to cocoa, and yet only small areas have ever been planted. The Amazon-Orinoco basin, the presumed botanical source of the cocoa tree and one of the world's greatest expanses of tropical forest, has witnessed much collection from the wild, but only limited cultivation. Successfully acclimatised in Monsoon Asia in the seventeenth century, cocoa did not become a truly significant crop there till the late twentieth century. Similarly, cocoa was introduced into the heart of the Congo basin at the end of the nineteenth century, without this great mass of forest ever becoming a supplier of any importance.

Cultivation tended to cling to the fringes of the world's three great masses of rainforest, especially where cheap transport by water was available, a crucial consideration before the railway age. Population also clustered on the edges of forests, easing labour supplies, and soils were often better. Cultivators also sought areas where it was possible to dry beans in the sun after the main harvest, as artificial drying was expensive and unsatisfactory. Conversely, when cocoa was cultivated as a monoculture, excessive rainfall throughout the year spread destructive fungal diseases. A potential disadvantage of ecologically excentred locations was the risk of drought, possibly worsened over time by the cumulative effects of deforestation.

While the decisive advantages of clearing virgin forest drove the cocoa frontier along, world cocoa output before 1914 was rarely such as to completely destroy the forest resources of a large region. Between the 1760s and the 1870s, the broad areas within which cocoa was produced remained quite stable, even though production moved around within regions, and the relative position of one region to another changed over time. The accumulation of skills in the production of cocoa may have reinforced this relative stability, only really broken by the great cocoa boom after the late 1870s.

The harvesting of cocoa pods from wild or feral trees persisted in the New World, but could not keep up with growing demand. Moreover, the over-exploitation of wild trees, and the clearing of forest for other agricultural purposes, displaced foci of collection. Unlike Hevea rubber, cocoa gathering easily blended into cultivation, as wild cocoa trees grew in dense clumps, which could be ameliorated and extended with little effort (Young 1994: 163–4).

Methods of cultivation and primary processing, especially those of small farmers, were often denounced as 'primitive'. In reality, they reflected a quest for maximum output at minimum cost. Large estates that adopted 'scientific' methods were sometimes successful at a purely technical level, but they failed to make sufficient returns. Techniques on the forest frontier mirrored the cheapness of land, the exploitation of the 'forest rent', the high price of labour, and the astronomical cost of capital. The improvement of planting material depended on a never ending process of seed selection. Experiments with grafting failed, in part because this technique weakened the already low resistance of cocoa trees to wind damage. A few simple hand tools sufficed for clearing, planting, weeding, pruning and harvesting. Hand-held sprayers were introduced shortly before 1914, but they had little immediate impact on the control of insects and disease. Fermenting beans in a heap in the fields, and drying them in the sun, yielded cocoa superior to that processed with complicated and expensive machinery.

Cultivation methods tended to move from an intensive to an extensive model, as elegantly simple smallholder solutions generally triumphed over fussily expensive estate routines. There was a steady decline in the cultivation of Criollo varieties, in favour of Forastero, which fruited earlier, yielded more, lived longer, was more resistant to disease, and required less care and attention. Forastero beans were bitter, but this could be countered by longer fermentation. Hybrids, often called Trinitarios, rarely bred true, usually reverting to a Forastero type. As Criollo and estates both declined, irrigation virtually disappeared, planting intervals were reduced, planting at stake became more common than transplanting seedlings, and weeding and pruning were reduced. There was no clear trend in the provision of shade, however, and the debate remains unresolved to our own day. The proponents of shade stressed the longer productive life of cocoa trees, while its opponents emphasised early bearing and high yields.

Techniques were not entirely reducible to the scale of cultivation. To be sure, the world's largest producer at the beginning of the liberal era, Venezuela, relied on Criollo raised on estates with horticultural intensity. At the end of the period, Gold Coast smallholders had taken the number one spot by growing Forastero in ways which were the despair of one British official. However, the techniques of Gold Coast farmers were ingenious and quite intensive in terms of labour inputs; indeed more so than traditional procedures on Ecuador's huge estates, also criticised by the very same British official.

The initial colonial assault on the forest

The Spaniards inherited a dependence on Criollo in Mesoamerica, associated with cultivation under shade (Scherr 1985: 34; Newson 1987: 52; Young 1994). They introduced iron tools, mules, and new forms of irrigation. The latter extended the range of cocoa on the Pacific side of the isthmus, albeit at high cost. There were no references to major diseases, but locusts and parrots were serious pests. Delicate Criollo trees matured slowly, and did not live long. Deforestation became a problem in some areas, and ageing cocoa groves were sometimes converted into pasture for newly introduced cattle (Touzard 1993: 34, 50–1, 57–8; MacLeod 1973: 76–7).

Planters in both Venezuela and Guayaquil began by ameliorating coastal stands of wild cocoa, but cultivation methods then diverged sharply. Venezuelans had either found or imported Criollo, which they grew in an increasingly intensive manner. A disease called *la alhorra* decimated coastal orchards from the late 1630s, but new estates sprang up in the inland valleys near Caracas, whence beans were sent by mule train for shipment (Ferry 1989; Tamaro 1988: 64–7). In contrast, Guayaquil planters had discovered a superior variety of Forastero, Arriba or Nacional, that only grew on the flat alluvial lands of the Guayas plain. They remained content with ameliorating wild stands, which proved remarkably healthy and high yielding. A superb network of waterways, allied with a strong boat-building tradition, further reduced their costs (Mahony 1996: 44; Chiriboga 1980: 16, 196–7; León Borja and Szászdi Nagy 1964: 43–50).

The collection of wild Forastero pods predominated elsewhere in Iberian America. The small bitter wild beans of the Amazon Basin, known as Maranhão cocoa, fetched the lowest prices on European markets. Jesuits experimented with cultivation, with some success (Alden 1976; Patiño 1963: 327). Jesuits also transferred lower Amazon planting material to Ilhéus some time after the 1660s, probably before a Portuguese settler planted it on the banks of the Rio Pardo in 1746 (Mahony 1996: 76–7, 86–7, 124–5; Monbeig 1937: 288). Criollo from Mesoamerica was probably introduced in the Amazonian piedmont of the Andes, for the Cuzco variety was later known as 'cacao Soconusco', distinguished from local 'cacao Chuncho' (*EUIEA*: XLIII, 1248). Moreover, Madrid connoisseurs of the late eighteenth century placed Mojos and Cuzco ahead of Soconusco and Tabasco (Kany 1932: 152).

Hurricanes were a constant menace in the Caribbean islands, volcanic eruptions were an occasional hazard, and disease ravaged delicate Criollo trees introduced by the Spaniards. Although it is not clear whether 'blasts' referred to diseases or hurricanes, severe crises afflicted cocoa in Jamaica in 1669–71, Saint-Domingue in 1713–16, and Martinique and Trinidad in 1727 (Patiño 1963: 297–8; Harwich 1992, 60–2; May 1930: 95). The Dutch pioneered cocoa cultivation in the Guianas, probably with both Forastero and Criollo (Reyne 1924–5: 3).

The transfer of cocoa to Asia was technically difficult. Beans lost their ability to germinate after less than two weeks, so that it was necessary to transport seedlings. These were difficult to keep alive on long and unpredictable sailing voyages, especially when water was rationed (Young 1994: 42). The Spanish introduction of Mesoamerican Criollo seedlings into the Philippines in the 1660s was thus something of a triumph (Jagor 1875: 94). An earlier Spanish introduction into northern Sulawesi in 1560 is almost certainly apocryphal, but the Dutch are said to have taken Venezuelan seedlings to Ceylon in 1634, and from there to Java in 1650 (Crow and Thomas 1983: 29–30). There was no recorded attempt to plant cocoa in Africa, which was seen merely as a source of slaves for the New World.

The cocoa frontier, 1760s–1820s

The boom in world demand drove a rapid extension of cultivation in the late eighteenth century. While disturbed conditions from 1796 brought expansion to a halt in some areas, it spurred it on in others. As no changes in methods of cultivation could be attributed to revolution and war, the period to the achievement of Latin American independence is treated here as a whole.

The shift of the Caracas cocoa frontier was clear. Coffee and cotton replaced cocoa, which was increasingly grown in eastern Barlovento. Planters were obliged to move on and clear virgin forest, as replanting cocoa in the same land resulted in weak low-yielding trees. Producers blamed soil exhaustion, while Humboldt thought that deforestation was altering the climate (Humboldt 1852: I, 288–9). Yields in more westerly areas of Barlovento were reported to have halved by the 1780s, whereas they were 1.5 kilos per tree on newly cleared land in the pioneer zones, high for Criollo. Acreage in the eastern sector was expanding rapidly, more than compensating for decline in the west (Tamaro 1988: 29–31, 62–3, 70–1).

The drive to eastern Barlovento cut down on a major cost for plantations: irrigation. On the old coastal estates, this took the form of diverting mountain streams into open trenches, which was fairly cheap to establish but quite laborious to maintain. Drought and an unspecified insect plague, possibly locusts, more than halved cocoa harvests in 1802–4, accentuating the shift to the east, where there was less need for irrigation (Tamaro 1988; 29–30, 52–3; McKinley 1985: 51, 139).

In other respects Barlovento producers retained the intensive cultivation traditions of Caracas. They totally cleared and burned forest, planted shade trees and wind breaks, dug irrigation and drainage channels, transplanted seedlings, and carefully pruned and weeded trees. Intervals between cocoa trees must have been quite wide, for it was noted that slaves adopted dense spacing on their little plots. Cocoa trees bore for only thirty years on average in Barlovento, compared to fifty years on the coast. The main disease was *la mancha*, a black 'stain' which killed trees. This was probably Phytophthora canker, a fungus particularly harmful to Criollo. Once harvested, beans were fermented for three days in a store, or exposed to the sun on patios in the daytime, and heaped up at night for light fermentation (Depons 1930: 226–35; Tamaro 1988: 52–63, 70–4; Walker 1822: II, 79–83, 86–7).

The intensity of cultivation lay in the use of labour rather than fixed capital. Debts were most likely to be incurred in the purchase of slaves, accounting for 20–30 per cent of the value of estates, whereas tools, animals and processing equipment represented a maximum of 2 per cent (McKinley 1985: 51). Many Barlovento estates even lacked stables and livestock, as mules were obtained from Caracas when necessary (Tamaro 1988: 108–9, 280).

An equally marked geographical shift was evident in eastern Venezuela (Harwich Vallenilla 1996: 23–4). Cotton and coffee replaced cocoa, which moved into virgin forest east of Cumaná. As trees only bore after eight to ten years, and quality was much superior to Guayaquil, producers must have been planting Criollo. The contrast was clear with the small bitter beans of the Orinoco, from trees which fruited abundantly in their fifth year (Humboldt 1852: I, 288–9; II, 335, 367, 422). However, the Barcelona Company complained in 1771 that the quality of Cumaná cocoa was 'very inferior' to that of Caracas, and fetched a much lower price (Oliva Melgar 1987: 300). Forastero or Trinitario cocoa may thus already have been cultivated in eastern Venezuela.

The cocoa frontier was moving in the opposite direction in western Venezuela, spilling over into the Nuevo Reino (Colombia) (Cardozo Galué 1991: 22–4, 53, 55, 63). The Coro region, seen as promising in 1720, was no longer even able to meet its own consumption needs in 1773 (Arcila Farias 1950: 50). In Cúcuta, Criollo was grown intensively on Caracas lines, with elaborate irrigation, permanent shade and wind-breaks. Small estates spread in 'wave-like' movement from the middle of the century. Groves were abandoned after thirty to fifty years, and producers moved on to clear the forest again (Brungardt 1974: 74–6, 88–90; Mollien 1824: 430). By 1796, indigo was taking over in parts of Cúcuta, and the cocoa frontier was moving south to Girón (Posada and Ibañez 1910: 354). Cocoa cultivation was also moving up the Magdalena river, with the areas around Neiva and Timaná producing about as much as Cúcuta and Girón by the 1810s (Patiño 1963: 317; Brungardt 1974: 93; Mollien 1824: 381).

Both Tabasco and Soconusco cocoa had an excellent reputation in

Madrid, indicating that Mesoamerica stuck to Criollo (Kany 1932: 152). The unbridled power of the great rivers which converged in Tabasco was a threat hanging over producers, with many cocoa estates swept away in 1782 (Gil y Saenz 1979: 144). Cocoa groves were vulnerable, as they stretched along the alluvial river banks (Gerhard 1979: 43). Tabascan production was also rocked by terrible plagues of locusts, especially in 1767–70 and again in 1801–5 (Ruiz Abreu 1989: 24; Ruz 1994: 243, 263–5). Locusts were a pest more widely in Mesoamerica, notably in Nicaragua and Guatemala at the turn of the century (Salvatierra 1939: II, 35; Newson 1987: 264; McCreery 1994: 19–20). While the old cocoa groves of Guatemala's Pacific piedmont were in decline, there was new planting, especially at either end of the cocoa belt (Solano 1974: 325–6, 340).

There were scattered references to wild cocoa in Mesoamerica, possibly feral trees, or perhaps *pataxte* (Theobroma Bicolor), sometimes mixed with true cocoa (Wood and Lass 1985: 11). Such pods were harvested in inland Guatemalan regions, and in northern Honduras, in the 1790s (Rubio Sánchez 1958: 91–2). Maya peoples also collected wild cocoa in southern Belize (*http*: 'The Maya Gold story'). Wild cocoa in Nicaragua came from eastern forests, not under Spanish control (Newson 1987: 72).

People in New Spain declared that Guayaquil cocoa came from 'almost wild trees', a partial exaggeration (Salvatierra 1939: II, 35). Stands of wild Forastero certainly remained important, shaded by a few high crowned jungle trees, but such stands were often rounded out with planted trees (Chiriboga 1980: 16, 196–7; Weinman 1970: 13–14). Trade liberalisation led to nearly 700,000 cocoa trees being sown in 1779–90 alone, set out in straight lines at intervals of about 3.5 metres (León Borja and Szászdi Nagy 1964: 31, 39–40). Five or more seeds were sown at stake, and the trunks of surviving trees were allowed to grow together. Irrigation was unnecessary, and the care of trees was limited to a little weeding, and scaring away monkeys (Baleato 1887: 65).

Aragonese Capuchin missionaries introduced Forastero into Trinidad in 1756, giving cocoa a new lease of life (Shephard 1937: III, 2). The new planting material was called 'Brazilian', but it may well have come from the Orinoco, and it hybridised with existing Criollo to form the original Trinitario. Missionaries propagated the planting of permanent shade trees at intervals of 13 metres, the fermentation of beans for three days under leaves, and sun drying. Drought was an occasional problem, as in 1772, when the cocoa crop failed (Newson 1976: 135–6; Giacottino 1976: II, 321, 328–9; John 1988: 11, 13).

Planters in the French possessions followed this Trinidadian model. In the 1730s, explorers had discovered abundant wild Forastero cocoa inland from Oyapock, and had planted some near Cayenne (Patiño 1963: 326). Forastero seedlings were sent to Martinique, encouraging small landowners to try the crop again from around 1765. The French knew that cocoa could only be grown successfully on newly cleared forest land, and in Martinique and Guadeloupe this meant steep slopes unsuitable for sugar (May 1930: 95–6; Arcy 1930: 16; Blérald 1986: 26, 97). In Saint-Domingue, cocoa spread in the rainy southwest corner of the island, where in 1767 it was planted 'in the middle of the forests, in the interior' (Léon 1963: 203). In 1808, either three seeds were sown at stake or seedlings were transplanted, and plantain shaded young trees. Beans were fermented in canoes covered with banana leaves for four to five days, the length of fermentation suggesting that this was Forastero or Trinitario. They were then dried in the sun, in courtyards (Street 1960: 156).

French refugees probably brought these methods to eastern Cuba after 1791. They certainly planted cocoa in land cleared of virgin forest, although they grew much more coffee at this stage, and do not appear to have inter-cropped the two. Officials in the Guantánamo region noted disparagingly in 1797 that cocoa was sown and then simply left to its fate (Marrero 1972–89: XI, 101, 133–4).

Hurricanes remained the major threat in Caribbean islands. An 'unprece-dented' run of tropical storms between 1780 and 1786 contributed to a fall in British Caribbean cocoa exports (Carrington 1988: 58, 180). Hurricanes in that decade were also blamed as one factor preventing exports from Santo Domingo (Sevilla Soler 1980: 93–4; Patiño 1963: 297; Moreau de Saint-Méry 1944: 99). The 1812 volcanic eruption in Saint Vincent destroyed most of the cocoa trees on the island (Ragatz 1977: 349). A precocious British concern with the desiccating effects of clearing primary forest may have hampered cocoa cultivation in the ceded islands, where forest reserves were established in the hills and mountains after 1763 (Grove 1995: ch. 6).

Cocoa cultivation shrank in parts of the Guianas, but expanded in others. In Berbice, exports fell as European planters drifted from the forested inte-rior to the swampy coastal plain, transformed into fertile sugar land by Dutch capital and technology (Kramer 1991). In French Guiana, where the same process was at work, cocoa exports also declined (Cardoso 1984: 27–9, 193). Surinam was the exception, as Forastero was planted in the northeast from around 1760. Prospective planters in 1770 were warned to stick to well drained virgin forest, as ninety years were needed to allow sufficient forest to regenerate on abandoned coffee estates. Little attention was given to cocoa once established, in terms of either weeding or pruning (Reyne 1924–5: 61–5, 118, 124). The lack of permanent shade may have accounted for a certain narrowing of the interval between cocoa trees, still generous at 4 metres. Seed was planted at stake, and nurseries probably served to fill gaps (Hall 1932: 338). Beans were fermented, dried in the shade, and packed in barrels (Stedman 1988: 479–80).

Late eighteenth-century accounts provide a rough guide to the picking of wild Forastero cocoa in the interior of South America. From the confluence with the Negro river eastwards, the alluvial terraces of the Amazon contained the most accessible stands, exploited by the Portuguese. The Madeira river, a great southern affluent, also yielded a fair amount. More wild pods were gathered in Spain's Andean piedmont, and in the contested Amazon-Orinoco watershed (Patiño 1963: 269–96; Humboldt 1852: II, 335, 367, 422). A little came from the interior of the Guianas (Reyne 1924–5: 7, 9).

Asia remained wedded to Criollo. The Philippines Company attempted to improve cocoa cultivation after 1785, in part by introducing seedlings from Guatemala (González Fernández 1875: 186). West Javanese experiments in the 1780s were conducted with seed from Manila (Haan 1910–12: III, 863).

Adjustment to economic crisis, 1820s–1840s

With prices low and labour scarce, Venezuelan producers were under great pressure to change their ways. Forastero or Trinitario rapidly became dominant in eastern Venezuela after independence (Harwich Vallenilla 1996: 26). Introductions into Barlovento were recorded in 1820 and 1825, the latter in El Guapo. Despite opposition from those who feared for the reputation of Venezuelan brands, 'inferior' trees spread rapidly. Coastal estates and Maracaibo remained bastions of Criollo, but the temptation to switch was even felt there (Middleton 1871; Erneholm 1948: 120–1; Tamaro 1988: 45; Patiño 1963: 331). Exceptionally dry years in the 1820s increased the pressure (Izard 1972: 134–6). The shift continued towards eastern Barlovento, more humid and with more forested land. While Caucagua had some 1.5 million cocoa trees in 1836, Rio Chico contained 3.6 million (Tamaro 1988: 51–3, 70). Venezuelan methods seem to have remained labour-intensive, although Boussingault's account may have drawn heavily on earlier writings by Humboldt and Depons (Boussingault 1851: I, 462–8). More telling was an anecdote of planters in the Aragua valley, making workers shout their heads off all day long to scare birds away from ripening pods, rather than wasting precious gunpowder (Boussingault 1974: 202).

Similar problems were encountered to the west. Ageing Criollo trees and the neglect of irrigation preceded the 1827–33 crisis in Maracaibo and Cúcuta. *La mancha*, probably Phytophthora canker, made black patches on trunks, eventually killing trees (Brungardt 1974: 85–7; Cardozo Galué 1991: 48). By the mid-nineteenth century, Cúcuta had turned to coffee (Camacho Roldán 1895: 664; Patiño 1963: 319). However, intensive methods of cultivating Criollo were apparently transferred to Tolima. Planters around Gigante prepared nurseries, protecting seedlings with a temporary thatch of palm leaves, and transplanted after six months. Cocoa trees were spaced widely, at intervals of 5 metres, and were watered. Yields were claimed to be 2 kilos of dry cocoa per tree, high for Criollo. There was also wild cocoa in the mountains, bitter but aromatic (Boussingault 1851: I, 462–3, 465, 469).

Mesoamericans were also intensive cultivators, who feared either too little or too much water. Tabasco's mighty and unpredictable rivers frequently flooded and changed their course, necessitating extensive dykes and drainage works (Arias *et al.* 1987: 33–4). In contrast, Nicaragua's delicate Criollo trees, already devastated by a hurricane, were nearly wiped out by a terrible drought in 1846 (Lanuza *et al.* 1983: 87).

In contrast, Ecuador's low costs were a boon in depressed markets. At the most basic level, planters continued to ameliorate stands of wild trees (Chiriboga 1980: 196–7). When they sowed cocoa, they did so at stake, dispensing with nurseries (Boussingault 1851: I, 464). The trick was to plant in alluvial terraces close enough to the water table to offset the dry season, but not so close as to kill the trees at the time of the annual flood (Kaerger 1901: II, 437–8). All harvesting had ceased by 1824 in the island of Puná, which had earlier produced some 50 tonnes of cocoa a year, and there were abandoned cocoa plantations near Naranjal in 1832 (Arosemena 1991: I, 25, 78, 181; Terry 1834: 66, 250–1). Most new cocoa groves in the 1830s seem to have been up the Daule river (Gosselman 1962: 96).

Lower Amazonian methods were similarly simple. Collection and cultivation merged imperceptibly around Cametá. Patches of forest on river banks were cleared and burned, and beans or seedlings were 'stuck in here and there almost at random' among numerous jungle trees, with banana trees for temporary shade. Trees bore precociously, after only three years, and were harvested by men standing in canoes with knives attached to the end of long sticks. Beans were rarely specially fermented, but pods remained piled up for long periods in canoes (Soares 1977: 112–16; Bates 1969: 78–9).

Cultivation was only slightly more intensive elsewhere in the Amazon, and in Bahia. Around Santarém, the forest was completely cleared, and trees were planted very densely in rows, without permanent shade. They were occasionally weeded. Some larger growers had wheeled covers to draw over the drying beans during showers. Fermentation and drying were poor, however, leading to complaints of mouldy beans (Bates 1969: 143; Wallace 1890: 98–9; Spruce 1908: I, 78, 80). In Mojos, Forastero from the surrounding jungle appears to have replaced Criollo, for trees fruited around five years of age. When banana trees had reached a certain height, cocoa seeds were sown at their foot (Orbigny 1992: 301). The timid revival of cocoa cultivation in southern Bahia stuck to well drained alluvial terraces, sandy banks serving to dry beans (Monbeig 1937: 280–3). The forest was completely cleared, and little or no permanent shade was provided (Mahony 1996: 318).

Despite patches of cultivation, most Amazon cocoa beans came from the wild, with Borba, on the lower Madeira, a major centre. From the upper reaches of the Negro, wild beans either came south to the Amazon, or descended the Orinoco (Soares 1977: 113; Patiño 1963: 327; Briceño de Bermúdez 1993: 146). Wild cocoa was picked in eastern Bolivia, especially around Apolobamba (Orbigny 1992: 74, 180, 301–2, 324). In British Guiana, some Amerindians near the Essequibo river had apparently planted cocoa in the past, but had abandoned their groves (Schomburgk 1840: 91, 107–8).

Most of the non-Hispanic Caribbean faced great ecological problems. There was little primary forest left on small and densely settled islands, much of it on dauntingly steep slopes, and yet, as one West Indian planter put it, cocoa 'requires virgin soil' (Great Britain 1831–2: para. 493). The humid and little developed southwest of Haïti was thus a favoured spot (Franklin 1828: 356; Street 1960: 175). Violent storms were a further hazard, especially in the Windward islands (Honychurch 1984: 92; Ragatz 1977: 375). French Guiana, where cocoa grew above the empoldered lands of Cayenne, had no convenient dry season, and beans dried over open fires had an unpleasant taste (Mam-Lam-Fouck 1986: 227). Trinidad's circumstances were thus exceptionally favourable. The island lay to the south of the hurricane belt, had high and well distributed rainfall, and retained good reserves of primary forest on gently sloping land (Giacottino 1977).

Producers in the Portuguese African islands of São Tomé and Príncipe usually intercropped cocoa with coffee, but cut out cocoa when prices favoured coffee. Cultivation was simple. One or two seeds were sown at stake, and there was little weeding or pruning. Beans were fermented in tins, and were spread to dry directly on the ground (Omboni 1846: 245; César 1969: 79, 87–8, 92).

In contrast, smallholders in the Philippines used fairly intensive techniques to grow Criollo for the internal market. They raised seedlings in nurseries, often in large leaves filled with soil, and planted them out in ditches about a metre and a half deep. Spacing was dense, at about a metre and a half, to keep down weeds. Banana trees served as temporary shade, and permanent shade was provided. Irrigation was sometimes necessary. Producers burned leaves to smoke out harmful insects, such as a worm which penetrated the bark and killed the trees, a technique learned from the Jesuits. Beans were sun dried (Buzeta and Bravo 1851: I, 203; Mas 1843: II; Mallat 1983: 86, 246; Jagor 1875: 95). However, the unsubdued highlanders of Negros appear to have treated cocoa like a wild tree, to be harvested but not cared for (Buzeta and Bravo 1851: I, 29).

Smallholder techniques in the ascendant, 1850s–1870s

Despite the partial recovery of prices and exports, the poor performance of cocoa relative to other crops meant that little attention was lavished on making production more 'scientific'. Smallholders took a larger share of production, and their simple and effective methods even tended to predominate on estates.

Ecuador was the prime example of large landowners successfully using techniques criticised in 1880 as 'ancient' and 'primitive'. Two to four seeds were planted directly in the ground. There was no attempt to select the strongest seedling, or to prune trees, and trunks grew into a tall and inter-twined *mata*. Plantations looked like jungles, and yields per *mata* were low. Men cut pods from high branches with knives attached to poles, children picked up pods, and women opened them. Beans were immediately set out to dry in the sun, probably being heaped up at night for light fermentation (Toscano 1960: 466–7).

Simple forms of cultivation also persisted along the Amazon, despite looming problems. In the little groves around Santarém, smallholders inter-planted cocoa with manioc in the 1860s, and with the occasional coffee or rubber tree (Agassiz and Agassiz 1969: 170, 174). Cocoa was still grown without permanent shade, and beans were sun dried. A crucial skill was judging whether fertile alluvial terraces were not likely to flood for long enough to kill cocoa trees, the presence of the Urucury palm being a favourable sign. As the harvest coincided with the slack period in collecting wild rubber, competition for labour was not yet overwhelming (Smith 1879: 94, 110–12). Older plantings on the Negro river were entirely abandoned, and signs of the end of a cycle appeared below Obidos, attributed to soil exhaustion but probably accelerated by the neglect of shade (Orton 1876: 251, 356, 361, 517). However, there appears to have been new planting up the Juruá, Purús and Madeira rivers (*Gordian*: XIX, 6301).

Wild cocoa was rarely available along the main stream of the Amazon, obliging collectors to go up the tributaries. Humble gatherers pushed into ever more remote areas of the forest, mainly exploring for wild rubber, but picking cocoa if they found any (Marcoy 1875: II, 427). The Madeira river, draining much of eastern Bolivia before entering Brazil, was of especial importance for wild cocoa (Orton 1876: 290; Brown and Lidstone 1878: 352).

The slow transition from estates to smallholdings in Venezuela was accompanied by less intensive cultivation. Some producers kept jungle trees for shade, and planting intervals were sometimes reduced to as little as two metres (Barral 1966: 84–7). The main change was the continuing progression of Trinitarios. Despite a proposal to flog anybody introducing them, they dominated much of Barlovento by 1870. Prices varied enormously, $40–45 being paid locally for a *fanega* of 'best creole', compared to only $18–22 for 'inferior Trinitario'. The extremely serious drought of 1868–9, in which only trees close to a supply of permanent water survived, hastened the process of substitution. For those concerned with preserving great brands, it was particularly shocking that Trinitario should have been introduced on the coast in 1854, close to the famous plantations of Chuao and Choroní. Coastal planters thus tried to reach agreement to uproot all Trinitarios (Middleton 1871: 452–7).

Trinidadian methods were somewhere in between intensive and extensive.

The foremost French planter wrote that, 'cacao plantations prosper only in virgin lands, and cannot be made to succeed any other cultivations'. The forest was completely cleared, and two types of shade tree were planted. Direct sowing of two cocoa beans at stake was the norm, the weaker seedling being removed if more than one germinated. Nurseries of seedlings were established, but only to fill gaps when both seeds failed. Trees usually bore well for forty years. Although no major diseases were reported, the same terrible drought that afflicted Venezuela reduced yields for five years after 1869. For rude British palates, beans were immediately spread to dry, and were only lightly fermented in heaps during the night. For more discriminating French and Spanish consumers, beans were thoroughly fermented for five to eight days, usually under banana or plantain leaves, but sometimes in wooden boxes. They were then dried in the sun (Verteuil 1858: 262–4; Giacottino 1976: II, 418–19; Shephard 1937: III, 7).

When coffee prices collapsed in the late 1840s, French planters in eastern Cuba were encouraged to plant cocoa and coffee together, a kind of inter-cropping not mentioned in treatises on coffee before the 1840s (Marrero 1972–89: XI, 135; Pérez de la Riva 1944: 149–73). Although rarely successful elsewhere, it had become standard practice by 1888. Virgin forest was fully cleared on mountain slopes up to 1,000 metres. Food crops such as maize and plantain were harvested for a few years, the latter providing temporary shade for the young trees. There was no mention of permanent shade, but rather of cocoa shading coffee. After ten to twelve years, declining coffee trees were cut out. The value of output over a cultivation cycle was roughly one quarter coffee to three quarters cocoa (United States 1888: 37, 117–19). Planters experimented with Venezuelan Criollo, but seem to have relied on Trinitario or Forastero (Mangin 1860: 37–8). Spain also tried to renew cocoa cultivation on Puerto Rico, but the island's coffee economy rebounded more quickly (Gil-Bermejo García 1970: 189; Palerm Rincón 1982: 686; United States 1888: 124).

Turning to cocoa was also a response to the coffee crisis for estate owners in Dominica and Surinam. However, the replanting of former coffee lands with cocoa in Dominica proved a poor substitute to chopping down virgin forest (Gordian; VIII, 3263–7). The same could be said of planting cocoa trees in the gaps left by dead coffee trees in Surinam (Panday 1959: 181, 185). The recovery of cocoa production in Surinam was due rather to the opening of a new pioneer front, as the planting of Forastero shifted from the northeast to the centre. The use of Erythrina Glauca as permanent shade may have spread, although the dating of this practice is unclear (Reyne 1924–5: 18, 62, 198; Hall 1932: 338).

The Forastero Amelonado variety, spreading outwards from Príncipe, was almost unchallenged in western Africa, although the Spaniards in Fernando Póo experimented with Forastero Arriba in the 1860s (Hall 1914: 91; Sorela 1884: 32). Cocoa was grown under shade in Gabon, almost certainly copying methods on Príncipe (Tornezy 1984: 170). Producers in São Tomé and Príncipe generally clung to the simplest and cheapest of techniques (Silva 1969: 147; Silva 1883: 18).

Colombian producers clung to delicate Criollo, and paid the price. *La mancha* caused the abrupt collapse of production in western Antioquia in 1850–5 (Brew 1977: 245–6; Patiño 1963: 297, 313, 319; Schenck 1953: 41; Beyer 1947: 36). Cultivation in Tolima continued, but in a costly manner. Forested land was felled on slopes up to around 1,000 metres. Producers used plantain for temporary shade, and planted Erythrina as permanent shade. Some irrigation was necessary, and average yields were only around 0.75 kilos per tree (*PP* 1888: vol. 100). Small farmers on the lower Magdalena fermented beans in old canoes, and dried them in the sun (Holton 1967: 46). In Cauca, former slaves grew cocoa and tobacco on raised river banks, with plantain as their staple food (Taussig 1977: 417). They suffered from locusts and drought in the late 1870s (Eder 1959: 168–9).

Mesoamerica's excellent Criollo was produced at even more fearful cost. Water storage facilities and lined irrigation channels were especially expensive in Nicaragua, but absolutely essential. The forest was completely felled, tree stumps were uprooted, and bananas provided temporary shade. Permanent shade and wind-breaks were planted, cocoa seedlings were transplanted from nurseries, and weeding was thorough. Trees were highly susceptible to pests and diseases, only bore fruit after seven or eight years, and yielded a mere 0.2 kilos per tree. Beans were fermented for about three days in old canoes, dried in the sun, and sorted. It took nine years to get any income, although profits of 25 per cent a year were eventually obtained by the patient and the lucky, as consumers were prepared to pay a hefty premium (Lévy 1873: 445, 458, 461, 465–70; Scherzer 1857: I, 123). Impatient Guatemalan landowners in the 1860s 'tore up flourishing cacao plantations to plant cotton that soon succumbed to diseases, and then coffee trees that withered and died in the heat' (McCreery 1994: 6). At the opposite extreme was the collection of 'wild' cocoa, probably feral Criollo, thriving on alluvial soils in northern Honduras (Squier 1970b: 140, 161–2; Mangin 1860: 19; Touzard 1993: 22).

There was a fall in the estimated number of cocoa trees in Tabasco, from around four million in 1854 to three million in 1890. While changes in taxation might account for this, there was also a bad drought in the Sierra in 1859–61, followed by a series of devastating floods (Scherr 1985: 39, 72). A particularly high flood afflicted the Sierra in 1868, possibly worsened by a neglect of water control measures in the unsettled political conditions of the time (Arias *et al.* 1987: 251). A plague of locusts was also reported in 1856 (Alejo Torre 1931: 14). Yields were allegedly lower in the 1860s than they had been earlier, suggesting ageing trees (Gil y Saenz 1979: 36–7). These problems may have led to the introduction of Forastero and simpler cultivation methods, for in the 1860s cocoa trees were reported to be bearing after four years, seed was planted at stake, and spacing was close, albeit under permanent shade (*Larousse*: XI, 200).

Asian cultivation also depended on Criollo, and again paid the price. Moluccan pioneer fronts moved rapidly along, as delicate Criollo trees lived only twelve years on average, thirty years at most, ravaged from the 1840s by the pod borer or cocoa moth, *Acrocercops* (*Conopomorpha*) *Cramerella*. Only found in Southeast Asia, the moth laid its eggs on cocoa pods, and the larvae burrowed inside, ate the pulp, and inhibited the growth of the beans. The Dutch recommended rooting out the worst affected trees, cutting off all pods at times of minimal fruiting, and burning such pods, or burying them deep in the ground. This was highly labour-intensive and rather ineffective, as the larvae also fed on wild plants. Undaunted, the Dutch ordered the uprooting of some 400,000 infected trees in 1867. Indigenous responses to the pod borer appear to have been more cost effective. Sick trees were given no care, but were harvested of any sound pods which they might bear. Farmers then moved further into the forest to plant again (Clarence-Smith 1998: 99–102). The dominant variety in Ceylon was 'Old Red', a Caracas Criollo with a fine taste but a low yield (Maclaren 1924: 194). On the Malabar coast of India, Criollo seedlings were transplanted and grown under permanent shade (Rice 1876–8: III, 48).

A greater problem for the Philippines was that the northern and central islands lay athwart the track of tropical storms sweeping in from the Pacific. The great typhoon of 1856 caused immense damage to delicate Criollo trees, discouraging large landowners from growing the crop for a generation (Jagor 1875: 96; Foreman 1890: 354–5). In the 1870s, it was said that violent storms afflicted cocoa growers almost every year (*PP* 1876: vol. 73). The first possible report of the pod borer moth dates from the late 1850s, but it does not appear to have been as devastating as in the Moluccas (Jagor 1875: 96). Indeed, pod borer seems to have been absent in Sulu as late as 1878 (Burbidge 1989: 221).

The 'modern estate' and its weaknesses, 1880s–1914

The great cocoa boom was accompanied by a conviction that science would transform tropical agriculture, and that biologically inferior tropical peoples would merely provide unskilled labour (Clarence-Smith 1995). As one expert put it, trees not in straight lines 'appear all awry and crooked, and will be an offence to the meticulous and mathematical eye' (Knapp 1923: 37). In the event, no capital- or labour-intensive techniques enjoyed any substantial economic success. Indeed, it was later discovered that the obsessive tidiness of estates hampered the breeding of pollinating insects, thus reducing yields (Young 1994: 167–8).

Estates were wrongfooted by staking their future on quality. 'Fine' cocoa accounted for 79 per cent of world exports in 1895, but only 32 per cent in

1912 (Hall 1914: 495–6). Indeed, these figures understate the change, as Hall's 'fine' category included not only Forastero Arriba from Ecuador, but also inferior Forastero from eastern Venezuela and elsewhere. As imports of 'bulk' beans overtook those of 'fine' beans, price differentials narrowed, as indicated in Table 7.1. The greatest differences were found within Venezuela, between coastal Criollos and eastern Forasteros.

Ecuador's great estates slowly ceased to be paragons of elegant simplicity, although stands of wild trees were still being discovered and improved quite late (Arosemena 1991: I, 234). One estate had 800,000 in production, some bearing heavily (Weinman 1970: 59). Thousands of wild trees were sometimes discovered at once in the 1890s, although they were apparently in a minority by 1900 (Preuss 1987: 84–5; Kaerger 1901: II, 437). As late as 1914, there were reports of workers improving wild stands, easily recognisable by their irregular spatial distribution (Enock 1914: 112, 328–9).

Preuss criticised Guayaquil's 'jungles', while conceding that landowners made good profits. In the Arriba region, virgin forest was cleared in the dry season. Selected jungle trees were retained for permanent shade, including some that yielded fruit, rubber or valuable timber. Brushwood was left to dry before being piled up and burned. Large stumps were left to rot for four to six years. No plant holes were dug, as the soil was loose and without stones. A number of seeds were sown at stake, at least two and as many as ten. Planting was in sinuous lines, following the contours of river banks. All seedlings were left to grow together as one *mata*, and suckers were not removed, so that a *mata* might eventually consist of as many as sixteen interwoven trunks and live for decades. Plantains and cassava provided temporary shade, and other food crops were interplanted. Weeding was only for food crops, being abandoned once the canopy had formed. This took only four years, due to planting intervals of about 2.5 metres. Cocoa trees were not pruned, watered, drained or fertilised. Any spaces were filled with

Table 7.1 Highest and lowest prices paid in Le Hâvre in 1913 (French Francs per 100 kilos)

Origin	Highest price	Lowest price
Venezuela	200	78
Ceylon	105	85
Pará	87	83
Guayaquil	86	78
Accra	86	76
São Tomé	84	81
Bahia	81	75
Trinidad	80	80
Haïti	78	68

Source: Tosta Filho 1957: 3

transplanted seedlings. Beans were fermented in heaps at night, under banana leaves or canvas, and were dried in the sun on split bamboo matting during the day. They were often dried again in Guayaquil, in large cement yards or in the open streets (Preuss 1987: 78, 82–7; Kaerger 1901: II, 437–47; Tudhope 1921).

Ecuadorian planters began to move away from these effective methods of cultivation, although initial changes were forced by circumstances. From the 1880s, the cocoa frontier began to spill out from the Guayas plain, pushing into the foothills of the Andes, where it was discovered that Arriba trees did not grow wild and could not be planted. Landowners sought to introduce Criollo, but the Venezolano that thrived turned out to be a sturdy Forastero. The quality was inferior, but while an Arriba tree yielded around half a kilo a year, a Venezolano produced three times as much (Crawford de Roberts 1980: 49–51; Chiriboga 1980: 127, 196–7, 210; Preuss 1987: 87–8; Tudhope 1921: 354–5). When European brokers and manufacturers complained in 1911 that quality was deteriorating, planters responded that new varieties still accounted for a small proportion of the harvest, while admitting that beans of different kinds were sometimes mixed together (*Gordian*: XVIII, 4527–30).

Some modernising planters, especially in the foothills, began to adopt new methods of cultivation from around 1900. They cleared the forest completely, planted shade trees, left lanes at regular intervals, raised seedlings in nurseries of bamboo wood, planted single seedlings in one spot, cut out suckers, spaced cocoa trees at intervals of up to 4 metres, grew them in straight rows, weeded intensively, and pruned the trees. However, they employed neither fertiliser nor fungicides. They achieved higher yields per tree, but it is far from clear that it was worth the cost (Chiriboga 1980: 202–6, 391; Kaerger 1901: II, 437–47; Preuss 1987: 82–4).

The number of planters who adopted new methods should not be exaggerated, nor the lengths to which they were prepared to go. In 1914, it was estimated that Ecuador deployed only 0.2 workers per hectare of cocoa, the lowest number in the world (Sociedade de Emigração 1915: 93). Most likely to experiment were the few planters who had raised capital in Europe, for local banks made loans according to the number of bearing trees, discouraging wide spacing (*Gordian*: XIV, 1981, 2184). Balao planters experimented with disc ploughs and harrows, but found that they could neither intercrop foodstuffs nor plant shade trees (Chiriboga 1980: 202–3). The Seminario brothers began fermenting on textbook lines, only to discover that Guayaquil merchants refused to pay a premium (Hall 1914: 303–4). Planters who bought expensive dryers were dismayed to discover that Western brokers classified artificially dried beans as inferior (Tudhope 1921: 355).

Ecuador's remarkable freedom from disease began to change, following the introduction of Forastero and the spread of cultivation into the wetter foothills (Tudhope 1921: 352–5; Ruf 1995: 162–72). In 1897, *la mancha* or *la mosquilla* was held responsible for the bankruptcy of some estates, diagnosed by Preuss as 'black pod' fungus (Chiriboga 1980: 391; Preuss 1987: 90; Kaerger 1901: II, 447). In 1901, a German botanist was hired to study means of combating the problem (Weilbauer 1974: 40). Much more serious was the discovery of the Moniliophthora (or Monilia) Roreri fungus in 1914, and the witches' broom fungus, previously confined to the eastern side of the Andes, after 1918. Together, these fungi contributed to a sharp postwar contraction in Ecuador's output (Wood and Lass 1985: 283, 293–5).

Cultivation methods became much more intensive on Trinidadian estates, as production soared, properties grew in size and newfangled theories spread. Not only was the forest cleared and burned, but the site was then cleaned up and burned a second time, before drainage ditches were dug. While three seeds might still be sown at stake, nurseries were also maintained. Planting intervals widened from some 3 metres to about 5 metres. Cocoa trees were pruned so thoroughly that even Preuss thought this was taken to extremes. Shade trees were planted every 9 metres or so, allowing one shade tree for two cocoa trees. Experimentation with different shade trees proved unsatisfactory, contributing to a gradual abandoning of permanent shade before 1914. Copied from Grenada, this also served to cut labour costs, increase yields, and combat pod rot, the main disease in the island (Preuss 1987: 30–9, 42; Hall 1914: 379). Experiments with grafting were also carried out, probably in Trinidad (Brown 1913: 48–9).

Primary processing was not only labour-intensive on estates, but also capital-intensive. Fermentation was usually for eight days in wooden boxes, but 'inferior Calabacillo' was fermented for an astonishing fourteen days. The fermented beans were then 'danced'. Workers trod on them with bare feet, to remove any remaining detritus and give them a smooth polished appearance. The most up-to-date drying machines were used, burning wood as fuel. Drying sheds had a light movable roofs on wheels, to allow for some sun drying (Preuss 1987: 40–59). In contrast, smallholders fermented beans under plantain leaves in their groves, and spread them out to dry on the ground in the sun, with makeshift sheds to keep the rain off. Venezuelan Panyols fermented for three days, followed by drying in the day and heaping up at night for extra fermentation (Moodie-Kublalsingh 1994: 20–2).

The ending of Trinidad's great cocoa boom after 1920 was not due to a lack of fresh forested land. The advance of cocoa, unusually well mapped, shows how cultivation pushed out into the central and eastern forests, with the help of a good network of roads and railways. Abandoned sugar lands proved ill adapted to cocoa, as did some sandy or swampy soils, and the British established forest reserves. However, there was still much land available for cocoa cultivation in the 1930s (Giacottino 1976: II, 397, 543–8, 553, 570–6, 586; Preuss 1987: 30).

Grenada was famous for not having permanent shade on most of its cocoa estates. This resulted in more rapid maturation and less fungal infestation, but the lifespan of cocoa trees was probably shortened. To compensate for the lack of shade trees, cocoa was planted at intervals of 3 metres, the soil was regularly forked, drains were installed, and chemical and organic fertiliser was applied. A relative abundance of labour on the island probably reduced the cost of these operations. However, Grenada's real problem by 1914 was a shortage of virgin forest (Williams 1922: 215–23; Preuss 1987: 34–5; Milstead 1940: 196–9). Replacing sugar with cocoa in the plains was a poor substitute for cutting down the jungle (Hall 1932: 395).

Cocoa estates elsewhere in the British Caribbean adopted 'modern' methods, but did poorly. Jamaica relied on 'elaborate systems of drainage'. Storms periodically wreaked havoc, even on estates tucked away in sheltered valleys (Knapp 1923: 35; Davies 1924: 165). Worthy Park's cocoa was wiped out by a great hurricane in 1902 (Craton and Walvin 1970: 250). Attempts at long-term intercropping with bananas failed. While some estates decided to convert from bananas to cocoa in the 1900s, the movement was often in the opposite direction. As in the other Antilles, Forastero was dominant (Hall 1932: 411–12). Dominica had much forest left, but planters complained that slopes were steep, soils heavy, and rainfall excessive. Wind-breaks were planted rather than permanent shade, but they gave little protection when the destructive hurricane of 1916 struck the island (Great Britain 1942: 189, 191, 196; Hall 1932: 401). Estates in British Guiana estates followed 'modern' norms, but only had about 750 hectares planted in 1913 (Preuss 1987: 21; Maclaren 1924: 193).

Venezuelan estate owners walked a tightrope between maintaining the reputation of their famous Criollo brands, while planting more Trinitario. Barlovento and Maracaibo had largely succumbed to Trinitario by 1911, leaving Criollo mainly confined to the coast between La Guaira and Puerto Cabello. A little was also grown to the west of the city of Caracas. However, pure groves of Criollo were now almost unknown, as almost all producers mixed varieties. When Criollo trees died, the gap was filled with a Trinitario, a dubious ploy even witnessed in the famous Chuao estate. Hybridisation allegedly resulted in trees close to Criollo in this area, contrasting with the usual reversion to Forastero. Prices varied more in Venezuela than in any other cocoa producing country, ranging from 131 marks for 50 kilos of fine coastal Criollo to 41 marks for the same amount of 'Carúpano' Forastero in 1897 (Preuss 1987: 64–70; Guislain and Vincart 1911: 69–73).

Where Criollo was grown, intensive and expensive methods of production persisted. The trees only yielded fully after nine years, and then only around 0.25 kilos per tree (Guislain and Vincart 1911: 69–71). Producers trans- planted seedlings, and took great care with irrigation and the manipulation of shade (Hall 1914: 373–4). Fermentation was short, a day or two at most (Preuss 1987: 66). There was no mention of *la mancha*, the disease which had caused so much trouble in the past, but Criollo was subject to the depre- dations of a 'gray moth' (Bell 1922: 256).

Preuss opined that cultivation of Trinitario 'is not intensive, and the preparation of the harvest is simple and almost primitive'. The forest was completely cleared, and shade trees were planted, usually a kind of Erythrina. Sowing was at stake, without plant holes, and nurseries were only established to fill gaps. Planting intervals were usually 3 metres, sometimes less, and food crops were interplanted. Trees fruited at about four years of age, and were in full bearing at seven. They were pruned and kept short, but weeding was lackadaisical. Simple irrigation involved diverting mountain streams into open unlined trenches. Trees were free of disease, apart from a little pod rot, and yields were variously estimated at 0.5–1 kilo per tree. Beans were fermented for up to eight days, according to the old practice of drying beans in the sun, and fermenting them at night in heaps under banana leaves, often in the open air. Before the final drying, beans were coated with red earth, customary for the Spanish and French markets, the earth allegedly protecting beans against insects and fungi. Artificial dryers were not in use (Preuss 1987: 68–72; Guislain and Vincart 1911: 69–72).

Constant experimentation was the rule in the foreign-owned estates of Colombia's Atlantic lowlands, albeit with few positive results. It was probably here that Forastero or Trinitario was introduced around 1890, although it did not reach Antioquia till the 1920s (Lass and Wood 1985: 549–50; Brew 1977: 249). Planters tried growing cocoa with no shade, with retained jungle trees, and with varying densities of planted shade. They initially planted seeds directly in the fields, but seem to have shifted to transplanting. They also varied pruning and irrigation, and intercropped with bananas and rubber. In the end, it proved most profitable to concentrate on bananas (Thomson 1895: 419–25; Posada Carbó 1996: 49–51).

Colombia's Tolima estates were coming to the end of a long cycle. In the late 1880s, it was reported that a 'most destructive disease' was attacking Criollo cocoa in this area, even relatively young trees (*PP* 1888: vol. 100). A similarly unspecified malady was again mentioned in the 1890s, albeit patchy in its impact, and cocoa groves were described as decrepit. Yields were very low, at only 0.25 kilos per tree (Thomson 1895: 423). No remedy could be found for the 'blight', and by 1913 the region's cocoa production was a shadow of what it had once been (Eder 1913: 210). Garzón was the only area where cocoa was prospering in 1914 (Lévine 1914: 161).

Techniques in the Amazonian piedmont of the Andes were intensive around Cuzco. Producers must still have been growing Criollo, as their beans fetched much more than those from Guayaquil (Orton 1876: 437). In the Urubamba valley, plant holes were dug, seedlings were transplanted from nurseries, and planting intervals were twice those in Ecuador. Moreover, trees were pruned, and irrigated in dry season. Beans were washed, fermented, and sometimes dried artificially (Kaerger 1901: II, 376–7). In Bolivia's Yungas valleys, however, estate owners concentrated scarce labour resources on coca bushes. They planted cocoa trees haphaz-ardly, giving them little care and attention (Walle 1925: 171–3).

An English traveller complained in the 1900s that Mexican methods were unsatisfactory. Nurseries were of poor quality, planting was too dense, Castilloa rubber trees were unsuitable as permanent shade, there was no pruning, and there were no publicly funded research stations (*Gordian*: XV, 3081). A German expert noted that Tabascans neither hoed nor fertilised the soil after planting, and sometimes employed no more than a sharpened digging stick to work the ground. Yields per tree were low and there was no treatment for the main disease, *la mancha* or *la broma*, which often followed a particularly high flood. This was probably Phytophthora canker, as dark patches appeared on the trunk and eventually killed the tree (Kaerger 1901: II, 494–508). Methods in Pichucalco were also described as backward, and wild or feral cocoa was collected in Palenque (Oficina de Informaciones 1895: 15, 18).

Such criticism was wide of the mark, as Mexican cocoa cultivation was probably more intensive than was wise. Producers clear-felled and burned the forest, digging drainage ditches where flooding was a problem. They planted shade trees in advance, experimenting with a variety of rubber trees. Seedlings from nurseries were transplanted into plant holes in straight lines. Estate owners gradually increased spacing between trees, excised suckers, and weeded three or four times a year when the canopy had not yet formed. They even tried some replanting in former cocoa groves. Beans were often washed before fermentation, and were sometimes sun dried on artificial surfaces. By-products were fed to the cattle of the numerous local ranches (Kaerger 1901: II, 494–508; Rabana 1895). Forastero varieties appear to have been introduced in greater numbers at this time, although numerous local names for varieties are confusing (Wood and Lass 1985: 556; Peña 1951: III, 929–31; Rabana 1895).

The intensive nature of Nicaraguan production certainly contributed to decline. Droughts, together with a volcanic eruption in 1883, reduced the number of cocoa trees to around 0.4 million by 1900. In a bid to improve returns and break into exports, Menier replaced Criollo with heavier-yielding Trinitario. However, construction and maintenance costs for irrigation remained excessively expensive. Water was collected in reservoirs and distributed through a network of channels, lined with cement, with a trench for each row of cocoa trees. The provision of one planted shade tree per cocoa tree was another heavy expense, especially as both shade and cocoa trees were heavily pruned to keep them low. Fermentation was in cement basins, two days being allowed for Criollo beans and four for Trinitario, and wheeled trays moved sun dried beans under cover when necessary (Preuss 1987: 95–8; *EUIEA*: XXXVIII, 528). Wild cocoa was also harvested by Miskito on the thinly populated Caribbean side of Nicaragua, and used to make bitter 'tiger chocolate' (Bell 1989: 257). This was probably *pataxte* (Theobroma Bicolor), sold cheaply on Managua markets in the late 1890s (Preuss 1987: 102).

Competition with coffee was alleged to have caused cocoa's decline in Guatemala's Pacific region, but landowners had learned the lesson of the 1860s. They now grew cocoa between 300 and 700 metres above sea level, confining Arabica coffee to above 900 metres. A shortage of virgin forest at lower altitudes was a problem for cocoa, together with the long maturation and low productivity of high-quality Criollo. Beans were fermented for a day, and sun dried (Winter 1909: 97–8, 106). The premium for fine beans on the world market was falling, but exports still benefited from the fabled brand name of Soconusco (Preuss 1987: 100–1).

A little Criollo was still produced in this manner on the Pacific side of Costa Rica, whereas United Fruit blended modern and traditional methods on the Caribbean side. Young Inga seedlings were dug out of the forest and positioned as permanent shade two years before cocoa was sown. The company planted only Forastero Amelonado, at stake and at wide intervals of around 5 metres, but still suffered from much fungal black pod rot. By 1923, beans were brought by rail to a single central factory in Puerto Limón, where they were fermented for four days. Conveyor belts ferried fermented beans to vast rotating dryers, which spewed out dried and polished beans after thirty-six hours, ready for loading on company ships. Such short periods of fermentation and artificial drying reduced final quality (Hall 1932: 415–21; Wilson 1947: 191–2; Bergmann 1957: 45). Small farmers retained forest trees as shade, planted more closely, kept all surviving seedlings, fermented in large heaps in cemented patios, and dried beans in the sun (Quesada Camacho 1977–8: 84–6, 88–90).

The tiny cocoa estates of Surinam were 'well-tended gardens', but they were not profitable. The coastal strip, naturally under water at high tide, necessitated a complex and expensive system of dykes, sluices, drains and canals, although these also provided cheap and convenient transport. Primary or secondary forest was meticulously cleared to the last stump, and planting was usually on the banks of rivers, to benefit from some drainage. Forastero Amelonado dominated, despite renewed experiments with Criollo. Permanent shade trees were put in at the same time as cocoa, at 15–20 metre intervals, usually Erythrina Glauca to enrich the soil. They were planted more thickly as wind-breaks, and to strengthen canal banks. Planting of cocoa seeds was mainly at stake, without plant holes, and at intervals of 4–6 metres. Seedlings were transplanted from nurseries to fill gaps. Wide spacing necessitated thorough weeding four times a year. Pruning of both cocoa and shade trees was vigorous, and some fertiliser was applied. An outbreak of witches' broom in 1895 revealed the weaknesses of this expensive way of growing cocoa. Caused by a fungus endemic to the Amazon, witches' broom extended throughout the colony by 1903. Heavy pruning and spraying with Bordeaux mixture proved no more than a palliative (Preuss 1987: 19–29;

Gordian: V, 1907–10; VII, 2884; Hall 1932: 338–51; Benjamins and Snelleman 1914–17: 187–91).

Primary processing was both labour- and capital-intensive. Fermentation was in long wooden boxes, divided into compartments, and placed over a cement floor. Beans were moved from one compartment to another every day, for 5–8 days, and temperature was carefully controlled. Drying was in the sun when possible, on cemented stone floors. Wheeled racks and roofs kept the rain off. Expensive artificial dryers were increasingly used, some driven by steam engines. Even sorting was mechanised on one estate, albeit not effectively (Preuss 1987: 23–7; Benjamins and Snelleman 1914–17: 192–3).

Estate owners in São Tomé and Príncipe began by copying simple but effective smallholder methods. They indebted themselves to buy slaves from Angola and more land, but not to improve production methods. Cocoa was grown up to around 500 metres above sea level in the drier northeastern part of both islands. Planting was at stake, in small holes, and was quite irregular, following the lie of the land. Spacing was at around one metre, the canopy formed quickly, and there was little weeding or pruning. Banana or plantain trees provided temporary shade, and selected jungle trees were retained for permanent shade, including semi-wild oil palms. If trees failed to grow, the soil was lightly worked over, and a new seed or seedling was planted. Manuring was limited to spreading empty pods around the trees. Processing was basic, relying on sun drying. Smallholders clung to these tried and tested methods up to 1914, and their trees remained remarkably free of disease, although damaged by rats (Nogueira 1893: 49, 103, 120, 168; Ferrer Piera 1900: 58–9; Ponsard 1912: 11; Hall 1914: 313–14, 327).

More labour- and capital-intensive methods were adopted from around the turn of the century. Among the pioneers of mechanisation in the 1880s was the partially German firm of Chamiço and Biester, owners of the Monte Café estate and closely tied to the Banco Nacional Ultramarino (AHU 1884). From the 1890s, a stream of gadgets graced the pages of the annual reports of the Companhia da Ilha do Príncipe, the largest corporation in the colony and established on both islands despite its name. About 1,500 kilometres of light railways, small ports, steamers, sailing boats, roads, mules and horses transformed transport. Electricity and telephones were installed, and 'truly modern cities' sprang up on estates (UBL 1909; Negreiros 1908: 222, 290, 318–21). Ever more expensive repair workshops were required to keep complicated machinery in working order (Faro 1908: 154–7). This quasi-industrialisation, pictured in photographs of the time, increased the pressure on the forest, as wood was both the usual building material and the fuel for machines (Sociedade de Emigração 1915: 20; Henriques 1917: 145–6).

Many estates processed cocoa beans in an intensive manner in the 1900s. Workers fermented beans for 3–6 days in wooden boxes, turning the beans and moving them into a new box every day. Beans were dried for some four days on large cemented floors, with wheeled trays to keep them out of showers. As cultivation moved into the rainier southwest, drying machines were imported, but they dried beans too quickly and consumed vast amounts of firewood (UBL 1909; Hall 1914: 230, 311–14, 490; Ponsard 1912: 25–7).

Cultivation methods required far more labour than before. Workers dug ever deeper planting holes, averaging 1.5 metres in the 1900s, which were filled with organic manure. Spacing widened, up to around 4 metres, and weeding and pruning became intensive, with weeding accounting for about half of all the hours worked on one estate in 1909. Banana or plantain trees continued to provide temporary shade, but Hevea rubber proved unsuitable as permanent shade. Influenced by Grenada's example, estate managers began to dispense with permanent shade, especially in the frontier zone of the southwest. Irrigation in the drier northeast became general, albeit simply by diverting mountain streams. Many 'fine' varieties of cocoa were tried, but they all reverted to Forastero Amelonado (Hall 1914: 91, 318–25; Anon. 1907; UBL 1909; Ponsard 1912; Velarde 1924: 86–8, 139–40). Yields varied from 0.75 kilos per ageing tree, in exhausted land, to a high 5 kilos per five-year-old tree in fertile land (*Gordian*: X, 4397).

The short life of cocoa trees in the islands, declining rapidly after twenty years, pushed the frontier into lands which were marginal for cocoa. The burst of new planting on São Tomé in the late 1870s was already on freshly cleared land, as the old plantations were 'tired' (Almada 1884: 21). However, planting was still in the northeast, where the dry spell was well timed for drying beans in the sun (Hall 1914: 323). As planters moved on into the southwest, they entered lands where rainfall was too high, slopes too sleep and soils too poor. Many estates carved out of the jungle at considerable cost were quickly abandoned (Campos 1908: 16–23; UBL 1909).

The price of São Tomé's estate cocoa gradually improved, relative to other types, but not enough to compensate for all these investments (UBL 1909; *Gordian*: XI, 228–9; Henriques 1917: 138–9). Indeed, some landowners clung prudently to tried and tested cheap methods. At the height of the boom, William Cadbury shrewdly observed that few estates made above average profits, most were mortgaged to the hilt, and many were losing money hand over fist (UBL 1909). The profit squeeze was all too evident by 1914, with thirty-seven of the sixty-five holders of Banco Nacional Ultramarino mortgages in arrears on their payments (Sociedade de Emigração 1915: 99–112, 200).

Crisis was not slow to follow. Thrips (*Selenothrips rubrocinctus*), probably always present in the islands, ravaged the plantations during the First World War, allegedly halving the area in cocoa to some 25,000 hectares (Velarde 1924: 142–3). This probably reflected the advancing age of some trees and the tendency to dispense with permanent shade in new plantings

(Wood and Lass 1985: 397–8). An additional problem may have been the absence of a parasite, *Dasycapus parvipennis*, which weakened thrips on the West African mainland (Urquhart 1956: 126–7).

German corporations in Cameroon followed São Tomé's evolution. Spacing, initially at about 2.5 metres, increased to between 4 and 5 metres. Three seeds were planted directly in holes dug in the dry season, but only one seedling was allowed to grow. Bananas or plantains gave temporary shade, while selected jungle trees were retained for permanent shade (*Gordian*: II, 548; IV, 1619). By 1912, the estate way to grow cocoa was summarised as clear felling, burning, digging plant holes, planting shade trees, spacing widely, weeding intensively, pruning thoroughly, and fertilising (ANC 1912). Despite rich volcanic soils, increasing amounts of chemical fertiliser were imported to combat low yields (Michel 1969: 204, 208). The first doubts about the wisdom of wide spacing and excessive shade began to be voiced shortly before 1914, as yields remained stubbornly lower than on Gold Coast and Samoan smallholdings (*Gordian*: XVIII, 5753–5).

Processing and transport on Cameroonian estates copied São Tomé's evolution towards more intensive methods, with railways, steamers, wharves, stone warehouses, workshops and housing (Michel 1969: 206; *Gordian*: XI, 142). At first, beans were fermented for 2–3 days, in an ill judged imitation of procedures for Criollo, and this gave Cameroonian beans a reputation for bitterness (Jumelle 1900: 201–2). Matters improved as fermentation periods were lengthened (Stollwerck 1907: 31). A greater problem was that wet weather prevented drying the main harvest in the sun. Some planters replaced cocoa with rubber, others cleared new cocoa plantations on the other side of Mount Cameroon, and yet others invested in costly drying machines, which consumed vast amounts of wood and never performed satisfactorily. Over time, a greater emphasis was placed on mobile trays to move beans out of showers, allowing better use of what sunshine there was (*Gordian*: IV, 1587, 1622; IX, 3846–7; XI, 228).

Mayombe estates went down the same road of 'modernity'. In the Congo Free State, the forest was clear-felled, plant holes were dug as deep as four metres, and seedlings were transplanted from nurseries. Weeding and pruning were recommended, albeit sometimes neglected for lack of labour, and irrigation was sometimes necessary. Fermentation was thorough, up to eight days, but washing was tried and abandoned. Despite the long dry spell, all sorts of expensive drying machines were in use (Belgium 1908: 61, 76–7, 87–8; T'serclaes de Wommersom 1911; Claessens 1914). Over the frontier in Cabinda, landowners planted at stake and dispensed with permanent shade (*Gordian*: VI, 2233–4).

Fernando Póo's small estates were initially closer to smallholders, but the fever of modernisation infected some producers. Planters might clear the forest completely without planting permanent shade trees, although most kept some jungle trees. Similarly, some transplanted seedlings and spaced them 5 metres apart, but most planted two or three seeds at stake, at about 2.5 metre intervals, letting trunks intertwine (Ferrer Pia 1900: 55–64; Baumann 1888: 14; Bravo Carbonell 1917: 122). Processing became somewhat more 'modern' over time, although one missionary sensibly asked what the point was of 'careful fermentation and drying, to secure small, if any, advantage' (MMSA 1915). Progressive estate owners fermented beans thoroughly in wooden boxes. They had drying trays on wheels, and used hot air dryers. However, others fermented for as little as three days in old canoes, covering the beans with banana leaves or cloth, and in wet weather they dried beans over open fires, giving them a smoky taste (Ferrer Piera 1900: 68; Jumelle 1900: 197). There was less evidence of the expensive forms of modern transport found on other Equatorial African cocoa estates (Clarence-Smith 1994a).

Estates in eastern Africa placed more emphasis on growing Criollo, as in northwestern Madagascar. This region was isolated from pests and diseases, was sheltered from tropical storms, had unusually large reserves of virgin forest, and had a clear spell to dry the main harvest. Forasteros and Trinitarios, introduced on the east coast of Madagascar around 1900, were dominant there by 1914, but the area was exposed to devastating tropical storms and rain throughout the year. In addition, Réunionais Creoles made the mistake of planting at wide intervals of around 6 metres in exhausted lands formerly planted in coffee (Campbell 1996: 195–7, 201–3). Many varieties were introduced into Uganda from 1901, as transport innovations made exports viable, and methods were intensive. Planters cleared virgin forest, planted shade trees, transplanted cocoa seedlings from nurseries into plant holes, and spaced widely (Brown and Hunter 1913).

Ceylon demonstrated a particularly strong emphasis on science and quality. Attacks of canker, a fungus penetrating the bark, led to the introduction of Forastero around 1878. Hybridisation, unusually, resulted in a tree close to Criollo (*Gordian*: VI, 2233; Maclaren 1924: 194). These were probably Trinidad seedlings, some of which were sent on to Malaya (Burkill 1966: 2189). Some planters attempted to return to 'Old Red' Criollo, as Forastero Amelonado proved susceptible to canker and produced beans of lower value (Wright 1907: 9). Spacing was wide, at 5 metres on average soils, and weeding and pruning consequently took up a lot of labour. Erythrina Lithosperma trees were planted as shade, but they had to be constantly pruned. Too little shade resulted in attacks by sap-sucking Helopeltis insects, but rubber trees, tried by many planters, cast a shade that was too dense. Chemical and organic fertilisers were applied on a fair scale, and sulphuric acid was sprayed against canker (Hall 1914: 398–401).

Ceylonese primary processing was equally thorough. Beans were fermented for up to three days, trampled, washed individually by hand in cement tanks, dried on mats in the sun when possible, dried by machine when necessary, and finally rubbed with sacking to improve their appearance. The best Criollo beans had a light colour and a sweet taste, and thus fetched high prices, but most beans did not reach these levels (Watt 1889–96: VI-4, 44; Hall 1914: 402–3).

The 'scientific' techniques preached by Dutch agronomists were taken to almost obsessive lengths by corporations in east Java, although cheap female labour loomed larger than expensive fixed capital. They used irrigation, deep drains, terracing, clear-felling, deep plant holes, elaborate seedling nurseries, wide spacing, planted shade trees, intensive weeding, hard pruning of both cocoa and shade trees, and regular tillage and fertilising of the soil. The transport of pods or beans was mainly by ox-cart and pack horse. Workers fermented beans for four days in perforated teak boxes, turning them every day, and then washed them in big buckets. Some estates artificially dried the whole crop, but it was more usual to begin drying in the sun, raking the beans several times for a day or two. Beans were then painstakingly sorted into twelve different categories (Roepke 1922).

In contrast, the authorities could scarcely conceal their irritation at the 'backward' techniques adopted by central Java's resident and creolised planters. Cocoa seedlings, or more rarely seeds, replaced Arabica coffee trees ravaged by leaf blight, in areas above the rice plains and up to around 600 metres. The former shade trees and close spacing of coffee groves were retained, and Robusta coffee was sometimes mixed in. Kapok, coconut palms and various types of rubber were interplanted as shade trees, while nutmeg and kola were used as wind-breaks. Pepper vines were sometimes trailed over other trees, leading officials to refer derisively to these estates as 'grocer's shops'. Poor and already depleted laterite soils required a yearly dose of fertiliser, which meant keeping a herd of cattle, buying dung from the colonial cavalry, composting, and planting leguminous shade trees. There was almost no tilling or pruning, and selective weeding was brought to a fine art, certain weeds being retained to protect and improve the soil. Drying was mainly in the sun. Yields per cocoa tree were poor on these estates, but they provided a reasonable living for their owners (Roepke 1922; Hall 1932: 474–5, 482–4).

There were repeated introductions of Forastero into Java from the 1880s, largely because of insect damage. Hybridisation with 'red' Criollo gave rise to a number of local varieties, with higher yields, a longer lifespan, and greater resistance to insect pests. Although they did not breed true, a significant proportion exhibited marked Criollo features. The Helopeltis menace was biologically controlled by black ants and white mealybugs, but the pod borer was not so easily dealt with. It attained pest status in Java from 1895, being especially virulent above 300 metres. The coordinated destruction of infested pods was not very effective, as the moth also bred in the wild (Roepke 1922; Hall 1932: 270–9, 474–81). Forastero varieties were not reported in the Moluccas, but there were experiments with Nicaraguan Criollo (Clarence-Smith 1998: 102).

Western Samoa grew cocoa quite intensively. Criollo, obtained from Ceylon and Java, was preferred by smallholders, but hybrids from Ceylon were introduced on estates in 1898, for their yields and resistance to disease. They marginalised Criollo through further hybridisation, and yet approximated Forastero more with every passing generation (Wright 1907: 10–11; Hall 1932: 494; *BII*: XII, 477–8). There was little virgin forest left on the island where estates were located, but secondary forest 60–80 years old was deemed adequate. Estate owners cleared and burned all vegetation, raised seedlings in nurseries, and spaced them out widely at 4.5 metres. Complex drying machines were commonly used. Frequent and violent tropical storms were a hazard, more or less wiping out the harvest in early 1903 (*Gordian*: VII, 2932; IX, 3786–7). This style of cultivation undoubtedly contributed to estates falling behind smallholders by 1914.

New Guinea provided a textbook example of everything that could go wrong with 'scientific' estates. The Kaiser Wilhelmsland Plantagen-Gesellschaft was set up in Hamburg to grow cocoa and coffee in 1890. It had a nominal capital of half a million marks, and obtained vast expanses of land in Astrolabe Bay from the chartered New Guinea Company. A Dutch planter, who had managed a cocoa estate in Trinidad, was hired to run the business. Seed came from Ceylon, and the company purchased complicated processing machinery. Hopelessly uneconomic, this venture collapsed within a year. Small estates in the Gazelle peninsula fared better, benefiting from fertile volcanic soil (Sack and Clark 1979: 50, 144, 344–5; Firth 1982: 28, 30, 35).

The triumph of smallholder methods, 1880s–1914

By 1914, smallholder ways of growing cocoa were emerging as dominant in the world, for the first time since the Spanish conquest of the Aztec empire. For all the talk of 'primitive' methods, smallholders were constantly experimenting, acutely aware of the balance between costs and returns, and they were quite prepared to adopt intensive techniques if prices were right.

A major reason for the remarkable triumph of smallholders in the Gold Coast lay in their sensible rejection of two methods preached by the Department of Agriculture. Attempts to control pests and diseases by thorough pruning, frequent harvesting, spraying, and burning or burying infected materials, achieved little. While Africans experimented with spraying, it was cheaper and more effective to deal with sap-sucking capsids, the main insect pest, by following the practice of 'weeds overgrown'. The infected area was allowed to return to bush for three years, after which the trees were often found to be healthy and could be cleared of undergrowth. The second departmental recommendation was wide spacing, to increase yields per tree and reduce losses from pod rot. However, this probably lowered yields per hectare, especially on poor soils, hugely increased the need for weeding, and raised the risk of capsid attacks, seen by farmers as a greater threat (Austin 1996: 164–8).

There was little capital investment in cultivation by smallholders in Akim (Akyem Abuakwa), but labour inputs tended to increase over time. Large jungle trees might be retained, as well as kola nut trees and oil palms, but no permanent shade trees were planted. Two to three Forastero Amelonado seeds were planted at stake at close intervals, with a food crop such as taro or plantain for temporary shade. The weaker seedlings in each clump were cut out after two or three years. Transplanting seedlings from nurseries, situated by streams, was at first limited to filling gaps, but it gradually became more common as a planting method. Weeding and pruning were minimal, and a thick canopy formed quickly. Even healthy trees aged quickly, but farmers simply moved further into the forest and planted again (*Gordian*: X, 4388–9; XVII, 4953; XIX, 7133; Tudhope 1917: 180–1, 184). Most expenditure was on cement houses with corrugated iron roofs, although farmers banded together to build toll bridges, one of which was completed in 1914 at a cost of £2,000 (Szereszewski 1965: 60, 64; Hill 1963: 190–1).

The Department of Agriculture was hardly more effective in influencing processing. Officials favoured fermenting in special wooden boxes, laboriously transferring beans between them every day for about a week. However, smallholders found that it was just as effective, and far easier, to cover beans with banana leaves and leave them (Austin 1996: 168). Smallholders experimented a great deal with fermentation and drying, but they wanted a price premium to reward their efforts, which only Cadbury's offered. Fermentation was for 3–8 days, compared to six or seven recommended by the Department. Beans were covered with mats or banana leaves, and were rarely turned. The heaps might be in pits, on the ground, in large baskets, or on planks raised a metre or so above the ground. Drying was in the sun, sometimes on the hard-baked surface of local roads. Some farmers used planks and trestles, which could be moved out of the rain. Richer producers installed cement floors, copied from those of traders who dried beans (*Gordian*: X, 4389; XVII: 4953; XIX, 7133; Tudhope 1917: 182).

Yoruba cultivation and processing techniques in Nigeria were so similar to those in Akim that there may have been some transfer of skills by migrant labourers. The extremely irregular appearance of planting was noted, as there was no attempt to place beans or seedlings in straight lines. Smallholders rarely fermented beans for more than three days, whereas Creole landowners did so for a good six days (Johnson 1917). Jacob Coker also experimented with planting kola trees as permanent shade in Agege, although they proved to cast too dense a shade (Webster 1962: 125–8; Wood and Lass 1985: 143).

Smallholders in Equatorial Africa ignored European criticisms, many of which had to be retracted. A plant pathologist in 1904 found no evidence that Bakweri groves were sources of disease around Mount Cameroon. The

Bakweri planted very densely, maximising the use of what land remained to them, cutting down on weeding, and reducing temporary shading with bananas and plantains, which attracted elephants that devastated cocoa orchards (Wirz 1972: 204–7; *Gordian*: VIII, 3434). In Spanish Río Muni to the south, coastal growers shaded densely planted cocoa with coconut palms (LCL 1908). Bubi cocoa farmers on Fernando Póo, much lampooned, were remarkably successful (Clarence-Smith 1994a: 185, 194–5). Cameroon's 'Viktorianer Kakao' was poorly fermented and had a smoky taste from drying over open fires, but it still found a ready market in Hamburg, albeit at a considerable discount to estate beans (*Gordian*: IV, 1559–60, 1622). To avoid having to process at all, some Africans sold fresh beans to traders or estate owners (ANC 1913).

Bahian farmers, rapidly emerging as the most dynamic in the New World, minimised their inputs. The cheapest way to establish a plot was to plant in parallel paths cleared through the forest, removing excess jungle as cocoa grew. However, seedlings were easily stifled, and they grew upwards, making them hard to harvest. Other farmers cleared more vigorously, keeping just a few mature forest trees for shade, but they found that jungle trees did great damage when they died and fell. Retaining young but fast growing forest trees was another option. Planting shade trees spread from around the 1880s, but was seen as expensive. By about 1910, most producers had decided to dispense with shade altogether (Zehntner 1914: 8–11, 17–18). The result was that trees died more quickly. There was a marked contrast in the 1930s between the venerable Rio Almada plantations, still producing under dense shade after a hundred years, and decrepit forty-year-old trees deprived of shade (Monbeig 1937: 288). Three Forastero beans were usually planted in holes, and if they all survived this interfered with the formation of the crown. Food crops were interplanted, planting was dense, and yields per tree low. However, yields per hectare were satisfactory (Zehntner 1914: 6, 9–13, 20). Infrequent weeding and minimal pruning were reported in the 1930s (Monbeig 1937: 288–9).

Simple primary processing was reflected in low prices (*Gordian*: III, 1145). Some producers did not ferment at all in 1907, and few bothered with more than three days (*Gordian*: XIII, 1365). About two thirds of Bahia's cocoa exports around 1910 were inadequately processed. Fermentation was carried out in old canoes, covered with banana leaves or old sacks, or in wooden boxes. Sun drying was general, on convenient sandy beaches where possible, but more often on jute material later used to make bags. Traders on the Jequitinhonha and Pardo rivers bought fresh cocoa beans for fermentation and drying, but this was only feasible where transportation by water was available. Estates had expensive sliding trays and roofs to cope with sudden downpours, and experimented with artificial drying (Zehntner 1914: 60–9).

The wild rubber boom sweeping through the Amazon caused a neglect of planted cocoa, not only in Brazil but also in Peru's Iquitos region (Bonilla 1975–6: II, 195, 235). Exceptionally high floods made matters worse, and many cocoa groves returned to bush, although new stands of wild cocoa were discovered by wandering rubber tappers (*Gordian*: XIX, 6301). Le Cointe criticised 'impenetrable jungles' of densely planted and poorly tended cocoa trees in the Amazon, but he conceded that they bore precociously, yielding a few pods after only three years. They were also remarkably healthy, especially when planted in their natural habitat of alluvial river terraces (Le Cointe 1922: II, 116, 123, 127, 136, 140). Trees showed no sign of witches' broom, the fungus which later constrained the region's development (Ruf *et al.* 1994: 28). Some smallholders in the lower Tocantins intercropped Hevea rubber with cocoa, which received little attention and was never pruned. Beans were not fermented, and were re-dried by local traders (Lange 1914: 88–91). However, Amazon beans still fetched a relatively good price, due to a high butter content and a low shell content (Tosta Filho 1957: 2).

Dominican Republic smallholders, almost as dynamic as their Bahian colleagues, moved rapidly westwards from Samaná Bay, chopping down virgin forest as they went (Baud 1982: 66–7; Hoetink 1988: 161; Bryan 1977: 150–2; Marte 1984: 228). The authorities recommended Criollo, but farmers preferred hardy Forastero Amelonado (Baud 1982: 66–7; Ciferri 1930: 17; Hall 1914: 380). They cleared the forest completely, without planting shade trees, so that cocoa trees did not live long. They sowed three seeds directly in the ground, sometimes allowing all surviving seedlings to grow together, and spaced closely. Plantain or cassava served as temporary shade, and maize was intercropped for food. Yields averaged about a kilo per tree. Smallholders rarely fermented beans, simply soaking them in water and then drying them on mats or on the bare earth. Merchants often re-dried prior to export. In contrast, estate methods were characterised by plant holes, transplanting after six months, wide spacing, permanent shade, and fermentation for up to eight days (Deschamps 1907: II, 328–30; Schoenrich 1918: 154–5; Hall 1914: 378–81).

Producers of cheap 'Carúpano' in eastern Venezuela favoured wide alluvial terraces by the slow rivers draining into the Gulf of Paria, although they were also expanding into the hills. Planting was close and 'unruly', but farmers provided thick permanent shade for their trees. Fermentation and drying were rudimentary, and traders often re-dried the beans, coating them with red earth for the Spanish market (*Gordian*: X, 4263).

Smallholders did fairly well elsewhere in the Caribbean and Guianas. Those in Cuba's eastern mountains interplanted coffee and cocoa in a 'primitive' and 'haphazard' fashion, shifting emphasis on each crop according to relative prices (Wright 1910: 447–8, 460). Drought and hurricanes harmed the region's cocoa, especially in 1907–10, the former possibly linked to deforestation (Hall 1914: 429; Pérez Junior 1989: 139–40, 156). Cocoa production began to increase in Baracoa from around 1900, as a replacement for coconut palms ravaged by disease (Marrero 1951: 660). Surinam small-holders planted on river banks, intercropping with maize or taro in early years (Benjamins and Snelleman 1914–17: 187–8). The scattering of plots at a fair distance from one another was taken by Van Lier to spring from a desire 'to avoid one's fellow-men', but it may have been a sensible way of limiting the impact of witches' broom and other diseases (Lier 1971: 229). Guadeloupe overtook Martinique as a cocoa exporter before 1914, as production moved from the northeastern plains of Grande Terre, where irrigation by hand was required, to the better watered southwest of Basse Terre, on the slopes of a volcano (Hall 1932: 401–2).

Colombia's small farmers were unusual in growing Criollo, a particularity explained by the premium obtainable from local consumers. As thick shade was the norm in the Cauca valley, this entailed waiting eight years for a crop, and twelve years for full maturity. Yields of a kilo per tree were reported on well kept plots, but the average was lower. However, trees bore to the age of sixty or over, bringing reliable profits for the patient (Eder 1913: 152, 204–5). Weeding and pruning were rare, and trees were allowed to grow 6 metres tall (Patiño 1963: 312). A high flood of the Cauca in 1886–7 destroyed millions of recently planted cocoa trees. This was a permanent danger, as cocoa was mainly planted on the margins of the river and its tributaries (Hyland 1982: 404). A 'tragedy of the commons' was played out in the forests near Santa Marta, where wild or feral cocoa trees grew high and spindly, reaching for light under the forest canopy. People simply felled these trees to obtain pods, roughly processing the beans. However, a process of claiming the land and ameliorating wild stands was under way in the 1890s (Thomson 1895–6: 418–20, 423–5).

Smallholders also grew Criollo in the Philippines, again for discriminating local consumers rather than for export. Beans were allegedly not fermented, being thoroughly washed and dried in the sun for 2–3 days (Forbes-Lindsay 1906: 337). Cocoa suffered so much from pests and diseases that every tree in the colony was allegedly affected in some way in the 1880s. An unnamed disease attacked the roots of trees, spreading quickly through a grove, and damage due to unspecified insects was considerable (Foreman 1890: 354–5). The pod borer may have been one of these insects, as it reached pest status in Mindanao by the 1930s (Lass and Wood 1985: 75).

Conclusion

The greatest difficulty in understanding how producers chose to grow cocoa lies in the interplay between economic and ideological factors. Economic historians feel most comfortable with explanations relating to the availability of labour or ecological conditions. However, cultivation methods were also influenced by mental models and 'path dependency', which require a great deal more research. In particular, the 'collective neurosis' of pseudo-scientific agriculture, which gripped so many educated people before 1914, needs to be understood, especially as it persists to our own day.

A more technical problem is the relation between cultivation techniques on the one hand, and pests, diseases and natural disasters on the other. Producers often treated the latter as unpredictable acts of God, but there were clearly links between how cocoa was grown and what it suffered from. What this chapter suggests is that disease was more likely to occur when intensive methods prevailed, although a great deal more work would be needed to demonstrate this. The problem in the historical record is often one of extreme vagueness as to what afflicted cocoa, which requires painstaking trawling through archives to resolve. In my own work on eastern Indonesia, the constant repetition of the uninformative term 'the sickness' only made sense when I stumbled across a report from the remote island of Buru, which at last described the symptoms in detail.

As the world runs out of tropical forest, a more intensive study of past agroforestry techniques would be of great utility. This should not be limited to smallholdings, as estates in Ecuador and Java both experimented in interesting ways with mimicking nature. One of the dangers of agronomy is the constant re-invention of the wheel, instead of studying how past generations confronted similar problems in growing particular crops.

8

COERCED AND FREE LABOUR

Coerced labour proved remarkably durable, despite a sustained liberal challenge from the mid-eighteenth century. This longevity is puzzling at first sight, as obtaining labour by force had many drawbacks. Paying in advance for slaves exacerbated the need for capital, always expensive on the frontier. Substantial recruitment costs were lost when labourers died or fled, which happened most often on arrival or soon after. Low productivity sprang from a mixture of demoralisation and active resistance, and the cost of supervision was correspondingly high. Such disadvantages more than offset low or non-existent payment, the ability to assign workers to any task, and the acquisition of skills through long residence (Clarence-Smith 1990).

The advantage of coerced labour was not that it was cheap, but that it was readily available. This was particularly important for estate owners, who usually found it difficult to recruit. There was thus an intimate relationship between the survival of estates and the persistence of coerced labour. Abolitionists did not always fully perceive this link, because they often saw the future of ex-slaves as wage workers, not as petty entrepreneurs. Workers on cocoa estates were rarely organised in disciplined gangs, as the production process did not require it.

The world's cocoa was mainly produced by free workers from the middle of the nineteenth century, partly because of labour reforms, and partly because of the spread of smallholdings. Although smallholders employed members of their family, they had to draw workers from outside the family whenever a major cocoa boom developed. Smallholders occasionally coerced labour, particularly in Africa, but they generally had recourse to cheap and flexible arrangements, such as sharecropping. Landowners in the New World frequently used contractors to establish estates, but this was unattractive when there was little local knowledge of cocoa cultivation. Pockets of unfree labour persisted here and there, and the resurgence of estates at the end of the nineteenth century led to a new wave of slavery and forced labour.

Labour under the ancien regime

While coercion loomed large in mercantilist cocoa production, it was not quite as widespread as has sometimes been assumed. Indigenous slavery quickly gave way to short stints of forced labour in Spanish America, until catastrophic demographic decline, due mainly to imported diseases, undermined the system (MacLeod 1973: chs 4, 5, 12, 18; Ferry 1989). Black slaves were an alternative source of labour, but foreign powers controlled the sea routes from Africa (Rout 1976: chs 2–3). The post-1650 decline of cocoa exports from Santo Domingo, where no Amerindians remained, was succinctly blamed on a 'lack of negroes' (Patiño 1963: 297). Venezuela, favourably located for contraband imports, made the greatest use of slaves in cocoa production (Ferry 1989). Slaves were more expensive in Guayaquil, due to the territory's remote location in the Pacific (Mahony 1996: 44). Cocoa planters in Mesoamerica, retaining access to quite abundant Amerindian labour, employed the fewest slaves (Romero Vargas 1976: 455–9; Rosés Alvarado 1982: 256–7; Gerhard 1979: 43, 170).

One solution to the Spanish dilemma was to turn to local free labour, as Amerindians staged a demographic recovery and a free mixed-race population grew rapidly in the eighteenth century. Guayaquil cocoa planters, lacking political clout to obtain Amerindians from the Andes, were pioneers in employing free people of mixed race (Laviana Cuetos 1987: ch. 2; Hamerly 1970). Mesoamerican cocoa estates also began to employ more free labour, both mixed-race and Amerindian (Gasco 1987: 175–6; Wortman 1982: 75–6, 78–81). Venezuelan landowners were most dependent on African slaves, but employed some day labourers, whether people of mixed race, manumitted slaves, Amerindians, or poor immigrants from the semi-tropical Canary Islands (Ferry 1989).

Amerindian slavery was crucial to the collection of wild cocoa in the Amazon, albeit in an indirect manner. The Portuguese tolerated the capture of slaves from 'rebel' peoples and the purchase of war captives. Settled in villages, most of these people were placed under the authority of missionaries, especially Jesuits. Villagers were sent on long canoe expeditions to gather cocoa from the forest, but they were paid, and were quick to desert if ill treated. The collection of forest produce was a skilled activity, and one that could not easily be regimented (MacLachlan 1973; Cardoso 1984). African slaves were not desired. They lacked knowledge of the forest and represented a major capital loss if they fled during expeditions (MacLachlan 1974: 120–3).

European interlopers mainly relied on African slaves to grow cocoa, with French Martinique as an early and influential example (May 1930: 95; Brizan 1984: 7, 38; Harwich 1992: 60). Only in the Guianas was Amerindian labour at all significant. Amerindian slaves made up 12 per cent of Dutch Berbice's estate workers in the 1750s, when cocoa production was peaking there (Kramer 1991: 60). The expulsion of the Jesuits in 1764 deprived French Guiana of half its labour force, previously supplied by mission stations (Coudreau 1886–7: I, 28; Cardoso 1984: 35–7).

The zenith of coerced labour, 1760s–1790s

The Caribbean model of servile labour achieved its greatest influence in the late eighteenth century. In a buoyant market for cocoa, politically influential estate owners particularly valued the ready availability of slaves, despite their high and rising price. Slave-grown cocoa thus became more common around the Caribbean Basin and in northern Brazil. On the Pacific side of the New World, however, African slaves were at their most expensive, and the expanding local population offered an alternative source of labour. Spanish reformers stamped out lingering relics of Amerindian slavery but sought to facilitate imports of African slaves. Measures to foster imports enjoyed uneven success, partly because of frequent bouts of warfare, and partly because Spanish attempts to secure a foothold in the African slave trade came to nothing (Rout 1976: 58–61; Sundiata 1996: 19).

Slavery remained central to cocoa cultivation in Venezuela, the largest producer in the world. Even small planters employed slaves, contrary to McKinley's supposition (McKinley 1985: 24). Humboldt painted a striking picture of humble cocoa pioneers in eastern Venezuela, setting off into the forest with a single slave, and living a frugal life for 6–8 years before their cocoa trees came into full production and their families came to join them (Humboldt 1941: II, 146).

In comparison to newer branches of agriculture, cocoa benefited from accumulated slave supplies (Lombardi 1971: 109). Just over half of the slaves in Caracas province at the turn of the century were located in the cocoa strongholds of Barlovento and the coast (Tamaro 1988: 256). Despite an alleged decline in slave imports from 1781, there was no sustained agitation on the part of planters, and the servile population of Caracas province rose from 53,055 in 1785–7 to 67,733 in 1800–9 (McKinley 1985: 10, 23–4, 100; Lucena Salmoral 1990: 57). The sale price of prime male slaves remained steady at between 200 and 250 pesos, suggesting that supplies were broadly in line with demand (Tamaro 1988: 235).

A partial solution to the riddle of rising numbers lies in Tamaro's argument that rural slaves were more than reproducing themselves, unlike their urban counterparts. Overall natural increase hovered around 1 per cent a year between 1770 and 1800 in Barlovento and the Chuao coastal estate, for which good parish records are available. Sex ratios were fairly even after the initial stages of establishing cocoa plantations, and legal marriages were the norm, because the bishop made planters pay the fee. Families were common, as women and children were valued for weeding and processing. Pregnant women were assigned light tasks, birth rates were high, and it was uncommon for families to be split up by sale. In particular, young children were very rarely separated from their mothers. Families usually had their own plots, and the Church acted as a check on planter abuses (Tamaro 1988: 60, 236–40, 245–58). This treatment of slaves owed little or nothing to provisions enshrined in the 'black code' of 1789, as settler pressure caused the legislation to be suspended in 1794 (McKinley 1985: 122).

The relative ease of manumission in Venezuela may have encouraged slave reproduction. A master was obliged to free any slave who could pay 300 pesos, even if the slave's market value was twice as high (Humboldt 1852, I, 398–9). Although this was a large sum, custom allowed some slaves to grow cocoa on their plots, which financed the manumission of slaves or their offspring. Indeed, the 300 pesos could be paid in cocoa trees (Brito Figueroa 1985: 116–19, 129; Tamaro 1988: 236, 239–40; Piñero 1994: 75). Manumission at the death of an owner was an alternative route to freedom, although wills indicated that less than 5 per cent of slaves were freed thus, and they were usually domestics (McKinley 1985: 24).

Employment on small plantations, with fellow slaves in charge of day-to-day affairs, was demographically favourable. In Barlovento, few estates had over fifty male slaves, and twenty or so was common. While a handful of really large estates were under a White manager, medium and small estates were usually run by a *mandador*, either a trusted slave or a man freed on condition that he take up the position. After the slave risings in Haïti in 1791, absentee planters in Caracas became nervous about this arrangement, but it remained remarkably common. A survey of part of the coast in 1800 revealed that twenty-one out of thirty-one estates were run by a *mandador* (Tamaro 1988: 106–7, 236, 284).

Internal demographic growth cannot explain everything, for the increase in the slave population of the main cocoa zones was about 2 per cent a year in 1783–1809, or twice the estimated natural rate of increase (Tamaro 1988: 230, 233, 258, 287). Imports must thus have been rising. Unlike some of those who have used his figures, Brito Figueroa stresses that legal imports may have fallen, but clandestine purchases of slaves soared, at least until Spain declared war on Britain in 1796. Whereas just over 12,000 slaves can be documented as having been imported into Venezuela between 1777 and 1799, the actual figure was certainly higher (Brito Figueroa 1978: 114–25). Other authors paint a similar picture of rising imports (Izard 1972: 85; Acosta Saignes 1984: 41–4, 62–84, 132–5). It is hard to accept Lombardi's contention that slave imports fell away from 1780, as returns on cocoa diminished (Lombardi 1971: 6).

There were marked regional disparities in the evolution of slave numbers in Barlovento, reflecting the onward march of the cocoa frontier. Slave numbers fell in western areas, giving a false impression of decline. In the booming frontier zone to the east, the slave population of El Guapo rose from 136 to 542 between 1784 and 1802. It was usually accepted that one male worker was needed for 1,000 cocoa trees, and women and children probably brought that figure up to around 2.5 labourers in all (Tamaro 1988: 60, 71, 283).

For all that, cocoa cultivation in Venezuela certainly did make use of abundant free labour, especially at harvest time (Izard 1972: 103). Free people of colour rarely resided on estates. They worked on a casual daily basis, usually for three reales in cash and kind, migrating to Barlovento as the cocoa frontier expanded (McKinley 1985: 9, 19–24, 50; Lucena Salmoral 1990: 57; Tamaro 1988: 109, 260, 282). Amerindians were another significant element among cocoa harvesters in the valleys to the west of Caracas, but not in Barlovento (Depons 1930: 233; Tamaro 1988: 109, 111, 205). Mission Amerindians were a basic source of labour for cocoa planters in eastern Venezuela (Harwich Vallenilla 1996: 34). Out of an estimated total of 100,000 Amerindians in the 1790s, there were said to be some 60,000 left in the east, many of them on Capuchin and Franciscan missions (Humbodlt 1852: I, 294–7).

Several thousand poor Canarians entered Venezuela between 1780 and 1810, as memories of an ill fated rebellion in 1749 died away (McKinley 1985: 14–15, 18). They sought to be accepted as Europeans, and thus not to break the taboo of engaging in manual labour for others. However, some poor Canarians in Ocumare del Tuy, unable to gain access to land, accepted seasonal employment on cocoa plantations (Tamaro 1988: 122).

African slave labour underpinned the development of cocoa in the Nuevo Reino. In Cúcuta, a former Jesuit plantation had 127 slaves and 40,000 cocoa trees in 1770. There were over a thousand slaves producing cocoa in Cúcuta prior to independence (Brungardt 1974: 88, 91). On the vast Cauca estates, where cocoa was a minor crop, mining magnates used the African slave labour to which they were accustomed. A fall in slave prices between 1760 and 1800 suggests that supplies were more than adequate (Colmenares 1997: 180–2, 185, 205, 256–7; Patiño 1963: 309–10).

Slave numbers shot up in a spectacular manner in Spanish-ruled Trinidad, albeit from a very low base and only partly for cocoa. The total population in 1776 had been a mere 3,432, excluding a few Amerindians outside Spanish control. Land grants to French settlers were proportionate to the number of slaves that they brought with them, although only three slaves entered for every two free persons between 1785 and 1790. Settlers were also allowed to import slaves free of duty for ten years, and at a reduced rate thereafter. By the end of Spanish rule in 1797, the total population had risen to 17,718, of whom 10,009 were slaves, while the Amerindian population had nearly halved (Sevilla Soler 1988: 26–32, 38, 46–7, 51, 110–11).

Spain proved unable to repeat this feat in Santo Domingo, where the dearth of labour contributed to restricted cocoa exports. Import duties on slaves were slashed in 1765, and abolished in 1786. Foreigners were offered a raft of concessions in 1789 and 1791 if they brought slaves with them, and subsidies were offered to Spanish captains importing slaves. However, workers could all too easily escape in this large and sparsely settled colony, and it made more sense to raise cattle for sale to the French (Sevilla Soler 1980: 90–2, 119, 125, 128–30).

Black slaves were crucial to rising cocoa exports from the non-Hispanic Caribbean. In Surinam, 1,000 cocoa trees required the attention of 1.3 African field slaves in 1770, with one 'negro officer' and one skilled labourer for every thirty field hands (Reyne 1924–5: 196–7). Imports of slaves into Surinam were hit by a severe credit crunch in the mid-1770s, worsened by a major slave rebellion, but labour relations were said to be better on cocoa estates than on sugar properties (Stedman 1988: 479–80; Stipriaan 1995b). Dependence on imports from Africa became absolute, as the remnants of Amerindian slavery withered away on estates in Dutch Berbice in the 1770s (Kramer 1991: 60). Black slaves remained the norm for cocoa in the islands, although French planters continued to employ few slaves per estate (Cox 1984: 64–5; Dupuy 1989: 26–7).

Slaves were rare in Guayaquil, the world's second largest cocoa producer, and some planters only used them as foremen (Contreras 1994: 206). Manumission eroded slave numbers (Chiriboga 1980: 18–19). There were only around 2,000 slaves in Guayaquil province between 1778 and 1800, despite a slight rise in the 1780s. The average price of a prime male slave in 1784–6 was 300–400 pesos, nearly twice Venezuelan levels, and officials ignored requests for subsidised sales. Moreover, only about a third of the servile population was employed in rural areas, where tobacco and timber competed with cocoa for labour (Laviana Cuetos 1987: 83, 126, 137–40; Hamerly 1970: 90–2). Even after a 1795 declaration of 'free trade in negroes' in the Spanish Pacific, only one prominent Lima merchant specialised in the business (Parrón Salas 1995: 259–60).

A report of 1785 asserted that Guayaquil was also the province with the fewest Amerindians in Spanish America. This may have been an exaggeration, but the indigenous peoples of the western part of the coastal strip rarely offered their services to cocoa planters. Although they were back to 1570s population levels by the 1790s, they were not subject to forced labour, and they kept control of their lands. They preferred to earn cash for their tribute by selling fish, salt and straw hats, together with some casual work in the shipyards (Laviana Cuetos 1987: 137, 151–2). Migrants from the highlands were an obvious alternative, especially as colonial free trade provided new competition for textile workshops (Deler 1981: 139–40; Hamerly 1973: 133; Contreras 1994: 196–200). However, there is little hard evidence of movement to the coast, even by temporary male migrants. The Quito elite's grip on coerced highland workers remained tight, and textile workshops may not have been as badly affected as was once believed.

The growing mixed-race population of the coastal strip was certainly the backbone of Guayaquil's small workforce (Hamerly 1970: 90–2, 116, 129; 1973: 103). The scarcity and expense of workers partly explained minimal labour inputs into cocoa cultivation. Workers had to be attracted by high salaries and cash advances, as they could easily subsist on their little plots and earn cash by catching and salting fish for sale in the highlands (Contreras 1994: 207–8; Baleato 1887: 69–70). In 1777, the rural wage was 4–8 reales for a short five-hour day. Around 1800, the wage was quoted at an average of six reales, with food added, for a six-hour day (Laviana Cuetos 1987: 172). This contrasted with a daily wage of one real in the highlands (Chiriboga 1980: 17).

Coerced highland Amerindians, the traditional labour force on Mesoamerican cocoa estates, became less freely available as reforms gathered momentum. From 1761, the authorities in Guatemala City began to reassert control over allocating forced labour, and monitored the system much more closely. Cocoa estates continued to draw on such workers, but the number of labour drafts fell significantly in the 1780s and early 1790s, and the authorities proposed abandoning the system altogether (McCreery 1994: 93–7; Wortman 1982: 173, 180). Nicaragua's Amerindian population was sparse and not firmly under Spanish control, so that only a few favoured estate owners obtained forced labour (Newson 1987: 260–1).

Highlanders increasingly migrated voluntarily to pay cash taxes, such as the group who arrived in Suchitepéquez in 1792 'to earn their tribute'. They usually came on a seasonal basis to perform piece work. Tempted with cash advances, they sometimes disappeared with the money (McCreery 1994: 48, 91–2). Zoque migrants going to Tabasco benefited from links of kinship in the Sierra, and devotion to certain saints (Ruz 1994: 199–200). Amerindian drifters were also recorded in Suchitepéquez in the 1770s, uprooted from their communities and wandering from one job to another (Wortman 1982: 174, 180–1). Some highlanders brought their families with them and settled on estates, as in Soconusco and Tabasco (Gasco 1987: 116; Scherr 1985: 35). A Guatemalan inquiry of 1802 noted that such settlers were indebted to landowners, and that many were fugitives from justice (McCreery 1994: 92, 99). Free wage labourers of mixed race joined them, also indebted (McCreery 1994: 48, 89; Ruz 1994: 185; Ruiz Abreu 1989: 29; Guerrero and Soriano 1966: 112, 116).

African slaves were usually an adjunct to the workforce, except on the small Matina cocoa estates of Costa Rica, well placed for contraband imports. However, even Matina plantations rarely had more than ten slaves (Touzard 1993: 38, 48). These slaves were sometimes seized by Miskitos and sold back to British traders, and a contract of 1753 offered manumission in exchange for opening up a new estate (Rosés Alvarado 1982: 257, 266). Despite access to forced labour and a rapidly growing free population, Tabasco's cocoa planters faced an acute labour shortage (Florescano and Gil Sánchez 1976: 278–9; Gerhard 1979: 43). There were only thirty-three slaves registered in 1766, but by the 1780s some Tabascan planters owned between five and twenty slaves, with forty-six as the maximum recorded (Ruz 1994: 202–5). Few slaves were imported into Guatemala after 1760, and numbers may have declined overall, although the price of a prime male slave was stable at the surprisingly low level of around 150 pesos (McCreery 1994: 89). One of the largest landowners in Rivas, the centre of Nicaragua's cocoa economy, owned a mere fifteen slaves in 1763, of whom only five were reported to be fit for work (Romero Vargas 1976: 455–6).

Amerindian collectors of wild cocoa in the Brazilian Amazon became scarce and expensive. Pombal attempted to stamp out indigenous slavery, appointed lay 'directors of Indians' to replace missionaries in 1757, and imported more African slaves, bearing diseases. Directors granted settlers half the labour time of adult male Amerindian villagers, many of whom died or fled into the jungle. Directors were abolished in 1798, but Amerindians remained liable to enrolment into a labour corps for public works under military discipline. Some 2,000 'tame' Amerindians were working for the government in 1800, out of an estimated 5,000 left. As the 'tame' Amerindian population declined drastically, shortages of skilled cocoa collectors pushed up wages, and free labour of mixed race became more common (MacLachlan 1973).

Cocoa cultivation with African slaves became significant for the first time. By 1803, African slaves grew cocoa on a fair scale around Santarém. The number of slaves landed at Belém fell slightly after the abolition of the Pará Company in 1778, some 25,000 being imported between 1778 and 1818, but more were retained in the Amazon than previously. It was estimated that 23 per cent of the population of Pará consisted of African slaves in 1801, more than the 20 per cent registered as 'tame Indians' (Cardoso 1984: 123–4, 127, 173; MacLachlan 1974: 128, 136). However, African slaves were rare in the distant fringes of the Amazon, where Amerindian cocoa collectors were not under Iberian control (Patiño 1963: 284–96).

The Spaniards had long ago abolished slavery in the Philippines, and sharecropping was the norm. Some cocoa may have been grown in this way, for religious orders or 'native' proprietors (Comyn 1969: 20–1). In contrast, slaves raided from all over Southeast Asia performed most tasks in the independent Muslim sultanate of Sulu, and this probably included tending cocoa trees (Warren 1981).

Revolutionary crisis and labour reforms, 1790s–1820s

The crisis in coerced labour at the turn of the century was unexpected, and its effects are debated. The French Revolution rejected slavery in a spectacular albeit temporary manner. A campaign launched by Quakers in the mid-eighteenth century led Denmark to ban the Atlantic slave trade in 1792, followed by Britain in 1807–8, and then by the new Hispanic American republics. However, neither slavery nor forced labour were permanently abolished in the New World, let alone in Africa and Asia. Furthermore, the portrayal of abolition as a kind of economic suicide conceals much uncertainty as to the efficacy of slavery (Oostindie 1995).

The whirlwind hit the French Caribbean first, in the aftermath of the revolution of 1789. Slaves began to liberate themselves in 1791, precipitating the French abolition of slavery in 1794. This was reversed by Napoleon in 1802, but it proved hard to force people back into slavery, and violence erupted. In southwestern Haïti, the chief centre of cocoa production, five plantations were burned in 1802, and numerous slaves were hanged in retaliation. French attempts at reconquest were defeated, and slavery came to an abrupt and permanent end (Fick 1990: 216–17, 223–4). Paradoxically, this stimulated slave-grown cocoa elsewhere in the Caribbean, as French planters fled with some of their slaves (Marrero 1951: 608; Harwich Vallenilla 1996: 34).

Revolutionary contagion spread to Britain's 'ceded islands', with their substantial and restive French populations. In 1795–6, French Creoles stirred up slaves in a bid to oust the British from Grenada, the largest producer of cocoa in the British Caribbean at the time. Julien Fedon, the cocoa and coffee planter who led the rising, set a revolutionary example by freeing his own slaves. The rebellion was suppressed at great cost, and some 7,000 slaves perished (Brizan 1984: 59–77). Dominica was shaken by a similar combination of servile risings and pro-French rebellions from 1791 (Honychurch 1984: 78–91).

The crisis in the Caribbean worsened with Britain's 1807 prohibition on slave imports from Africa, effective in 1808, and also applied to occupied Dutch possessions. As slave populations generally did not reproduce themselves, planters transferred shrinking labour resources out of secondary and less profitable crops such as cocoa. Even on Trinidad, the largest British cocoa producer, only 1,040 slaves worked on cocoa estates in 1813, out of 17,087 plantation slaves. Conditions were better on cocoa estates, however, with lower mortality and higher fertility (John 1988). In Surinam, the Alkmaar estate had been responsible for about a tenth of cocoa exports in 1775, but it grew nothing but sugar by 1818 (Reyne 1924–5: 198–9). The 1807 act provoked a similar rush into sugar in the western section of the Dutch possessions, retained by Britain after the war (Farley 1956: 95).

British blockades from 1796 disrupted the flow of slaves to Venezuela. Prices of prime male slaves edged up to around 300 pesos by 1810 in Caracas province, and planters complained of labour shortages. There were nearly three times as many free persons of colour as slaves by this date, and even free blacks were about half as numerous as slaves (Lucena Salmoral 1990: 52, 56–7). However, eastern Venezuela received an influx of slaves, as French planters came from Haïti and Grenada, or moved over the straits after the British seizure of Trinidad in 1797. By 1800 there were 3,000 or

6,000 slaves in the region, according to different estimates (Harwich Vallenilla 1996: 34–5; Acosta Saignes 1984: 192; Humboldt 1852: I, 398–9).

Shortages of slaves in Mesoamerica contributed to a temporary recrudescence of forced labour. The collapse of Costa Rica's cocoa plantations was partly caused by difficulties in importing fresh slaves (Quesada Camacho 1989: 107). Forced labour drafts rose in Guatemala after 1795, as control of labour shifted back to landowners (McCreery 1994: 95–6). In 1805, Tabascan cocoa estates monopolised about two thirds of the scarce labour available for agriculture (Ruz 1994: 263). The liberal Spanish parliament abolished forced labour throughout the empire in 1812. The measure was revoked by the king in 1814, and then reinstated by the liberals in 1820. However, Spanish control was ebbing away, and the decline of forced labour in Central America owed more to economic crisis than to legislation in distant Spain (McCreery 1994: 110–11).

The attack on slavery widened with the wars of independence, particularly in Venezuela and Colombia. Rebels banned the slave trade in 1810, but did not dare abolish the institution of slavery itself. Caracas planters protested strongly at the freeing of slaves who enlisted in opposing armies from 1812, many of them to desert at the first opportunity. Other slaves escaped without enlisting, some to join bands of maroons (Lombardi 1971: ch. 2; Rout 1976: ch. 6). Estimates for the number of slaves before and after the wars are contradictory, but, according to a contemporary estimate, the number of slaves in Venezuela and Colombia fell by about a third (Hall 1824: 15).

Regional variations complicated the picture. As masters fled across the straits to Trinidad in the late 1810s, slaves escaped to the forests of eastern Venezuela (Harwich Vallenilla 1996: 25, 34–5; Moodie-Kublalsingh 1994: 154). Cúcuta was almost denuded of slaves by 1820 (Brungardt 1974: 82–6). In contrast, the proportion of slaves in the population of Barlovento only declined from 48 to 45 per cent during the liberation wars (Tamaro 1988: 74–5). Similarly, few slaves from Chuao joined the armed forces of either side, or escaped to maroon settlements in the mountains (Brito Figueroa 1985: 128–30). Guayaquil was touched little and late by the wars of independence, although some slaves were liberated in the closing years of the struggle (Humphreys 1940: 228).

Brazil experienced little foreign or domestic strife, and the Portuguese did no more in 1808 than to promise to end the slave trade. African slavery remained undisturbed on the cocoa estates of the middle Amazon (Cardoso 1984). In Ilhéus, pioneer German and Swiss planters relied on a mixture of African slaves and casual 'tame' Amerindian workers, the latter especially skilled at clearing the forest. Captured 'rebel' Amerindians might also be pressed into obligatory labour for ten years (Spix and Martius 1976: II, 54, 159, 161).

Abolition opened up a vista of producing cocoa with free labour in

Africa. Denmark, the first nation to abolish the slave trade, dreamed of using free labour on Gold Coast plantations, although in the event, slaves were employed and only coffee was grown in Akwapim (Macau 1973; 25–7; Nørregard 1966: 175, 178, 182). As for Sierra Leone's freed slaves, they were keener to engage in trade than in risky tropical agriculture in poor soils (Peterson 1969: chs 1–2).

Resistance to the abolition of coerced labour, 1820s–1840s

The progress of labour reform was agonisingly slow with the return of peace. Idealistic declarations that Amerindians were free and equal citizens of new republics were soon drowned out by politically dominant landowners clamouring for labour. Hispanic American governments put an end to the slave trade, but tried to salvage what they could of slavery where it remained economically important. Most Western countries paid no more than lip service to the British crusade against the slave trade, and it was 1848 before any European power emulated Britain's 1833–4 abolition of slavery.

Not only was slavery kept until 1854 in Venezuela, but transitional arrangements made a mockery of the laws enacted by Gran Colombia in 1821, and kept on the statute book after independence in 1830. Cocoa planters mounted a tenacious rearguard action, as slaves were not only a labour force, but also collateral for loans. Manumission boards, starved of funds, only freed a handful of old and sick slaves. Children born to slave mothers became *manumisos*, tied to their masters till the age of eighteen, and legally bought and sold as late as 1852. As the time for liberation loomed, the age of freedom was raised to twenty-one, and then again to twenty-five (Lombardi 1971; Rout 1976: 249–52; Brito Figueroa 1985: 274–5). The press was full of advertisements seeking the return of fugitives, and many small rebellions were recorded (Brito Figueroa 1985: 260, 263).

There was some free labour on Venezuelan cocoa estates, including poor Canarians. They began to immigrate again as soon as independent Venezuela relaxed restrictions, even though emigration remained illegal in Spanish eyes until 1853. The great majority of the 12,610 immigrants entering Venezuela between 1832 and 1857 were Canarians, coming via Cuba or Puerto Rico. They paid off the cost of their passage by signing stringent labour contracts for four years or more (Rodríguez Campos 1989: 157–64, 191, 204–22). Most Canarians worked initially as estate labourers, and those in eastern Venezuela were almost certainly growing cocoa (Zawisza 1975: 17–18, 29).

In neighbouring Colombia, the constitution of 1832 failed to mention manumission boards, and the abolition of slavery was delayed till 1851 (Rout 1976: 236–40). Whereas there had been over a thousand slaves growing cocoa in Cúcuta before independence, only 205 were left in 1835 (Brungardt 1974: 91). However, this was compensated by the growth of cocoa estates in western Antioquia, through transfers of slaves out of declining gold mines (Brew 1977: 243). Cauca also depended on servile labour, and slave prices remained quite steady (Colmenares 1989: 163–8).

Even Ecuador showed considerable ambivalence about slavery. Slaves continued to be employed on coastal estates, and the legal status of slavery was retained until 1851 (Chiriboga 1980: 16–19, 27). As Ecuador was becoming the greatest cocoa producer in the world, labour was in short supply. Part of the cocoa harvest remained unpicked in the early 1820s (Walker 1822: I, 366). The British consul wrote in 1826 that the manumission of slaves during the independence struggle 'has very seriously affected the agricultural interest of this province' (Humphreys 1940: 228). Compared to 2,226 slaves registered in the province in 1790, Laviana Cuetos puts the number at 2,168 in 1825, only a fraction down (Laviana Cuetos 1987: 126, 140). However, Hamerly cites a figure of 1,778 for 1825, and refers to slaves dying and fleeing (Hamerly 1970: 91–2). Slaves were even being imported from Colombia in 1830, although the size of the trade is unknown (Colmenares 1989: 164).

Free labour continued to be the norm on Ecuador's cocoa plantations. In addition to contractors for the establishment of plantations, cocoa estates in 1832 employed day labourers on a casual basis. An 1840 census for five cantons in the province of Guayaquil listed only 318 slaves and 221 *conciertos*, Amerindians tied to the land. This compared to 6,816 free persons of colour and 20,175 free Amerindians, although most of those in the latter two categories were not labourers. Coastal Amerindians, clustered in the west, had secure title to their land, and earned sufficient money through fishing, making salt and straw hats, and smuggling tobacco. Moreover, many of them refused to pay their tribute after independence (Hamerly 1973: 102–4).

By 1840, there existed nuclei of highland Amerindians in Guayaquil province, where wages were three to five times higher than in the Andes. However, they seem to have come more from parishes of the Andean piedmont than from the densely populated intramontane basins of the high Andes, where many Amerindians remained tied to the land (Deler 1981: 140, 169; Chiriboga 1980: 20). Highlanders were very vulnerable to malaria, which decimated the population in 1825 and 1829, and to yellow fever, which killed some 8,500 people in the two coastal provinces of Guayaquil and Manabí in the epidemic of 1842–3 (Hamerly 1973: 138–40).

The slave trade was banned at independence in Mesoamerica, and slavery was abolished in 1824 in the Central American Federation, and in 1829 in Mexico (Rout 1976: 261, 279). Tabasco's landowners lost the services of several hundred former slaves, who migrated to Yucatán in the 1830s (Reed 1964: 20). There were few slaves left on the Pacific side of the isthmus, although some still laboured on Soconusco's cocoa estates in 1820–1 (Carvalho 1994: 85). Guatemalan abolition had the advantage of attracting runaways from the neighbouring British territory of British Honduras (Belize), until slavery came to an end there in 1834 (Solórzano 1963: 276; McCreery 1994: 90; Shoman 1994: 56).

Debt peonage remained the major form of labour control. Tabascan regulations in 1826 abolished colonial forced labour for Amerindian communities, but outlawed vagrancy, obliged workers to remain under contract unless debts were paid off, allowed for the transfer of debt between employers, sanctioned the inheritance of debt from father to son, and made children of debtors work for their father's employer until marriage or the age of twenty-five (Arias *et al.* 1987: 85–7, 222–3). Tabascan debt peons on cocoa estates, mainly Amerindians who accepted cash advances, suffered from corporal punishment and were forced to marry against their will (*Larousse*: XI, 200). Colonial forced labour was abolished at independence in Guatemala, but then re-introduced in 1829 for both Amerindians and non-Amerindians (McCreery 1994: 111–12).

Southern Bahia retained both African and Amerindian slavery. Ilhéus was a major centre of illegal but tolerated slave imports from Africa after 1830, and some were retained for local uses (Mahony 1996: 251–2). The enslavement of Amerindian children was a by-product of ruthless frontier wars in the 1830s and 1840s. Every small farmer was said to possess such slaves in the south of the state, where the going price for a child was 100 milreis (Hemming 1987: 365–6). Free agricultural workers, paid per task or per day, came from settled Amerindian communities, notably former Jesuit missions (Mahony 1996: 354; Métreaux 1946: 531). German, Swiss and Irish immigrants became smallholders rather than labourers (Mahony 1996: 229–33).

African slaves merely trickled into the Brazilian Amazon, where the serious and prolonged Cabanagem rebellion of 1835–9 allowed numerous slaves to gain their freedom. Attempts to resurrect the colonial forced labour corps in the wake of this rebellion proved a dismal failure (Weinstein 1983: 40–3). The ownership of a dozen slaves was considered great wealth by Santarém cocoa producers in the 1840s, and most smallholders relied on family labour and cooperation between neighbours at harvest time. Indeed, lack of labour was cited as the main reason for the slow clearing of forest to plant cocoa (Bates 1969: 83–4, 132–3, 141–3, 186). Planters around Santarém in 1846 not only suffered from a shortage of African slaves, but also found that Amerindians had become 'difficult to catch' (Ross 1978: 205). Relics of Amerindian slavery lingered on upstream, where young victims of inter-tribal wars were 'redeemed out of servitude' and forced by their masters to collect produce from the jungle (Bates 1969: 278–82).

When the British inter-island trade in slaves was prohibited in 1824, Trinidad had 1,622 slaves on 101 cocoa estates. Abolitionists praised conditions, as slaves worked in the shade, were spared night work, and had free time for their provision grounds under a task system. On the smallest estates, owned by free persons of colour, slaves were allegedly treated as members of the family. Spanish law also facilitated manumission through self-purchase (Williams 1952: 273, 294–5, 329–32; John 1988: 106).

The abolition of slavery in British crown colonies was decreed in 1833, became effective in 1834, and was cushioned by an apprenticeship period of four years and financial compensation. Many landowners sought to concentrate on sugar, as early efforts at recruiting indentured labour met with indifferent success (Shephard 1937: III, 6–7). Estate cultivation of cocoa in British Guiana collapsed, and sugar reigned supreme (Schomburgk 1840: 107).

Although the legal status of slavery was retained in the non-British Caribbean, a similar flight from cocoa was blamed on restricted slave imports. When the British returned Surinam to the Netherlands in 1814, the ban on the slave trade remained in force, and the 50,000 existing slaves fell to around 40,000 by 1850 (Panday 1959: ch. 3). As the number of slaves employed in sugar roughly doubled by 1850, cocoa and other secondary crops languished (Stipriaan 1995a: 125). France banned the slave trade in 1818 and introduced 'free womb' laws in the 1830s, making cocoa in Martinique another victim of sugar monoculture (Tomich 1990: 91). In 1840, there were only 259 slaves producing cocoa in French Guiana, on eleven small estates (*PP* 1847: vol. 64).

The dawn of cocoa in Portuguese Africa was under the sign of slavery. After Brazil's independence in 1822, the Portuguese feared the imminent ending of the slave trade, and cast around for means to employ slaves in Africa (Clarence-Smith 1985: ch. 2). It was no coincidence that it was in 1822 that José Ferreira Gomes brought cocoa seedlings from Brazil to Príncipe (César 1969: 20–1, 38, 47). However, the slave trade to Brazil continued at high levels, and slaves were used more to grow coffee than cocoa in São Tomé and Príncipe (Lima 1844: 2–3, 10, 33).

Southeast Asia generally stuck to free labour. The few cocoa estates that emerged in the Spanish Philippines probably followed the established usage of making advances to sharecroppers or wage workers (Mallat 1983: 174, 441–4). The Dutch kept the ban on the slave trade on regaining their possessions in 1816, and encouraged manumission, causing slave numbers to fall. To supply labour to the anaemic cocoa estates of northern Sulawesi, it was proposed in 1846 that slaves be 'redeemed from servitude' in areas not directly ruled by the Dutch, and be obliged to sign ten-year contracts. However, this proposal was not accepted (Clarence-Smith 1998: 103–4).

The incomplete triumph of liberalism, 1850s–1870s

Around the world, the campaign against coerced labour moved into high gear following the wave of liberal revolutions in 1848. The expansion of smallholdings further undermined the use of coercion in cocoa cultivation.

However, significant pockets of slave-grown cocoa remained, and some countries resurrected colonial forced labour.

The abolition of Venezuelan slavery in 1854 was much more than the 'nonevent' that Lombardi has called it (Lombardi 1974). As one contemporary put it, 'the cultivation of cocoa especially was all at once checked, and for some time deranged, by the sudden and unlooked for liberation of the slaves' (Middleton 1871: 454). The cocoa sector held a disproportionately high number of the dwindling stock of slaves, and compensation was paid little and late, if at all. Furthermore, the figure of 13,000 slaves in Venezuela in 1854 was thoroughly misleading. *Manumisos* were technically 'free', but in reality they were still treated as slaves. Indeed, what really angered landowners in 1854 was not that slavery had ended, but that the *manumiso* system had been abolished (Lombardi 1971: 135–42). Some 27,000 *manumisos* were freed in 1854, more than twice the number of slaves (Landaeta Rosales 1963: II, 229).

Difficulties in obtaining free labour contributed to the decline of Venezuelan cocoa estates, particularly in Barlovento, where some 20,000 Blacks and 2,000 Capaya Amerindians had no wish to work on estates (Middleton 1871: 454–5). The coffee sector was better placed to attract seasonal workers from the Andes and the southern cattle plains, although eastern Venezuela's cocoa estates obtained some labour from Caribbean islands (Rangel 1974: 78–83). However, there was much competition from Trinidad estates across the straits (Moodie-Kublalsingh 1994: ch. 1). Furthermore, a terrible cholera epidemic carried off some 15,000 Venezuelans in 1854–5, mainly rural labourers (Polanco Martínez 1960: II, 208).

Colombia was equally severely affected by the ending of slavery in 1851, with cocoa exports falling to their lowest level of the nineteenth century. Brew argues that abolition was not an important factor in the sudden demise of the cocoa zone of western Antioquia in the early 1850s, because so few slaves were left, but he ignores the question of *manumisos* (Brew 1977: 245). In Cauca, near Cali, the Arboleda family handed over plots of virgin forest to 174 former slaves in 1853, in return for ten days' labour per month to plant sugar-cane and cocoa on the estate (Mina 1975: 54–7; Taussig 1977: 410). Tolima cocoa planters faced severe competition for Amerindian labour from the eastern highlands, owing to a boom in tobacco exports (McGreevey 1971: 111–13; Taussig 1977: 399).

The 1851 abolition of slavery in Ecuador compounded problems in finding free labour for rapidly expanding cocoa estates. Short-term labour crises, due to natural and social disasters, led to violent and unpredictable fluctuations in Ecuador's cocoa exports. Repeated outbreaks of yellow fever occurred from 1842 to 1886, decimating the free coloured coastal population and dissuading Amerindians from coming down from the highlands (Hamerly 1973: 112, 138–40). Destructive civil wars rocked the country from the mid-1840s to the mid-1870s, and many workers were forcibly recruited into contending armies. Stringent vagrancy laws could not be enforced. The mobility of highland peasants was restricted by debt peonage, while employment in highland towns was stimulated by a renaissance of artisanal activities. Amerindians in the dry west of the coastal strip did not need to work on cocoa estates, compensating for a crisis in exports of straw hats in the 1870s by gathering wild rubber, 'vegetable ivory', and other forest products (Chiriboga 1980: 18–22, 26–8, 50).

The bargaining position of coastal Ecuadorian workers was thus strong. A skilled contractor cleared the forest and planted cocoa for the landowner, who paid a fixed sum per tree when the grove was handed over. Agreements at this time were for the unusually long period of ten years, allowing the contractor to sell the first few cocoa harvests on his own account. As for permanent workers, they were given a house and a plot of land, in addition to wages. They worked eight hours a day, but not on Sundays and feast days, of which there were many in Ecuador (Toscano 1960: 466–8). A local newspaper in 1867 denounced the rising level of wages on cocoa estates (Chiriboga 1980: 21).

The Dutch abolition of slavery in Surinam in 1863, followed by a lengthy ten-year apprenticeship, was unexpectedly positive for cocoa estates. Apprentices had to contract for plantation labour, but were free to choose their employer, only had to sign up for a year, and could change employer at the end of each contract. Former slaves thus rushed on to cocoa plantations, where conditions were better. The number of small cocoa estates shot up, and cocoa exports roughly tripled between the early 1860s and 1873, whereas estates producing sugar, cotton and coffee declined, especially the latter. Export figures show a rise in cocoa output a little before 1863, however, possibly reflecting the recruitment of a few hundred Chinese, Madeiran Portuguese and Barbadian workers in the 1850s (Emmer 1993: 101, 113; Panday 1959: 90–3, 102–3, 108, 113, 124–7, 132–3, 181, 185).

The disruptions caused by the abolition of slavery in the British Caribbean were receding by mid-century, notably in Trinidad. Steady supplies of South Asian indentured labour were secured by an agreement with British India in 1851. Though overwhelmingly employed on sugar estates, they reduced competition for ex-slave labour (Brereton 1981: 92; Shephard 1937: III, 7). Day labour was common on cocoa estates in 1861, paid 25–35 cents, whereas task work prevailed in sugar (Giacottino 1976: II, 420–1).

Sharecropping rapidly became the preferred option of former slaves on Grenada, although estate owners were less enthusiastic. Sharecropping was only officially approved in 1848, but the Lieutenant-Governor wrote in 1854 that 'the cocoa and coffee estates throughout the island are managed almost without exception upon the *metairie* system, and with success' (Brizan 1984: 128–37, 179–80). Cocoa estates sometimes also employed South Asian labourers, on five-year indentures (Brizan 1984: 183, 193–4; Mahabir 1987: 372–3). One successful cocoa estate in 1856 relied on Portuguese families, probably Madeirans who had completed their indentures (*PP* 1857–8: vol. 40).

Forced labour raised its ugly head again in Mexico. Labour shortages worsened after cholera decimated the population of the south in the 1850s (Alejo Torre 1931: 17). The prefect appointed in Tabasco by Emperor Maximilian formally revived the Spanish forced labour system in 1864. Planters could requisition Amerindian villagers to work on estates for a month at a time, and this retrograde law remained on the statute book after the execution of Maximilian. Increasing numbers of Amerindians accepted debt peonage instead. Apart from food and other payments in kind, debt peons were paid three pesos a month in cash. Many escaped to earn up to four times more in forestry enterprises. However, the entrepreneurial Chontal Maya generally avoided forced labour and debt peonage, providing no more than casual labour for estates (Arias *et al.* 1987: 222–3, 234, 253).

Parts of Central America also lurched back towards the colonial past, but free labour was the rule and debt peonage was rare on Nicaraguan cocoa estates in the early 1870s. Amerindians and free peasants had enough land not to have to work for wages, pushing up the supply cost of labour (Lévy 1873: 446–9, 453–4). The Menier estate employed some 300 'native' workers growing cocoa in the 1860s, and French overseers complained of indiscipline (Cerfberr de Medelsheim 1867: 16). Guatemala legally revived forced labour for Amerindians in 1851, but implementation was patchy before 1871 (Dunkerley 1988: 15).

The Amazonian piedmont of the Andes was another area where colonial traditions of forced labour were in evidence. Near Cuzco, whole families were obliged to travel over considerable distances to harvest cocoa on estates around 1870 (Marcoy 1875: I, 313). Despite Bolivia's grant of legal equality to the Mojos in 1842, they were still subjected to forced labour. A millenarian rebellion broke out in 1881, and was put down with considerable bloodshed (Osborne 1955: 87).

Slave-grown cocoa became more common in southern Bahia, despite the enforcement of Brazilian prohibitions on slave imports from 1850. Clandestine landings continued for a decade in southern Bahia, and although most of these slaves were probably sent south, in 1851 Swiss planters of Ilhéus expressed an interest in buying some (Verger 1968: 432; Bethell 1970: 285, 358, 374). The Bahian authorities did not object to slaves being switched from sugar to cocoa within the state, though they tried to prevent sales to southern coffee estates. Cocoa presented a particular advantage, in that both aged and child slaves could be productively employed. In 1870–2 there were over 1,000 slaves registered in Ilhéus, accounting for around a fifth of the sparse population. The local price for slaves increased at least fourfold between 1850 and the 1870s, reaching as high as 1,250 milreis. Nevertheless, slaves were still being purchased shortly before 1888 by planters in southern Bahia (Mahony 1996: 253–4, 317, 321, 326–31, 343). Moreover, the continuing enslavement of Amerindian children was reported in the 1870s (Hemming 1987: 380).

The distribution of slave ownership was uneven. Inventories made at the death of individuals between 1850 and 1888 show that the Sá clan possessed some 300 slaves in the 1860s, and the Cerqueira Lima family up to 100. While still employed to some extent in sawmills and sugar, these slaves were increasingly transferred into cocoa. A more numerous group of deceased persons owned fewer than ten slaves, and some 60 per cent owned none at all. Managers of estates were white and free, often becoming planters and slave owners. Slaves were allowed plots, on which they could grow cocoa and other cash crops. They could buy their freedom, especially when they were over fifty years of age and likely to become a burden (Mahony 1996: 279–82, 335–6, 343–4, 350–5).

Free immigrants from the drought-prone backlands, paid in cash and kind, worked side-by-side with slaves in cocoa cultivation. These free people of mixed race were mainly drawn from Bahia, receiving some assistance from the state government to migrate. A substantial minority came from the state of Sergipe to the north, and a few from an even wider area of north-eastern Brazil. The usual picture of these migrants as half-starved victims of successive droughts in the dry backlands needs to be qualified. Not a few paid their own passage to Ilhéus, and some came with enough capital to buy cocoa plots, without first having to work for wages. They had large families and organised mutual help between neighbours, to minimise their own need for hired labour (Mahony 1996: 256–67, 352–7).

Small groups of Amerindians engaged in casual labour on the fringes of the Bahia cocoa zone. Paid in food, rum and tobacco, they rarely stayed more than a few days, before melting back into the forest. Settlers were keen to retain access to this labour, even though its productivity was low, and they complained that Italian Capuchins were interfering (Hemming 1987: 372, 380). To add insult to injury, Capuchins tried to turn Amerindians into producers of cash crops, including cocoa (Nembro 1958: 294–7, 303–13).

Slavery was moribund in the Brazilian Amazon, but a few remaining owners of cocoa estates clung to their dwindling stock of slaves (Tosta Filho 1957: 2). In contrast, the rising group of cocoa smallholders relied heavily on their families and neighbours at harvest time (Soares 1977: 115). The state's forced labour corps was disbanded in the 1860s, but the population was depleted by epidemics of yellow fever and cholera in the 1850s (Weinstein 1983: 43; Bates 1969: 18).

Cuba was the other great bastion of slavery in Latin America, although cocoa was less of a slave crop than sugar. The Spaniards choked off illicit slave imports into Cuba in the late 1860s, declared that all slave children born after 1870 would be free, and in 1886 put an end to slavery itself.

Chinese workers, indentured in conditions almost indistinguishable from slavery, were imported until 1875, but essentially for work in the sugar sector (Clarence-Smith 1984). Two cocoa plantations in Remedios were run on classic lines in the 1850s, presumably with slave or indentured labour, but nothing was said of the more numerous units in eastern Cuba (Fisher 1858: 59, 120). While there were quite a few slaves in eastern Cuba in 1868, there were more free persons of colour than was usual in the island, and slavery was further undermined during the Ten Years War that ravaged the region after that date (Pérez de la Riva 1944: 90–4).

São Tomé and Príncipe's slave system came to a sudden end in 1875, albeit a temporary one. From 1858 slaves legally became *libertos* or freedmen, but nothing significant changed in their condition (Clarence-Smith 1985: 30–1, 74–6). The self-liberation of slaves in 1875 thus came like a bolt out of the blue. Encouraged by Gregório Ribeiro, a liberal governor, some 6,000 *libertos* announced that the time of their servitude was legally over, deserted their estates, and marched on the capital. In a panic, landowners agreed to cancel a two-year apprenticeship foreseen by law, and to waive compensation. Former *libertos* then signed contracts for a maximum of two years, and changed employers frequently. Cocoa probably benefited, as ex-slaves preferred employment with small African planters, more likely to grow cocoa than coffee. It took the Portuguese a few years to decide to allow a renewal of the clandestine slave trade (Clarence-Smith 1993b).

The Spaniards abolished slavery in Fernando Póo in 1859, to ensure British support for direct administration, initiated the previous year. However, slaves intercepted by anti-slavery patrols and landed in Cuba were sometimes sent to Fernando Póo, joining those previously landed by the British. Cubans were also transported for political offences. Runaway slaves from Príncipe arriving in the island were contracted to planters. The conditions of all these workers were close to slavery. Free Kru from Liberia could not be treated this way, but they were expensive and rarely worked in agriculture (Sundiata 1972: 89–91, 155–61; Sanz Casas 1983: 53–61).

The drift to freedom, 1880s–1914

The last vestiges of slavery were swept away in the New World in the 1880s, and the predominance of free labour became unquestionable. Free labour was also the norm in West Africa and Asia, where population was dense, commerce well developed, smallholdings widespread, and colonial officials prevented abuses.

Ecuador's cocoa estates continued to demonstrate that large-scale ownership of land could coincide with free labour, especially through the contractor system. However, the average contract period was 5–6 years, shorter than before. Estate owners preferred men with families and prior experience. Contracts could take a written form, but were often verbal, and the contractor controlled the entire labour process. He was allocated a stretch of virgin forest to clear and sow with cocoa and shade trees. He was allowed to interplant food between the seedlings, mainly rice, with plantains and cassava serving as temporary shade. The contractor owned his tools and employed casual day labourers, paid with cash advances obtained from the planter. At the end of the stipulated period, the contractor received 0.2 sucres per bearing tree. If his debts were greater than the lump sum, he might enter into another agreement or become a permanent labourer. If not, he was free to move elsewhere (Chiriboga 1980: 199–203; Kaerger 1901: II, 449; Guislain and Vincart 1911: 66; Weinman 1970: 59–61).

There were few permanent workers on Ecuadorian estates, and their bargaining power was great. One woman estate owner had only 108 resident peons for 500,000 trees in 1893 (Pineo 1996: 17). An observer considered in 1887 that the workers 'impose their will on landowners, because they understand full well that they are needed, due to the scarcity of labour' (Chiriboga 1980: 28, 176–7). The engrossing of so much land by the Guayaquil elite was the reason for there being a labour force at all, although it is not clear whether this was a deliberate strategy.

Conditions for permanent workers had to be attractive. A house, a plot of land and pasture for a horse or a cow were customary benefits provided to such workers, together with rudimentary medical care. Advances were expected for special occasions, such as marriage, building a house, or the birth of a child. However, this was not debt peonage. Wages were high, at 0.6–0.7 sucres a day around 1900, and interest on advances was usually waived as an added bonus. The proud and independent coastal workers could easily borrow from other sources, notably shopkeepers. If labourers perceived that debt was being unfairly manipulated, they absconded, got another landowner to pay off their debt, or resorted to violence (Crawford de Roberts 1980: 79–81; Preuss 1987: 90–1; Chiriboga 1980: 118, 216–18; Kaerger 1901: II, 448–9).

Single men housed in barracks were employed for seasonal tasks, notably the two main harvests. They were paid on a daily basis without written contracts, and were attracted by wages that rose from around 0.5 to about 1.1 sucres a day in the course of the 1880s. This was far above the 0.1 sucres routinely earned on estates and public works in the highlands. Workers enjoyed much independence, bargaining over remuneration, and benefiting from expanding urban employment (Chiriboga 1980: 28, 177, 186, 213–21; Crawford de Roberts 1980: 78–9; Preuss 1987: 90). Alternatively, workers were employed at a fixed rate per task, the landowner usually providing tools and draught animals (Kaerger 1901: II, 448–9). Variations in wages were to the advantage of the skilled coastal population. Pod cutters were particularly well paid. They used a sharp knife attached to a bamboo cane, which might be thrown at the highest pods (Preuss 1987: 85–6).

There remains much uncertainty as to the numbers and origins of workers on Ecuadorian cocoa estates. A tentative figure of around 15,000 workers in the cocoa sector in 1893 can be derived from a large sample (Chiriboga 1980: 191; Preuss 1987: 78; Pineo 1996: 17; Guerrero 1980: 37). Crawford de Roberts maintains that the expanding population of the coastal strip met most labour needs, and that migration from the Andes was still a trickle in 1914. Although tying labour in the highlands was legally abolished in 1895, this was only enforced after 1918 (Crawford de Roberts 1980: 76–81). However, Chiriboga contends that highland landlords found it increasingly difficult in practice to prevent debt peons from leaving, and sometimes even rented them to cocoa planters. Moreover, there were free communities, which suffered from heavy taxes, the sub-division of plots, debt, and a shortage of employment. A planter journal in 1904 claimed that migration to cocoa estates was increasing (Chiriboga 1980: 184–7).

Foreign workers were few. The importation of Chinese 'coolies' was forbidden from 1899, and planters were fined in the 1900s for enticing Jamaicans building the railway to Quito (Chiriboga 1980: 182). Peruvian and Colombian employees in the 1890s were mainly foremen (Preuss 1987: 90). More workers came from these two countries after the turn of the century, but still not in great numbers (Maiguashca 1996: 76; Chiriboga 1980: 191).

Ecuadorian estate owners began to question their flexible and efficient labour system before 1914, but the timing and extent of changes remain unclear. Deler sees a major shift around 1890, whereas Chiriboga plumps more cautiously for 1910. A few wealthy landowners experimented with replacing contractors with gang labour, but such 'modern' practices required numerous and expensive supervisors (Deler 1981: 167, illustration XI; Chiriboga 1980: 202). In 1911, and again in the 1930s, the contractor system was reported to be the norm (Guislain and Vincart 1911: 66; Ruf 1995: 168).

Contractors were in general use on Trinidad, but the system was more closely monitored than in Ecuador. The landowner cleared the forest and dug the main drains with casual labour. Written contracts were then drawn up for up to three *quarrées* (about four hectares), the landowner often providing seed and cash advances. Venezuelans skilled in cocoa cultivation were preferred, and personal reputation was important, as contractors could spend advances in 'riotous living' and then disappear into the forest. The contractor employed about five workers, in addition to his family. He finished clearing the land, sold any residual timber, dug minor drains, and planted cocoa and shade trees in straight lines, at specified intervals. Workers were allowed to interplant food crops, sometimes providing a small surplus for sale. In slack periods, some or all of the workforce might perform casual labour. At the end of the agreed period, the contractor received the contracted sum per bearing cocoa tree, usually approaching 25 cents, half for immature trees over three years of age, quarter for trees between two and three years old, and nothing for seedlings. Empty spaces resulted in a deduction from the final payment. Most contractors then took on another contract, or became smallholders (Shephard 1937: IV, 3–6; Preuss 1987: 31–2).

Indentured South Asian workers became more common as permanent labourers on Trinidadian cocoa estates, and the portrayal of this type of labour as a 'new slavery' is clearly mistaken (Northrup 1995). South Asians came on five-year contracts, received free accommodation, food, medical services and other payments in kind, as well as 25 cents a day for male workers, compared to the going rate of 35–50 cents. As most cocoa estates were too small to have a hospital and pay for regular visits by a doctor, they clubbed together to comply with the law (Shephard 1937: IV, 6–7; V, 2–3). On expiry of their indentures, a few South Asians worked for estates too small to import indentured workers, but they preferred to set up on their own account (Head 1903: 40–1). Although cocoa estates paid less than sugar estates, the incidence of disease and death was lower (Williams 1964: 106 9, 113). Local Creoles were still employed for piecework and casual day labour, notably weeding and harvesting (Preuss 1987: 31–2).

Trinidadian estates had high supervisory costs. For some forty permanent workers and forty temporary harvesters in the 1900s, an estate in the northeast employed one highly paid European general manager and three overseers (Harrison 1979: 67). One of the first effects of the postwar depression was the sacking of expensive European plantation managers, replaced by 'visiting plantation attorneys', often of Venezuelan extraction (Moodie-Kublalsingh 1994).

Unusually high population densities on smaller Caribbean islands coincided with sharecropping. Dominica, losing labour through emigration, made some use of the contractor system for cocoa in the 1890s, but estates were usually divided into plots of up to eight hectares, tended by sharecroppers (Trouillot 1988: 81–7, 94–113). Seasonal labour by owners of small plots was common in Grenada, where emigration was also running at high levels (Great Britain 1942: 142, 144; Brizan 1984: 216–17, 227). Tobago had a tradition of sharecropping, although the contract system was copied from Trinidad as cocoa developed from the 1880s (Brereton 1981: 210).

Labour-intensive estates in Surinam suffered from a dependence on expensive Asian indentured labour (Preuss 1987: 23). After the ending of apprenticeship in 1873, the authorities supplied low-interest loans to facilitate labour imports from British India and Java. Some 32,000 South Asians and 11,000 Javanese were brought under five-year contracts of indenture to Surinam up to 1914 (Panday 1959: 132–59). Without this help from the authorities, estates would undoubtedly have collapsed much sooner.

The abolition of slavery in 1888 may have dealt the final blow to Amazonian cocoa estates, but the same was not true in Bahia. Southern

Bahia's landowners fought abolition tooth and nail, and Salvador's commercial association fruitlessly petitioned the government for an apprenticeship system (Pereira Filho 1959: 27–9, 49; Ridings 1977: 233–4). To their surprise, estate owners found that the labour situation actually improved, as thousands of freed slaves flocked to the cocoa frontier from depressed sugar and ranching zones of the northeast. While many families moved straight to the forest frontier to become smallholders, others undertook a spell of wage labour on estates to acquire expertise and a little capital (Mahony 1996: 332, 423–4; Caldeira 1954: 11; Pereira Filho 1959: 67–8; Freitas 1979: 54). A similar flow of northeasterners to the Amazon had quite different results, as collecting wild rubber proved more attractive (Weinstein 1983).

Contractors in Bahia obtained an advance to clear and plant land, receiving an agreed sum per bearing tree, normally after five years. Agreements were verbal rather than written. Contractors interplanted manioc, bananas, maize and beans for their own consumption, and sold any early cocoa crop. They either moved on to clear a new patch of forest for the same estate owner, or became producers on their own account (Caldeira 1954: 37–8). Farmers with more resources preferred to obtain plots, clear and plant them, and sell them to estates at the going rate when trees reached a certain age (Zehntner 1914: 23).

Casual labourers in Bahia sought piecework, which allowed for autonomy and the accumulation of savings to set up as smallholders. Large landowners often negotiated with jobbers, rather than with individual workers, granting cash advances, tools and food. Work on estates rarely lasted more than eight months in a year (Caldeira 1954: 39–41, 44, 46). Landowners alleged that piecework led to careless work, and that about a fifth of the advances that they made were not repaid (Tosta Filho 1957: 17; Zehntner 1914: 150).

Bahia's more affluent cocoa smallholders were also employers of labour. Of applicants for land titles in 1900–9, more than half had two or more workers resident on their property. Most of the rest had at least one (Mahony 1996: 459). Whether labour relations differed on smallholdings remains to be determined.

Venezuelan cocoa estates experienced severe and growing labour problems, as new opportunities in gold mining and wild rubber caused seasonal labour from the southern cattle plains to dry up (Rangel 1974: 78–83, 87, 165). Aspirant smallholders could not be denied land, at least in eastern Venezuela and Trinidad, where squatting was common (Harwich Vallenilla 1996: 37–8; Moodie-Kublalsingh 1994: ch. 1). Cocoa estates in eastern Venezuela depended on densely populated British Caribbean islands such as Barbados and Dominica (Harwich Vallenilla 1996: 36; Trouillot 1988: 113). However, growing xenophobia and racism led to a ban on permanent immigration from Caribbean islands in 1903. European migrants were no alternative, as they wanted land not labour contracts (Norbury 1970: 137–8,

142). Moreover, Barbadians flocked in ever increasing numbers to Panama from 1904, to build the canal (Beckles 1990: 142–7).

Estates in Bolivia's Yungas valleys were similarly hamstrung by labour shortages. There were typically 40–50 permanent Amerindian labourers on such estates in 1912, most of them employed in cultivating coca leaf rather than cocoa. They had their own allotments, were only obliged to work for four days a week, were much addicted to alcohol, and were prompt to abandon an unpopular employer. Casual day labour was expensive, at the equivalent of a shilling a day, and a plantation manager cost £80 plus perks (Walle 1925: 173–4, 179–83).

Costa Rican cocoa estates employed Caribbean island workers, especially Jamaicans hired by the United Fruit Company (Bergmann 1957: 48). They were joined by migrants from the interior of Costa Rica and from Nicaragua, attracted by high wages, although wages for casual labourers on the coast fell around 1900 (Quesada Camacho 1989: 96, 109; 1977–8: 81–2, 96, 97).

Cocoa estates in the Dominican Republic were able to recruit locally, whereas sugar planters were obliged to import thousands of seasonal wage workers a year, mainly from the British Caribbean. Task work was the norm on cocoa estates, imposed against the wishes of reluctant masters, and such work seems often to have been a temporary phase before setting up as small-holders (Hoetink 1988: 166–7, 171–2). The French owners of La Evolución estate made an attempt to employ German immigrants in 1888, but sold out to Suchard within two years (Baud 1982: 70). Labour relations on estates could be tense, for the German manager of Suchard's plantation was murdered 'by the Blacks' in 1913 (*Gordian*: XIX, 6394).

The smallest farmers in the Dominican Republic disposed of less than 2.5 hectares and relied mainly on family members and mutual help arrange-ments between groups of neighbours to clear and prepare the land. However, even small farmers usually paid for a little outside help with the two main harvests. Wages rose as a result of the cocoa boom, and so did the social status of the landless. Heads of households with more land continued to work with their families, but routinely employed outside labour and with-drew from jobs such as weeding. Any farmer with over 25 hectares was likely to have almost all tasks performed by piece workers, typically paying $2–2.5 to clear and prepare a *tarea* of land (0.6 hectares) (Deschamps 1907: II, 328–9; Schoenrich 1918: 154; Baud 1982: 67, 72–3).

Even larger amounts of labour were required for the burst of small-holder production that catapulted the Gold Coast to the position of largest producer in the world in 1911. Even excluding the laborious busi-ness of transporting beans to market, it was estimated that cocoa cultivation must have required 37 million labour days in 1911, equivalent to about 185,000 workers (Szereszewski 1965: 57). While family labour was undoubtedly important, with labour time released by buying food, there were probably as many labourers as farmers by 1910 in Akim and Akwapim (Hill 1963: 187).

Farmers planting over 500 trees at any one time in Akim usually took on workers. These were mainly sharecroppers, who received a third of the harvest, and many of them came from German Togo. They required a minimum of supervision and no working capital. They were highly motivated, as they hoped to set up their own cocoa farms, either where they worked, or on their return home. However, larger farmers preferred to pay wages, retaining closer control of production decisions, land and profits. Cash in hand was then needed and wages were high, up to 15 shillings a month, and double that during the harvest (Hill 1963: 17, 186–90; *Gordian*: X, 4388–9; XIX: 7133).

Other kinds of labour were involved. Numerous workers were needed to carry loads, or roll barrels to the rail-head, and they came increasingly from the savannah regions to the north. It even proved economical for European firms to introduce some of the earliest lorries on the flat lands near the coast (Harris 1968: 46, 255–7). Transport workers were paid even more than harvesters, allegedly up to 3–5 shillings a day at the height of the season (*Gordian*: XIX, 7133).

Smallholders mobilising labour through cooperative work groups probably formed the basic labour pattern in Ashanti, and some commoners also hired out their services for payment. To some extent, this was labour reallocated from older pursuits, such as warfare, hunting and gold mining. However, chiefs utilised a medley of pawns, slaves and corvée labour to create their cocoa farms. The British banned the slave trade in 1896, prohibited the giving and taking of pawns in 1902, and made slavery illegal in 1908, but they were cautious in enforcing this legislation, for fear of a rebellion (Austin 1984: 329, 381–2, 430–40, 454–7, 472–85, 507–10, 523; 1987: 260–3; 1997: xvii).

The Yoruba of Nigeria, another hierarchical society with a strong slaving tradition, had a similar mix. Family labour was the key for smaller producers, benefiting from a reallocation of males from fighting to agriculture, and cooperative work groups were used to clear the forest. Sharecropping and hired labour were not common. Chiefs employed slaves and pawns to establish farms, as slavery was not abolished till 1916 outside Lagos (Berry 1975: 51–3, 128–35, 140–1).

British officials refused to provide forced local labour to European planters, and rejected calls for indentured Chinese or South Asian labour, in order to avoid rebellions and social tension (Phillips 1989: ch. 3). European cocoa planters on the Gold Coast, using inappropriately intensive methods of cultivation, were thus hamstrung by the cost of free workers and inordinately expensive European employees. In contrast, small estates owned by Africans were viable. The owner of Koransan, in Akim, started planting in 1904 and had 36 hectares in cocoa in 1936, tended by hired labour (Austin 1996).

Creole cocoa planters in Nigeria initially coped with high wages, although this probably contributed to their fall after 1918. They recruited Yoruba from inland on one year contracts. Foremen received 30 shillings a month, and labourers 15–20 shillings, exclusive of board and lodging, wages that were considerably higher than on European estates elsewhere in western Africa (Harris 1968: 46, 263). Jacob Coker employed about 200 workers a year on his Agege cocoa estate after 1904, in groups of six to twelve under a headman. He provided housing, food plots, entertainment, medical facilities, education for children and adults, and Christian services. Labourers saw this as a training period, during which they learned the gospel of 'coffee, cocoa, cotton and work, as well as the scriptures'. Coker also obtained labour services as repayment for small loans of under £5 (Webster 1962: 126–9).

Free labour was the norm on cocoa estates around the Indian Ocean, although the French supplied prison labour to corporations for cocoa cultivation from 1911 in Madagascar (Campbell 1996: 202–3). Ceylon's cocoa estates depended on Tamils from southern India, with a few local Sinhalese recruited on a casual daily basis (Hall 1932: 469; Maclaren 1924: 195). The resident workforce for cocoa cultivation was never greater than 1.5 per hectare, and jobs such as weeding were done on a piecework basis (Hall 1914: 400, 404). As Ceylon was close to the Tamil heartland, labour was not indentured. Landowners loaned money to foremen, who travelled to Tamil villages and advanced money to workers. Foremen kept day-to-day control over their workers, most of whom did not stay for more than a few months. This was a flexible and cheap system, which removed much administration from managers and owners, but it was not easy to be sure that labour would be available when needed (Kurian 1989: 89–94).

The low cost of Javanese labour was an essential ingredient in the success of cocoa estates, and this was a largely female workforce. Women, crucial for harvesting, received 15–25 cents a day, compared to 25–40 cents for men (Hall 1914: 406–7; Hall 1932: 312). Large numbers were needed because of intensive methods of cocoa cultivation, especially in the struggle against insect pests. Casual day labour from neighbouring villages was the norm (Hunger 1913: 422). Many children were also employed, especially to control insects (Roepke 1922: 66–9, 77–8, 124–5, 133, 155).

The imposition of German rule in 1899 curbed excesses in Western Samoa, but local people preferred to work on their own coconut and cocoa farms, and were considered expensive as day labourers (*Gordian*: IX, 3786–7). Bringing a cocoa tree to bearing cost 6.5 marks with local labour, compared to 5 marks with Chinese workers (*BII*: XII, 478). The Germans thus agreed to the recruitment of Chinese on three-year contracts. Workers were allowed free passage home, but increasingly preferred to sign new contracts at higher rates of pay. By 1914, there were 2,184 Chinese and 877 Melanesians under indenture in the colony, and Chinese workers had become the mainstay of cocoa estates (Keesing 1934: 352–5; Maclaren 1924: 197).

The resurgence of coerced labour, 1880s–1914

The unprecedented demand for labour during the great cocoa boom led to exceptions in the drift to freedom. Much of Mesoamerica witnessed an intensification of forced labour, and there were notorious abuses in the South Pacific. Even more striking was the extent to which slavery and coerced labour contributed to the rapid rise of cocoa in Equatorial Africa, where population densities were low, markets stunted, and colonial regimes reactionary.

In São Tomé and Príncipe, briefly the largest cocoa producer in the world, a backlash followed the abolition of slavery in 1875. When landowners complained that the cost of importing free labour from West Africa was ruining them, the Portuguese authorities allowed the slave trade to resume in the early 1880s. The great majority of slaves came from Angola, with a few from Dahomey and Gabon, and some 300 indentured labourers from China. Slaves purchased in the backlands of Angola were obliged to sign a labour contract, and were then sold on the islands by transferring contracts. Some 70,000 slaves were imported in this way between 1880 and 1908. When contracts came to an end, they were 'automatically renewed'. Furthermore, all children of slaves were obliged to sign contracts when they grew up. The export of slaves from Angola was stopped in 1908, and the repatriation of existing slaves was imposed by the Republicans after 1910 (Clarence-Smith 1990; Duffy 1967).

Rising slave prices and international humanitarian agitation led the Portuguese to search for supplementary sources of labour from their colonies. Some 14,000 drought-stricken Cape Verdeans voluntarily signed contracts between 1903 and 1915. About 33,000 Mozambicans were sent to the islands over the same period, mostly under administrative compulsion, together with 7,500 from Angola after 1908. Overall, these figures were nearly as high as for slaves, but contract workers only went to the islands for one to three years (Clarence-Smith 1990: 153–4).

The expense of this labour system was greatly magnified by death, flight, low productivity, and high supervisory costs. Rates of mortality reached 8 per cent a year on São Tomé, and double that on Príncipe, where a sleeping-sickness epidemic raged until 1914. Mortality and flight were concentrated in early months, so that purchase costs were lost for almost no return. The provision of food, clothing, shelter and medical services improved over time, but productivity was undermined by illness, homesickness and corporal punishment. Expenditure on European skilled and supervisory employees was a further drag on profitability, worsened by intensive methods of production (Clarence-Smith 1990; 1993b).

Many of the labourers entering Fernando Póo before 1900 were recruited on the African coast by Creole landowners. Many were runaway slaves and victims of the 1896 tax rebellion in Sierra Leone (Sundiata 1972: 238–9; Phillips 1989: 34, 36; Crowder 1966: 155). Another large group came from Angola's Cabinda enclave in the 1880s (Baumann 1888: 138–9). Kru were expensive, but many of those called Kru were Liberians of other origins, more likely to accept work on estates (Sanz Casas 1893: 84; Davis 1976: 49–54). The Vai of Liberia sold slaves and pawns to recruiters, technically as indentured labourers, and 'Vai-Boys' became a name for all Liberians on the island (Holsoe 1977: 297–8; Chevalier 1906: 295). Runaway slaves from Príncipe or São Tomé continued to be handed over to estate owners on long contracts (Clarence-Smith 1994a: 192).

A strike by workers from southwestern Nigeria in 1900 led Britain to close her possessions to recruitment for Fernando Póo, leaving Liberia as the main source of labour. The Liberian government, perpetually on the verge of bankruptcy, benefited from recruitment fees, bonds to guarantee repatriation, and deferred wage payments. It thus turned a blind eye to corrupt, deceitful and violent recruiting practices, but made strenuous efforts to secure repatriation (Sundiata 1974). Some prisoners of war, seized in pacification expeditions inland, were offered to labour recruiters on four-year contracts (BAAP 1898). Many pawns and domestic slaves also found themselves contracted to 'Nanny Po' (Davis 1976: 57).

The Spaniards were thrown back on their own resources in 1908, when Liberia suspended labour exports, in response to demands from Americo-Liberian planters (Sundiata 1974: 105). Attempts to force the indigenous Bubi to work on estates resulted in mass protests, which turned violent in 1910. Madrid ordered a halt the following year, leaving Bubi chiefs in peace to use domestic slaves and pawns to grow their cocoa (Clarence-Smith 1994a: 193–4). Spanish officials in the coastal enclave of Río Muni were little enamoured of losing scarce labour, but packed off some 'rebels' to Fernando Póo as 'pacification' campaigns gathered way from 1910 (Sanz Casas 1983: 223–8, 300). In 1913, there were some 6,000 workers on Fernando Póo, mostly on cocoa estates (Sundiata 1972: 286).

The Germans in Cameroon and Togo were more ruthless, and had a larger area from which to draw forced labour. The Cameroonian authorities initially hesitated, but Jesko von Puttkamer swept away doubts when he became governor in 1895. He mounted yearly 'pacification' campaigns, sending 'rebels' to work for long years on estates, often the equivalent of a death sentence. Puttkamer also winked at disguised forms of slavery, and permitted labour recruiters to bend or break the law (Clarence-Smith 1993a: 192, 200–3; Rüger 1960). In Togo, Germany's 'model colony', estates were kept ticking over by receiving some 5,000 tax defaulters a year, drawn from the north (Sebald 1988: 373). British agronomists praised the modernity of the Kpeve cocoa estate, taken over as part of the spoils of the First World

War, but its running costs with free labour were hopelessly uneconomic (Austin 1996: 159–60).

Puttkamer's recall in 1906 signalled a desire for change, but labour scandals tarnished the record of German colonialism till its demise. While slavery and the deportation of war captives were stamped out, the authorities proved all too willing to 'help' labour recruiters to meet their quotas. The Bakweri people of Mount Cameroon were subjected to stints of forced labour on cocoa estates in 1913, despite close relations with missionaries. Appalling death rates on cocoa estates actually increased, with 30.5 per cent of one group of workers dying over a mere seven months in 1913. Reports painting estates as death camps sent shockwaves through Berlin, but the war intervened before any action could be taken (Clarence-Smith 1993a: 208–11). German estates made their problems worse by adopting intensive methods of production and a racist division of labour. There were nearly 18,000 workers on Cameroonian estates at the beginning of 1913, producing mainly cocoa, and the ratio of White to Black employees stood at 1:96 (Hausen 1970: 220, 249; Michel 1969).

European planters were not alone in Cameroon in using coerced labour to grow cocoa. The Duala elite of the capital city found a new use for slaves formerly producing palm oil, putting them to work on their small cocoa estates, alleging that they treated them like children. The Germans clamped down on the internal trade in slaves from 1901, and the resulting scarcity and high cost of slaves gradually obliged Duala estate owners to shift to free wage labour, drawn from the highlands of southwestern Cameroon. Some came to earn their tax money, while others aspired to become cocoa producers themselves (Monga 1996: 128–31; Austen and Derrick 1999: 118).

In the densely populated Mayombe region, local labour predominated, routinely described as free. However, it seems that Yombe chiefs initially hired out their slaves to estates. As the Belgian authorities clamped down on slavery after 1908, workers were probably former slaves with little access to land (Vellut 1996: 130). There were some 3,000 workers on Mayombe estates by 1914 (Claessens 1914: 217). Over the frontier, Cabinda had over 1,000 workers on the main cocoa estates by 1915, drawn from the area to the south of the Congo estuary (AHA 1915). A great rebellion in this area was in part provoked by forced labour in 1914 (Sociedade de Emigração 1915: 49–51, 198). The thousand or so workers on the cocoa estates of the French Congo were recruited under administrative pressure and paid wages that were among the lowest in western Africa, often in kind (Vennetier 1968: 206, 210; Harris 1968: 46, 141).

'Blackbirded' labour was common in the South Pacific. Solomon Islanders were kidnapped, sent to work on Samoan cocoa estates, and harshly treated, although this traffic was repressed after the establishment of German rule in 1900 (McLynn 1994: 368, 398–9, 421–2, 443). Melanesians working on German New Guinea's cocoa estates came on three-year indentures from islands in the Bismarck and Solomon archipelagos, and abuses were widespread under the New Guinea Company. With the establishment of direct German rule in 1899, a head tax replaced administrative coercion, and mortality rates on estates fell. Even so, considerable pressure was required to prevent labour drifting to the British Solomon islands, where wages were higher (Firth 1982).

The freeing of labour did not even extend to all New World cocoa producers, as old-fashioned coercion surged ahead in Mesoamerica, notably in the northern Chiapas district of Pichucalco. A press campaign in 1885 denounced the chaining and beating of labourers, the appalling conditions in which they worked and died, the timidity of officials in punishing landowners who broke the law, and ever-mounting hereditary debts. The root cause of these abuses was the forced recruitment of Amerindians, ignorant of their rights. The creation of debts through advances, fines and other mechanisms mainly served to delay or prevent repatriation (García Cantú 1969: 382–97). Pichucalco had 3,242 debt peons officially registered in 1897, mainly from the central highlands of Chiapas, with an average debt of over 150 pesos per person (Benjamin 1989: 28, 38–9, 64–5, 87–9). Indebtedness was higher in Pichucalco in 1896 than anywhere else in Chiapas (Baumann 1983: 16). Workers were effectively bought and sold through the transfer of debts between planters, and individual debts reached 500 pesos and more by 1910 (Wasserstrom 1983a: 52).

Chiapas landowners expressed considerable unhappiness with this labour system, and sought alternatives. Naked force provoked flight and violence, including the murder of a plantation manager in Pichucalco. Cash advances tied up working capital, led to serious losses when workers died or fled, and undermined productivity. Advances were actively sought by some Amerindians, who fled without repaying. More and more capital was tied up in ruinous competition between planters to bind labourers to estates. When the revolutionary government in Chiapas cancelled all debts in 1914, planters bemoaned the fact that they had lost both their capital and their workers at a stroke (Baumann 1983: 13–24, 44–5; García Cantú 1969: 385–6, 391, 397).

Debt peons only made up a third to a half of Chiapas' labour force by 1910, and seasonal workers became of increasing importance as the authorities clamped down on illegal forced labour (Benjamin 1989: 89). The state authorities promulgated strict vagrancy laws in 1880, and raised the head tax in 1892. Landowners sent out recruiters to enlist highlanders, squeezed by growing land alienation (Wasserstrom 1983a: 115–16, 152). Cash advances were the rule, and casual workers were paid 5 reales a day, rather than the 4 reales earned by permanent workers in 1900. Day labourers also received higher bonuses at harvest time, and were paid more per task. Such seasonal labour, drawn mainly from the central highlands, became common on Pichucalco's cocoa estates (Baumann 1983: 38, 42).

Conditions were equally bad in Guatemala, where a law of 1877 autho-rised forced labour for estates producing coffee, sugar, cocoa and bananas. Forced labour was briefly abolished in 1893, but indebted labourers resident on estates growing specified crops, including cocoa, were exempted from obligatory labour on public works and military conscription. Forced labour was reinstated in 1897–8, and lasted till 1920 (McCreery 1983: 742–3; Trümper 1996: 19–20). Some Maya preferred to emigrate to British Honduras, a few of them finding employment on cocoa and coffee planta-tions there in the 1880s (Shoman 1994: 104–5).

Forced recruitment was less significant in Tabasco, most of whose popu-lation were classed as Mestizos in the 1895 census (Arias *et al.* 1987: 253, 273–4, 287). However, Tabascan planters were accused of inflicting corporal punishment on their workers in the 1880s (García Cantú 1969: 390). The main illegality was when officials apprehended fugitive debtors and brought them back to estates, for breach of contract was a civil matter. Permanent workers received food, free medical services, a house and a plot of land, but their money wages, at 25 centavos or 2 reales a day, were half those of casual labourers. Competition was driving up wages in 1900, amidst complaints that the population was too small and could too easily obtain land. One estate near Villahermosa was offering 75 centavos a day to casual workers by the turn of the century (Kaerger 1901: II, 508–9). Even so, oral evidence reveals that some debt peons were unhappy when they were freed in 1914, because they lost the patron who had looked after them (Arias *et al.* 1987: 273, 332).

Conclusion

The eighteenth-century Quaker dream of free labour was not entirely realised by 1914, in large part because estates continued to produce cocoa. Even though some estates employed free labour, and some smallholders had recourse to coercion, there can be little doubt that ending all support for estates would have considerably speeded up the freeing of labour around the globe. It remains all the more puzzling that abolitionists did not promote land reform earlier and more vigorously, and more research is needed to determine what stood in the way.

The hoary old myth that coerced labour was cheap still survives, making the assessment of the economic and social consequences of labour coercion more difficult. In reality, the low productivity of such labourers almost inevitably outweighed their low remuneration, so that they did not even hasten the primary accumulation of capital. In addition, coerced labour left a legacy of bitter and twisted social relations, of which Colombia's upper Cauca valley was a good example in the cocoa world. While a simple corre-lation between slave labour and subsequent economic woes is misleading, the relationship needs to be explored further.

One other urgent item on the research agenda concerns labour recruitment by smallholders. This chapter has largely focused on estate labour, because of paucity of data relating to smallholdings, and yet it is important not to reinforce another hoary old myth, that smallholders only employed family labour. No major smallholder cocoa boom has ever occurred without the employment of masses of outsiders, and an understanding of how this was achieved should be an integral part of the cocoa story. Sharecropping contracts and their evolution need to be particularly carefully examined, as these may have been one of the key reasons for the efficiency of small farmers.

CONCLUSION
Lessons from the past

Cocoa was the fifth most valuable food commodity exported by developing countries in 1991, despite prices being at a historical low, and yet there were no 'tiger economies' among cocoa producers (Dand 1993: ix). A fundamental premise of this book has been that exporting primary agricultural commodities is not necessarily an economic dead end. Indeed, it may be the only possible route to development for certain countries or regions (Clarence-Smith and Ruf 1996). Some lessons from the liberal era may thus be of use to today's 'cocoa actors', even though the past is another country.

The relatively steady growth of world demand for chocolate has been an great advantage, but optimistic allegations that consumers are 'hooked', and will continue to crave for chocolate whatever happens, are not supported historically. The need to keep chocolate competitive with similar products is a powerful argument against forcing up the price of cocoa beans, whether through public and private cartels, or through excessive taxation and inappropriate regulation. It is an equally powerful argument against allowing the world chocolate industry to drift any further towards oligopoly.

Competition is equally vital at the level of much maligned intermediaries, from dealers and brokers to humble peddlers. Liberal immigration policies and checks on social discrimination are vital preconditions for the effective working of a commodity chain, as entrepreneurial minorities may be the greatest single neglected resource for economic development. As a rule of thumb, the more competition there is between highly skilled traders, the higher is the percentage of the world price that accrues to direct producers. The unhappy marketing-board page in the history of commercialisation needs to be turned, once and for all. Enforcing accurate labelling is about the only task that the state can perform better than the private sector.

Supplying credit to smallholders should also be left to entrepreneurial communities. They have an intimate knowledge of the needs and desires of their customers, and work more cheaply than banks. Given the low capital requirements of cocoa cultivation, the emphasis should in any case be shifted towards mechanisms for saving profits garnered from the 'golden bean'.

As estates suffer from diseconomies of scale and inappropriate 'modes of cultivation', it is all the more remarkable that they should once again have been touted as a 'solution' to the woes of the sector in the 1970s and 1980s. Estates should never be favoured in any way. They can be left to compete on a level playing field, on which, nine times out of ten, they will not survive for long. This might seem a utopian recommendation, given the powerful pressures brought to bear on weak and often corrupt governments, but it could usefully be incorporated into conditions required by lending agencies.

The nature of cocoa production not only argues strongly against the use of gang labour on estates, but possibly against the use of wage labour by any producer. Conversely, sharecropping should never be labelled as 'backward' or 'primitive'. It needs to be recognised as a flexible, efficient and highly motivating labour contract, well adapted to the seasonal nature of cocoa production, requiring minimal amounts of supervision, and allowing for easy adaptation to swings in cocoa prices.

Last but not least, cocoa poses a serious threat to shrinking tropical forests. Cocoa cultivation in the liberal era engendered massive deforestation on small islands such as Grenada and São Tomé, but now a general crisis looms, as millions of trees are cleared with chainsaws to satisfy a much larger and wealthier body of 'chocoholics'. When all the forests of the tropical world suited to cocoa cultivation have been chopped down, or effectively protected, consumers will have to pay substantially more for their chocolate. This makes it necessary to intensify research into agroforestry techniques and the biological control of pests and diseases, taking full account of smallholder experiences in interacting with their environment. The record of the past is important here. Sustainable techniques have long been used, contrasting with the short-term consumption of forest rent, at times without even the provision of permanent shade. Mesoamerica, the cradle of cocoa cultivation all those centuries ago, may hold particularly important lessons for the producers of today (Young 1994: 163–73).

Many of these points can be applied more widely than to cocoa. Other tropical trees generate pioneer fronts which contribute to the rapid destruction of the world's remaining forests, notably coffee and rubber, and estates are probably not the most efficient means of growing any of them. The long lead time between planting and harvesting magnifies the impact on prices for all tree crops, and causes the effects of sharp price movements to linger on for decades. Problems of marketing, processing and consumption vary more, according to the physical properties of commodities and the uses to which they are put, but there are many common points. The history of cocoa and chocolate in the liberal era can thus hopefully be a source of inspiration for all those striving to achieve economic development in the tropical world.

APPENDIX 1

Cocoa prices

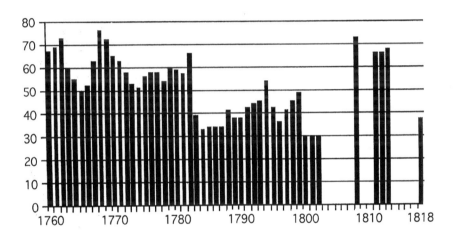

Figure A1.1 Caracas cocoa, annual average wholesale price on the
Amsterdam exchange, 1760–1818, in hundredths of guilders per
pond, deflated by author's weighted wholesale price index
(1721–45 = 100)

Source: Posthumus 1946: I, ci, 196–7

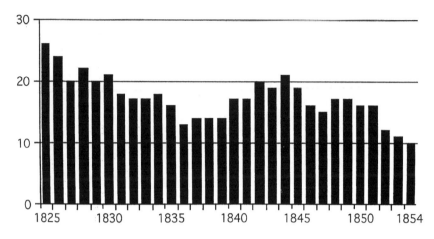

Figure A1.2 Caracas cocoa, price in Philadelphia, 1825–54, in cents per pound. Deflated by the Warren and Pearson price index (1910–14 = 100)

Sources: (Commodity Research Bureau 1939: 335; Cook and Waller 1998: 189–90)

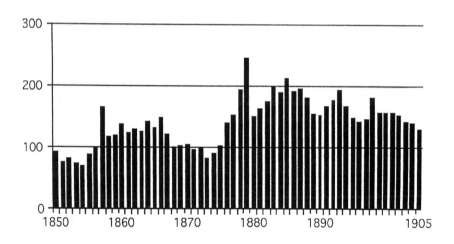

Figure A1.3 Cocoa of no specified origin, average import price in Hamburg, 1850–1905, in pfennigs per kilo. Deflated by the German wholesale price index (1913 = 100)

Sources: (*Gordian*: III, 1108; XII, 959; Mitchell 1992: 840–2)

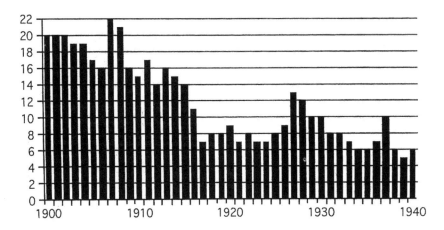

Figure A1.4 Cocoa, possibly Accra, average import price in the United Kingdom, 1900–40, in pence per pound, deflated by United Kingdom general wholesale price index (1947–9 = 100)

Source: FAO 1955: 93

APPENDIX 2

Cocoa exports

Figure A2.1 is a graph of world cocoa exports from 1765 to 1913. Figures A2.2–A2.6 provide details by country. All exports are in tonnes. Estimates are italicised. Names and political allegiances of territories are based on 1914 status. Sources are indicated below.

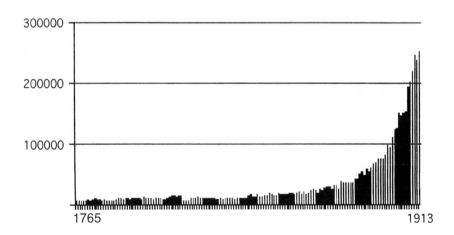

Figure A2.1 World exports of cocoa in tonnes, 1765–1914

EXPORTS-TONNES	1765	1766	1767	1768	1769	1770	1771	1772	1773	1774	1775	1776	1777	1778	1779
Nicaragua	250	250	250	250	250	250	250	250	250	250	250	250	363	250	250
Costa Rica		6					11	28	20						
Dominican Republic	2	2	2	2	2	2	2	2	2	2	2	2	2	2	2
St. Domingue [Haïti]	75	75	73	75	75	75	75	75	75	77	276	250	250	100	100
Guadeloupe	21	17	23	23	39	26	30	33	22	47	42	22	29	16	
Martinique	593	300	290	334	574	597	417	664	655	598	456	480	881		
Jamaica	8	8	8	10	15	11	42	42	42	42	42				
Dominica	9						22	22	22	22	22	40	40	40	40
Saint Lucia					21	20	13	25							
Saint Vincent	50	50	50	50	112	48	47	70	106	91	61				
Grenada	81	110	98	135	106	139	256	174	156	143	135	121	109	108	101
Trinidad and Tobago	2	2	2	2	2	2	4	4	4	4	4	4	20	20	22
Curaçao	300	300	300	300	335	318	300	300	300	300	300	300	300	300	150
St Eustatius	101	39	11	158	20	40	44		15				215	46	32
West Dutch Guiana	58	346	266	172	101	38	115	51	37	89	117	41	42	96	71
Surinam	80	123	125	216	163	103	256	192	194	288	389	275	315	389	390
French Guiana		80	45	50	60	70	45	50	70	50	60	70	61	80	70
Venezuela	2750	1900	3096	3100	3198	3061	2719	4133	4000	3431	3773	2510	2815	2500	2500
N. Reino [Colombia]	200	200	200	200	200	200	200	200	200	200	200	300	300	481	300
Ecuador	1118	1200	1247	1500	1544	2500	1750	1529	2815	1863	1671	1255	2012	1435	1729
Brazil	464	469	429	602	14	753	566	799	863	60	1071	861	1014	885	854
WORLD	6162	5477	6515	7179	6831	8253	7164	8643	9848	7557	8971	6781	8768	6748	6611

Figure A2.2 World exports of cocoa in tonnes, 1765–94

EXPORTS-TONNES	1795	1796	1797	1798	1799	1800	1801	1802	1803	1804	1805	1806	1807	1808	1809
Mexico								33	341	1257		224	213	234	620
Nicaragua	250	250	200	200	200	200	200	200	200	200	200	200	200	200	200
Costa Rica	41	6				3	10	1		1					
St. Domingue/Haïti	334	250	250	250	250	250	317	100	100	99	100	100	100	100	200
Guadeloupe									8	10	10	16	12	53	38
Martinique	100	100	100	100	100	100	100	100	100	100	100	100	100	100	100
Jamaica															
Dominica															
Saint Lucia															
Saint Vincent															
Grenada	150	150	150	150	150	150	150	150	150	150	150	150	150	150	150
Trinidad and Tobago	418	400	44	75	117	129	147	63	164	228	239	267	161	303	326
Surinam	173	50	50	50	50	50	50	50	50	64	137	93	69	60	55
French Guiana	80	75	240	65	55	560	80	80	60	65	65	60	130	120	75
Venezuela	5500	4000	6000	5500	5500	4500	4500	2000	2000	2000	6000	5983	6000	6000	5500
Colombia	400	800	100	500	300	300	200	1000	500	500	400	500	500	800	700
Ecuador	2787	2965	2441	1023	2462	2449	3596	3000	2332	3894	2394	4512	3700	3942	3700
Brazil	1078	713	1092	1393	1256	2331	1005	2042	2707	1588	1671	3170	2292	246	3047
WORLD	11311	9759	10667	9306	10440	11022	10355	8819	8712	10156	11466	15375	13627	12308	14711

Figure A2.3 World exports of cocoa in tonnes, 1795–1824

1780	1781	1782	1783	1784	1785	1786	1787	1788	1789	1790	1791	1792	1793	1794
250	250	250	250	250	250	250	250	250	250	250	250	250	250	250
	14		8						9	6			27	14
2	2	2	2	2	2	2	2	2	2	2	2	2	2	2
100	100	250	250	250	250	250	250	73	294	80	73	150	150	273
		65	16	25	51	132	38	24	22	27	31	21		
	66	763	790	643	555	692	427	483	300	337	97			
								4						
40	40	40	40	40	40	40	61	40	40	40	40	40	40	40
		150	150	150	150	150	192	150	139	157				
								7						
201	100	100	100	100	100	100	123	100	100	100	100	100	100	200
20	2	9	14	20	21	31	31	70	95	110	118	142	149	418
150	150	150	150	150	150	103	103	103	103	103	103	103	100	100
205			1	38	54	82	94	50	20					
100	100	100	150	50	50	50	50	50	50	50	50			
310	93	420	521	306	335	329	401	163	329	259	286	60	15	175
50	50	50	50	60	100	50	50	50	55	50	45	70	55	65
2500	2500	2500	4000	4000	4000	4000	4500	4500	5500	5000	5000	5500	5000	6000
300	300	300	300	200	249	336	525	238	459	212	543	410	413	895
1301	1682	2129	2972	2958	1914	2304	1971	1661	2317	1899	2169	2564	2487	2786
890	601	750	750	1481	512	1236	1137	589	855	739	676	600	573	889
6419	6050	8028	10513	10676	8727	10159	10204	8649	10966	9435	9583	10012	9361	12107

1810	1811	1812	1813	1814	1815	1816	1817	1818	1819	1820	1821	1822	1823	1824
162	134						7		4		30		24	
200	200	200	200	200	200	200	200	200						
150	150	150	150	150	150	150	150	160	139	213	130	227	163	226
1		2			9	1	2	22	33	21	32	13	5	21
100	100	100	100	100	150	150	150	241	221	140	274	168	121	113
					6	6	6	6						
						2	2	2	2	2				
							30	30	30	30	30	30	30	30
				2	2	2	2	2	2	5	6	7	4	11
150	150	150	150	150	150	150	150	150	150	150	150	150	150	150
329	291	624	467	525	483	479	608	559	683	791	551	808	1100	1207
44	56	60	50	52	50	45	57	49	17	4	5	30	34	36
75	75	75	58	82	101	50	50	50	50	50	50	50	50	50
7353	2500	2500	2500	2500	2500	2500	3000	3000	3000	3000	2500	2500	3000	2500
800	100	300	300	300	300	300	1000	300	300	100	100	100	100	400
2766	860	800	781	3700	3700	3700	4723	3700	3700	4845	4262	5256	5345	3989
1561	974	1437	1285	2610	2134	1878	1850	1493	1500	1290	1376	2001	714	1251
13691	5590	6398	6041	10371	9965	9643	11987	9964	9837	10641	9496	11340	10840	9984

EXPORTS-TONNES	1825	1826	1827	1828	1829	1830	1831	1832	1833	1834	1835	1836	1837	1838	1839
Mexico	5	8													
Guatemala															
Nicaragua															
Costa Rica															
Cuba															15
Dominican Republic	2	4													
Haiti	178	247	344	237	398	224	152	171	177	181	195	245	130	222	234
Guadeloupe	10	5	3	5	8	3	6	7	2	9	5	9	11	8	12
Martinique	171	170	180	188	170	142	122	115	142	118	98	134	110	109	146
Jamaica							3	2	1	1		1		8	
Dominica									3	4	3		1	1	3
Saint Lucia		45	36	34	43	70	44	24	41	27	22	22	22	18	25
Saint Vincent	9	12	6	8	6		3			2		1	1	1	
Grenada	100	100	100	100	100	100	167	89	142	155	123	139	159	176	149
Trinidad and Tobago	1252	1339	1677	1171	1250	747	857	604	1402	1526	1245	1446	1137	1167	1322
British Guiana										1					
Surinam	58	8	23	65	47	9	23	12	8	4	16	64	42	79	27
French Guiana	30	30	30	30	30	30	52	47	40	33	31	23	25	28	36
Venezuela	2500	2000	2000	2000	2463	3336	2280	3319	2522	2447	1952	2411	3119	2673	2989
Colombia	78	76	224	161	150	150	150	150	150	259	118	100	354	116	143
Ecuador	3318	3500	3500	3500	3500	4995	4696	4203	3081	5061	6350	5022	3920	3311	5594
Brazil	1545	1614	1996	667	1221	654	858	1599	796	1201	839	1342	1216	2780	2961
São Tomé & Príncipe						1	1	1	1	1		1	5	5	10
Angola															
Réunion							6			6	13	4	8	3	1
Dutch East Indies	3	2	4		3				15	16	19	41	62	94	59
Philippines															
WORLD	9259	9160	10123	8166	9389	10461	9417	10349	8532	11057	11018	11014	10317	10796	13726

Figure A2.4 World exports of cocoa in tonnes, 1825–54

EXPORTS-TONNES	1855	1856	1857	1858	1859	1860	1861	1862	1863	1864	1865	1866	1867	1868	1869
Mexico															
Guatemala															
Nicaragua												10		2	
Costa Rica															
Cuba	419	448	491	276	300	766	487	619	633	1046	1037	1134	805	100	100
Dominican Republic														19	21
Haiti	500	500	500	728	684	774	639	854	1145	685	800	800	800	800	800
Guadeloupe	19	15	53	53	68	59	73	72	68	69	79	65	91	106	79
Martinique	211	212	244	249	201	223	268	284	258	221	258	301	362	354	351
Jamaica															
Dominica	26	13	29	57	24	44	51	82	46	62	67	70	86	78	102
Saint Lucia	63	95	114	78	90	96	108	87	114	101	131	87	130	117	123
Saint Vincent															
Grenada	406	438	469	500	355	465	604	584	531	480	587	641	773	755	900
Trinidad and Tobago	2462	2225	2127	2401	2158	2215	3843	1973	3182	2272	2999	2556	3466	3519	2844
British Guiana						79								41	47
Surinam	119	154	180	185	230	272	283	356	308	380	331	456	505	652	425
French Guiana										10		26	27	6	
Venezuela	3742	4572	3500	2000	2000	3300	2000	2000	2000	3036	1812	3000	4600	2000	1617
Colombia	18	78	78	71							5	57	57	57	6
Ecuador	6941	6152	6792	9117	6265	7710	8592	7372	7545	5267	6563	10354	9074	9768	7980
Brazil	2173	2413	3532	3620	4133	3181	4005	2985	3873	3445	3195	2604	2888	3884	2802
Spanish Guinea															
São Tomé & Príncipe	60	100	130	180	176	176	396	237	193	211	290	258	316	263	261
Angola			28			10									
Ceylon															
Dutch East Indies	59	105	59	163	111	105	201	153	169	124	92	82	100	86	86
WORLD	17218	17520	18326	19678	16795	19475	21550	17658	20065	17409	18256	22491	24082	22605	18544

Figure A2.5 World exports of cocoa in tonnes, 1855–84

1840	1841	1842	1843	1844	1845	1846	1847	1848	1849	1850	1851	1852	1853	1854
								1					1	
			21											
	40	1				44	105	40	50	50	81	98	290	263
								1	1					
217	314	204	347	251	409	308	573	443	325					
16	13	22	18	13	20	15	11	12	8	14	11	11	5	16
128	132	141	134	154	161	181	134	153	150	150	149	169	186	194
5	8	39	35		7	8	17	9	30	6	3			
4	2	9	3	5	11	6	13	17	13	13	16	32	41	24
37	35	25	22	8	13	5	7	7	3	41	56	61	85	68
4	1	1	1	4	1	2	2	2	2	2	3	4		
109	133	138	131	247	212	243	135	234	170	222	209	182	207	200
1469	1416	1425	1272	1499	1147	1824	1696	1341	2145	1731	2272	1926	2197	1706
1		2	5								4			
91	43	58	62	36	52	9	41	76	59	83	74	117	112	116
29	29	18	32	28	23	33	23	36	20	20	20	20	20	20
4034	3522	4432	4102	4170	3483	4251	3467	4000	3447	3379	3754	5025	3531	4572
150	302	10	302	221	205	200	246	648	614	500	400	300	200	100
6563	5249	3086	7113	3944	4475	5153	5554	9663	6548	5090	4401	6424	6092	5056
2966	2046	2678	2226	2787	1950	2935	3022	2365	3697	4146	3859	4280	3378	4646
10	15	15	20	20	30	30	30	30	30	30	51	40	40	28
								1						
	2	7		1	2									
89	51	59	36	71	36	64	62	27	46	49	49	50	37	76
2														
15924	13353	12368	15858	13485	12237	15311	15141	19104	17357	15527	15413	18736	16421	17085

1870	1871	1872	1873	1874	1875	1876	1877	1878	1879	1880	1881	1882	1883	1884
									2				3	1	7
														4	1
3	40													4	10
															4
100	100	100	100	100	100	100	250	450	900	450	400	800	1053	895
17	17	39	50	60	70	80	90	100	110	126	176	184	267	321
800	800	800	800	800	800	800	800	800	800	1336	1500	1500	1500	1500
93	55	103	77	85	100	124	125	234	156	210	248	167	194	193
303	306	343	288	318	324	320	458	466	587	500	578	472	530	481
					20									
61	92	93	85	86	88	152	167	156	187	195	344	173	215	177
117	89	112	127	116	126	181	110	232	205	199	238	137	139	226
1097	2739	2557	3140	3386	3653	1753	1264	1888	1602	2142	2662	2234	2355	2806
3113	2952	3184	3491	4262	2845	4299	4412	4496	5280	4989	4903	4977	5284	5855
128	137	139	139	99	216	164	254	120	294	241	329	280	260	240
534	547	849	1649	1103	1153	1348	1399	556	1113	858	1883	1156	1876	1450
34	21	20	6		4		6	24	13	16	26	22	14	21
1771	2500	3308	2749	3164	4329	4875	5311	4618	3310	3200	3101	5260	6498	3709
57	12	12	12	1	12	35	35	35	119	119	119	180	240	300
10725	7931	8612	10914	11385	4761	10166	9444	4864	14839	15372	10303	9743	7206	8413
4578	4471	5547	4327	4612	5340	5165	5827	4469	6763	4972	6805	7501	6763	6957
									45	50	50	50	92	50
361	434	500	491	500	400	489	655	486	774	702	750	900	850	1100
								1	2	6	14	44	172	469
127	137	198	224	81	203	237	212	305	124	147	75	186	100	93
24019	23380	26516	28669	30158	24544	30288	30819	24300	37225	35830	34504	35969	35617	35278

EXPORTS-TONNES	1885	1886	1887	1888	1889	1890	1891	1892	1893	1894	1895	1896	1897	1898	1899
Mexico	30	4	1	1		8			1	2	84	3	3	3	4
British Honduras															
Guatemala															
El Salvador									27						
Nicaragua															
Costa Rica	7	3	5	8	13	11	1	8	3	2	10	6	5	5	12
Panama															
Cuba	705	700	750	700	1070	1350	1116	1252	1001	1428	1420	1793	70	43	656
Dominican Republic	369	398	494	721	670	617	1029	1145	1944	1975	1660	2250	3655	3993	2895
Haiti	1545	1928	1779	1922	400	2399	1640	2007	1509	1698	1141	1120	1370	2018	2038
Guadeloupe	235	235	164	314	238	202	282	305	347	300	346	396	411	533	416
Martinique	426	582	440	672	585	481	490	158	408	398	354	401	99	635	511
Jamaica	154	196	175	241	267	326	279	432	524	246	466	515	408	801	1050
Dominica	213	292	227	264	335	210	372	223	329	346	340	472	296	557	434
Saint Lucia	205	248	277	359	368	420	448	397	471	491	369	568	478	471	441
Saint Vincent										87	86	96	132	93	2
Grenada	2496	2641	3140	3385	2814	3876	3391	3829	4759	3631	4208	4510	4256	4003	3945
Trinidad and Tobago	6228	8125	5410	9685	6956	9776	7343	11359	8667	9801	13363	10651	10814	11041	13257
British Guiana										40	46	21	47	25	62
Surinam	1344	1575	1720	1542	2043	2181	2211	1689	3498	3249	4456	3303	3585	2830	3860
French Guiana										11	14	7		11	
Venezuela	6691	5110	6975	7232	7197	6984	7334	6500	5916	7352	7112	8930	8867	7661	8301
Colombia	250	250	275	792	500	270	450	530	250	250	250	178	248	553	500
Ecuador	11832	12733	16310	13287	11811	18052	10446	16101	19955	19027	17542	17343	16478	20847	26608
Peru									36	41	25	24	119	604	53
Brazil	6214	4237	7840	10107	9613	6815	11552	7611	11350	10149	10846	11264	11388	11562	14473
Sierra Leone															
Liberia															
Ivory Coast															
Gold Coast [Ghana]									?	9	13	39	71	100	324
Togo															
Dahomey															
Nigeria				2	1	6	7	7	8	18	21	13	46	35	72
Cameroon						10	20	45	78	83	132	133	169	208	222
Spanish Guinea	50	50	50	9	52	193	260	320	380	500	500	1000	1561	941	1200
São Tomé & Príncipe	1200	1400	2250	2000	2292	3208	3599	5037	3448	6157	7023	6771	7700	9203	12462
Gabon/French Congo												5	8	16	23
Belgian Congo															
Angola															
Madagascar															
Comoros															
Réunion										4					
German East Africa															
Ceylon [Sri Lanka]	379	663	887	621	958	810	1017	974	1513	1158	1398	1837	2222	2434	2379
Dutch East Indies	116	168	60	116	184	270	408	381	546	873	960	885	893	977	1089
Portuguese Timor															
German New Guinea															
New Caledonia															
New Hebrides															
Fiji															
Western Samoa															
WORLD	40689	41539	49229	53980	48367	58475	53695	60310	66970	69326	74185	74534	75399	82291	97289

Figure A2.6 World exports of cocoa in tonnes, 1885–1914

1900	1901	1902	1903	1904	1905	1906	1907	1908	1909	1910	1911	1912	1913	1914
	3	2	2	2	2	1	1	3	1	1	1			
				2		19							22	9
			˙ 23								47	36	65	62
14	22	60	81	119	149	176	278	340	235	184	343	309	385	330
			5	10	20	30	40	43	26	12	30	45	44	36
1671	1750	1875	2540	2697	1768	3272	1714	827	1940	1412	1252	1599	767	2229
5963	6850	7975	7325	13558	13092	14539	9954	18984	14800	16606	19828	20833	19471	20745
2112	1963	1990	2175	2531	2162	1820	2226	2709	2122	1851	1485	3128	1900	3300
294	351	588	599	625	638	675	782	744	594	779	1060	919	909	1125
732	488	435	334	319	470	473	503	530	593	571	603	502	525	454
1002	1350	1525	1697	1650	1358	2506	2219	2694	3214	1743	2783	3400	2355	3673
518	450	478	594	493	589	573	584	488	551	573	576	603	483	451
659	765	765	785	800	859	703	780	615	553	743	940	900	741	723
7					62					106	128	100	95	102
4476	4768	5192	4828	6010	5797	4932	4612	5108	5441	5846	5948	5500	5349	5216
13782	13678	17049	16399	18486	21962	12506	22558	22289	23394	26245	22585	18836	21826	28780
49	34										10	10	25	22
2927	3163	2355	2225	854	1682	1481	1625	1699	1897	2043	1594	966	1528	1893
7			9	17				23	18					
5082	8768	8418	8548	14677	11661	13777	11956	15750	16282	16117	18039	14508	12772	16887
500	500	500	500	500	654	528	847	621	730	297	340	116	218	200
18922	23603	24664	22964	28216	21724	23140	19743	31836	31769	36733	38803	38225	41869	47210
99	110	174	174	174	195	103	200	348	361	200	200	200	200	
16916	18324	22371	21738	23160	21090	25135	24528	32956	33818	29158	34994	30492	30598	40767
														4
					6						6		10	
				1	2	2	2	3	5	8	15	21	47	36
545	996	2435	2581	5773	5620	9739	10451	12946	20533	22989	40356	39260	51309	53735
			1	11	13	29	52	83	134	137	231	283	335	450
								4	4	2			7	7
205	209	312	286	539	478	735	948	1388	2367	2978	4471	3643	3679	5018
260	528	688	913	1142	1413	1252	1797	2447	3322	3431	3532	4552	5265	3200
734	1224	1499	1480	2057	1915	1788	2627	2814	2799	2114	2807	3983	5313	4835
13935	16983	17619	22051	20496	25669	24620	24194	28560	27846	37810	35512	36091	35311	32064
14	47	58	50	91	50	90	75	98	103	92	108	73	158	140
9	4	16	89	231	195	402	549	612	769	902	681	845	914	482
		1	1	1	1	3	11	10	12	21	27	32	71	90
4	8	25	15	33	21	25	44	22	45	54	46	60	39	46
				13				5	22	26				
				2				1	3	4	2			
											8	11		
1890	2697	2673	3075	3255	3225	2510	4700	2836	3570	4069	3064	3720	3507	2499
1342	1267	890	1470	1018	1084	1850	1838	2359	2408	2527	2399	2099	2292	1604
									6		11	7	29	
									7	40	65	74	140	150
			2	1										
											2		5	40
													3	3
2	6	9	5	20	28	92	117	204	387	505	642	734	890	1050
94672	110909	122641	125553	149577	145612	149618	152459	192830	202674	219114	245564	236715	251471	279867

APPENDIX 2

Sources

Several territories

EUIEA; *Gordian*; *Larousse*; *PP*; *SAC*; *SYB*; *TGCF*; Chevalier 1906; Food and Agriculture Organisation 1955; Hall 1914; Hall 1932; Maclaren 1924; Rouma 1948–9; Schneider 1981; Wright 1907.

Mexico

Colegio de México 1960; Herrera Canales 1980; Lerda de Tejada 1853; Peña 1951: III, 926.

Central America

Brigham 1887: 312; Fernández Molina 1992: 425–39; Lanuza *et al.* 1983: 52, 87–8; Newson 1987: 264; Preuss 1987: 99; Quesada Camacho 1989: 88, 102; Salvatierra 1939: II, 207–8; Squier 1970a: 106. Also, Fernández Molina, e-mail 10 February 1999.

Cuba

AEE; *EGCEE*; Alzola 1895: 81, 83, 165; Fisher 1858: 123; Mangin 1860: 38; Marrero 1972–89: XI, 135; Pezuela 1863–6: I, 60.

Dominican Republic

Ciferri 1930: 127; Marte 1984: 72, 84, 267; Oliva Melgar 1987: 299; Olivares 1988: 84.

Haïti

Arcy 1930: 16; Ardouin 1853–60: X, 53–4; XI, 238; Benoit 1954: 36; Franklin 1828: 322, 325; Geggus 1982: 402; Léon 1963: 203–4, 206; Lepkowski 1968: I, 83; Mackenzie 1971: II, 298–302; Marte 1984: 77, 85; Moral 1959: 114; Rouzier 1892–3: I, 204; II, 130–41; Saint John 1971: 372–6; Street 1960: 181; Tarrade 1972: I, 34.

French Caribbean

Arcy 1930: 16; Boyer-Peyreleau 1823: II, app. 8; Cardoso 1984: 76, 162; Légier 1905: 183–6; Mam-Lam-Fouck 1986: 228; Schnakenbourg 1977: 116, 120; Tarrade 1972: II, 748–9. Also, personal communication, C. Schnakenbourg.

British Caribbean

Ashcraft 1973: 58; Breen 1970: 319; Brizan 1984: 40–1, 102; Carrington 1988: 16–17, 31, 43, 59, 176, 179; Edwards 1801: I, 287, 430, 447; Kramer 1991: 54–5; Milstead 1940: 200; Nardin 1969: 236; Newson 1976: 135, 213–16; Ragatz 1977: 39–40, 123, 132, 318, 348, 350; Sevilla Soler 1988: 110–11, 154; Shephard 1971: app.; Trouillot 1988: 59, 61. Also, personal communications, C. Schnakenbourg and A. van Stipriaan.

Dutch Caribbean

Erneholm 1948: table 21; Klooster 1998: 187–8, 226–7; Panday 1959: 20; Postma 1994: 20–1; Stipriaan 1993: app. 1.

Venezuela (excluding Maracaibo till independence, and excluding Trinidad before 1797)

Anon 1827: 162; Arcila Farías 1950: 310–12; Arcila Farías 1973: I, 157; Brito Figueroa 1966: I, 216, 228; Cuenca Esteban 1981: 416–17; Depons 1930: 323; Dias 1971: 361–75; Erneholm 1948: table 15; Hall 1824: 26; Harwich Vallenilla 1996: 25, 31; Humboldt 1811: II, 436; 1941: III, 174–5; Humphreys 1940: 275–7; Izard 1972: 106, 135, 139; Lerda de Tejada 1853: tables 15–35; Lucena Salmoral 1990: 158; McKinley 1985: 36; Martínez 1988, I, 82–3, 152, 188, 212, 214; II, 184; Nuñez 1972: 550; Oliva Melgar 1987: 299, 314–5; Piñero 1993: 26; Polanco Martínez 1960: II, 35; Tandrón 1976: 127, 161.

Colombia (including exports through Maracaibo till independence)

AEC 1875: 169; Arcila Farias 1950: 79, 310–11; Camacho Roldán 1895: 657; Colombia 1975: 186; Dias 1971: 361–75; Erneholm 1948: 63; Gosselman 1962: 123; Lerda de Tejada 1853: tables 15–35; McFarlane 1993: 371; Ocampo 1984: 103; Pohl 1963: 277; Vergara y Velasco 1901: 745, 822–3. Also, German consular reports, provided by T. Fischer.

Ecuador (including Callao exports till independence)

Anna 1979: 115; Arcila Farias 1950: 310–11; Arosemena, 1991: I, 182, 224; Baleato 1887: 84; Chiriboga 1980: 10, 41, 133–4; Contreras 1990: 143–6; Erneholm 1948: table 13; Humboldt 1811: II, 436; Humphreys 1940: 231–5; Laviana Cuetos, 1987: 186; Lerda de Tejada 1853: tables 30–5; Mollien 1824: 456; Parrón Salas 1995: 353. Also, personal communication, M. T. Hamerly.

Peru (excluding re-exports through Callao till independence)

Bonilla 1975–6: I, 327; II, 215, 304; Enock 1925: 235.

Brazil

AHTT 1820, Alden 1976: 127, 133–4; Arruda 1980: table 62; Bondar 1938: 27; Garcez and Freitas 1975: 35, 66; Instituto Brasileiro de Geografia e Estatística 1987: 310; Le Cointe 1922: II, 141; Mahony 1996: 203; Soares 1977: 119; Zehntner 1914: 102–6.

Liberia

Great Britain 1919c: 46.

Ivory Coast

Great Britain 1919b: 18; Lopo 1963: 33.

Togo

Sebald 1988: 394.

Dahomey

Great Britain 1919a: 33.

Nigeria

Berry 1975: app. 3; Ciferri 1930: 120.

Cameroun

ANC, FA, 1/774, 'Entwicklung und Aussichten der Europäischen Pflanzungen'.

Spanish Guinea

Nosti 1948: 46; Sorela 1884; Sundiata 1972: 235; Sundiata 1990: 24. Also, AGA, A-G, C682, E1, 'Protesto', 25 January 1901, and C144, E11, 'Apuntes', 20 June 1903, and C104, E3, 'Total del cacao exportado'; LCL, 380, HOL-I, 9/1, A. R. Green 10 April 1913.

São Tomé and Príncipe

AGC 1929: 172–3; Almada 1884: 96–7; Almeida 1878: 221; Banco Nacional Ultramarino 1890: 105; César 1969: 88–9; Corvo 1883–7: I, 124; Freitas 1867: 86–7; Moreira Júnior 1905: I, 122; II, 121–2; Negreiros 1906: 96; Nogueira 1893: 51; Ribeiro 1877: 454–5, 478; Rodrigues 1974: 70–1; Silva 1958: 103; 1969: 146; Tams 1850: II, 208. Also, AHU, STP, P507, Report, Governor of Príncipe 1871, and P511, Labour Inspector, 31 December 1877; AHSTP, 1-a-C, 3. fl. 165.

French Equatorial Africa

Coquery-Vidrovitch 1972: 471–2.

Belgian Congo

Wildeman 1902: 115.

Angola

Lopo 1963: 36–7, 41; Mesquita 1918: 43; Moreira Júnior 1905: I, 195.

Réunion

Lami 1885: II, 87.

German East Africa

Great Britain 1916: 236; 1920b: 63–4. Also, BAAP, RKA, 8003, 'Kakao und die Deutschen Kolonien'.

Uganda

Great Britain 1920a: 232.

Dutch East Indies

KV. Also, ANRI, 31, 167, 'Aantekeningen betreffende de kakao', 23 April 1859.

Portuguese Timor

Anon. 1910: 15; Great Britain 1920c: 21.

Philippines

Mas 1843: II, Estadística Comercial, 11.

German New Guinea

Sack and Clark 1979: 316, 331, 348.

Fiji

Great Britain 1920d: 93.

APPENDIX 3
Cocoa output in selected countries and decades

Figure A3.1 gives details for cocoa output in selected countries and decades. All figures are annual averages, in tonnes, and include exports where relevant. These patchy figures, often based on extremely uncertain data, merely suggest an order of magnitude for countries which consumed all their crop, or a substantial part of it. No figures could be found for other Central American republics or Bolivia. Sources are indicated below.

Sources

Mexico

AEM; *DP*: I, 428; Enock 1909: 289; Gil y Saenz 1979: 252; Hall 1914: 472; Instituto de Economia e Finanças da Bahia 1960: 179; Kaerger 1901: II, 509; Pelletier 1861: 40; Peña 1951: III, 926; Ruiz Abreu 1989: 61–2.

Central America

Hall 1914: 474; Lanuza *et al.* 1983: 85; Quesada Camacho 1989: 87–8; Rubio Sánchez 1958: 90–1, 93–6; Salvatierra 1939: II, 207–8; Touzard 1993: 40.

Cuba

EUIEA: XVI, 817; *Larousse*: V, 616; Marrero 1972–89: X, 94; XI, 134–5; XII, 212, 214.

Haïti

Rouzier 1892–3: II, 129.

	A	B	C	D	E	F	G	H	I	J	K	L	M	N	O	P
1	OUTPUT-TONNES	1770s	1780s	1790s	1800s	1810s	1820s	1830s	1840s	1850s	1860s	1870s	1880s	1890s	1900s	1910s
2	Mexico			900						1400				1200	3000	3000
3	Guatemala	200	200	200									400	150	150	250
4	Nicaragua	400									400					
5	Costa Rica	200	200	150						100						
6	Cuba						250	200	350		2000				4500	
7	Haiti												2500			
8	Venezuela			7000				4000	5000					11000		
9	Colombia			1500								1000		3000		3600
10	Ecuador															
11	Peru														2500	
12	Philippines										200				350	600

Figure A3.1 Cocoa output in selected countries and decades

Venezuela

Izard 1970: 73–9; Humboldt 1941: III, 176 (adjusted); Middleton 1871: 457; *PP* 1847: vol. 64.

Colombia

AEC 1875: 144; Erneholm 1948: 126; Leal 1984; 496; Schenck 1953: 41. Also German consular reports, kindly supplied by T. Fischer.

Peru

Bonilla 1975–6: II, 228.

Philippines

Cavada 1876: I, table 22; II, table 21; Hall 1932: 493; Miller 1920: 469; United States 1905: IV, 325.

APPENDIX 4

Weights, measures and currency

Standard pre-metric units of weight, in kilogrammes

From McCusker (1974), but Lisbon *arroba* and *quintal* based on *libra* of 0.45905 kilos.

	kilogrammes
1 pound, England	0.4536
1 *pond*, Amsterdam	0.4941
1 *pfund*, Hamburg	0.4844
1 *livre*, Paris	0.4895
1 *libra*, Castile	0.4601
1 *arrátel* or *libra*, Lisbon	0.4591
1 quarter, England = 28 pounds	12.7008
1 *arroba*, Castile = 25 *libras*	11.5023
1 *arroba*, Lisbon = 32 *libras*	14.6896
1 'long' or English hundredweight = 112 pounds	50.8023
1 'short' or US hundredweight =100 pounds	45.3592
1 Amsterdam *centenaar* = 100 *ponden*	49.4094
1 German *zentner* (metric)	50
1 Paris *quintal* = 100 *livres*	48.9506
1 Castile *quintal* = 100 *libras*	46.0093
1 Lisbon *quintal* = 128 *libras*	58.7584
1 tonne, metric	1,000
1 'long' or English ton = 2,240 pounds	1,016.0640
1 'short' or US ton = 2,000 pounds	907.2

Regional units of weight, in kilogrammes (alphabetical)

From León Borja and Szászdi Nagy 1964: 3; Patiño 1963: 314; Ward 1828: II, 694, 698; unless otherwise stated.

	kilogrammes
1 *arroba*, Colombia, after 1836 (Schneider 1981: II, 699)	12.5
1 *carga*, Acapulco (Kicza 1983: 70)	35.8878
1 *carga*, Guatemala	27.606
1 *carga*, Guayaquil	37.2681
1 *carga*, Colombia (Lévine 1914: 188)	115.025
1 *carga*, Tabasco	27.606
1 *carga*, Veracruz	27.606
1 *cavan*, Philippines (González Fernández 1875: 136)	38.1883
1 *fanega*, Caracas	50.611
1 *fanega*, Maracaibo	44.1696
1 *fardo*, Nicaragua (Salvatierra 1939: II, 35–6)	57.5125
1 *medio*, Nicaragua (Lévy 1873: 469; Touzard 1993: 16)	2.3005
1 *millar*, Cartagena	1.8404
1 *pico*, Manila (Sancianco y Goson 1881: 255–6)	63.2638
1 *pikul*, Dutch East Indies (*ENI*: II, 688)	61.7613
1 *pikul*, Singapore (Sancianco y Goson 1881: 255–6)	60.48
1 *quintal*, Colombia, after 1836 (Schneider 1981: II, 699)	50
1 *tercio*, Colombia (McFarlane 1993: xiii)	46.0093
1 *tercio*, Nicaragua (Salvatierra 1939: II, 35–6)	57.5125
1 *tercio*, Veracruz	55.212

Note: A sack of cocoa usually weighed between 50 and 100 kilos. See Mangin 1860: 117–26, and Sociedade de Emigração 1915: 94.

Units of surface area, in hectares

	hectares
1 acre	0.405
1 *carreau*, Haïti (Schoenrich 1918: 402–3)	1.298
1 *manzana*, Costa Rica (Saenz Maroto 1970: 554–7)	0.699
1 *quarrée*, Trinidad (Shephard 1937: IV, 3)	1.298
1 *tarea*, Dominican Republic (Schoenrich 1918: 402–3)	0.0629

A note on currency

Colonial Latin America and the Philippines used the silver dollar or peso, divided into eight reales. After independence, the peso sometimes changed its name and became decimalised, and usually depreciated against the US dollar from the 1880s. In Ecuador, the peso became a sucre in 1884, at par with the US dollar, depreciated, and was fixed at a tenth of a pound sterling 1898–1914. A Venezuelan bolívar was worth 19.3 US cents 1880–1913.

The Brazilian milreis fell gradually from a seventh of a pound sterling 1836–40, to a fifteenth 1906–10.

In the main Western countries, one pound sterling, from 1871 to 1914, equalled 20.4 German marks, 25.2 French francs, and 4.9 US dollars.

For more details on exchange rates around the world, see the handbooks by Jürgen Schneider, published in Stuttgart by Franz Steiner; McCusker, J. J. (1978) *Money and Exchange in Europe and America: A Handbook*, London: Macmillan; and Bidwell, R. L. (1970) *Currency Conversion Tables: A Hundred Years of Change*, London: Rex Collins.

APPENDIX 5

Maps

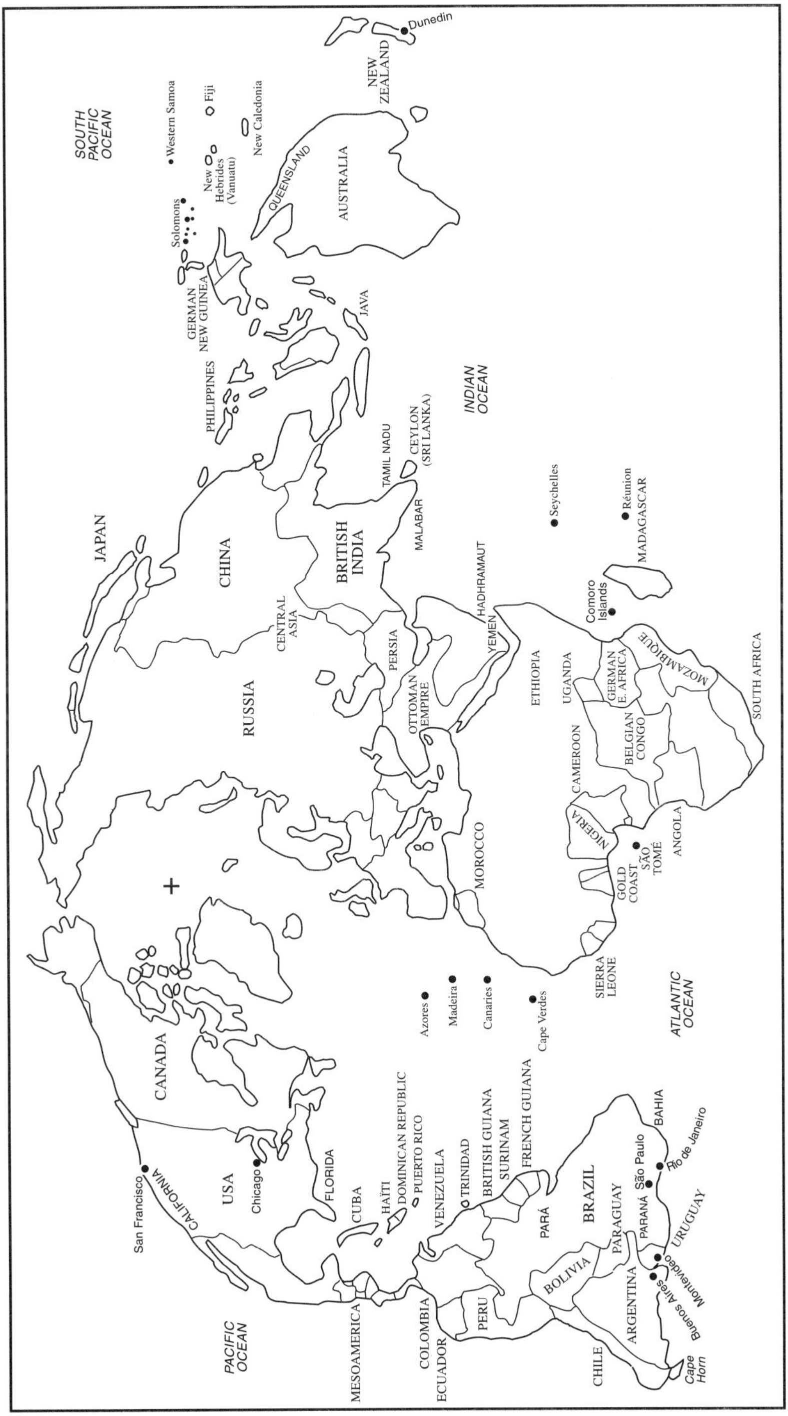

Map 1 The cocoa and chocolate world in 1914

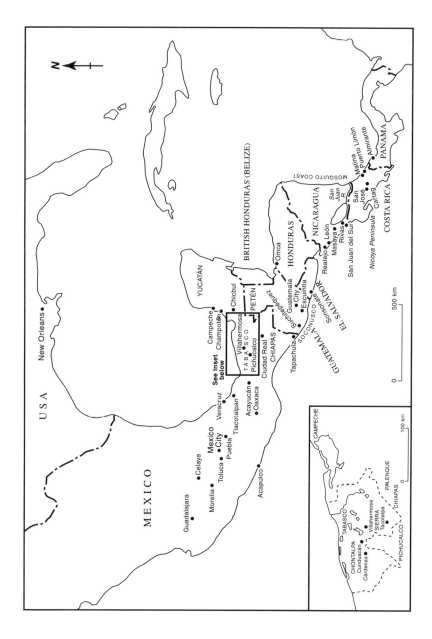

Map 2 Mesoamerica and the Gulf of Mexico

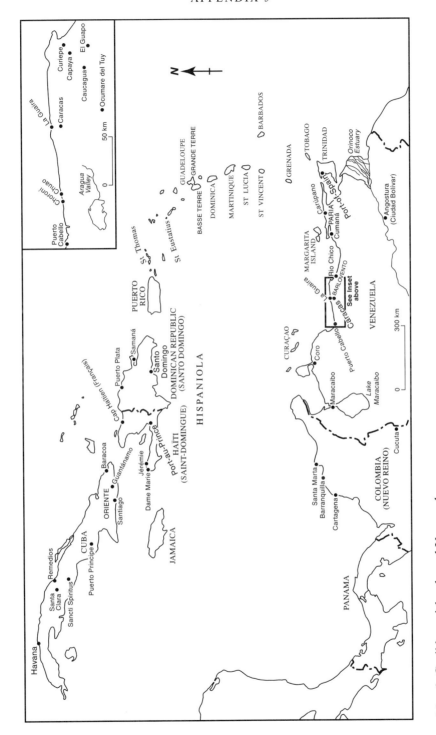

Map 3 Caribbean islands and Venezuela

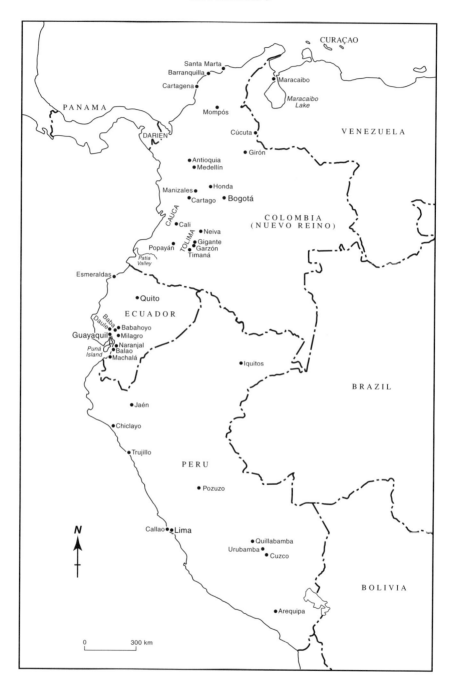

Map 4 Colombia, Ecuador and Peru

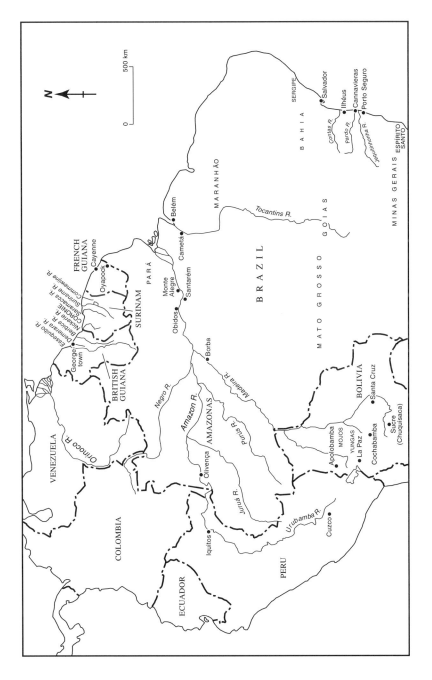

Map 5 Brazil, Bolivia and the Guianas

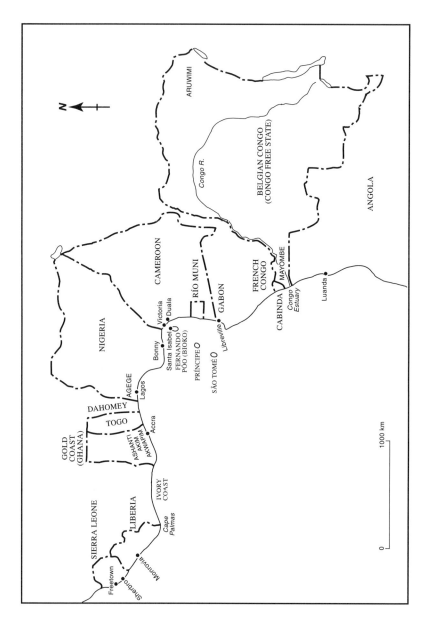

Map 6 West and Equatorial Africa

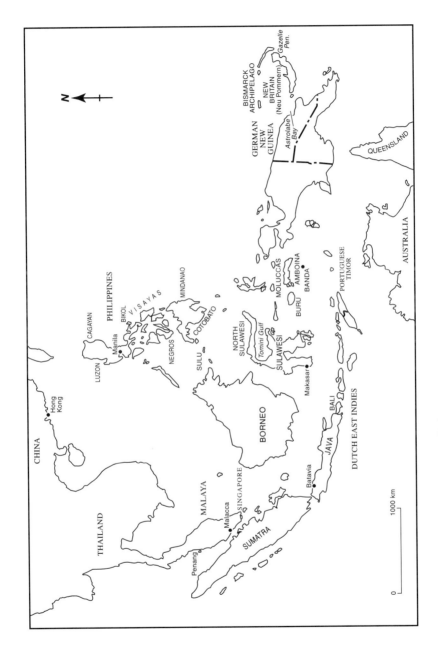

Map 7 Southeast Asia and New Guinea

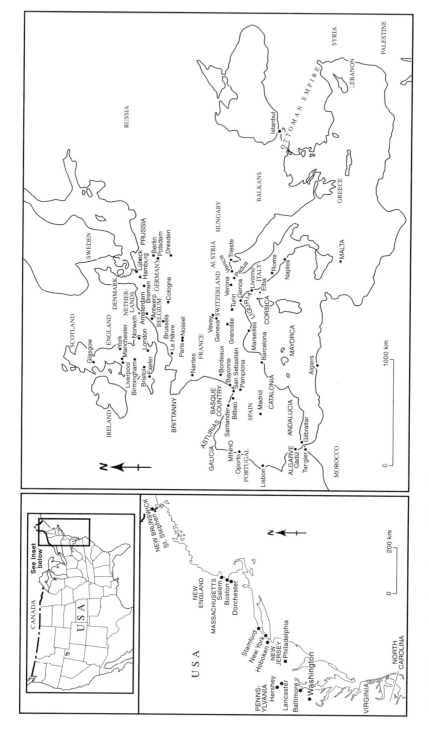

Map 8 Europe, the Near East and North America

REFERENCES

Archival references

ABM 1906: E-10.22, 20, Schmidt, 3 March, in Archiv der Basler Mission (Cameroon files), Basel, Switzerland.

AGA 1901: C682, E1, Informe, R.E. 23, 19 June, in Archivo General de la Administración (Africa-Guinea), Alcalá de Henares, Spain.

AGA 1904–14: C104, E3, Exportación de cacao y su régimen arancelario, in *ibid.*

AGA 1905: C144, E11, Coll y Astrell, in *ibid.*

AGA 1913: C104, E3, Governor, 17 March in *ibid.*

AGA 1914: C148, E7, Governor, undated, in *ibid.*

AHA 1912: 5362, 13–3-9, Estatística geral, in Arquivo Histórico de Angola (Avulsos), Luanda, Angola.

AHA 1915: 5361, 13–4-4, Cacongo report, April, in *ibid.*

AHSTP 1900: 1-a-C, 4, Governor of São Tomé, 27 December, in Arquivo Histórico de São Tomé e Príncipe, São Tomé, São Tomé and Príncipe.

AHTT 1820: Junta do Comercio, Balança do Comercio, in Arquivo Histórico da Torre do Tombo, Lisbon, Portugal.

AHU 1872: P507, Governor of Príncipe, Report, 1 March, in Arquivo Histórico Ultramarino (São Tomé *Pastas*), Lisbon, Portugal.

AHU 1880: P517, Governor of São Tomé, 17 June, in *ibid.*

AHU 1884: P534, Governor of São Tomé, 22 July, in *ibid.*

ANC 1896: 1/808, Governor, 29 December, in Archives Nationales du Cameroun (Fonds Allemand), Yaoundé, Cameroun.

ANC 1912: 1/808, 'Anleitung für Eingeborene zum Kakaobau', in *ibid.*

ANC 1913: 1/806, Dr Fickendey, 14 March, in *ibid.*

ANRI 1859: 29, 1538, J. Schmeddings, 15 February, in Arsip Nasional Republik Indonesia (Residency Archives), Jakarta, Indonesia.

ANRI 1870a: 52, 60, Report for outer possessions, in *ibid.*

ANRI 1870b: 52, 1659, Java cultivation report, in *ibid.*

BAAP 1898: 3226, J. Thormählen, 29 September, in Bundesarchiv Abteilung Potsdam (Reichskolonialamt), Potsdam, Germany (now in Berlin).

BAAP 1906: 8003, 'Kakao und die deutschen Kolonien', in *ibid.*

BAAP 1907a: 8056, C. W. Metzer, 6 February, in *ibid.*

BAAP 1907b: 8003, L. Stollwerck, 21 March 1907, in *ibid.*

BAAP 1908a: 8003, Redaktion des Gordians, 29 January, in *ibid.*

BAAP 1908b: 8057, L. Stollwerck, 26 September, in *ibid.*
BAAP 1908c: 8003, L. Stollwerck, 11 May, in *ibid.*
BAAP 1908d: 3417, VKP report, in *ibid.*
BAAP 1908e: 7844, Tecklenburg, 13 May, in *ibid.*
BAAP 1917: 7844, Dr Fickendey, report.
GCR 1879: German consular report, Bucamaranga, Colombia, courtesy of T. Fischer.
ICR 1863 and 1892, Italian consular reports, Guayaquil, Ecuador, courtesy of J. Maiguashca.
LCL 1893–99: 380, H0L I, 1/8, 3/1, 3/3, various documents, in Liverpool Central Libraries (Holt Papers), Liverpool, UK.
LCL 1908: 380, HOL-I, 9/1, Bata letter, 3 March, in *ibid.*
LCL 1911: 380, HOL-I, 9/1, Herschell letter, 7 April, in *ibid.*
MMSA 1915: PM 1157, microfilm 7, 256, J. Bell, 28 July, in Methodist Missionary Society Archives, School of Oriental and African Studies, London, UK.
UBL 1903: 180/336, W. Cadbury, 17 March, in University of Birmingham Library (Cadbury Papers), Birmingham, UK.
UBL 1907: 180/365, W. Cadbury, 19 November, in *ibid.*
UBL 1909: 299–300, W. Cadbury, 'Note-book', in *ibid.*
UBL 1910: 180/2, Cadbury Brothers, 16 December, in *ibid.*

References from series and encyclopaedias

AEC: *Anuário Estadístico de Colombia*, Bogotá: Imprenta de Medardo Rivas.
AEE: *Anuário Estadístico de España*, Madrid: Imprenta Nacional.
AEM: *Anuário Estadístico de Mexico*, Mexico City: Imprenta Nacional.
BII: *Bulletin of the Imperial Institute*, London: John Murray.
DP: *Diccionario Porrúa de História, Biografía y Geografía de México*, Mexico City: Editorial Porrúa.
EB: *Encyclopaedia Britannica*, London and Chicago: 1911, 1929 and 1993 editions.
EUIEA: *Enciclopedia Universal Ilustrada Europeo-Americana*, Barcelona: Espasa.
EGCEE : *Estadística General del Comercio Exterior de España*, Madrid: Dirección General de Aduanas (title varied).
ENI: *Encyclopaedie van Nederlandsch-Indië*, The Hague: M. Nijhoff.
GEPB: *Grande Enciclopédia Portuguesa e Brasileira*, Lisbon: Editorial Enciclopédia.
Gordian: *Der Gordian, Zeitschrift für die Kakao- Schokoladen- und Zuckerwarenindustrie*, Hamburg: Der Gordian.
KV: *Koloniaal Verslag*, The Hague: Algemeene Landsdrukkerij (title varied).
Larousse: *Grand Dictionnaire Universel du XIXe Siècle*, Paris: Librairie Larousse et Boyer.
MGCP: *Mappas Geraes do Commercio de Portugal com as suas Possessões Ultramarinas e as Nações Estrangeiras*, Lisbon: Direcção Geral das Alfândegas (title varied).
MP: *Mercurio Peruano*, Lima: Biblioteca Nacional del Perú (facsimile reprint).
PA: *Portugal em Africa*, Lisbon: Typ. da Casa Catholica.
PP: *Parliamentary Papers* (House of Commons Sessional Papers) London.

SAC: *Statistical Abstracts for the Several Colonial and Other Possessions of the United Kingdom in each Year*, London: HMSO (title varied).
SYB: *Statesman's Year-book*, London: Macmillan.
TGCF: *Tableau Général du Commerce de la France avec ses Colonies et les Puissances Etrangères*, Paris: Direction Générale des Douanes (title varied).

Internet references, alphabetically by title

'Brest96: le centenaire du Belem', *http://www.fr.msn.com/BREST96/Belem100.htm*
'Cadbury fact sheet, the story of Cadbury Limited', *http://www.cadbury.co.uk/facts/html/cadst*
'Cadbury Limited at Somerdale, and the history of J. S. Fry and Sons', *http://www.cadbury.co.uk/facts/html/fry1.htm*
'Caffarel, i nostri 170 anni', *http://www.caffarel.com/170anni_ita.html*
'Carob', *http://ds.dial.pipex.com/town/place/vu87/carob.shtml*
'Chocolat Basque', *http://visite-online.tm.fr/pbe/dossierculture/produits/chocolat.htm*
'Chocolates y turrones', *http://www.6tems.com/lascomas/esp.html*
'Ganong, our history', *http://www.gulliver.nb.ca/pcsolve/ganong/history.htm*
'Ghirardelli Square', *http://www.thelowell.org/lowell/dec10–96/page28/ghirardelli.html*
'Maté (Ilex Paraguariensis)', by G. C. Giberti, *http://www.hort.purdue.edu/newcrop/1492/mate.html*
'The Maya Gold story', by Green and Black, *http://www.earthfoods.co.uk/ gbs.maya.html*
'Menier – Nestlé', *http://www.ucad.fr/pub/virt/mp/menier_nestle_anglais.html*
'A modern herbal', originally published by M. Grieve in 1931, *http:// www.botanical.com/botanical/mgmh/mgmh/html*
'Our history, a proud tradition', *http://www.cadburynz/story.htm*
'Profile – Domenico Ghirardelli', *http://www.sacbee.com/goldrush/profiles/ pro_ghirardelli.html*
'Tropical plant database', compiled by Leslie Taylor for Raintree, *http://www.raintree.com/*

Books, articles, chapters, theses and papers

Note: Names in the Spanish tradition are entered under the first surname, those in the Portuguese tradition under the second surname, and those beginning with Mc as though they started with Mac.

Abel, C. (1985) 'Politics and the economy of the Dominican Republic, 1890–1930', in C. Abel and C. Lewis (eds) *Latin America: Economic Imperialism and the State*, 339–66, London: Athlone Press.
Acheson, T. W. (1982) 'The national policy and the industrialization of the Maritimes', in M. S. Cross and G. S. Kealey (eds) *Canada's Age of Industry, 1849–1896*, 62–94, Toronto: McClelland and Stewart.
Acosta Saignes, M. (1984) *Vida de los Esclavos Negros en Venezuela*, Valencia: Vadell Hermanos.
Agassiz, L. and Agassiz, E. (1969) *A Journey in Brazil*, New York: Praeger.
AGC (Agencia Geral das Colonias) (1929) *S. Tomé e Príncipe*, Lisbon.

Aguiar Filho, A. (1978) *Sul da Bahia, Chão de Cacau*, Rio de Janeiro: Civilização Brasileira.

Aizenberg, I. (1978) 'Los intentos de estabelecer un cementerio judío en la Caracas del siglo XIX', *Boletín Histórico, Fundación John Boulton*, 47, 243–54.

Alden, D. (1976) 'The significance of cacao production in the Amazon region during the late colonial period: an essay in comparative history', *Proceedings of the American Philosophical Society*, 120, 2, 103–35.

Alejo Torre, L. (1931) *Apuntes Históricos de Tabasco*, Mexico City: C. Rivadeneyra.

Almada, V. Pinheiro Lobo Machado de Mello e (1884) *Relatório do Governador de S. Thomé e Príncipe, Referido ao Anno de 1880*, Lisbon: Academia Real das Sciencias.

Almeida, E. X. d'Assumpção e (c. 1878) *Relatório do Governador da Provincia de S. Thomé e Príncipe, 1877 e 1878* (no place: no publisher).

Almeida, M. (1996) 'Phoenicians of the Pacific: Lebanese and other Middle Easterners in Ecuador', *The Americas*, 53, 1, 87–111.

Alvárez, M. M. (1963) *Comercio y Comerciantes, y Sus Proyecciones en la Independencia Venezolana*, Caracas: Tip. Vargas.

Alzola, P. de (1895) *Relaciones Comerciales entre la Península y las Antillas*, Madrid: M. Minuesa de los Rios.

Anna, T. E. (1979) *The Fall of the Royal Government in Peru*, Lincoln: University of Nebraska Press.

——(1983) *Spain and the Loss of America*, Lincoln: University of Nebraska Press.

Anon. (1827) *The Present State of Colombia*, London: John Murray.

——(1849) 'Laboean, Serawak, de Noord-Oostkust van Borneo en de Sultan van Soeloe', *Tijdschrift voor Nederlandsch Indië*, 66–83, 97–111, 237–42.

——(1890) *Universal-Lexicon der Kochkunst*, Leipzig: J. J. Weber.

——(1907) *A Ilha de S. Thomé e o Trabalho Indígena*, Lisbon: Revista Portuguesa Colonial e Marítima.

——(c. 1910) *A Nossa Província de Timor* (no place: no publisher).

Appadurai, A. (ed.) (1988) *The Social Life of Things: Commodities in Cultural Perspective*, Cambridge: Cambridge University Press.

Arcila Farías, E. (1950) *Comercio entre Venezuela y México en los Siglos XVII y XVIII*, Mexico City: El Colégio de México.

——(1973) *Economia Colonial de Venezuela*, Caracas: Italgráfica.

Arcy, F. d' (1930) 'Les débuts du cacao des isles', *Revue Historique des Antilles*, 5, 11–16.

Ardouin, B. (1853–60) *Etudes sur l'Histoire d'Haïti*, Paris: Dezobry et E. Magdeleine.

Are, L. A. and Gwynne-Jones, D. R. G. (1974) *Cacao in West Africa*, Ibadan: Oxford University Press.

Arias, M. E., Lau, A. and Sepúlveda, X. (1987) *Tabasco: Una Historia Compartida*, Villahermosa: Instituto Móra.

Arosemena, G. (1991) *El Fruto de los Dioses: El Cacao en Ecuador, Desde la Colonia hasta el Ocaso de su Industria, 1600–1983*, Guayaquil: Editorial Graba.

Arruda, J. Jobson de (1980) *O Brasil no Comércio Colonial*, São Paulo: Editora Atica.

Ashcraft, M. (1973) *Colonialism and Underdevelopment: Processes of Political and Economic Change in British Honduras*, New York: Teachers College Press.

Atkinson, F. W. (1905) *The Philippine Islands*, Boston: Ginn & Co.

Aubin, E. (1910) *En Haïti: Planteurs d'Autrefois, Nègres d'Aujourd'hui*, Paris: Armand Colin.

Austen, R. A. and Derrick, J. (1999) *Middlemen of the Cameroons Rivers: The Duala and Their Hinterland*, c. *1600*–c. *1960*, Cambridge: Cambridge University Press.

Austin, G. (1984) 'Rural capitalism and the growth of cocoa farming in South Ashanti to 1914', Ph.D. thesis, Birmingham University.

——(1987) 'The emergence of capitalist relations in South Asante cocoa farming, c. 1916–1933', *Journal of African History*, 28, 259–79.

——(1996) 'Mode of production or mode of cultivation: explaining the failure of European cocoa planters in competition with African farmers in colonial Ghana', in W. G. Clarence-Smith (ed.) *Cocoa Pioneer Fronts since 1800: The Role of Smallholders, Planters and Merchants*, 154–75, London: Macmillan.

——(1997) 'Introduction', in Polly Hill, *Migrant Cocoa-farmers of Southern Ghana: A Study in Rural Capitalism*, ix–xxvii, Oxford: James Currey.

Baardewijk, F. van (1994) 'Rural response to intensifying colonial exploitation: coffee and society in Central and East Java, 1830–1880, in G. J. Schutte (ed.) *State and Trade in the Indonesian Archipelago*, 151–76, Leiden: KITLV.

Balbi, A. (1822) *Essai Statistique sur le Royaume de Portugal et d'Algarve*, Paris: Rey et Gravier.

Baleato, A. (1887) *Monografía de Guayaquil, Escrita por Andrés Baleato en Lima en en Año de 1820*, Guayaquil: Imprenta de la Nación.

Balmori, D., Voss, S. F. and Wortman, M. (1984) *Notable Family Networks in Latin America*, Chicago: University of Chicago Press.

Banco Nacional Ultramarino (1890) *Relatórios do Banco Nacional Ultramarino desde o Anno de 1865 a 1889*, Lisbon.

Banko, C. (1988) 'Los comerciantes alemanes en La Guaira, 1821–1848', *Jahrbuch für Geschichte von Staat, Wirtschaft und Gesellschaft Lateinamerikas*, 25, 61–81.

——(1990) *El Capital Comercial en La Guaira y Caracas, 1821–1848*, Caracas: Academia Nacional de la Historia.

Bannister, R. (1890) 'Sugar, coffee, tea and cocoa: their origin, preparation and uses; lecture IV', *Journal of the Society of Arts*, 7 November, 1038–52.

Barbier, J. A. (1990) 'Commercial reform and comercio neutral in Cartagena de Indias, 1788–1808', in J. R. Fisher, A. J. Kuethe and A. McFarlane (eds) *Reform and Insurrection in Bourbon New Granada and Peru*, 96–120, Baton Rouge: Louisiana State University Press.

Barr, A. (1998) *Drink: A Social History*, London: Pimlico.

Barral, J. A. (1966) *Porvenir de las Grandes Explotaciones Agrícolas Estabelecidas en las Costas de Venezuela*, Caracas: Ediciones del Cuatrocentinario de Caracas.

Barreta, C. J. (1841) *Manuel Complet, Théorique et Pratique, du Chocolatier*, Paris: Mathias.

Basadre, J. (1963–68) *Historia de la República del Perú*, Lima: Editorial Panamérica

Bates, H. W. (1969) *The Naturalist on the River Amazons*, London: Dent.

Baud, M. (1982) 'Agricultural transformation in a Caribbean region: tobacco and cacao cultivation in the Cibao (Dominican Republic) in the late nineteenth century', MA thesis, University of Groningen.

——(1988) 'German trade in the Caribbean: the case of Dominican tobacco, 1844–1940', *Jahrbuch für Geschichte von Staat, Wirtschaft und Gesellschaft Lateinamerikas*, 25, 83–115.

Bauer, P. T. (1963) *West African Trade: A Study of Competition, Oligopoly and Monopoly in a Changing Economy*, London: Routledge & Kegan Paul.

Baumann, F. (1983) 'Terratenientes, campesinos y la expansión de la agricultura capitalista en Chiapas, 1896–1916', *Mesoamérica*, 4, 5, 8–63.

Baumann, O. (1888) *Eine Afrikanische Tropen-Insel: Fernando Póo und die Bube*: Vienna: E. Hölzel.

Beckles, H. (1990) *A History of Barbados, from Amerindian Settlement to Nation-state*, Cambridge: Cambridge University Press.

Belgium (1908) *Manuel Pratique de la Culture du Caféier et du Cacaoyer au Congo Belge*, Brussels: Ministère des Colonies.

Bell, P. L. (1922) *Venezuela: A Commercial and Industrial Handbook, with a Chapter on the Dutch West Indies*, Washington D.C.: U.S. Department of Commerce.

Bell, C. N. (1989) *Tangweera: Life and Adventures among Gentle Savages*, Austin: University of Texas Press.

Benjamin, T. (1989) *A Rich Land, a Poor People: Politics and Society in Modern Chiapas*, Albuquerque: University of New Mexico Press.

Benjamins, H. and Snelleman, J. F. (eds) (1914–17) 'Cacao', *Encyclopaedie van Nederlandsch West-Indië*, 185–94, The Hague and Leiden: M. Nijhoff and E. J. Brill.

Benoit, P. V. (1954) *Cent Cinquante Ans de Commerce Extérieur d'Haïti, 1804–1954*, Port-au-Prince: Institut Haïtien de Statistique.

Bensaúde, A. (1936) *Vida de José Bensaúde*, Oporto: Litografia Nacional.

Bergad, L. W. (1983) *Coffee and the Growth of Agrarian Capitalism in Nineteenth Century Puerto Rico*, Princeton: Princeton University Press.

Bergmann, J. F. (1957) 'Cacao and its production in Central America', *Tijdschrift voor Economische en Sociale Geografie*, 48, 43–8.

Bergquist, C. W. (1986) *Coffee and Conflict in Colombia, 1886–1910*, Durham NC: Duke University Press.

Bernard, B. (1996) 'Est-il moral de boire du chocolat?', in E. Collet (ed.) *Chocolat: De la Boisson Elitaire au Bâton Populaire*, 83–90, Brussels: CGER.

Bernecker, W. L. (1989) 'Comercio y comerciantes extranjeros en las primeras décadas de la independencia mexicana', in R. Liehr (ed.) *América Latina en la Epoca de Simón Bolívar: La Formación de las Economías Nacionales y los Intereses Ecónomicos Europeos, 1800–1850*, 87–114, Berlin: Colloquium.

Berry, S. S. (1975) *Cocoa, Custom and Socio-economic Change in Rural Western Nigeria*, Oxford: Clarendon Press.

Bethell, L. (1970) *The Abolition of the Brazilian Slave Trade: Britain, Brazil and the Slave Trade Question*, Cambridge: Cambridge University Press.

Beyer, R. C. (1947) 'The Colombian coffee industry: origins and major trends, 1740–1940', Ph.D. thesis, University of Minnesota.

Bhat, S. (n.d.) 'Plant interaction in a mixed crop community of arecanut and cacao', Ph.D. thesis, University of Mysore.

Bizière, J.-M. (1979) 'Hot beverages and the enterprising spirit in eighteenth-century Europe', *Journal of Psychohistory*, 7, 2, 135–45.

Blair, E. H. and Robertson J. A. (1903–7) *The Philippine islands*, Cleveland: (no publisher).

Blanchard, I. (1989) *Russia's Age of Silver: Precious Metal Production and Economic Growth in the Eighteenth Century*, London: Routledge.

Blérald, A.-P. (1986) *Histoire Economique de la Guadeloupe et de la Martinique du XVIIe Siècle à Nos Jours*, Paris: Karthala.

Blouet, B. (1977) 'The post-emancipation origins of the relationship between the estates and the peasantry in Trinidad', in K. Duncan and I. Rutledge (eds) *Land and Labour in Latin America: Essays on the Development of Agrarian Capitalism in the Nineteenth and Twentieth Centuries*, 435–52, Cambridge: Cambridge University Press.

Boin J. and Serulle Ramia, J. (1981) *El Proceso de Desarollo del Capitalismo en la Republica Dominicana, 1844–1930, Tomo Segundo, el Desarrollo de Capitalismo en la Agricultura, 1875–1930*, Santo Domingo: Gramil.

Bologne, J.-C. (1996) 'Le chocolat et la littérature Française et Européenne des XIXe et XXe siècles', in E. Collet (ed.) *Chocolat: De la Boisson Elitaire au Bâton Populaire*, 223–36, Brussels: CGER.

Bondar, G. (1938) *A Cultura de Cacau na Bahia*, São Paulo: Revista das Tribunaes.

Bonilla, H. (ed.) (1975–6) *Gran Bretaña y el Perú: Informes de los Cónsules Británicos*, Lima: Instituto de Estudios Peruanos.

Bonin, H. (1997) 'L'industrie agro-alimentaire du grand sud-ouest, XIXe-XXe siècles: un renversement historique du positionnement dans les flux économiques', in J. Marseille (ed.) *Les Industries Agro-alimentaires en France: Histoire et Performances*, 121–65, Paris: Le Monde-Editions.

Borchart de Moreno, C. R. (1984) *Los Mercaderes y el Capitalismo en la Ciudad de México, 1759–1778*, Mexico City: Fondo de Cultura Económica.

Botero Herrera, F. (1984) *La Industrialización en Antioquia, Génesis y Consolidación, 1900–1930*, Medellín: Uniersidad de Antioquia.

Bourgaux, A. (1935) *Quatre Siècles d'Histoire du Cacao et du Chocolat*, Brussels: E. Guyot.

Boussingault, J.-B. (1851) *Economie Rurale, Considérée dans ses Rapports avec la Chimie, la Physique, et la Météorologie*, Paris: Béchet Jeune.

——(1974) *Memorias*, Caracas: Centauro.

Boyer-Peyreleau, E.-E. (1823) *Les Antilles Françaises, Particulièrement la Guadeloupe, depuis leur Découverte*, Paris: Librairie de Brissot-Thivars.

Brading, D. A. (1971) *Miners and Merchants in Bourbon Mexico, 1763–1810*, Cambridge: Cambridge University Press.

Bravo Carbonel, J. (1917) *Fernando Póo y el Muni: Sus Misterios y Riquezas; su Colonización*, Madrid: Alrededor del Mundo.

Breen, H. H. (1970) *Saint Lucia, Historical, Statistical and Descriptive*, London: Cass.

Brenner, J. G. (1999) *The Chocolate Wars: Inside the Secret Worlds of Mars and Hershey*, London: HarperCollins.

Brereton, B. (1974) 'The experience of indentureship, 1845–1917', in J. G. La Guerre (ed.) *Calcutta to Caroni, the East Indians of Trinidad*, 25–38, London: Longman.

——(1981) *A History of Modern Trinidad, 1783–1962*, London: Heinemann.

Brew, R. (1977) *El Desarollo Económico de Antioquia desde la Independencia hasta 1920*, Bogotá: Banco de la Republica.

Briceño de Bermúdez, T. (1993) *Comercio por los Rios Orinoco y Apure durante la Segunda Mitad del Siglo XIX*, Caracas: Tropykos.

Brigham, W. T. (1887) *Guatemala: The Land of the Quetzal*, New York: Charles Scribners' Sons.

Brillat-Savarin, J. A. (n.d.) *La Physiologie du Goût, Tome 1*, Paris: Henri Piazza.

Brisseau Loaiza, J. (1981) *Le Cuzco dans sa Région: Etude de l'Aire d'Influence d'une Ville Andine*, Talence: Institut Français d'Etudes Andines.

Brito, J. Rodrigues de (1821) *Cartas Economico-politicas Sobre a Agricultura e Commercio da Bahia*, Lisbon: Imprensa Nacional.

Brito Figueroa, F. (1966) *Historia Económica y Social de Venezuela: Una Estructura para su Estudio*, Caracas: Universidad Central de Venezuela.

——(1978) *La Estructura Económica de Venezuela Colonial*, Caracas: Universidad Central de Venezuela.

——(1985) *El Problema Tierra y Esclavos en la Historia de Venezuela*, Caracas: Universidad Central de Venezuela.

Brizan, G. (1984) *Grenada, Island of Conflict: From Amerindians to People's Revolution, 1498–1979*, London: Zed Books.

Brown, C. B. and Lidstone, W. (1878) *Fifteen Thousand Miles on the Amazon and its Tributaries*, London: E. Stanford.

Brown, E. and Hunter, H. H. (1913) *Planting in Uganda: Coffee, Para Rubber, cocoa*, London: Longmans Green & Co.

Brown, R. F. (1995) 'Profits, prestige and persistence: Juan Fermín de Aycimena and the spirit of enterprise in the kingdom of Guatemala', *Hispanic American Historical Review*, 75, 3, 405–40.

Browning, D. (1975) *El Salvador: La Tierra y el Hombre*, San Salvador: Ministerio de Educación.

Brungardt, M. P. (1974) 'Tithe production and patterns of economic change in central Colombia, 1764–1833', Ph.D. thesis, University of Texas at Austin.

Bryan, P. F. (1977) 'The transformation of the economy of the Dominican Republic, 1870–1916', Ph.D. thesis, University of London.

Buckley, C.B. (1965) *An Anecdotal History of Singapore in Old Times*, Kuala Lumpur: University of Malaya Press.

Buley, E. C. (1914) *North Brazil*, London: Pitman.

Bullock, W. (1824) *Six Months Residence and Travel in Mexico*, London: John Murray.

Bulmer-Thomas, V. (1994) *The Economic History of Latin America Since Independence*, Cambridge: Cambridge University Press.

Burbidge, F. W. (1989) *The Gardens of the Sun: A Naturalist's Journal of Borneo and the Sulu Archipelago*, Singapore: Oxford University Press.

Burkill, I. H. (1966) *A Dictionary of the Economic Products of the Malay Peninsula*, Kuala Lumpur: Ministry of Agriculture and Co-operatives.

Burnett, J. (1999) *Liquid Pleasures: A Social History of Drinks in Modern Britain*, London: Routledge.

Burns, E. B. (1991) *Patriarch and Folk: The Emergence of Nicaragua, 1798–1858*, Cambridge: Harvard University Press.

Bushnell, D. (1970) *The Santander Regime in Gran Colombia*, Westport: Greenwood Press.

Butel, P. (1974) *Les Négociants Bordelais, l'Europe et les Iles au XVIIIe Siècle*, Paris: Aubier.

Buzeta, M. and Bravo, F. (1851) *Diccionario Geográfico-Estadístico-histórico de las Islas Filipinas*, Madrid: J. C. de la Pona.

Cadbury Brothers (1880) *Cocoa and its Manufacture*, Carlisle: Hudson Scott & Sons.

Caldeira, C. (1954) *Fazendas de Cacau na Bahia*, Rio de Janeiro: Serviço de Informação Agrícola.

Calderón, F. (1955) *Historia Moderna de México: La República Restaurada; la Vida Económica*, Mexico City: Editorial Hermes.

Camacho Roldán, S. (1895) *Escritos Varios, Tercera Serie, Hacienda Pública, Política General, Variedades*, Bogotá: Libreria Colombiana.

Campbell, G. R. (1996) 'The cocoa frontier in Madagascar, the Comoro Islands, and Réunion, c. 1820–1970', in W. G. Clarence-Smith (ed.) *Cocoa Pioneer Fronts since 1800: The Role of Smallholders, Planters and Merchants*, 195–211, London: Macmillan.

Campos, E. dos (1908) *A Ilha de São Thomé*, Lisbon: Sociedade de Geografia de Lisboa.

Capie, F. H. (1994) *Tariffs and Growth: Some Insights from the World Economy, 1850–1914*, Manchester: Manchester University Press.

Cardoso, C. F. S. (1984) *Economia e Sociedade em Areas Coloniais Periféricas: Guiana Francesa e Pará, 1750–1817*, Rio de Janeiro: Graal.

Cardozo Galué, G. (1991) *Maracaibo y su Región Histórica: El Circuito Agroexportador 1830–1860*, Maracaibo: Editorial de la Universidad de Zulia.

Carr, R. (1982) *Spain 1808–1975*, Oxford: Clarendon Press.

Carrington, D. (1971) *Granite Island: A Portrait of Corsica*, London: Longman.

Carrington, S. H. H. (1988) *The British West Indies during the American Revolution*, Dordrecht: Foris.

Cartay, R. (1988) *Historia Económica de Venezuela, 1830–1900*, Valencia: Vadell Hermanos.

Carvalho, A. M. (1994) *La Ilustración del Despotismo en Chiapas, 1774–1821*, Mexico City: Consejo Nacional para la Cultura y las Artes.

Casey, J. D. (1981) *Bordeaux, Colonial Port of Nineteenth Century France*, New York: Arno Press.

Cavada, A. de la (1876) *Historia Geográfrica, Geológica y Estadística de las Filipinas*, Manila: Ramírez y Giraudier.

Cerfberr de Medelsheim, A. (1867) *Le Cacao et le Chocolat, Considérés aux Points de Vue Hygiénique, Agricole et Commercial*, Paris: Société des Livres Utiles.

César, A. (1969) *O Primeiro Barão d'Agua-Izé*, Lisbon: Agência Geral do Ultramar.

Chalot, C. and Luc, M. (1906) *Le Cacaoyer au Congo Français*, Paris: A. Challamel.

Chauveau, J.-P. and Léonard, E. (1996) 'Côte d'Ivoire's pioneer fronts: historical and political determinants of the spread of cocoa cultivation', in W. G. Clarence-Smith (ed.) *Cocoa Pioneer Fronts since 1800: The Role of Smallholders, Planters and Merchants*, 176–94, London: Macmillan.

Chávez Suárez, J. (1944) *Historia de Moxos*, La Paz: Fénix.

Chevalier, A. (1906) 'Le cacao, sa production et sa consommation dans le monde', *Annales de Géographie*, 15, 82: 289–98.

Chiriboga, M. (1980) *Jornaleros y Gran Propietarios en 135 Años de Exportación Cacaotera, 1790–1925*, Quito: Consejo Provincial de Pichincha.

Ciferri, R. (1930) *Informe General sobre la Industria Cacaotera de Santo Domingo*, Santo Domingo: Estación Agronómica de Moca.

Claessens, J. (1914) 'Note relative à la culture du cacaoyer au Mayumbe, Congo Belge', *Bulletin Agricole du Congo Belge*, 5, 2, 215–46.

Clarence-Smith, W. G. (1984) 'The Portuguese contribution to the Cuban slave and coolie trades in the nineteenth century', *Slavery and Abolition*, 5, 1, 24–33.

——(1985) *The Third Portuguese Empire, 1825–1975: A Study in Economic Imperialism*, Manchester: Manchester University Press.

——(1990) 'The hidden costs of labour on the cocoa plantations of São Tomé and Príncipe, 1875–1914', *Portuguese Studies*, 6, 152–72.

——(1991) 'The economic dynamics of Spanish colonialism in the nineteenth and twentieth centuries', *Itinerario*, 15, 1, 71–90.

——(1993a) 'Plantation versus smallholder production of cocoa: the legacy of the German period in Cameroon', in P. Geschiere and P. Konings (eds) *Itinéraires d'Accumulation au Cameroun*, 187–216, Paris: Karthala.

——(1993b) 'Labour conditions in the plantations of São Tomé and Príncipe, 1875–1914', *Slavery and Abolition*, 14, 1, 149–67.

——(1994a) 'The contribution of Africans and Europeans to cocoa cultivation on Fernando Póo, 1882–1914', *Journal of African History*, 35, 2, 179–200.

——(1994b) 'The organization of "consent" in British West Africa, 1820s–1960s', in D. Engels and S. Marks (eds) *Contesting Colonial Hegemony: State and Society in Africa and India*, 55–78, London: British Academic Press.

——(1995) 'Cocoa plantations in the Third World, 1870s–1914: the political economy of inefficiency', in J. Harriss, J. Hunter and C. Lewis (eds) *The New Institutional Economics and Third World Development*, 157–71, London: Routledge.

——(1997) 'Hadhramaut and the Hadhrami diaspora in the modern colonial era: an introductory survey', in U. Freitag and W. G. Clarence-Smith (eds) *Hadhrami Traders, Scholars and Statesmen in the Indian Ocean, 1750s–1960s*, 1–18, Leiden: Brill.

——(1998) 'The rise and fall of Maluku cocoa production in the nineteenth century: lessons for the present', in S. Pannell and F. von Benda-Beckmann (eds) *Old World Places, New World Problems: Exploring Resource Management Issues in Eastern Indonesia*, 113–42, Canberra: Centre for Resource and Environmental Studies.

Clarence-Smith, W. G. and Ruf, François (1996) 'Cocoa pioneer fronts: the historical determinants', in W. G. Clarence-Smith (ed.) *Cocoa Pioneer Fronts since 1800: The Role of Smallholders, Planters and Merchants*, 1–22, London: Macmillan.

Clark, W. J. (1899) *Commercial Cuba: A Book for the Businessman*, London: Chapman and Hall.

Coatsworth, J. H. (1989) 'The decline of the Mexican economy, 1800–1860', in R. Liehr (ed.) *América Latina en la Epoca de Simón Bolívar: La Formación de las*

Economías Nacionales y los Intereses Ecónomicos Europeos, 1800–1850, 27–53, Berlin: Colloquium.

Coe, S. D. and Coe, M. D. (1996) *The True History of Chocolate*, London: Thames and Hudson.

Cole, F. (1997) 'Great Britain and the Syrian question in Sierra Leone, late 1880s–1930: a study of economic and social relations', paper given at the African History Seminar, SOAS, London, 26 November.

Colegio de México (1960) *Estadísticas Económicas del Porfiriato: Comercio Externo de México, 1877–1911*, Mexico City.

Collet, E. (ed.) (1996) *Chocolat: De la Boisson Elitaire au Bâton Populaire*, Brussels: CGER.

Colmenares, G. (1989) 'Popayán, continuidad y discontinuidad regionales en la época de la independencia', in R. Liehr (ed.) *América Latina en la Epoca de Simón Bolívar: La Formación de las Economías Nacionales y los Intereses Ecónomicos Europeos, 1800–1850*, 157–81, Berlin: Colloquium.

——(1997) *Historia Económica y Social de Colombia, II: Popayán, una Sociedad Esclavista, 1680–1860*, Bogotá: TM Editores.

Colombia (1975) *Estadísticas Históricas*, Bogotá: Departamento Administrativo Nacional de Estadística.

Commodity Research Bureau (1939) *Commodity Year Book*, New York.

Comyn, T. de (1969) *State of the Philippines in 1810*, Manila: Filipiniana Book Guild.

Contreras, C. (1990) *El Sector Exportador de una Economía Colonial: La Costa del Ecuador, 1760–1830*, Quito: Colección Tesis Historia.

——(1994) 'Guayaquil y su región en el primer boom cacaotero, 1750–1820', in J. Maiguashca (ed.) *Historia y Región en el Ecuador, 1830–1930*, Quito: Corporación Editora Nacional.

Cook, C. and Waller, D. (1998) *The Longman Handbook of Modern American History, 1763–1996*, Harlow: Addison Wesley Longman.

Coolhaas, W. P. (1960–) *Generale Missieven van Gouverneurs-generaal en Raden aan Heren XVII der Verenigde Oostindische Compagnie*, The Hague: M. Nijhoff (in progress).

Coquery-Vidrovitch, C. (1972) *Le Congo au Temps des Grandes Compagnies Concessionnaires, 1898–1930*, Paris: Mouton.

Corvetto, P. M. de (1886) *Les Industries Françaises à Buenos Aires*, Buenos Aires: Librairie Française.

Corvo, J. de Andrade (1883–7) *Estudos sobre las Provincias Ultramarinas*, Lisbon: Academia Real das Ciencias.

Cosio Villegas, D. (1932) *La Cuestión Arancelaria en México, Vol. III: Historia de la Política Aduanal*, Mexico City: Centro Mexicano de Estudios Económicos.

Costa, A. da (1911) *O Problema da Emigração*, Lisbon: Imprensa Nacional.

Coudreau, H. A. (1886–7) *La France Equinoxiale*, Paris: Challamel Ainé.

Cox, E. L. (1984) *Free Coloureds in the Slave Societies of St Kitts and Grenada, 1763–1833*, Knoxville: University of Tennessee Press.

Craton, M. and Walvin, J. (1970) *A Jamaican Plantation: The History of Worthy Park, 1670–1970*, London: W. H. Allen.

Crawford de Roberts, L. (1980) *El Ecuador en la Epoca Cacaotera: Respuestas Locales al Auge y Colapso en el Ciclo Monoexportador*, Quito: Editorial Universitaria.

Crow, B. and Thomas, A. (1983) *Third World Atlas*, Milton Keynes: Open University Press.

Crowder, M. (1982) *West Africa under Colonial Rule*, London: Hutchinson.

Cruikshank, B. (1982) 'Continuity and change in the economic and administrative history of nineteenth century Samar', in A. W. McCoy and E. de Jesús (eds) *Philippine Social History, Global Trade and Local Transformations*, 219–49, Quezon City: Ateneo de Manila University Press.

Cuenca Esteban, J. (1981) 'Statistics of Spain's colonial trade, 1792–1820: consular duties, cargo inventories and balance of trade', *Hispanic American Historical Review*, 61, 3, 381–428.

——(1984) 'The United States balance of payments with Spanish America and the Philippine Islands, 1790–1819: estimates and analysis of principal components', in J. A. Barbier and A. J. Kuethe (eds) *The North American Role in the Spanish Imperial Economy, 1760–1819*, 28–70, Manchester: Manchester University Press.

Dalence, J. M. (1975) *Bosquejo Estadístico de Bolivia*, La Paz: Universidad Boliviana.

Daly, V. T. (1975) *A Short History of the Guyanese People*, London: Macmillan.

Dand, R. (1993) *The International Cocoa Trade*, Cambridge: Woodhead.

Davis, R. W. (1976) *Ethnohistorical Studies on the Kru Coast*, Newark: University of Delaware.

Davies, S. H. (1924) 'Cocoa cultivation in the British tropical colonies' *Journal of the Royal Society of Arts*, January, 158–68.

Debay, A. (1864) *Les Influences du Chocolat, du Thé et du Café sur l'Economie Humaine*, Paris: E. Dentu.

Deeds, S. M. (1995) 'Indigenous responses to mission settlement in Nueva Vizcaya', in E. Langer and R. H. Jackson (eds) *The New Latin American Mission History*, Lincoln: University of Nebraska Press.

Deler, J.-P. (1981) *Genèse de l'Espace Equatorien: Essai sur le Territoire et la Formation de l'Etat National*, Paris, Institut Français d'Etudes Andines.

Dellheim, C. (1987) 'The creation of a company culture: Cadburys, 1861–1931', *American Historical Review*, 92, 1, 13–44.

Depons, F. (1930) *Viaje a la Parte Oriental de Tierra Firme en la América Meridional*, Caracas: Tipografia Americana.

Deschamps, E. (1907) *La República Dominicana: Directorio y Guía General*, Santiago de los Caballeros: J. Cunill.

Descola, J. (1968) *Daily Life in Colonial Peru, 1710–1820*, London: Allen and Unwin.

Diaper, S. (1988) 'J. S. Fry and Sons: growth and decline in the chocolate industry, 1753–1918', in C. Harvey and J. Press (eds) *Studies in the Business History of Bristol*, 33–54, Bristol: Bristol Academic Press.

Dias, M. Nunes (1971) *El Real Consulado de Caracas, 1793–1810*, Caracas: Academia Nacional de la Historia.

Dias, A. Gomes, and Diniz, A. do Nascimento (1988) 'Os Angolares: da autonomia à inserção na sociedade colonial, segunda metade do século XIX', *Ler Historia*, 13, 53–75.

Díaz Arenas, R. (1838) *Memoria sobre el Comercio y Navegación de las Islas Filipinas*, Cadiz: Domingo Fèros.

——(1850) *Memorias Históricas y Estadísticas de Filipinas, y Particularmente de la Grande Isla de Luzón*, Manila: Diario de Manila.

Díaz-Trechuelo, M. L. (1964) 'Philippine development plans, 1746–1779', *Philippine Studies*, 12, 2, 203–31.

——(1965) *La Real Compañía de Filipinas*, Seville: Escuela de Estudios Hispano-Americanos.

Dickson, K. (1969) *A Historical Geography of Ghana*, Cambridge: Cambridge University Press.

Dobbin, C. (1996) *Asian Entrepreneurial Minorities: Conjoint Communities in the Making of the World Economy, 1570–1940*, Richmond: Curzon Press.

Dorchy, H. (1996) 'Le moule à chocolat et l'imagerie populaire', in E. Collet (ed.) *Chocolat: De la Boisson Elitaire au Bâton Populaire*, 195–210, Brussels: CGER.

Douglass, W. A. and Bilbao, J. (c. 1986) *Amerikanuak, los Vascos en el Nuevo Mundo*, Bilbao: Universidad del País Vasco.

Dowell, S. (1888) *A History of Taxation and Taxes in England*, London: Longman Green & Co.

Drummond, J. C. and Wilbraham A. (1939) *The Englishman's Food: A History of Five Centuries of the English Diet*, London: Jonathan Cape.

Duffy, J. (1967) *A Question of Slavery*, Cambridge: Harvard University Press.

Dunkerley, J. (1988) *Power in the Isthmus: A Political History of Modern Central America*, London: Verso.

Dunn, H. (1829) *Guatimala, or the Republic of Central America, in 1827 to 1828*, London: James Nisbet.

Dupeux, G. (1969) 'L'activité économique; le port', in L. Desgraves and G. Dupeux (eds) *Bordeaux au XIXe siécle*, 375–95, Bordeaux: Delmas.

Dupuy, A. (1989) *Haïti in the World Economy: Class, Race and Underdevelopment since 1700*, Boulder: Westview Press.

Echaúz, R. (1978) *Sketches of the Island of Negros,* Athens: Ohio University Press.

Eckert, A. (1996) 'Cocoa farming in Cameroon, c. 1914–c. 1960: land and labour', in W.G. Clarence-Smith (ed.) *Cocoa Pioneer Fronts since 1800: The Role of Small-holders, Planters and Merchants*, 137–53, London: Macmillan.

Eder, F. J. (1985) *Breve Descripción de las Reducciones Mojos, c. 1772*, Cochabamba: Historia Boliviana.

Eder, P. J. (1913) *Colombia*, London: Fisher and Unwin.

——(1959) *El Fundador, Santiago M. Eder: Recuerdos de su Vida y Acotaciones para la História Económica del Valle del Cauca*, Bogotá: Antares Ltda.

Edwards, B. (1801) *The History, Civil and Commercial, of the British Colonies in the West Indies*, London: John Stockdale.

Eisner, G. (1961) *Jamaica 1830–1930: A Study in Economic Growth*, Manchester: Manchester University Press.

Elkin, J. L. (1980) *Jews of the Latin American Republics*, Chapel Hill: University of North Carolina Press.

Elson, R. (1994) *Village Java under the Cultivation System, 1830–1870*, Sydney: Allen and Unwin.

271

Emerson, E. R. (1908) *Beverages Past and Present: An Historical Sketch of Their Production, together with a Study of the Customs Connected with Their Use*, New York: G. P. Putnam's Sons.

Emmanuel, I. S. and Emmanuel, S. A. (1970) *History of the Jews of the Netherlands Antilles*, Cincinnati: American Jewish Archives.

Emmer, P. C. (1993) 'Between slavery and freedom: the period of apprenticeship in Suriname (Dutch Guiana), 1863–1873', in M. Twaddle (ed.) *The Wages of Slavery: From Chattel Slavery to Wage Labour in Africa, the Caribbean and England*, 87–113, London: Cass.

Enjalbert, H. (1952–3) 'La renaissance économique de la République Dominicaine', *Cahiers d'Outre-Mer*, 5, 20, 330–56, and 6, 21, 61–87.

Enock, C. R. (1909) *Mexico: Its Ancient and Modern Civilisation, History and Political Conditions, Topography, Natural Resources, Industries and General Development*, London: Fisher and Unwin.

——(1914) *Ecuador: Its Ancient and Modern History, Topography, Natural Resources, Industry and Social Development*, London: Fisher and Unwin.

——(1925) *Peru: Its Former and Present Civilisation, History and Existing Conditions, Topography and Natural Resources, Commerce and General Development*, London: Fisher and Unwin.

Epale, S. J. (1985) *Plantations and Development in Western Cameroon, 1885–1975*, New York: Vantage Press.

Erneholm, I. (1948) *Cacao Production of South America: Historical Development and Present Geographical Distribution*, Gothenburg: C. R. Holmqvists Boktryckeri.

Euraque, D. A. (1998) 'The Arab-Jewish economic presence in San Pablo Sula, the industrial capital of Honduras: formative years, 1880s–1930s', in I. Klich and J. Lesser (eds) *Arab and Jewish Immigration in Latin America: Images and Realities*, 94–124, London: Cass.

Farley, R. E. G. (1956) 'Aspects of the economic history of British Guiana, 1781–1852: a study of economic and social change on the southern Caribbean frontier', Ph.D. thesis, University of London.

Faro, Conde de Sousa e (1908) *A Ilha de S. Thomé e a Roça Agua-Izé*, Lisbon: Annuario Commercial.

Farré, J. (1979) 'Relations commerciales entre la Catalogne et le Vénézuela à la fin du XVIIIe siècle: essai de quantification', *Cahiers du Monde Hispanique et Luso-Brésilien*, 32, 19–38.

Farriss, N. M. (1984) *Maya Society under Colonial Rule: The Collective Enterprise of Survival*, Princeton: Princeton University Press.

Fawcett, P. H. (1953) *Exploration Fawcett*, London: Hutchinson.

Fawcett, Louise L'E. (1992) 'Lebanese, Palestinians and Syrians in Colombia', in A. Hourani and N. Shehadi (eds) *The Lebanese in the World: A Century of Emigration*, 361–77, London: I. B. Tauris.

Fendyan, M. (1991) *Guittard Family Recipes: Cooking with Chocolate*, Burlingame: Guittard Chocolate Co.

Ferguson, J. (1903) *Ceylon in 1903*, Colombo: A. M. and J. Ferguson.

Fernández Molina, J. A. (1992) 'Colouring the world in blue: the indigo boom and the Central American market, 1750–1810', Ph.D. thesis, University of Texas at Austin.

Ferrer Piera, P. (1900) *Fernando Póo y sus Dependencias, Descripción, Producciones y Estado Sanitario*, Barcelona: A. López Robert.

Ferry, R. J. (1989) *The Colonial Elite of Early Caracas: Formation and Crisis, 1567–1767*, Berkeley: University of California Press.

Fick, C. F. (1990) *The Making of Haïti: The Saint-Domingue Revolution from Below*, Knoxville: University of Tennessee Press.

Fincke, H. (1936) *Handbuch der Kakaoerzeugnisse*, Berlin: Julius Springer.

Firth, S. (1982) *New Guinea under the Germans*, Melbourne: Melbourne University Press.

Fisher, R. S. (ed.) (1858) *The Spanish West Indies: Cuba and Porto Rico, Geographical Political and Industrial*, New York: J. H. Colton & Co.

Fisher, J. R. (1981) 'Imperial "free trade" and the hispanic economy, 1778–1796', *Journal of Latin American Studies*, 13, 1, 21–56.

——(1985a) 'The imperial response to "free trade" Spanish imports from Spanish America, 1778–1796', *Journal of Latin American Studies*, 17, 1, 35–78.

——(1985b) *Commercial Relations between Spain and Spanish America in the Era of Free Trade, 1778–1796*, Liverpool: Centre of Latin American Studies, University of Liverpool.

——(1997) *The Economic Aspects of Spanish Imperialism in America, 1492–1810*, Liverpool: Liverpool University Press.

Fitchett, L. S. (1906) *Beverages and Sauces of Colonial Virginia, 1607–1907*, New York: Neale Publishing Co.

Fitzgerald, R. (1995) *Rowntree and the Marketing Revolution, 1862–1969*, Cambridge: Cambridge University Press.

Florescano, E. and Gil Sánchez, I. (eds) (1976) *Descripciones Económicas Regionales de Nueva España, Provincias del Centro, Sudeste y Sur, 1766–1827*, Mexico City: INAH.

Floyd, T. S. (1967) *The Anglo-Spanish Struggle for Mosquitia*, Albuquerque: University of New Mexico Press.

Fonseca, E. (1986) *Costa Rica Colonial: La Tierra y el Hombre*, San José: Universidad Centro-Americana.

Fonssagrives (1875–6) 'Cacao' and 'Chocolat', in *Dictionnaire Encyclopédique des Sciences Médicales*, XI, 359–64, 724–36, Paris: G. Masson & P. Asselin.

Food and Agriculture Organization (1955) *Cacao: A Review of Current Trends in Production Price and Consumption*, Rome (Commodity Series Bulletin no. 27).

Forbes-Lindsay, C. H. (1906) *The Philippines under Spanish and American Rules*, Philadelphia: J. C. Winston Co.

Foreman, J. (1890) *The Philippine Islands*, London: Kelly and Walsh.

——(1906) *The Philippine Islands*, Shanghai: Kelly and Walsh.

Fortune, S. A. (1984) *Merchants and Jews: The Struggle for British West Indian Commerce, 1650–1750*, Gainesville: University Presses of Florida.

Franceschini, A. (1908) *L'Emigrazione Italiana nell'America del Sud*, Rome: Forzani.

Franklin, J. (1828) *The Present State of Hayti (Saint Domingue)*, London: John Murray.

Fraser, W. H. (1981) *The Coming of the Mass Market, 1850–1914*, London: Macmillan.

Fréchou, H. (1955) 'Les plantations Européennes en Côte d'Ivoire', *Cahiers d'Outremer*, 8, 29, 56–83.

Freeman, W. G. and Chandler, S. E. (1907) *The World's Commercial Products: A Descriptive Account of the Economic Plants of the World and their Commercial Uses*, London: Pitman.

Freitas, J. J. Rodrigues de (1867) *Notice sur le Portugal*, Paris: P. Dupont.

Freitas, A. F. Guerreiro de (1979) 'Os donos dos frutos de ouro', M.A. thesis, Salvador: Universidade Federal da Bahia.

Fuentes, C. (1992) *The Buried Mirror: Reflections on Spain and the New World*, London: Houghton Mifflin.

Gárate Ojanguren, M. (1990) *La Real Compañía Guipuzcoana de Caracas*, San Sebastián: Sociedad Guipuzcoana de Ediciones y Publicaciones.

Garavaglia. J. C. (1983) *Mercado Interno y Economía Colonial*, Mexico City: Grijalbo.

Garcez, A. N. Rolim and Freitas, A. F. Guerreiro de (1975) *História Económica e Social da Região Cacaueira*, Ilhéus: CEPLAC.

García Cantú, G. (c. 1969) *El Socialismo en México, Siglo XIX*, Mexico City: Ediciones Era.

Gardella, R. (1994) *Harvesting Mountains, Fujian and the China Tea Trade, 1757–1937*, Berkeley: University of California Press.

Gardiner, A. G. (1923) *Life of George Cadbury*, London: Cassell.

Gasco, J. L. (1987) 'Cacao and the economic integration of native society in colonial Soconusco, New Spain', Ph.D. thesis, University of California, Santa Barbara.

Geggus, D. P. (1982) *Slavery, War and Revolution: The British Occupation of Saint-Domingue, 1793–1798*, Oxford: Clarendon Press.

Gerhard, P. (1979) *The Southeast Frontier of New Spain*, Princeton: Princeton University Press.

Gereffi, G. and Korzeniewicz, M. (eds) (1994) *Commodity Chains and Global Capitalism*, Westport: Greenwood Press.

Giacottino, J.-C. (1976) 'Trinidad-et-Tobago: étude géographique', doctoral thesis, Université de Bordeaux III.

Gil y Saenz, M. (1979) *Compendio Histórico y Estadístico del Estado de Tabasco*, Villahermosa: Consejo Editorial del Gobierno del Estado de Tabasco, 1st ed. 1872.

Gil-Bermejo García, J. (1970) *Panorama Histórico de la Agricultura en Puerto Rico*, Seville: Escuela de Estudios Hispano-Americanos.

Girault, A. (1916) *The Colonial Tariff Policy of France*, Oxford: Clarendon Press.

González Fernández, R. (1875) *Manual del Viajero en Filipinas*, Manila: Tip. de Santo Tomás.

Goslinga, C. C. (1985) *The Dutch in the Caribbean and in the Guianas, 1680–1791*, Assen: Van Gorcum.

Gosselman, C. A. (1962) *Informes sobre los Estados Sudamericanos en los Años de 1837 y 1838*, Stockholm: Ibero-Amerikanska Biblioteket och Institutet.

Great Britain (1807) 'Report from the committee on the commercial state of the West India colonies', in *Parliamentary Papers* 1807: IV.

——(1831–2) 'Report of the select committee on the commercial state of the West India colonies', *Parliamentary Papers*, 1831–2: XX.

——(1845) 'Import Duties 1840–1845', *Parliamentary Papers*, subject volumes.

——(1848) 'Select committee on sugar and coffee planting', *Parliamentary Papers*, subject volumes.

——(1916) *A Handbook of German East Africa*, London: Admiralty, Naval Intelligence Division.

——(1919a) *Dahomey*, London: Foreign Office, Historical Section.

——(1919b) *Ivory Coast*, London: Foreign Office, Historical Section.

——(1919c) *Liberia*, London: Foreign Office, Historical Section.

——(1920a) *A Handbook of the Uganda Protectorate*, London: Admiralty, Naval Intelligence Division.

——(1920b) *Tanganyika – German East Africa*, London: Foreign Office, Historical Section.

——(1920c) *Portuguese Timor,* London: Foreign Office, Historical Section.

——(1920d) *British Possessions in Oceania,* London: Foreign Office, Historical Section.

——(1942) *Agriculture in the West Indies*, London: Colonial Office.

Green, W. A. (1991) *British Slave Emancipation: The Sugar Colonies and the Great Experiment, 1830–1865*, Oxford: Oxford University Press.

Greenhill, R. G. (*c.* 1972) 'Britain and the cocoa trade in Latin America before 1914', Working Paper 8, Cambridge Centre of Latin American Studies.

——(1977) 'Shipping 1850 to 1914', and 'Merchants and the Latin American trades: an introduction', in D. C. M. Platt (ed.) *Business Imperialism 1840–1930: An Inquiry Based on British Experience in Latin America*, 119–97, Oxford: Clarendon Press.

——(1996) 'A cocoa pioneer front, 1890–1914: planters, merchants and government policy in Bahia', in W. G. Clarence-Smith (ed.) *Cocoa Pioneer Fronts since 1800: The Role of Smallholders, Planters and Merchants*, 86–104, London: Macmillan.

Groff, D. H. (1987) 'Carrots, sticks and cocoa pods: the spread of cocoa production in Assikasso, Ivory Coast, 1908–1920', *International Journal of African Historical Studies*, 20, 3 , 401–16.

Grove, R. (1995) *Green Imperialism: Colonial Expansion, Tropical Island Edens and the Origins of Environmentalism, 1600–1860*, Cambridge: Cambridge University Press.

Guardino, P. F. (1996) *Peasants, Politics and the Formation of Mexico's National State: Guerrero, 1800–1857*, Stanford: Stanford University Press.

Guedes, A. Pinto de Miranda (1911) *S. Thomé, Seis Meses de Governo e Administração*, Oporto: Guedes.

Guerrero, A. (1980) *Los oligarcas del cacao: ensayo sobre la acumulación originaria en el Ecuador; hacendados, cacaoteros, banqueros, exportadores y comerciates en Guayaquil, 1890–1910*, Quito: El Conejo.

Guerrero, J. N. and Soriano, L. (1966) *Rivas, Monografía*, Managua: IFAGAN.

Guislain, L. and Vincart, L. (1911) 'La culture du cacaoyer au Vénézuéla et à l'Equateur', *L'Agronomie Tropicale*, III, 4, 65–73.

Haan, F. de (1910–12) *Priangan: de Preanger-Regentschappen onder het Nederlandsch bestuur tot 1811*, Batavia: Bataviaasch Genootschap van Kunsten en Wetenschappen.

Haarer, A. E. (1956) *Modern Coffee Production*, London: L. Hill.

Haber, S. H. (1989) *Industry and Underdevelopment: The Industrialization of Mexico, 1890–1940*, Stanford: Stanford University Press.

Hall, C. J. J. van (1914) *Cocoa*, London: Macmillan.

——(1932) *Cacao*, London: Macmillan.

Hall, F. (1824) *Colombia: Its Present State in respect of Climate, Soil, Productions and Government*, London: Baldwin, Cradock and Joy.

Hamerly, M. T. (1970) 'A social and economic history of the city and district of Guayaquil during the late colonial and independence periods', Ph.D. thesis, University of Florida.

——(1973) *Historia Social y Económica de la Antigua Provincia de Guayaquil, 1763–1842*, Guayaquil: Archivo Histórico del Guayas.

Hardy, G. (1947) *Histoire de la Colonisation Française*, Paris: Librairie Larose.

Harris, J. H. (1968) *Dawn in Darkest Africa*, London: Cass.

Harrison, D. (1979) 'The changing fortunes of a Trinidad peasantry' in M. Cross and A. Marks (eds) *Peasants, Plantations and Rural Communities in the Caribbean*, 54–85, Guildford: University of Surrey.

Hart, J. H. (1911) *Cacao: A Manual on the Cultivation and Curing of Cacao*, London: Duckworth & Co.

Harwich, N. (1992) *Histoire du Chocolat*, Paris, Editions Desjonquères.

Harwich Vallenilla, N. (1996) 'The eastern Venezuela pioneer front, 1830s–1930s: the role of the Corsican trade network', in W. G. Clarence-Smith (ed.) *Cocoa Pioneer Fronts since 1800: The Role of Smallholders, Planters and Merchants*, 23–44, London: Macmillan.

Hashimoto, Y. (1992) 'Lebanese population movements, 1920–1939', in A. Hourani and N. Shehadi (eds) *The Lebanese in the World: A Century of Emigration*, 393–410, London: I.B. Tauris.

Hausen, K. (1970) *Deutsche Kolonialherrschaft in Afrika, Wirtschaftsinteressen und Kolonialverwaltung in Kamerun vor 1914*, Zurich: Atlantis.

Have, J. J. ten (1913) *Beknopte Aardrijkskunde van Nederlandsch Oost- en West- Indië*, The Hague: J. Ykema.

Head, B. (1903) *The Food of the Gods: A Popular Account of Cocoa*, London: George Routledge & Sons.

Heer, J. (1966) *World Events, 1866–1966: The First Hundred Years of Nestlé*, Lausanne: Imprimeries Réunies.

Hemming, J. (1987) *Amazon Frontier: The Defeat of the Brazilian Indians*, London: Macmillan.

Henriques, J. A. (1917) *A Ilha de S. Tomé sob o Ponto de Vista Histórico-natural e Agrícola*, Coimbra 1917: Imprensa da Universidade.

Herrera Canales, I. (1980) *Estadística del Comercio Exterior de México, 1821–1875*, Mexico City: Instituto Nacional de Antropologia e Historia.

Hewett, C. (1862) *Chocolate and Cocoa: Its Growth and Culture, Manufacture, and Modes of Preparation for the Table*, London: Simpkin, Marshall & Co.

Hill, P. (1963) *Migrant Cocoa-farmers of Southern Ghana: A Study in Rural Capitalism*, Cambridge, Cambridge University Press.

Hinkle, S. F. (1964) *Hershey: Far-sighted Confectioner, Famous Chocolate, Fine Community*, New York: Newcomen Society.

Historicus (R. Cadbury) (1892) *Cocoa: All about it*, London: Sampson Low, Marston & Co.

Hodges, T. and Newitt, M. (1988) *São Tomé and Príncipe: From Plantation Colony to Microstate*, Boulder: Westview Press.

Hoetink, H. (1970) 'The Dominican Republic in the nineteenth century: some notes on stratification, immigration and race', in M. Mörner (ed.) *Race and Class in Latin America*, 96–121, New York: Columbia University Press.

——(1988) 'Labour "scarcity" and immigration in the Dominican Republic, *c*. 1875–*c*. 1930', in M. Cross and G. Heuman (eds) *Labour in the Caribbean: From Emancipation to Independence*, 160–75, London: Macmillan.

Hogendorp, C. S. W. de (1830) *Coup d'Oeil sur l'Ile de Java et les Autres Possessions Néerlandaises dans l'Archipel des Indes*, Brussels: C. J. de Mat.

Holsoe, S. (1977) 'Slavery and economic response among the Vai', in S. Miers and I. Kopytoff (eds) *Slavery in Africa: Historical and Anthropological Perspectives*, 287–303, Madison: University of Wisconsin Press.

Holton, I. F. (1967) *New Granada: Twenty Months in the Andes* (abridged edn) Carbondale: Southern Illinois University Press.

Honychurch, L. (1984) *The Dominica Story: A History of the Island*, Roseau: The Dominica Institute.

Hopkins, A. G. (1973) *An Economic History of West Africa*, London, Longman.

——(1978) 'Innovation in a colonial context: Nigerian cocoa farming, 1880–1920', in C. Dewey and A. G. Hopkins (eds) *The Imperial Impact: Studies in the Economic History of Africa and India*, 83–96, London, Athlone Press.

Horlings, E. (1995) 'An economic explanation of the late abolition of slavery in Suriname', in G. Oostindie (ed.) *Fifty Years Later: Antislavery, Capitalism and Modernity in the Dutch Orbit*, 105–16, Leiden: KITLV.

Humboldt, A. von (1811) *Essai Politique sur le Royaume de la Nouvelle Espagne*, Paris: F. Schoell.

——(1852) *Personal Narrative of Travels to the Equinoctial Regions of America during the Years 1799 to 1804*, London: George Routledge and Sons.

——(1941) *Viaje a las Regiones Equinocciales del Nuevo Continente*, Caracas: Ministerio de Educación.

Humphreys, R. A. (1940) *British Consular Reports on the Trade and Politics of Latin America, 1824–1826*, London: Royal Historical Society.

Hunger, F. W. T (1913) 'Cacao', in H. C. Prinsen Geerlings (ed.) *Dr K. W. van Gorkom's Oost-Indische Cultures, Opnieuw Uitgegeven*, II, 357–458, Amsterdam: J. H. de Bussy.

Hussey, R. D. (1934) *The Caracas Company, 1728–1784: A Study in the History of Spanish Monopolistic Trade*, Cambridge: Harvard University Press.

Hyland, R. P. (1982) 'A fragile prosperity: credit and agrarian structure in the Cauca valley, Colombia, 1851–87', *Hispanic American Historical Review*, 62, 3, 369–406.

Ileto, R. C. (1971) *Magindanao 1860–1888: The Career of Datu Uto of Buayan*, Ithaca: Cornell University Press.

Instituto Brasileiro de Geografia e Estatística (1987) *Estatísticas Históricas do Brasil*, Rio de Janeiro.

Instituto de Economia e Finanças da Bahia (1960) *A Zona Cacaueira*, Salvador: Universidade da Bahia.

Israel, J. I. (1989) *European Jewry in the Age of Mercantilism, 1550–1750*, Oxford: Clarendon Press.

——(1990) *Dutch Primacy in World Trade, 1585–1740*, Oxford: Clarendon Press.

Izard, M. (1970) *Series Estadísticas para la Historia de Venezuela*, Mérida.

——(1972) 'La agricultura venezolana en una época de transición, 1777–1830', *Boletín Histórico, Fundación John Boulton*, 28, 81–145.

——(1979) *El Miedo a la Revolución: La Lucha por la Libertad en Venezuela, 1777–1830*, Madrid: Tecnos.

Jackson, J. C. (1968) *Planters and Speculators: Chinese and European Agricultural Enterprises in Malaya, 1786–1921*, Kuala Lumpur: University of Malaya Press.

Jagor, F. (1875) *Travels in the Philippines*, London: Chapman and Hall.

Janes, H. and Sayers, H. J. (1963) *The Story of Czarnikow*, London: Harley.

Jeandelle, R. and Robert, P. (1994) 'Noisiel, un nouveau destin pour la chocolaterie Menier', *La Revue du Musée des Arts et Métiers*, 6, 51–8.

Jesús, E. C. de (1980) *The Tobacco Monopoly in the Philippines: Bureaucratic Enterprise and Social Change, 1766–1880*, Quezon City: Ateneo de Manila University Press.

Joachim, B. (1972) 'Commerce et décolonisation: l'expérience Franco-Haïtienne au XIXe siècle', *Annales: Economies, Sociétés, Civilisations*, 27, 1497–1525.

John, A. M. (1988) *The Plantation Slaves of Trinidad, 1783–1816: A Mathematical and Demographic Enquiry*, Cambridge: Cambridge University Press.

Johnson, H. (1987) 'Merchant credit and the dispossession of the cocoa peasantry in Trinidad in the late nineteenth century', *Peasant Studies*, 15, 1, 27–38.

Johnson, W. H. (1917) 'Cocoa in the southern provinces and colony of Nigeria', *Transactions of the Third International Congress of Tropical Agriculture, 1914*, II, 189–99, London: John Bale, Sons, and Danielson.

Johnston, J. (1865) *The Chemistry of Common Life*, London: W. Blackwood.

Jong, T. P. M. (1966) *De Krimpende Horizon van de Hollandse Kooplieden: Hollands Welvaren in het Caribisch Zeegebied, 1780–1830*, Assen: Van Gorcum.

Jumelle, H. (1900) *Le Cacaoyer: Sa Culture et son Exploitation dans tous les Pays de Production*, Paris: Augustin Challamel.

Kaerger, K. (1901) *Landwirtschaft und Kolonisation im Spanischen Amerika*, Leipzig: Duncker und Humbolt.

Kany, C. E. (1932) *Life and Manners in Madrid, 1750–1800*, Berkeley: University of California Press.

Karlsson, W. (1975) *Manufacturing in Venezuela: Studies on Development and Location*, Stockholm: Almqvist & Wiksell.

Katz, S. (1992) 'Un regard juif sur l'exotisme, Peretz Hirschbein au Brésil, 1914', *Cahiers du Brésil Contemporain*, 19, 25–41.

Keesing, F. M. (1934) *Modern Samoa: Its Government and Changing Life*, London: Allen and Unwin.

Keller, F. (1874) *The Amazon and Madeira Rivers: Sketches and Descriptions from the Note-book of an Explorer*, London: Chapman and Hall.

Kicza, J. E. (1983) *Colonial Entrepreneurs: Families and Business in Bourbon Mexico City*, Albuquerque: University of New Mexico Press.

Kidder, D. P. (1845) *Sketches of Residence and Travel in Brazil*, London: Wiley and Putnam.

King, A. R. (1974) *Coban and the Verapaz: History and Cultural Process in Northern Guatemala*, New Orleans: Tulane University Press.

Klooster, W. (1997) 'Contraband trade by Curaçao's Jews with countries of idolatry, 1660–1800', *Studia Rosenthaliana*, 31, 1–2, 58–73.

——(1998) *Illicit Riches: Dutch trade in the Caribbean, 1648–1795*, Leiden: KITLV.

Klopstock, F. (1937) *Kakao: Wandlungen in der Erzeugung und der Verwendung des Kakaos nach dem Weltkrieg*, Leipzig: Bibliographisches Institut.

Knaap, G. J. (1987) *Memories van Overgave van Gouverneurs van Ambon in de Zeventiende en Achtiende Eeuw*, The Hague: M. Nijhoff.

Knapp, A. W. (1920) *Cocoa and Chocolate: Their History from Plantation to Consumer*, London: Chapman and Hall.

——(1923) *The Cocoa and Chocolate Industry: The Tree, the Bean, the Beverage*, London: Pitman.

——(1930) *The Cocoa and Chocolate Industry: The Tree, the Bean, the Beverage*, London: Pitman.

Knight, F. W. (1990) *The Caribbean: The Genesis of a Fragmented Nationalism*, New York: Oxford University Press.

Kramer, K. (1991) 'Plantation development in Berbice from 1753 to 1779: the shift from the interior to the coast', *Nieuwe West-Indische Gids*, 65, 1–2, 51–65.

Kurian, R. (1989) 'State, capital and labour in the plantation industry in Sri Lanka, 1834–1982', Ph.D. thesis, University of Amsterdam.

Laan, H. L. van der (1997) *The Trans-oceanic Marketing Channel: A New Tool for Understanding Tropical Africa's Export Agriculture*, Binghampton: International Business Press.

Ladd, D. M. (1976) *The Mexican Nobility at Independence, 1780–1826*, Austin: University of Texas Press.

Lambert Ortiz, E. (1968) *The Complete Book of Mexican Cooking*, New York: Bantam Books.

Lami, E. A. (1885) *Dictionnaire Encyclopédique et Biographique de l'Industrie et des Arts Industriels*, vol. 2, 26–8; vol. 3, 293–348, Paris.

Landaeta Rosales, M. (1963) *Gran Recopilación Geográfica, Estadística e Histórica de Venezuela*, Caracas: Banco Central de Venezuela.

Lange, A. (1914) *The Lower Amazon*, New York: G. P. Putnam's Sons.

Langer, Erick (1989) *Economic Change and Rural Resistance in Southern Bolivia, 1880–1930*, Stanford: Stanford University Press.

Lanuza, A., Vázquez, J. L., Barahona, A. and Chamorro, A. (1983) *Economía y Sociedad en la Construcción del Estado en Nicaragua*, San José: ICAP.

Larson, B. (1988) *Colonialism and Agrarian Transformation in Bolivia, Cochabamba, 1550–1900*, Princeton: Princeton University Press.

Lass, R. A. and Wood, G. A. R. (1985) *Cocoa Production: Present Constraints and Priorities for Research*, Washington: World Bank (Technical Paper no. 29).

Lasserre, G. (1961) *La Guadeloupe: Etude Géographique*, Bordeaux: Union Française d'Impression.

Laviana Cuetos, M. L. (1987) *Guayaquil en el Siglo XVIII: Recursos Naturales y Desarollo Económico*, Seville: Escuela de Estudios Hispano-Americanos.

Le Cointe, P. (1922) *L'Amazonie Brésilienne*, Paris: A. Challamel.

Leal, I. (1984) 'La provincia de Maracaibo en 1791 segun un informe del segundo intendente de Caracas, Don Francisco de Saavedra', *Boletín de la Academia Nacional de la Historia*, 64, 267, 487–503.

Légier, E. (1905) *La Martinique et la Guadeloupe: Considérations sur l'Avenir et la Culture de la Canne, la Production du Sucre et du Rhum, et les Cultures Secondaires dans les Antilles Françaises*, Paris: Bureaux de la Sucrerie Indigène et Coloniale.

Léon, H. (1893) *Histoire des Juifs de Bayonne*, Paris: A. Durlacher.

Léon, P. (1963) *Marchands et Spéculateurs Dauphinois dans le Monde Antillais: Les Dolle et les Raby*, Paris: Les Belles Lettres.

León Borja, D. and Szászdi Nagy, A. (1964) 'El comercio del cacao de Guayaquil', *Revista de Historia de América*, 57–58, 1–50.

Leonard, P. G. (1973) 'A drinke called chocolate', *Mankind Magazine*, 4, 3, 44–51.

Lepkowski, T. (1968) *Haití*, Havana: CASA.

Lerda de Tejada, M. (1853) *Comercio Esterior de México, desde la Conquista hasta Hoy*, Mexico City: Rafael Rafael.

Lesser, J. H. (1996) '(Re)creating ethnicity: Middle Eastern immigration to Brazil', *The Americas*, 53, 1, 45–63.

Leubuscher, C. (1962) *The West African Shipping Trade, 1909–1959*, Leiden: A. W. Sythoff.

Lévy, P. (1873) *Notas Geográficas y Económicas sobre la República de Nicaragua*, Paris: Libreria Española de E. D. Schmitz.

Lévine, V. (1914) *Colombia: Physical Features, Natural Resources, Means of Communication, Manufactures and Industrial Development*, London: Pitman.

Libert, M. (1996) 'La consommation du chocolat dans les Pays-Bas Autrichiens', in E. Collet (ed.) *Chocolat: De la Boisson Elitaire au Bâton Populaire*, 75–80, Brussels: CGER.

Liehr, R. (1989) 'La deuda exterior de la Gran colombia frente a Gran Bretaña, 1820–1860', in R. Liehr (ed.) *América Latina en la Epoca de Simón Bolívar: La Formación de las Economías Nacionales y los Intereses Ecónomicos Europeos, 1800–1850*, 465–80, Berlin: Colloquium.

Lier, R. A. J. van (1971) *Frontier Society: A Social Analysis of the History of Surinam*, translated from Dutch, The Hague: M. Nijhoff.

Lieuwen, E. (1965) *Venezuela*, London: Royal Institute of International Affairs.

Lima, J. J. Lopes de (1844) *Ensaio sobre a Statistica das Ilhas de S. Thomé e Principe no Golfo de Guiné e sua Dependencia o Forte de S. João Baptista de Ajudá na Costa de Léste Chamada dos Popós além da Mina*, Lisbon: Imprensa Nacional

Linhares, T. (1969) *Historia Econômica do Maté*, Rio de Janeiro: Livraria José Olympio.

Liniger-Goumaz, M. (1979) *La Guinée Equatoriale: Un Pays Méconnu*, Paris: L'Harmattan.

Lobdell, R. A. (1988) 'British officials and the West Indian peasantry, 1842–1938', in M. Cross and G. Heuman (eds) *Labour in the Caribbean: From Emancipation to Independence*, 195–207, London: Macmillan.

Lombardi, J. V. (1971) *The Decline and Abolition of Negro Slavery in Venezuela, 1820–1854*, Westport: Greenwood Press.

——(1974) 'The abolition of slavery in Venezuela: a nonevent', in R. B. Toplin (ed.) *Slavery and Race Relations in Latin America*, 228–52, Wesport: Greenwood Press.

Loney, N. (1964) *A Britisher in the Philippines*, Manila: National Library.

Lopo, J. de Castro (1963) 'Para a história do cacau de Angola', *Actividade Económica de Angola*, 65, 33–56.

Lovejoy, P. (1995) 'Kola nuts, the "coffee" of the central Sudan', in J. Goodman, P. Lovejoy and A. Sherratt (eds) *Consuming Habits: Drugs in History and Anthropology*, 103–25, London: Routledge.

Lucena Salmoral, M. (1984) 'The commerce of La Guaira with the United States during the Venezuelan revolutionary juncture', in J. A. Barbier and A. J. Kuethe (eds) *The North American Role in the Spanish Imperial Economy, 1760–1819*, 158–76, Manchester: Manchester University Press.

——(1990) *Características del Comercio Exterior de la Provincia de Caracas durante el Sexenio Revolucionario, 1807–1812*, Madrid: Instituto de Cooperación Iberoamericana.

——(1992) *Los Mercados Exteriores de Caracas a Comienzos de la Independencia*, Caracas: Academia Nacional de la Historia.

Lynn, M. (1997) *Commerce and Economic Change in West Africa: The Palm Oil Trade in the Nineteenth Century*, Cambridge: Cambridge University Press.

Macau, J. (1973) *La Guinée Danoise*, Aix-en-Provence: IHPO.

McCoy, A. W. (1982) 'A queen dies slowly: the rise and decline of Iloilo city', in A. W. McCoy and E. de Jesús (eds) *Philippine Social History, Global Trade and Local Transformations*, 297–358, Quezon City: Ateneo de Manila University Press.

McCreery, D. (1983) 'Debt servitude in rural Guatemala, 1876–1936', *Hispanic American Historical Review*, 63, 4, 735–59.

——(1994) *Rural Guatemala, 1760–1940*, Stanford: Stanford University Press.

McCusker, J. J. (1974) 'Les équivalents métriques des poids et mesures du commerce colonial aux XVIIe et XVIIIe siècles', *Revue Française d'Histoire d'Outre-Mer*, 61, 224, 349–65.

McFarlane, A. (1993) *Colombia before Independence: Economy, Society and Politics under Bourbon Rule*, Cambridge: Cambridge University Press.

McGreevey, W. P. (1971) *An Economic History of Colombia, 1845–1930*, Cambridge: Cambridge University Press.

Macgregor, J. (1843–50) *Commercial Statistics: A Digest*, London: Whitaker Publishers.

Mackenzie, C. (1971) *Notes on Haiti, Made During a Residence in the Republic*, London: Cass.

McKinley, P. M. (1985) *Pre-revolutionary Caracas: Politics, Economy and Society, 1777–1811*, Cambridge: Cambridge University Press.

MacLachlan, C. M. (1973) 'The Indian labour structure in the Portuguese Amazon, 1700–1800', in D. Alden (ed.) *Colonial Roots of Modern Brazil*, 199–230, Berkeley and Los Angeles: University of California Press.

——(1974) 'African slave trade and economic development in Amazonia, 1700–1800', in R. B. Toplin (ed.) *Slavery and Race Relations in Latin America*, 112–45, Wesport: Greenwood Press.

Maclaren, W. A. (1924) *Rubber, Tea and Cacao, with Special Sections on Coffee, Spices and Tobacco*, London: Benn.

MacLeod, M. (1973) *Spanish Central America: A Socioeconomic History, 1520–1720*, Berkeley: University of California Press.

McLynn, F. (1994) *Robert Louis Stevenson: A Biography*, London: Pimlico.

MacMicking, R. (1967) *Recollections of Manilla and the Philippines during 1848, 1849 and 1850*, Manila: Filipiana Book.

MacMillan, H. F. (1925) *Tropical Gardening and Planting, with Special Reference to Ceylon*: Colombo: Times of Ceylon.

Mahabir, N. (1987) 'East Indians in Grenada: a study in absorption', in I. Singh (ed.) *Indians in the Caribbean*, 370–404, New Delhi: Sterling Publishers.

Mahony, M. A. (1996) 'The world cacao made: society, politics and history in southern Bahia, Brazil, 1822–1919', Ph.D. thesis, Yale University.

Maiguashca, J. (1996) 'Ecuadorian cocoa production and trade, 1840–1925', in W. G. Clarence-Smith (ed.) *Cocoa Pioneer Fronts since 1800: The Role of Smallholders, Planters and Merchants*, 65–85, London: Macmillan.

Malaurie, A. and Gazzano, J. M. (1888) *La Industria Argentina y la Exposición del Paraná*, Buenos Aires: J. M. Gazzano e Cía.

Mallat, J. (1983) *The Philippines: History, Geography, Customs, Agriculture, Industry and Commerce of the Spanish Colonies in Oceania*, Manila: National Historical Institute.

Mam-Lam-Fouck, S. (1986) 'Apogée, déclin et disparition du système esclavagiste, première moitié du XIXe siècle', in A.-M. Bruleaux, R. Calmont and S. Mam-Lam-Fouck (eds) *Deux Siècles d'Esclavage en Guyane Française, 1652–1848*, 119–282, Paris: L'Harmattan.

Mangin, A. (1860) *Le Cacao et le Chocolat, Considérés aux Points de Vue Botanique, Chimique, Physiologique, Agricole, Commercial, Industriel et Economique*, Paris: Guillaumin et Cie.

Mantero, F. (1910) *A mão d'Obra em S. Thomé e Principe*, Lisbon: Annuario Commercial.

Marcoy, P. (1875) *Travels in South America, from the Pacific Ocean to the Atlantic Ocean*, London: Blackie & Son.

Marrero, L. (1951) *Geografía de Cuba*, Havana: Alfa.

——(1972–89) *Cuba: Economía y Sociedad*, Madrid: Playor.

Marte, R. (1984) *Estadísticas y Documentos Históricos sobre Santo Domingo, 1805–1890*, Santo Domingo: Museo Nacional de Historia y Geografía.

Martínez, M. A. (1988) *Aspectos Económicos de la Epoca de Bolívar*, Caracas: Academia Nacional de la Historia.

Martínez Assad, C. (1991) *El Laboratorio de la Revolución: El Tabasco Garridista*, Mexico City: Siglo XXI.

Mas, S. de (1843) *Informe sobre el Estado de las Islas Filipinas en 1842*, Madrid: (no publisher).

Mathew, W. M. (1981) *The House of Gibbs and the Peruvian Guano Monopoly*, London: Royal Historical Society.

——(1989) 'Britain and the Bolivarian republics, 1820–1850, the interimperium and the tariff', in R. Liehr (ed.) *América Latina en la Epoca de Simón Bolívar: La Formación de las Economías Nacionales y los Intereses Económicos Europeos, 1800–1850*, 397–421, Berlin: Colloquium.

May, L.-P. (1930) *Histoire Economique de la Martinique, 1635–1763*, Paris: Les Presses Modernes.

Mbokolo, E. (1981) *Noirs et Blancs en Afrique Equatoriale: Les Sociétés Côtières et la Pénétration Française, vers 1820–1874*, Paris: Ecole des Hautes Etudes en Sciences Sociales.

Mecklenburg, A. F., Duke of (1913) *From the Congo to the Niger and the Nile: An Account of the German Central African Expedition of 1910 to 1911*, London: Duckworth & Co.

Medina, C. (1900) *Le Nicaragua en 1900*, Paris: Kugelmann.

Medina Hernández, A. (1993) 'Los Mames', in Víctor M. Esponda Jimeno (ed.) *La Población Indígena de Chiapas*, 399–482, Tuxtla Guttiérez: Gobierno del Estado de Chiapas.

Mentz, B. von, Radkau, V., Scharrer, B. and Turner, G. (1982) *Los Pioneros del Imperialismo Alemán en México*, Mexico City: Casa Chata.

Merril Lynch (1972) *Cocoa*, New York.

Mesquita, J. (1918) *Dados Estatísticos para o Estudo das Pautas de Angola: Exportação pelas Alfândegas do Círculo e do Congo nos Anos de 1888 a 1913*, Luanda: Imprensa Nacional.

Métraux, A. (1946) 'The Botocudo', in J. H. Steward (ed.) *Handbook of South American Indians*, I, 531–40, Washington: Government Printing Office.

Michel, M. (1969) 'Les plantations allemandes du Mont Cameroun, 1885–1914', *Revue Française d'Histoire d'Outremer*, 57, 2, 183–213.

Middleton (1871) 'Report by Mr. Consul-General Middleton upon the production of cocoa and coffee in Venezuela', *Parliamentary Papers* 1871, House of Commons, LXV, c. 343.

Milburn, W. (1825) *Oriental Commerce*, London: Kingsbury, Parbury and Allen.

Miller, H. H. (1920) *Economic Conditions in the Philippines*, Boston: Ginn & Co.

Milstead, H. P. (1940) 'Cacao industry of Grenada', *Economic Geography*, 16, 2, 195–203.

Mina, M. (1975) *Esclavitud y Libertad en el Valle del Río Cauca*, Bogotá: Fundación Rosca.

Mintz, S. W. (1985) *Sweetness and Power: The Place of Sugar in Modern History*, New York: Viking.

Mitchell, B. R. (1992) *International Historical Statistics, Europe 1750–1988*, London: Macmillan.

Mitchell, K. L. (1942) *Industrialization in the Western Pacific*, New York: Institute of Pacific Relations.

Mollien, G. T. (1824) *Travels in the Republic of Colombia in the Years 1822 and 1823*, London: C. Knight.

Monbeig, P. (1937) 'Colonisation, peuplement et plantation de cacao dans le sud de l'état de Bahia', *Annales de Géographie*, 46, 278–99.

Monga, Y. D. (1996) 'The emergence of Duala cocoa planters under German rule in Cameroun: a case study', in W. G. Clarence-Smith (ed.) *Cocoa Pioneer Fronts Since 1800: The Role of Smallholders, Planters and Merchants*, 119–36, London: Macmillan.

Moodie-Kublalsingh, S. (1994) *The Cocoa Panyols of Trinidad: An Oral Record*, London: British Academic Press.

Moor, J. H. (ed.) (1968) *Notices of the Indian Archipelago and Adjacent Countries*, London: Cass.

Moorne (1893) *Las Industrias Fabriles en Buenos Aires*, Buenos Aires: Librairie Française de Joseph Escary.

Moral, P. (1959) *L'Economie Haïtienne*, Port-au-Prince: Imprimerie de l'Etat.

——(1961) *Le Paysan Haïtien: Etude sur la Vie Rurale en Haïti*, Paris: G. P. Maisonneuve et Larose.

Moreau de Saint-Méry, M. L. F. (1944) *Descripción de la Parte Española de Santo Domingo*, Ciudad Trujillo: Editora Montalvo.

Moreira Júnior, M. A. (1905) *Relatorio Referente ás Provincias Ultramarinas e ao Districto Autonomo de Timor*, Lisbon: Imprensa Nacional.

Mörner, M. (1985) *Adventurers and Proletarians: The Story of Migrants in Latin America*, Pittsburgh: University of Pittsburgh Press.

——(1992) 'Immigration into Latin America, especially Argentina and Chile', in P. C. Emmer and M. Mörner (eds) *European Expansion and Migration: Essays on the Intercontinental Migration from Africa, Asia and Europe*, 211–43, Oxford: Berg.

——(1996) 'Inserción del fenómeno vasco en la emigración europea a América', in R. Escobedo Mansilla *et al.* (eds) *Emigración y Redes Sociales de los Vascos en América*, 15–30, Vitoria-Gasteiz: Euskal Herriko Unibertsitatea.

Mulhall, M. G. (1899) *Dictionary of Statistics*, London: George Routledge & Co.

Multatuli (E. Douwes Dekker) (1991) *Max Havelaar, of de Koffiveilingen der Nederlandsche Handelmaatschappy*, Amsterdam: Querido.

Nardin, J.-C. (1969) *La Mise en Valeur de l'Ile de Tabago, 1763–1783*, Paris: Mouton.

Negreiros, A. de Almada (*c.* 1908) *Les Colonies Portugaises: Etudes Documentaires; Produits d'Exportation*, Paris: A. Challamel.

Nembro, M. da (1958) *Storia dell'Attività Missionaria dei Minori Cappuccini nel Brasile, 1538?–1889*, Rome: Institutum Historicum OFMC.

Newman, R. (1995) 'Opium smoking in late imperial China: a reconsideration', *Modern Asian Studies*, 29, 4, 765–94.

Newson, L. A. (1976) *Aboriginal and Spanish Colonial Trinidad: A Study in Culture Contact*, London: Academic Press.

——(1987) *Indian Survival in Colonial Nicaragua*, Norman: University of Oklahoma Press.

Nicholls, D. (1992) 'Lebanese of the Antilles: Haïti, Dominican Republic, Jamaica and Trinidad', in A. Hourani and N. Shehadi (eds) *The Lebanese in the World: A Century of Emigration*, 339–60, London: I. B. Tauris.

——(1996) *From Dessalines to Duvalier: Race, Colour and National Independence in Haiti*, London: Macmillan.

Nichols, R. F. (1933) 'Trade relations and the establishment of the United States consulates in Spanish America, 1779–1809', *Hispanic American Historical Review*, 13, 3, 289–313.

Niephaus, H.-T. (1975) *Genuas Seehandel von 1746–1848: Die Entwicklung der Handelsbeziehungen zur Iberischen Halbinsel, zu West- und Nordeuropa, sowie den Überseegebieten*, Cologne: Böhlau.

Nogueira, A. F. (1893) *A Ilha de S. Thomé, a Questão Bancaria no Ultramar e o nosso Problema Colonial*, Lisbon: Jornal As Colonias Portuguezas.

Norbury, F. (1970) 'Venezuela', in W. A. Lewis (ed.) *Tropical Development, 1880–1913*, 128–46, Evanston: Allen and Unwin.

Norero, A. (1910) *El Cacao y su Cultivo: Ensayo sobre la Agricultura del Ecuador*, Madrid: Librería General de Victoriano Suárez.

Nørregard, G. (1966) *Danish Settlements in West Africa, 1658–1850*, Boston: Boston University Press.

Northrup, D. (1995) *Indentured Labor in the Age of Imperialism, 1834–1922*, Cambridge: Cambridge University Press.

Nosti, J. (1948) *Agricultura de Guinea, Promesa para España*, Madrid, IEA.

Novais, F. A. (1979) *Portugal e Brasil na Crise do Antigo Sistema Colonial, 1777–1808*, São Paulo: Editora Hucitec.

Nuñez, E. B. (1972) *Cacao*, Caracas: Banco Central de Venezuela.

Ocampo, J. A. (1984) *Colombia y la Economia Mundial, 1830–1910*, Bogotá: Siglo XXI.

Oficina de Informaciones de Chiapas (1895) *Chiapas, su Estado Actual, su Riqueza, sus Ventajes para los Negocios*, Mexico City.

Oficina del Periodismo (1921) *Guia Comercial e Industrial del Perú*, Lima: Empresa Tip. Unión.

Oliva Melgar, J. M. (1987) *Cataluña y el Comercio Privilegiado con América en el Siglo XVIII: La Real Compañia de Comercio de Barcelona a Indias*, Barcelona: Universitat de Barcelona.

Olivares, F. R. (1988) *El Cacao, Introducción y Fomento en República Dominicana*, Santo Domingo: 1988.

Olivier, J. (1834–37) *Reizen in den Molukschen Archipel naar Makassar en z., in het Gevolg van den Gouverneur-Generaal van Nederlandsch-Indië*, Amsterdam: G. J. A. Beijerinck.

Omboni, T. (1846) *Viaggi nell'Africa Occidentale*, Milan: Civelli.

Oostindie, G. (ed.) (1995) *Fifty Years Later: Antislavery, Capitalism and Modernity in the Dutch Orbit*, Leiden: KITLV.

Orbigny, A. d' (1992) *Descripción Geográfica, Histórica, y Estadística de Bolivia, Departamento del Beni, Provincia Caupolicán y Moxos*, Santa Cruz: Gobierno Municipal de Santa Cruz.

Ortiz de la Tabla, J. (1978) *Comercio Exterior de Veracruz, 1778–1821: Crisis de Dependencia*, Seville: Ecscuela de Estudios Hispano-Americanos.

Orton, J. (1876) *The Andes and the Amazon*, New York: Harper & Bros.

Osborne, H. (1955) *Bolivia: A Land Divided*, London: Royal Institute of International Affairs.

Ospina Vázquez, L. (1955) *Industria y Protección en Colombia, 1810–1930*, Medellín: Santafé.

Othick, J. (1976) 'The cocoa and chocolate industry in the nineteenth century', in D. Oddy and D. Miller (eds) *The Making of the Modern British Diet*, 77–90, London: Croom Helm.

Owen, N. G. (1984) *Prosperity without Progress: Manila Hemp and Material Life in the Colonial Philippines*, Berkeley: University of California Press.

Paixão, Braga (c. 1964) *Cem Anos do Banco Nacional Ultramarino, 1864–1964*, Lisbon: Banco Nacional Ultramarino.

Palerm Rincón, C. (ed.) (1982) *Depachos de los Consules Norteamericanos en Puerto Rico, 1818–1866, Tomo I*, San Juan: Universidad de Puerto Rico.

Panday, R. M. N. (1959) *Agriculture in Surinam, 1650–1950: An Enquiry into the Causes of its Decline*, Amsterdam: H. J. Paris.

Parrón Salas, C. (1995) *De las Reformas Borbónicas a la República: El Consulado y el Comercio Marítimo de Lima, 1778–1821*, San Javier (Murcia): Academia General del Aire.

Patch, R. W. (1993) *Maya and Spaniard in Yucatan, 1648–1812*, Stanford: Stanford University Press.

Paterson, D. (1972) *A Topographical Description of the Island of Grenada*, St George's (Grenada): Carenage Press.

Patiño, V. M. (1963) *Plantas Cultivadas y Animales Domesticos en America Equinoccial, Tomo I: Frutales*, Cali: Imprenta Departamental.

Pedler, F. (1974) *The Lion and the Unicorn in Africa: The United Africa Company, 1787–1931*, London: Heinemann.

Pelletier, E. and Pelletier, A. (1861) *Le Thé et le Chocolat dans l'Alimentation Publique*, Paris: Compagnie Française des Chocolats et des Thés.

Peña, M. T. de la (1951) *Chiapas Económico*, Tuxtla Gutiérrez: Dto. de Prensa y Turismo.

Pereira, M. Halpern (1981) *A Política Portuguesa de Emigração, 1850–1930*, Lisbon: A Regra do Jogo.

——(1983) *Livre-Câmbio e Desenvolvimento Económico, Portugal na Deguna Metade do Século XIX*, Lisbon: Sá da Costa.

Pereira Filho, C. (1959) *Ilhéus, Terra de Cacau*, Rio de Janeiro: Andes.

Pérez de la Riva, F. (1944) *El Café, Historia de su Cultivo y Explotación en Cuba*, Havana: J. Montero.

Pérez Junior, L. A. (1989) *Lords of the Mountain: Social Banditry and Peasant Protest in Cuba, 1878–1918*, Pittsburgh: University of Pittsburgh Press.

Peterson, J. (1969) *Province of Freedom: A History of Sierra Leone, 1787–1870*, London: Faber and Faber.

Pezuela, J. de la (1863–66) *Diccionario Geográfico, Estadístico, Histórico de la Isla de Cuba*, Madrid: Mellado.

Phillips, A. (1989) *The Enigma of Colonialism: British Policy in West Africa*, London: J. Currey.

Phillips, J. D. (1947) *Salem and the Indies*, Boston: Houghton Mifflin Co.

Phillips Lewis, K. (1996) 'The Trinidad cocoa industry and the struggle for Crown land during the nineteenth century', in W. G. Clarence-Smith (ed.) *Cocoa Pioneer Fronts since 1800: The Role of Smallholders, Planters and Merchants*, 45–64, London: Macmillan.

Pineo, R. F. (1996) *Social and Economic Reform in Ecuador: Life and Work in Guayaquil*, Gainesville: University Press of Florida.

Piñero, E. (1988) 'The cacao economy of the eighteenth-century province of Caracas and the Spanish cacao market', *Hispanic American Historical Review*, 68, 1, 75–100.

——(1992) 'Accounting practices in a colonial economy: a case study of cacao haciendas in colonial Venezuela', paper, later published in *The Colonial Latin America Historical Review*.

——(1993) 'Cacao output, world demand and the domestic economy of Venezuela, 1800–1860', paper for conference 'Cocoa production and economic development in the 19th and 20th centuries', London, School of Oriental and African Studies and London School of Economics and Political Science.

——(1994) *The Town of San Felipe and Colonial Cacao Economies*, Philadelphia: American Philosophical society (Transactions, 84, 3).

Plummer, B. G. (1988) *Haiti and the Great Powers, 1902–1915*, Baton Rouge: Louisiana State University Press.

——(1998) 'Between privilege and opprobrium: the Arabs and Jews in Haïti', in Ignacio Klich and Jeffrey Lesser (eds) *Arab and Jewish Immigration in Latin America: Images and Realities*, 80–93, London: Cass.

Pohl, H. (1963) *Die Beziehungen Hamburgs zu Spanien und dem Spanischen Amerika in der Zeit von 1740 bis 1806*, Wiesbaden: Franz Steiner Verlag.

Polanco Martínez, T. (1960) *Esbozo sobre Historia Económica Venezolana*, Madrid: Ediciones Guadarrama.

Ponsard, R. Mesnier de (1912) *Plantation Roça Porto-Alegre*, Lisbon: Tip. do Comercio

Posada, E. and Ibáñez, P. M. (eds) (1910) *Relaciones de Mando: Memorias Presentadas por los Gobernantes del Nuevo Reino de Granada*, Bogotá: Imprenta Nacional.

Posada Carbó, E. (1996) *The Colombian Caribbean: A Regional History, 1870–1950*, Oxford: Oxford University Press.

Poskin, A. (1900) *Bilans Congolais: Etude sur la Valeur Commerciale du Congo par Rapport à la Belgique*, Brussels: Société Belge de Librairie.

Posthumus, N. W. (1946) *Inquiry into the History of Prices in Holland, Volume 1: Wholesale Prices at the Exchange of Amsterdam 1585–1914; Rates of Exchange at Amsterdam, 1609–1914*, Leiden: E. J. Brill.

Postma, J. (1994) 'The fruits of slave labour: tropical commodities from Surinam to Holland, 1683–1794', unpublished paper supplied by the author.

Potash, R. A. (1959) *El Banco de Avío de México: El Fomento de la Industria, 1821–1846*, Mexico City: Fondo de Cultura Económica.

Potthast, B. (1998) *Die Mosquitoküste im Spannungsfeld britischer und spanischer Politik*, 1502–1821, Cologne: Böhlau.

Prados de la Escosura, L. (1982) 'Comercio exterior y cambio económico en España, 1792–1849', in Josep Fontana (ed.) *La Economia Española al Final del Antiguo Régimen, III: Comercio y Colonias*, 173–249, Madrid: Alianza

Preuss, P. (1987) *Cocoa: Its Cultivation and Preparation*, Brussels: International Office of Cocoa and Chocolate.

Preziosi, A. (1976) *Fermenti Patriottici, Religiosi, e Sociali all'Isola d'Elba, 1821–1921*, Florence: L. S. Olschki.

Quesada Camacho, J. R. (1977–78) 'Algunos aspectos de la historia económica del cacao en Costa Rica, 1880–1930', *Revista de Historia* (San José), 5, 65–100, and 6, 69–110.

——(1989) 'El cacao: el grano de oro de la Región Atlántica', in G. Carvajal (ed.) *Estado de la Investigación Científica y de la Acción Social sobre la Región Atlántica de Costa Rica*, 85–111, San José: Universidad de Costa Rica.

Rabana, R. (1895) *Estado de Chiapas: Geografía y Estadística*, Mexico City: Cuerpo Especial de Estado Mayor.

Ragatz, L. J. (1928) *Statistics for the Study of British Caribbean Economic History*, London: Bryan Edwards Press.

——(1977) *The Fall of the Planter Class in the British Caribbean, 1763–1833*, New York: Octagon Books.

Rangel, D. A. (1974) *Capital y Desarollo, Tomo Primero: La Etapa Agraria*, Caracas: Universidad Central de Venezuela.

Reed, N. (1964) *The Caste War of Yucatán*, Stanford: Stanford University Press.

Rego, A. da Silva (1966) *Relações Luso-Brasileiras, 1822–1953*, Lisbon: Panorama.

Reid, A. (1988) *Southeast Asia in the Age of Commerce, 1450–1680, volume 1: The Lands below the Winds*, New Haven: Yale University Press.

Renucci, J. (1973) 'Corse traditionelle et Corse nouvelle: la géographie d'une île', Ph.D. thesis, Université de Lyon II.

Reyne, A. (1924–5) 'Geschiedenis der cacaocultuur in Suriname', *De West-Indische Gids*, 6, 1–20, 49–72, 107–26, 193–216.

Ribeiro, M. Ferreira (1977) *A Provincia de S. Thomé e Principe e Suas Dependencias*, Lisbon: Imprensa Nacional.

Rice, L. (1876–8) *Mysore and Coorg: A Gazetteer Compiled for the Government of India*, Bangalore: Government Press.

Ridings, E. W. (1977) 'Interest groups and development: the case of Brazil in the nineteenth century', *Journal of Latin American Studies*, 9, 2, 225–50.

—— (1985) 'Foreign predominance among overseas traders in nineteenth century Latin America', *Latin American Research Review*, 20, 2, 3–27.

Rinman, T. and Brodefors, R. (1983) *The Commercial History of Shipping*, Gothenburg: Rinman & Lindén.

Rippy, J. F. (1946) 'The dawn of manufacturing in Peru', *Pacific Historical Review*, 15, 2, 147–57.

Roberts, J. S. (1984) *Drink, Temperance and the Working Class in Nineteenth Century Germany*, Boston: Allen and Unwin.

Rocchi, F. (1997) 'Building a nation, building a market: industrial growth and the domestic economy in turn-of-the-century Argentina', Ph.D. dissertation, University of California, Santa Barbara.

Rodney, W. (1981) *A History of the Guyanese Working People, 1881–1905*, London: Heinemann.

Rodrigues, F. M. de Carvalho (1974) *S. Tomé e Príncipe, sob o Ponto de Vista Agrícola*, Lisbon: JICU.

Rodríguez Campos, M. (1989) *La Libranza del Sudor: El Drama de la Inmigración Canaria en Venezuela entre 1830 y 1859*, Caracas: Academia Nacional de la Historia.

Rodríguez Demorizi, E. (ed.) (1960) *Informe de la Comisión de Investigación de los E. U. A. en Santo Domingo en 1871*, Ciudad Trujillo: Editora Montalvo.

Roepke, W. (1922) *Cacao*, Haarlem: H. D. Tjeenk Willink & Zoon.

Romero, E. (1961) *Geografía Económica del Perú*, Lima: Universidad Nacional Mayor de San Marcos.

Romero Vargas, G. J. (1976) 'Les structures sociales du Nicaragua au XVIIIème siècle', doctoral thesis, Université de Paris-IV.

Roseberry, W., Gudmundson, L. and Samper Kutschbach, M. (eds) (1995) *Coffee, Society and Power in Latin America*, Baltimore: Johns Hopkins University Press.

Rosenzweig, F. (1965) 'La industria', in D. Cosío Villegas (ed.) *Historia Moderna de México: El Porfiriato, la Vida Económica*, 311–481, Mexico City: Hermes.

Rosés Alvarado, C. (1982) 'El ciclo del cacao en la economía colonial de Costa Rica, 1650–1794', *Mesoamérica*, 3, 4, 247–78.

Ross, E. B. (1978) 'The evolution of the Amazon peasantry', *Journal of Latin American Studies*, 10, 2, 193–218.

Rouma, G. (1948–9) *L'Amérique Latine*, Brussels: La Renaissance du Livre.

Rout Jr, L. B. (1976) *The African Experience in Spanish America, 1502 to the Present*, Cambridge: Cambridge University Press.

Rouzier, S. (1892–3) *Dictionnaire Géographique et Administratif Universel d'Haïti*, Paris: C. Blot.

Rubinstein, H. (1982) *The Chocolate Book*, London: Penguin.

Rubio Sánchez, M. (1958) 'El cacao', *Anales de la Sociedad de Geografía e Historia de Guatemala*, 31, 81–129.

——(1976) *Historia del Añil o Xiquilite en Centro America*, San Salvador: Ministerio de Educación.

Rudin, H. R. (1968) *Germans in the Cameroons, 1884–1914*, New York: Greenwood Press.

Ruf, F. (1991) 'Les crises cacaoyères: la malédiction des âges d'or?', *Cahiers d'Etudes Africaines*, 31, 121–2, 83–134.

——(1995) *Booms et Crises du Cacao: Les Vertiges de l'Or Brun*, Paris: Karthala.

Ruf, F., Forget, M. and Gasparetto, A. (1994) *Production de Cacao et Replantation à Bahia, Brésil*, Montpellier: CIRAD.

Rüger, A. (1960) 'Die Entstehung und Lage der Arbeiterklasse unter dem Deutschen Kolonialregime in Kamerun, 1885–1905', in H. Stoecker (ed.) *Kamerun unter Deutscher Kolonialherrschaft*, I, 149–242, Berlin: Rütten und Loenig.

Ruiz Abreu, C. (1989) *Comercio y Milicias de Tabasco en la Colonia*, Villahermosa: Gobierno del Estado de Tabasco.

Ruz, M. H. (1994) *Un Rostro Escondido: Los Indios del Tabasco Colonial*, Mexico City: CIESAS.

Sack, P. and Clark, D. (eds) (1979) *German New Guinea: The Annual Reports*, Canberra: Australian National University.

Saenz Maroto, A. (1970) *Historia Agrícola de Costa Rica*, San José: Universidad de Costa Rica.

Sagra, R. de la (1963) *Cuba 1860: Selección de Artículos sobre Agricultura Cubana*, Havana: Edit. Nacional de Cuba.

Saint John, S. (1971) *Hayti, or the Black Republic*, London: Cass.

Salvatierra, S. (1939) *Contribución a la Historia de Centroamérica: Monografías Documentales*, Managua: Tip. Progreso.

Sánchez Mantero, R. (1981) 'La decadencia comercial de Cádiz y el sindrome de Gibraltar', *Primeras Jornadas de Andalucía y América: La Rabida*, I, 75–82, Huelva: Instituto de Estudios Onubense.

Sancianco y Goson, G. (1881) *El Progreso de Filipinas*, Madrid: Va. de J. M. Pérez.

Sandgruber, R. (1986) *Bittersüsse Genüsse: Kulturgeschichte der Genussmittel*, Vienna: H. Böhlaus.

Sanger, J. P. (1900) *Report on the Census of Cuba, 1899*, Washington: Government Printing Office.

Sanz Casas, G. (1983) 'Política colonial y organización del trabajo en la isla de Fernando Póo, 1880–1930', doctoral thesis, University of Barcelona.

Sapper, C. (1897) *Das Nördliche Mittel-Amerika nebst einem Ausflug nach dem Hochland von Anahuac; Reisen und Studien aus den Jahren 1888–1895*, Braunschweig: F. Vieweg.

Sarraut, A. (1923) *La Mise en Valeur des Colonies Françaises*, Paris: Payot.

Schenck, F. von (1953) *Viajes por Antioquia en el Año de 1880*, Bogotá: Banco de la República.

Scherr, S. J. (1985) *The Oil Syndrome and Agricultural Development: Lessons from Tabasco*, New York: Praeger.

Scherzer, C. (1857) *Travels in the Free States of Central America: Nicaragua, Honduras and San Salvador*, London: Longman, Brown, Green, Longmans and Roberts.

Schinzinger, F. (1984) *Die Kolonien und das Deutsche Reich; die Wirtschaftliche Bedeutung der Deutschen Besitzungen in Übersee*, Stuttgart: F. Steiner.

Schivelbusch, W. (1992) *Tastes of Paradise: A Social History of Spices, Stimulants and Intoxicants*, New York: Pantheon Books.

Schnakenbourg, C. (1977) 'Statistiques pour l'histoire de l'économie de plantation en Guadeloupe et en Martinique, 1635–1835', *Bulletin de la Société d'Histoire de la Guadeloupe*, 31.

Schneider, J. (1981) *Frankreich und die Unabhängigkeit Spanisch-Amerikas: Zum Französischen Handel mit den Entstehenden Nationalstaaten, 1810–1850*, Stuttgart: Klett-Cotta.

——(1998) 'Die neuen Getränke: Schokolade, Kaffee und Tee, 16.–18. Jahrhundert', in S. Cavaciocchi (ed.) *Prodotti e Tecniche d'Oltremare nelle Economie Europee, Secc. XIII–XVIII*, 541–90, Florence: F. Datini.

Schoenrich, O. (1918) *Santo Domingo: A Country with a Future*, New York: Macmillan.

Scholliers, P. (1996) 'De la boisson élitaire à la barre populaire; la production et la consommation du chocolat en Belgique aux XIXe et XXe siècles', in E. Collet (ed.) *Chocolat: De la Boisson Elitaire au Bâton Populaire*, 161–184, Brussels: CGER.

Schomburgk, R. H. (1840) *A Description of British Guiana, Geographical and Statistical*, London: Simpkin Marshall & Co.

Schrover, M. (1991) *Het Vette, het Zoete en het Wederzijdse Profijt: Arbeidsverhoudingen in de Margarine-industrie en in de Cacao- en Chocolade-Industrie in Nederland, 1870–1960*, Hilversum: Verloren.

Schurz, W. L. (1921) *Bolivia: A Commercial and Industrial Handbook*, Washington: Government Printing Office.

——(1959) *The Manila Galleon*, New York: E. P. Dutton.

Schuyler, R. L. (1945) *The Fall of the Old Colonial System: A Study in British Free Trade, 1770–1870*, New York: Oxford University Press.

Scidmore, E. R. (1984) *Java: The Garden of the East*, Singapore: Oxford University Press.

Scott, J. M. (1964) *The Tea Story*, London: Heinemann.

Sebald, P. (1988) *Togo 1884–1914: Eine Geschichte der Deutschen 'Musterkolonie' auf der Grundlage Amtlicher Quellen*, Berlin: Akademie-Verlag.

Sevilla Soler, M. R. (1980) *Santo Domingo, Tierra de Frontera, 1750–1800*, Seville: Escuela de Estudios Hispano-Americanos.

——(1988) *Inmigración y Cambio Socio-económico en Trinidad, 1783–1797*, Seville: Escuela de Estudios Hispano-Americanos.

Shephard, C. (1971) *Historical Account of the Island of Saint Vincent*, London: Cass.

Shephard, C. Y. (1937) *The Cacao Industry of Trinidad: Some Economic Aspects*, Port of Spain: Government Printing Office.

Sherratt, A. (1995) 'Introduction, peculiar substances', in J. Goodman, P. Lovejoy and A. Sherratt (eds) *Consuming Habits: Drugs in History and Anthropology*, 1–10, London: Routledge.

Shoman, A. (1994) *Chapters of a History of Belize*, Belize City: The Angelus Press.

Silva, A. Mansuy-Diniz (1987) 'Imperial reorganization 1750–1808', in Leslie Bethell (ed.) *Colonial Brazil*, 244–283, Cambridge: Cambridge University Press.

Silva, F. Teixeira da (*c.* 1883) *Província de S. Thomé e Príncipe* (no place: no publisher).

Silva, H. Lains e (1958) *São Tomé e Príncipe e a Cultura do Café*, Lisbon: Junta de Investigações do Ultramar.

Silva, L. A. Rebello da (1969) *Relatórios do Ministro e Secretário de Estado dos Negócios da Marinha e do Ultramar, 1870*, Lisbon: Ministério do Ultramar.

Simmonds, P. L. (1888) *The Popular Beverages of Various Countries*, London: J. G. Smith.

Sims, H. D. (1990) *The Expulsion of Mexico's Spaniards, 1821–1836*, Pittsburgh: University of Pittsburgh Press.

Slijper, H. J. (1927) *Technologie en Warenkennis, Tweede Deel, Organische Producten en Eenige ook voor Ned.-Indië Belangrijke Cultures*, Purmerend: J. Muusses.

Smith, H. H. (1879) *Brazil: The Amazons and the Coast*, New York: Charles Scribner's Sons.

Smith, M. S. (1980) *Tariff Reform in France, 1860–1900*, Ithaca: Cornell University Press.

Smith, S. D. (1996) 'Accounting for taste: British coffee consumption in historical perspective', *Journal of Interdisciplinary History*, 27, 2, 183–214.

Soares, S. Ferreira (1977) *Notas Estatísticas sobre a Produção Agrícola e Carestia dos Generos Alimentícios no Império do Brasil*, Rio de Janeiro: IPEA/INPES.

Sociedade de Emigração para S. Thomé e Principe (1915) *Relatório da Direcção, Parecer do Conselho Fiscal, e Lista dos Accionistas: Segundo Anno, 1914*, Lisbon.

Sociedade de Geografia de Lisboa (1912–15) 'Colónias portuguesas em países estrangeiros', *Boletim da Sociedade de Geografia de Lisboa*, March 1912–January 1915.

Solano, F. de (1974) *Los Mayas del Siglo XVIII, Pervivencia y Transformación de la Sociedad Indígena Guatemalteca durante la Administración Borbónica*, Madrid: Cultura Hispánica.

Solórzano, V. (1963) *Evolución Económica de Guatemala*, Guatemala City: J. de Pineda Ibarra.

Sorela, Lt. (1884) *Les Possessions Espagnoles du Golfe de Guinée: Leur Présent et leur Avenir*, Paris: A. Lahure.

Spix, J. B. and Martius, C. F. P. von (1976) *Viagem pelo Brasil, 1817–1820*, Rio de Janeiro: Melhoramentos.

Spruce, R. (1908) *Notes of a Botanist on the Amazon and Andes*, London: Macmillan.

Squier, E. G. (1970a) *Nicaragua: Sus Gentes y Paisajes*, San José: Editorial Universitaria Centroamericana.

——(1970b) *Honduras: Descriptive, Historical and Statistical*, New York: AMS Press.

Stedman, J. G. (1988) *Narrative of a Five Years Expedition against the Revolted Negroes of Surinam*, Baltimore: Johns Hopkins University Press.

Stephens, J. L. (1993) *Incidents of Travel in Central America, Chiapas and Yucatán*, abridged edn, Washington: Smithsonian Institution Press.

Stipriaan, A. van (1993) *Surinaams Contrast: Roofbow en Overleven in een Caraïbische Plantagekolonie, 1750–1863*, Leiden: KITLV.

——(1995a) 'Suriname and the abolition of slavery', in Gert Oostindie (ed.) *Fifty Years Later: Antislavery, Capitalism and Modernity in the Dutch Orbit*, 117–41, Leiden: KITLV.

——(1995b) 'Debunking debts: image and reality of a colonial crisis; Suriname at the end of the eighteenth century', *Itinerario*, 19, 1, 69–84.

Stollwerck, W. (1907) *Der Kakao und die Schokoladenindustrie: Eine Wirtschafts-statistische Untersuchung*, Jena: Fischer.

Stols, E. (1996) 'Le cacao: le sang voluptueux du nouveau monde', in E. Collet (ed.) *Chocolat: De la Boisson Elitaire au Bâton Populaire*, 37–56, Brussels: CGER.

Street, J. M. (1960) 'Historical and economic geography of the southwest peninsula of Haïti', Ph.D. thesis, University of California, Berkeley.

Sundiata, I. K. (1972) 'The Fernandinos: labour and community in Santa Isabel de Fernando Póo, 1827–1931', Ph.D. thesis, Northwestern University.

——(1974) 'Prelude to scandal: Liberia and Fernando Po, 1880–1930', *Journal of African History*, 15, 1, 97–112.

——(1990) *Equatorial Guinea: Colonialism, State Terror, and the Search for Stability*, Boulder: Westview Press.

——(1996) *From Slaving to Neoslavery: The Bight of Biafra and Fernando Po in the Era of Abolition, 1827–1930*, Madison: University of Wisconsin Press.

Swaelen, L. (1996) 'La Flandre et le chocolat', in E. Collet (ed.) *Chocolat: De la Boisson Elitaire au Bâton Populaire*, 57–74, Brussels: CGER.

Szereszewski, R. (1965) *Structural Changes in the Economy of Ghana, 1891–1911*, London: Weidenfeld and Nicolson

Tamaro, D. C. (1988) 'A New World plantation region in colonial Venezuela: eighteenth century cacao cultivation in the Tuy valley and Barlovento', Ph.D. thesis, Boston University.

Tams, G. (1850) *Visita ás Possessões Portuguezas na Costa Occidental d'Africa*, Oporto: Typ. da Revista.

Tandrón, H. (1976) *El Real Consulado de Caracas y el Comercio Exterior de Venezuela*, Caracas: Instituto de Estudios Hispanoamericanos.

Tarrade, J. (1972) *Le Commerce Colonial de la France à la Fin de l'Ancien Régime*, Paris: Presses Universitaires de France.

——(1992) 'Le commerce entre les Antilles Françaises et les possessions Espagnoles', in P. Butel (ed.) *Commerce et Plantations dans la Caraïbe, XVIIIe et XIXe Siècles*, 27–43, Paris: Maison des Pays Ibériques.

Taussig, M. (1977) 'The evolution of rural wage labour in the Cauca valley of Colombia, 1700 to 1970', in K. Duncan and I. Rutledge (eds) *Land and Labour in Latin America: Essays on the Development of Agrarian Capitalism in the Nineteenth and Twentieth Centuries*, 397–434, Cambridge: Cambridge University Press.

Teiser, R. (1945) *An Account of Domingo Ghirardelli and the Early Years of the D. Ghirardelli Company*, San Francisco: D. Ghirardelli Co.

Tenreiro, F. (1961) *A Ilha de São Tomé: Estudo Geográfico*, Lisbon: Junta de Investigações do Ultramar.

Terán, M. de (1962) *Síntesis Geográfica de Fernando Póo*, Madrid: IEA.

Terry, A. R. (1834) *Travels in the Equatorial Regions of South America in 1832*, Hartford: Cooke & Co.

Tetzlaff, R. (n.d.) *Koloniale Entwicklung und Ausbeutung: Wirtschafts- und Sozialgeschichte Deutsch-Ostafrikas, 1885–1914*, Berlin: Duncker und Humblot.

Thénard, Baron (1868) 'Matériel de la chocolaterie', in Michel Chevalier (ed.) *Exposition Universelle de 1867 à Paris: Rapports du Jury International*, VIII, 360–6, Paris: P. Duport.

Thomasset, H. (1891) 'Agricultura, industria y obras públicas: informe dirijido al Sr. Ministro de Fomento y Obras Públicas', *Gaceta Oficial de Santo Domingo*, 857, 24 January 1891.

Thomson (1895–6) 'Informe sobre una excursión a la Sierra Nevada de Santa Marta, para investigar sus capacidades agrícolas', *El Agricultor* (Bogotá), XI, 416–26; XII, 80–9.

Thurber, F. B. (1881) *Coffee, from Plantation to Cup: A Brief History of Coffee Production and Consumption*, New York: American Grocer Publishing Association.

Tomich, D. W. (1990) *Slavery in the Circuit of Sugar: Martinique and the World Economy, 1830–1848*, Baltimore: Johns Hopkins University Press.

Topik, S. and Wells, A. (eds) (1998) *The Second Conquest of Latin America: Coffee, Henequen and Oil during the Export Boom, 1850–1930*, Austin: University of Texas Press.

Tornezy, O. (1984) 'Les travaux et les jours de la mission Sainte-Marie du Gabon, 1845–1880: agriculture et modernisation', *Revue Française d'Histoire d'Outre-Mer*, 71, 3–4, 147–90.

Toscano, H. (ed.) (1960) *El Ecuador Visto por los Extranjeros: Viajeros de los Siglos XVIII y XIX*, Puebla: J. M. Cajica Jr.

Tosta Filho, I. (1957) *Cocoa Economy in Brazil*, Rio de Janeiro: FAO and Bank of Brazil.

Touzard, J.-M. (1993) *L'Economie Coloniale du Cacao en Amérique Centrale*, Montpellier: CIRAD.

Trouillot, M.-R. (1988) *Peasants and Capital: Dominica in the World Economy*, Baltimore: Johns Hopkins University Press.

Trümper, K. (1996) *Kaffee und Kaufleute: Guatemala und der Hamburger Handel, 1871–1914*, Hamburg: LIT Verlag.

T'serclaes de Wommersom, C. de (1911) *A travers les Plantations du Mayombe et de San-Thomé*, Louvain: L'Editorial.

Tudhope, W. S. D. (1917) 'The Gold Coast cocoa industry', *Transactions of the Third International Congress of Tropical Agriculture, 1914*, II, 176–88, London: John Bale, Sons, and Danielson.

——(1921) 'The cocoa industry of Ecuador', *Bulletin of the Imperial Institute*, 21, 3, 348–60.

Twinam, A. (1982) *Miners, Merchants and Farmers in Colonial Colombia*, Austin: University of Texas Press.

United States (1888) *Cultivation of, and Trade in, Coffee in Central and South America*, Washington (50th Congress, House of Representatives, 1st session, Consular Reports on Commerce etc., no. 98).

——(1905) *Census of the Philippine Islands*, Washington: Bureau of the Census.

Urquhart, D. H. (1956) *Cocoa*, London: Longmans Green & Co.

Vannini de Gerulewicz, M. (1966) *Italia y los Italianos en la Historia y la Cultura de Venezuela*, Caracas: OCI.

Vantieghem, L. (1996) 'La culture du cacao au Mayombe, Congo Belge, 1885–1914', in E. Collet (ed.) *Chocolat: De la Boisson Elitaire au Bâton Populaire*, 143–60, Brussels: CGER.

Vaussard, M. (1962) *Daily Life in Eighteenth-century Italy*, London: Allen and Unwin.

Vázquez, M. C. (1970) 'Immigration and "mestizaje" in nineteenth century Peru', in M. Mörner (ed.) *Race and Class in Latin America*, 73–95, New York: Columbia University Press.

Vega, B. and Cordero Michel, E. (eds) (1993) *Asuntos Dominicanos en Archivos Ingleses*, Santo Domingo: Fundación Cultural Dominicana.

Velarde, A. de Mantero (1924) *L'Espansione Politica e Coloniale Portoghese, con Speciale Riguardo alle Isole di São Thomé e Principe*, Rome: Istituto Cristoforo Colombo.

Vellut, J.-L. (1996) 'Le cacao dans l'économie politique de l'ancien Congo Belge', in E. Collet (ed.) *Chocolat: De la Boisson Elitaire au Bâton Populaire*, 123–42, Brussels: CGER.

Vennetier, P. (1968) *Pointe-Noire et la Façade Maritime du Congo-Brazzaville*, Paris: ORSTOM.

Vergara y Velasco, F. J. (1901) *Nueva Geografía de Colombia*, Bogotá: Imprenta de Vapor.

Verger, P. (1968) *Flux et Reflux de la Traite des Nègres entre le Golfe de Bénin et Bahia de Todos os Santos, du XVIIe au XIXe Siècle*, Paris: Mouton.

Vernon, A. (1958) *A Quaker Business Man: The Life of Joseph Rowntree, 1836–1925*, London: Allen and Unwin.

Verteuil, L. A. A. (1858) *Trinidad: Its Geography, Natural Resources, Present Condition and Prospects*, London: Ward and Lock.

Wagner, G. (1987) *The Chocolate Conscience*, London: Chatto and Windus.

Wagner, R. (1991) *Los Alemanes en Guatemala, 1828–1944*, Guatemala City: Editorial IDEA.

Waldeck, F. de (1838) *Voyage Pittoresque et Archéologique dans la Province d'Yucatan, Amérique Centrale, pendant les Années 1834 et 1836*, Paris: Bellizard Dufour.

Walker, A. (1822) *Colombia, Being a Geographical, Statistical, Agricultural, Commercial and Political Account of that Country*, London: Baldwin, Craddock and Joy.

Wallace, A. R. (1890) *A Narrative of Travels on the Amazon and Rio Negro*, London: Ward, Lock & Co.

Walle, P. (1925) *Bolivia: Its People and its Resources, its Railways, Mines and Rubberforests*, London: Fisher and Unwin.

Walter, R. (1985) *Los Alemanes en Venezuela, desde Colón hasta Guzmán Blanco*, Caracas: Asociación Cultural Humboldt.

——(1989) 'German and US American commercial relations with Venezuela, 1810–1830', in R. Liehr (ed.) *América Latina en la Epoca de Simón Bolívar: La Formación de las Economías Nacionales y los Intereses Ecónomicos Europeos, 1800–1850*, 439–52, Berlin: Colloquium.

Waltz, H. (1917) *Das Konzessionswesen im Belgischen Kongo*, Jena: G. Fischer.

Walvin, J. (1997) *Fruits of Empire, Exotic Produce and British Taste, 1660–1800*, Basingstoke: Macmillan.

Ward, H. J. (1828) *Mexico in 1827*, London: Henry Colburn.

Warren, J. F. (1981) *The Sulu Zone, 1768–1898: The Dynamics of External Trade, Slavery and Ethnicity in the Transformation of a Southeast Asian Maritime State*, Singapore: Singapore University Press.

Wasserstrom, R. (1983a) *Class and Society in Central Chiapas*, Berkeley and Los Angeles: University of California Press.

——(1983b) 'Spaniards and Indians in colonial Chiapas, 1528–1790', in Murdo J. Macleod and Robert Wasserstrom (eds) *Spaniards and Indians in Southeastern Mesoamerica: Essays on the History of Ethnic Relations*, 92–126, Lincoln: University of Caifornia Press.

Watt, G. (1889–96) *A Dictionary of the Economic Products of India*, London: Department of Revenue and Agriculture.

Webster, J. B. (1962) 'Agege plantations and the African church', *Nigerian Institute of Social and Economic Research, Conference Proceedings*, 8, 124–30.

——(1963) 'The bible and the plough', *Journal of the Historical Society of Nigeria*, 2, 4, 418–34.

Weilbauer, A. (1974) *Die Deutschen in Ecuador: Historische Studie*, Quito: Colegio Alemán.

Weinman, L. (1970) 'Ecuador and cacao: domestic responses to the boom-collapse monoexport cycle', Ph.D. thesis, University of California.

Weinstein, B. (1983) *The Amazon Rubber Boom, 1850–1920*, Stanford: Stanford University Press.

Werlich, D. P. (1978) *Peru: A Short History*, Carbondale: Southern Illinois University Press.

Wickberg, Edgar (1965) *The Chinese in Philippine life, 1850–1898*, New Haven: Yale University Press.

Wildeman, E. de (1902) *Les Plantes Tropicales de Grande Culture*, Brussels (no publisher).

Williams, C. T. (1953) *Chocolate and Confectionery*, London: L. Hill.

Williams, E. (1952) *Documents on British West Indian History, 1807–1833*, Port of Spain: Trinidad Publishing Co.

——(1964) *History of the People of Trinidad and Tobago*, London: Andre Deutsch.

Williams, I. A. (1931) *The Firm of Cadbury, 1831–1931*, London: Constable.

Williams, R. O. (1922) 'Cacao cultivation in Grenada', *Bulletin of the Department of Agriculture of Trinidad and Tobago*, 19, 4, 215–23.

Wills, W. (1831) *Observaciones sobre el Comercio de la Nueva Granada, con un Apendice Relativo al de Bogotá*, Bogotá: Imprenta del Gobierno.

Wilson, C. M. (1947) *Empire in Green and Gold: The Story of the American Banana Trade* (no place): Henry Holt & Co.

Winter, N. O. (1909) *Guatemala and her People of To-day*, Boston: L. C. Page & Co.

Wirz, A. (1972) *Vom Sklavenhandel zum Kolonialen Handel: Wirtschaftsräume und Wirtschaftsformen in Kamerun vor 1914*, Zürich: Atlantis.

Wolf, E. R. and Mintz, S. W. (1957) 'Haciendas and plantations in Middle America and the Antilles', *Social and Economic Studies* (Jamaica), 6, 3, 380–412.

Wolff, E. and Wolff, F. (1975) *Os Judeus no Brasil Imperial*, São Paulo: Universidade de São Paulo.

Wood, G. A. R. and Lass, R. A. (1985) *Cocoa*, Harlow: Longman.

Wortman, M. L. (1982) *Government and Society in Central America, 1680–1840*, New York: Columbia University Press.

Wright, A. and Cartwright, H. A. (1908) *Twentieth Century Impressions of British Malaya*, abridged edn, London: Lloyds Greater Britain Publishing Co.

Wright, H. (1907) *Theobroma Cacao, or Cocoa, its Botany, Cultivation, Chemistry and Diseases*, Colombo: A. M. and J. Ferguson.

Wright, I. A. (1910) *Cuba*, New York: Macmillan.

Young, A. M. (1994) *The Chocolate Tree: A Natural History of Cocoa*, Washington: Smithsonian Institute Press.

Zawisza, L. M. (1975) 'Colonización agrícola en Venezuela', *Boletín Histórico, Fundación John Boulton*, 37, 15–59.

Zehntner, L. (1914) *Le Cacaoyer dans l'Etat de Bahia*, Berlin: Friedländer & Sohn.

Zieger-Witschi, B. (1988) 'Schweizerische Kaufleute in Brasilien im 19. Jahrhundert', *Jahrbuch für Geschichte von Staat, Wirtschaft und Gesellschaft Lateinamerikas*, 25, 141–67.

INDEX